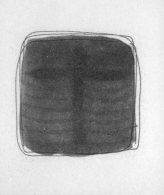

I went to an exhibition featuring masks from around the world. Even though I've been creating *Bleach* all this time, I only just now realized that I like masks.

-Tite Kubo

BLEACH is author Kubo's second title. Kubo made his debut with *ZOMBIEPOWDER.*, a four-volume series for *WEEKLY SHONEN JUMP*. To date, *BLEACH* has been translated into numerous languages and has also inspired an animated TV series that began airing in the U.S. in 2006. Beginning its serialization in 2001, *BLEACH* is still a mainstay in the pages of *WEEKLY SHONEN JUMP*. In 2005, *BLEACH* was awarded the prestigious Shogakukan Manga Award in the *shonen* (boys) category.

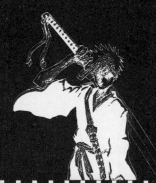

BLEACH
VOL. 69: AGAINST THE JUDGEMENT
SHONEN JUMP Manga Edition

STORY AND ART BY
TITE KUBO

Translation/Joe Yamazaki
Touch-up Art & Lettering/Mark McMurray
Design/Kam Li
Editor/Alexis Kirsch

Printed in the U.S.A.

Published by VIZ Media, LLC
P.O. Box 77010
San Francisco, CA 94107

10 9 8 7 6 5 4 3 2 1
First printing, March 2017

www.viz.com

THE WORLD'S
MOST POPULAR MANGA
SHONEN JUMP
www.shonenjump.com

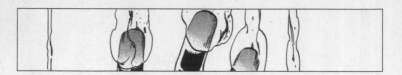

Bullet, Claw, Battle Flag, Short Sword
With my fingers bent, I wait for you.

BLEACH 69 | AGAINST THE JUDGEMENT

Shonen Jump Manga

ALL STARS ★ AND

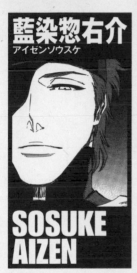

藍染惣右介
アイゼンソウスケ

SOSUKE AIZEN

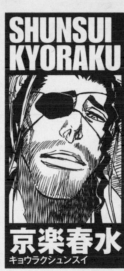

SHUNSUI KYORAKU

京楽春水
キョウラクシュンスイ

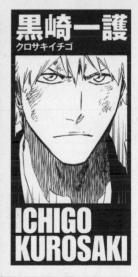

黒崎一護
クロサキイチゴ

ICHIGO KUROSAKI

plot ★

Ichigo Kurosaki meets Soul Reaper Rukia Kuchiki and ends up helping her eradicate Hollows. After developing his powers as a Soul Reaper, Ichigo befriends many humans and Soul Reapers and grows as a person...

Ichigo and friends finally reach Reiokyu, but awaiting them there is the Soul King's body, pierced by Yhwach's sword. With Reio now dead, the Soul Society and the Land of the Living begin to crumble. Ukitake uses a special ritual called Kamikake to restore order, but that power is soon taken by Yhwach as well. Hope seems lost, but Kyoraku then reveals that he has freed Aizen!

BLEACH

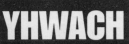

YHWACH

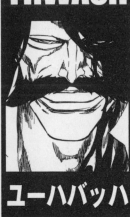

ユーハバッハ

ユーグラム・
ハッシュヴァルト

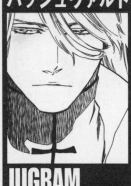

JUGRAM
HASCHWALTH

BAZZ-B

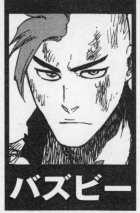

バズビー

STORIES

BLEACH 69

AGAINST THE JUDGEMENT

CONTENTS

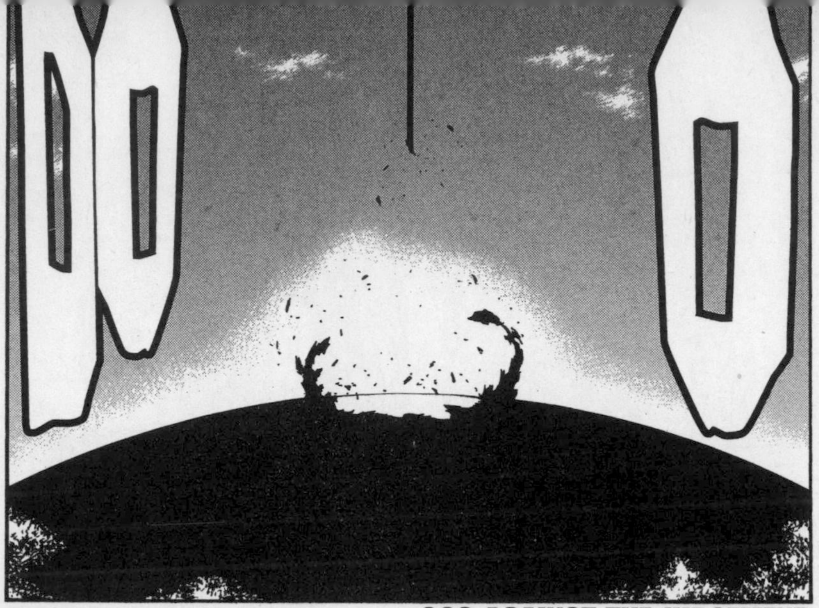

623.AGAINST THE JUDGEMENT

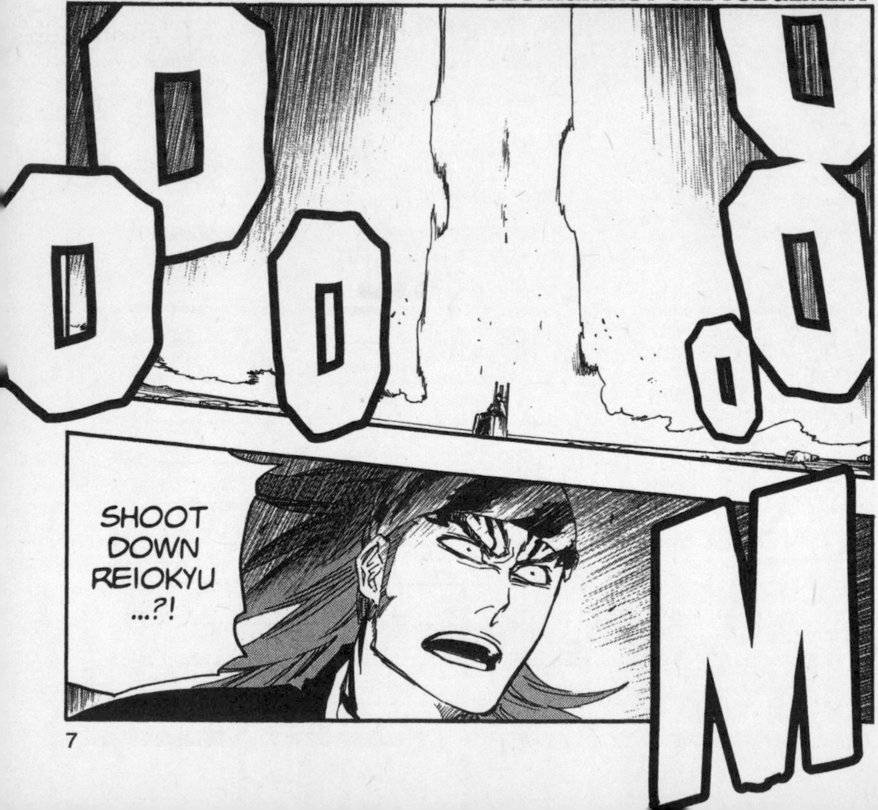
SHOOT DOWN REIOKYU ...?!

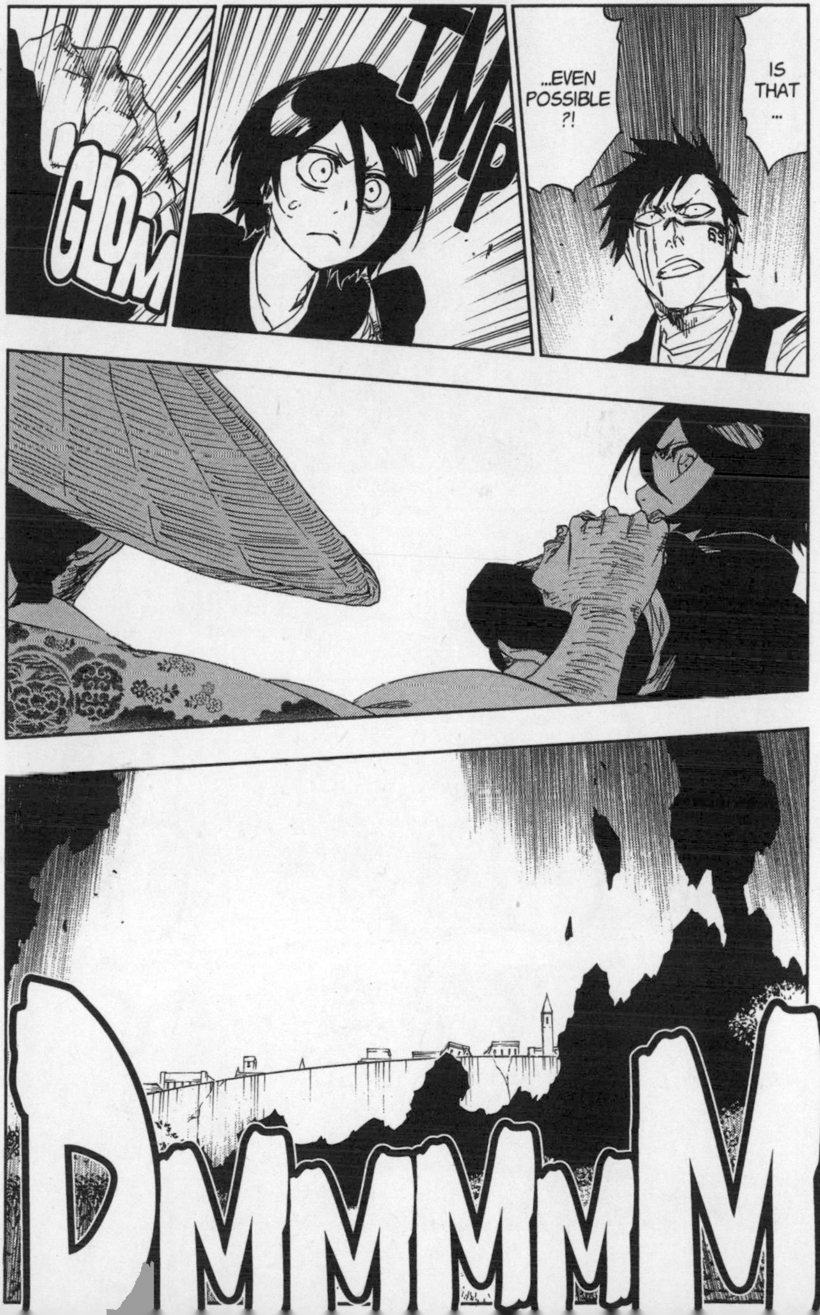
IS THAT ...
...EVEN POSSIBLE ?!
TMP
GLOM
DMMMMM

READ THIS WAY

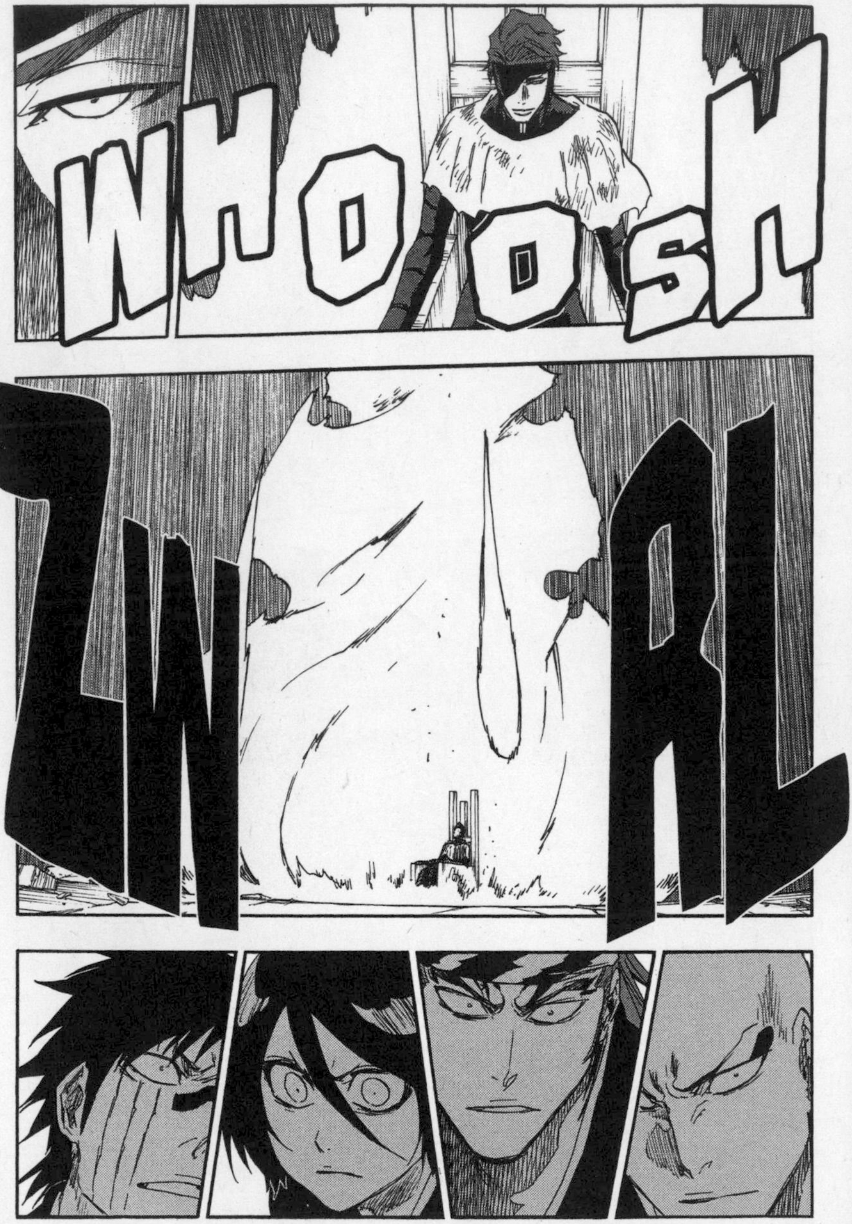
WHOOSH
ZWAL

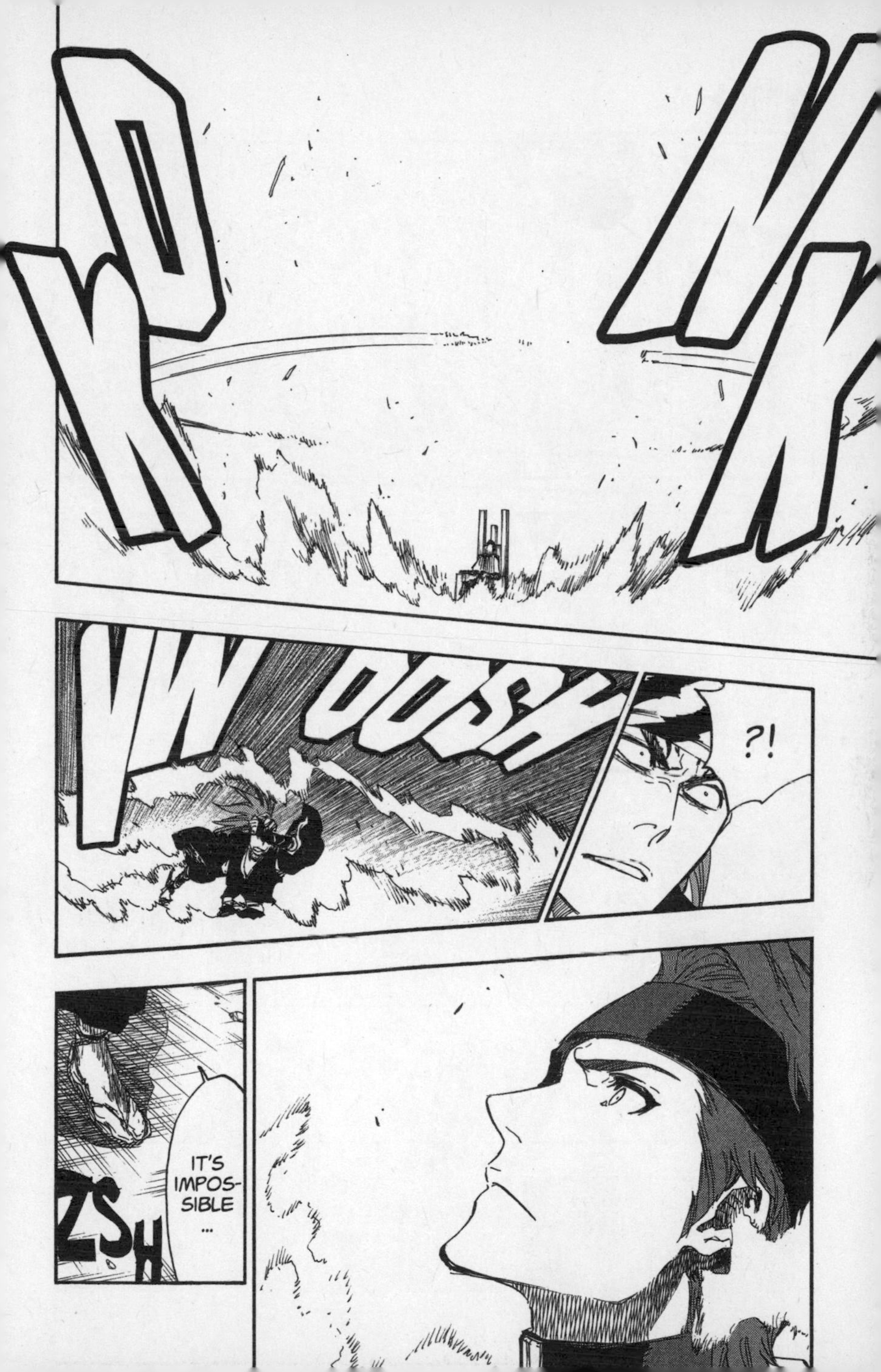
?!
IT'S IMPOSSIBLE ...
ZSH

READ THIS WAY

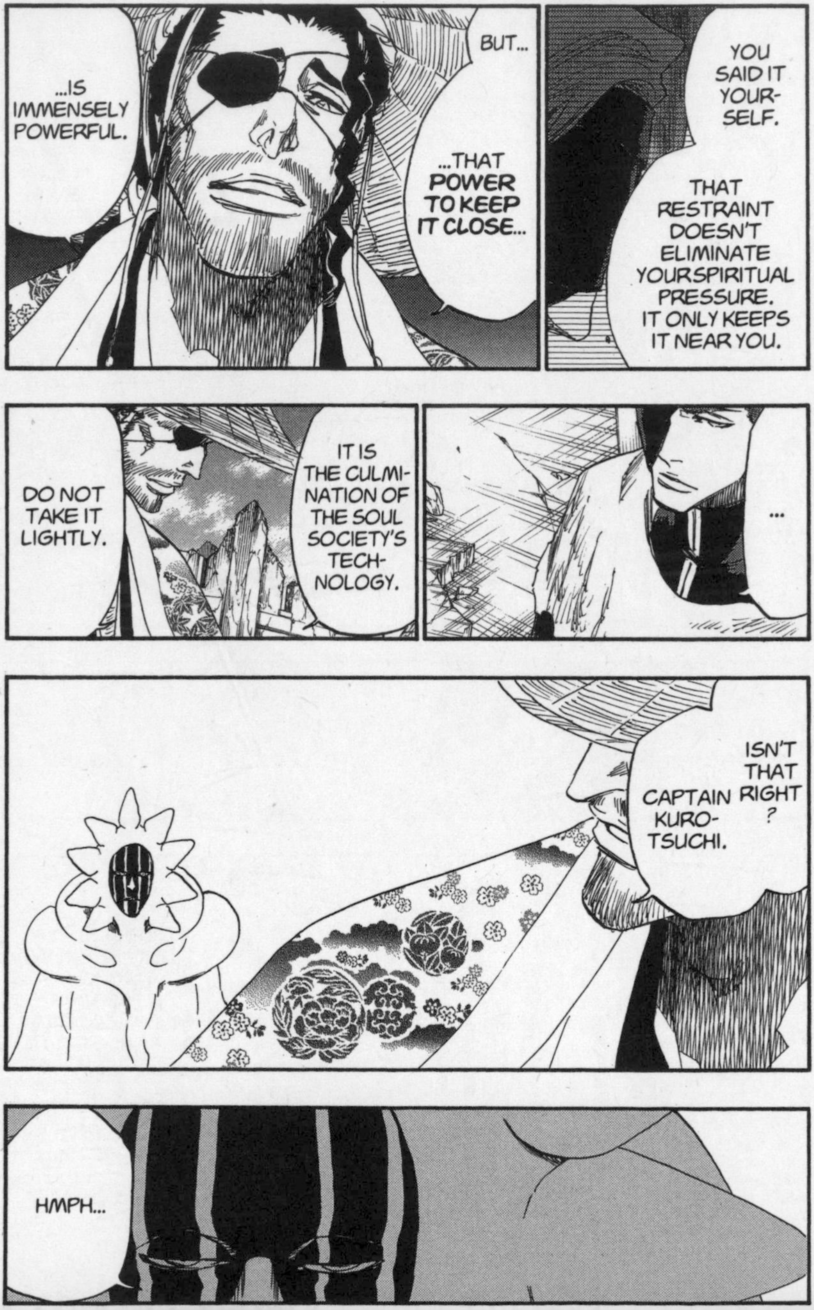
YOU SAID IT YOURSELF.
THAT RESTRAINT DOESN'T ELIMINATE YOUR SPIRITUAL PRESSURE. IT ONLY KEEPS IT NEAR YOU.
BUT...
...THAT POWER TO KEEP IT CLOSE...
...IS IMMENSELY POWERFUL.
...
IT IS THE CULMINATION OF THE SOUL SOCIETY'S TECHNOLOGY.
DO NOT TAKE IT LIGHTLY.
ISN'T THAT RIGHT?
CAPTAIN KUROTSUCHI.
HMPH...

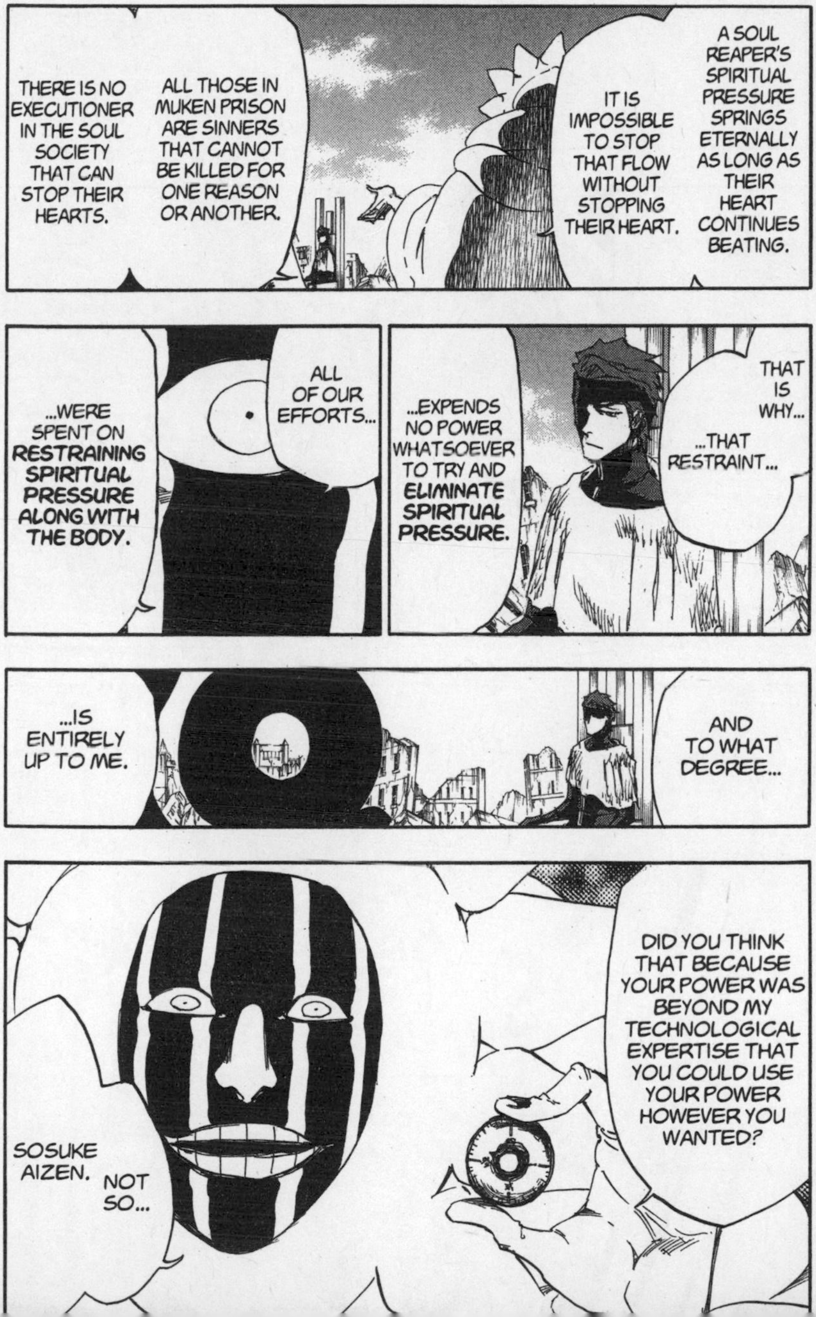
A SOUL REAPER'S SPIRITUAL PRESSURE SPRINGS ETERNALLY AS LONG AS THEIR HEART CONTINUES BEATING.
IT IS IMPOSSIBLE TO STOP THAT FLOW WITHOUT STOPPING THEIR HEART.
ALL THOSE IN MUKEN PRISON ARE SINNERS THAT CANNOT BE KILLED FOR ONE REASON OR ANOTHER.
THERE IS NO EXECUTIONER IN THE SOUL SOCIETY THAT CAN STOP THEIR HEARTS.
THAT IS WHY...
...THAT RESTRAINT...
...EXPENDS NO POWER WHATSOEVER TO TRY AND **ELIMINATE SPIRITUAL PRESSURE.**
ALL OF OUR EFFORTS...
...WERE SPENT ON **RESTRAINING SPIRITUAL PRESSURE ALONG WITH THE BODY.**
AND TO WHAT DEGREE...
...IS ENTIRELY UP TO ME.
DID YOU THINK THAT BECAUSE YOUR POWER WAS BEYOND MY TECHNOLOGICAL EXPERTISE THAT YOU COULD USE YOUR POWER HOWEVER YOU WANTED?
NOT SO...
SOSUKE AIZEN.

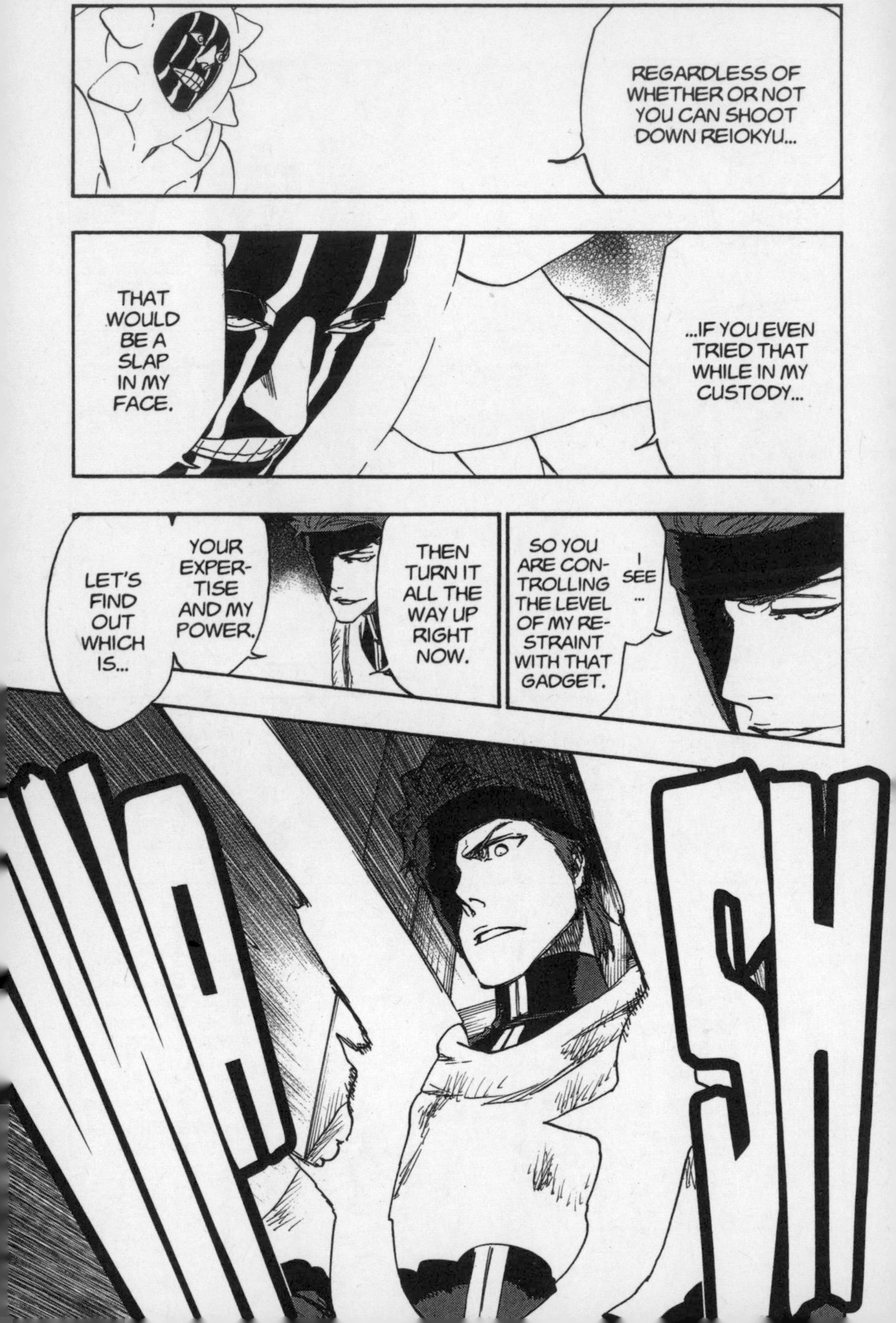
REGARDLESS OF WHETHER OR NOT YOU CAN SHOOT DOWN REIOKYU...
...IF YOU EVEN TRIED THAT WHILE IN MY CUSTODY...
THAT WOULD BE A SLAP IN MY FACE.
I SEE...
SO YOU ARE CONTROLLING THE LEVEL OF MY RESTRAINT WITH THAT GADGET.
THEN TURN IT ALL THE WAY UP RIGHT NOW.
YOUR EXPERTISE AND MY POWER.
LET'S FIND OUT WHICH IS...

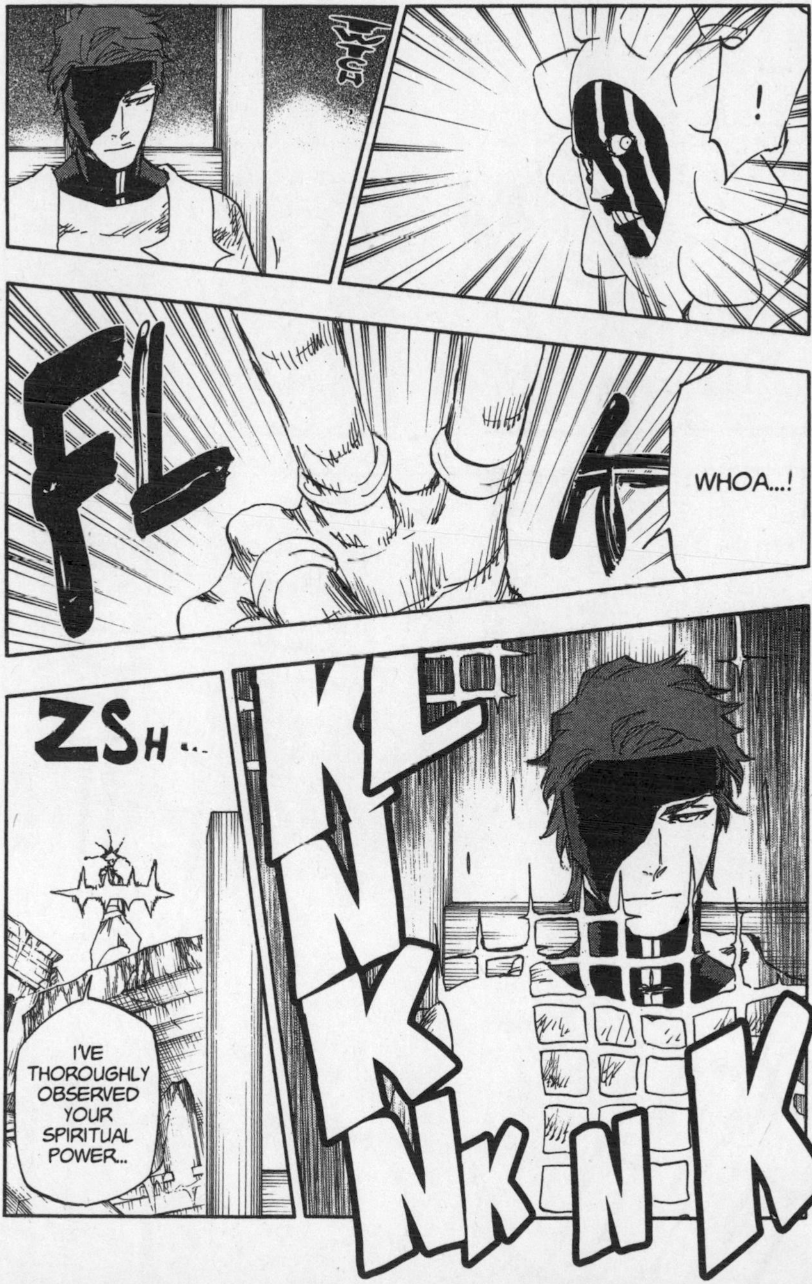
!
WHOA...!
ZSH...
I'VE THOROUGHLY OBSERVED YOUR SPIRITUAL POWER...

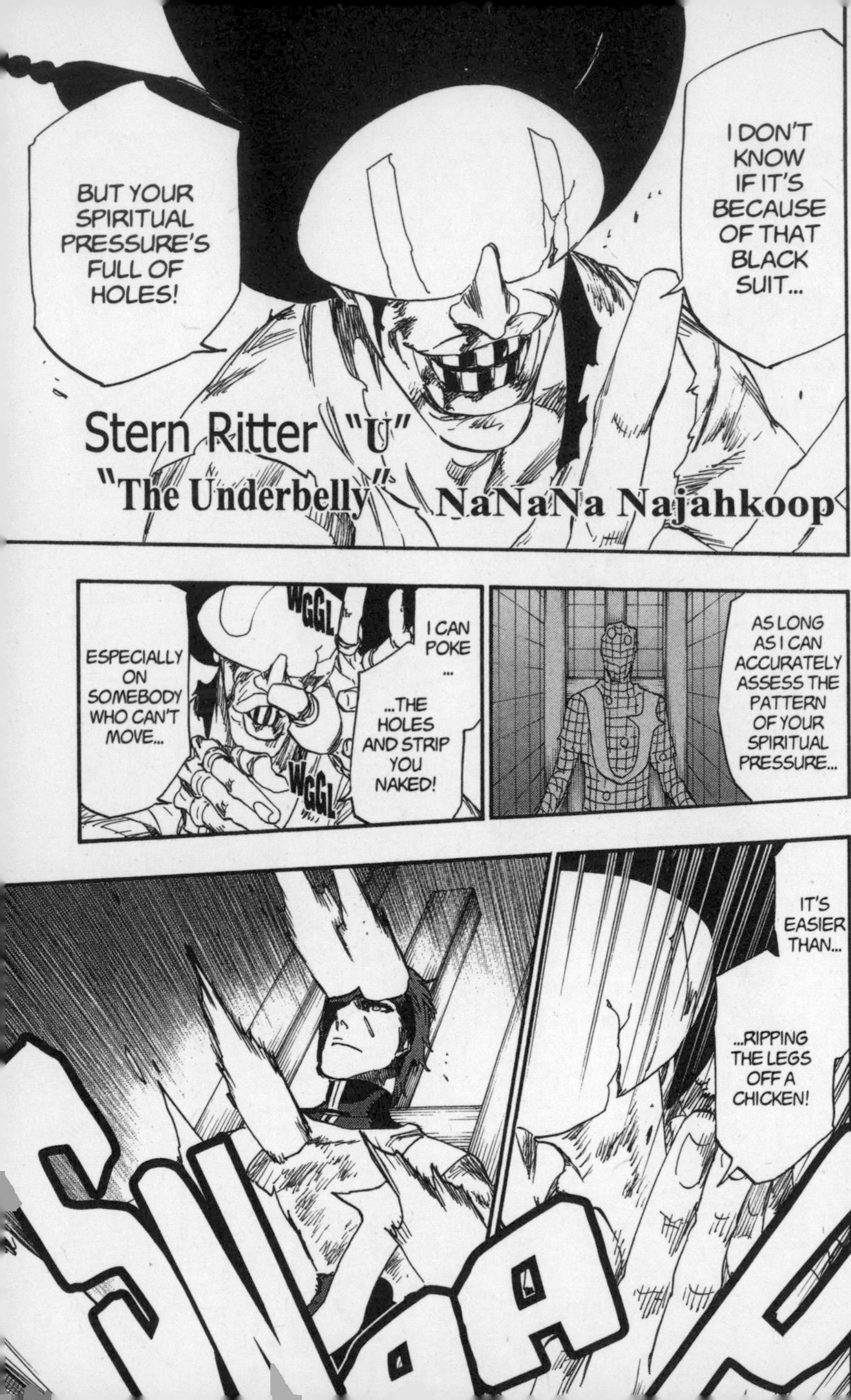
I DON'T KNOW IF IT'S BECAUSE OF THAT BLACK SUIT...
BUT YOUR SPIRITUAL PRESSURE'S FULL OF HOLES!
Stern Ritter "U"
"The Underbelly" NaNaNa Najahkoop
AS LONG AS I CAN ACCURATELY ASSESS THE PATTERN OF YOUR SPIRITUAL PRESSURE...
WGGL
I CAN POKE ...
...THE HOLES AND STRIP YOU NAKED!
ESPECIALLY ON SOMEBODY WHO CAN'T MOVE...
WGGL
IT'S EASIER THAN...
...RIPPING THE LEGS OFF A CHICKEN!

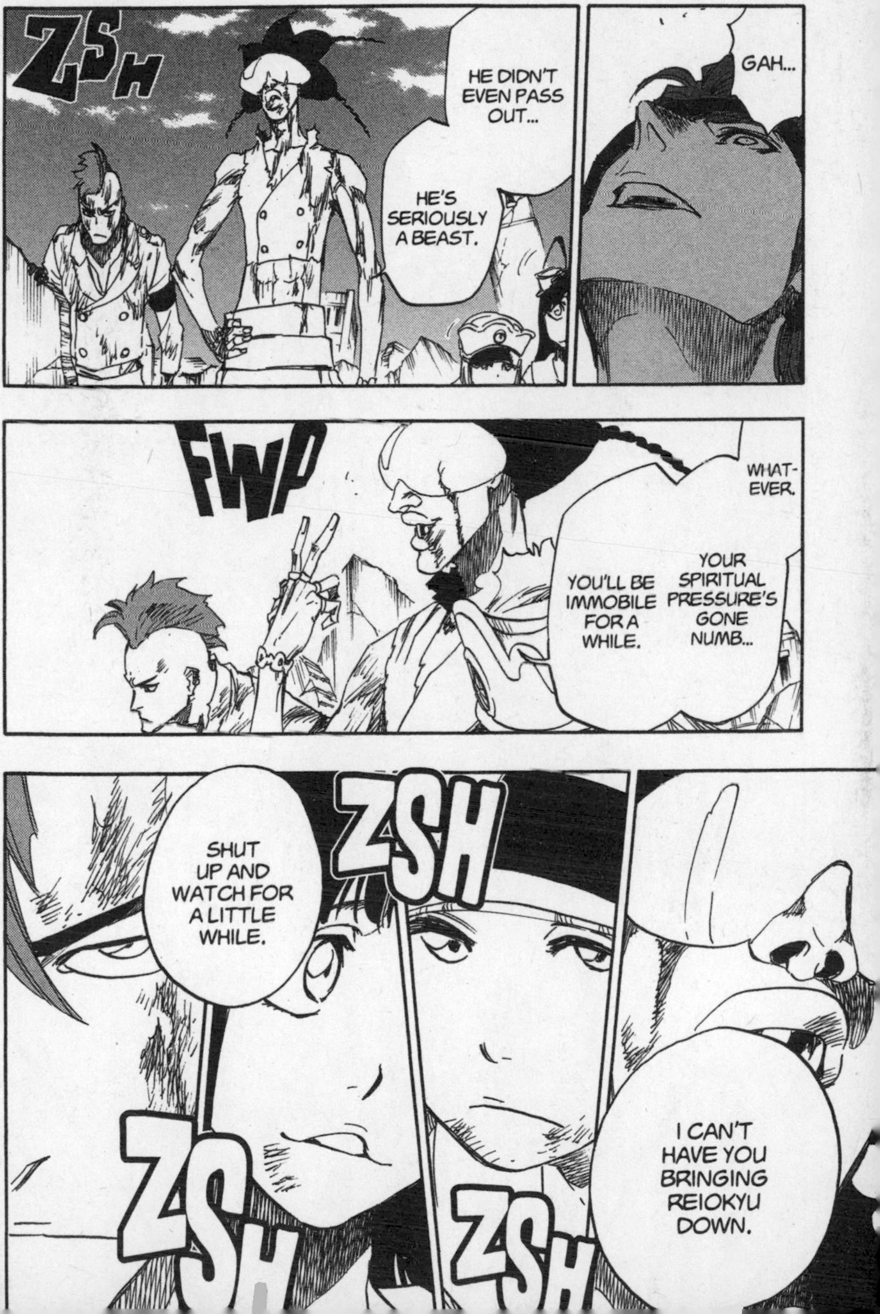
GAH...
ZSH
HE DIDN'T EVEN PASS OUT...
HE'S SERIOUSLY A BEAST.
WHAT-EVER.
YOUR SPIRITUAL PRESSURE'S GONE NUMB...
YOU'LL BE IMMOBILE FOR A WHILE.
FWP
I CAN'T HAVE YOU BRINGING REIOKYU DOWN.
ZSH
ZSH
SHUT UP AND WATCH FOR A LITTLE WHILE.
ZSH

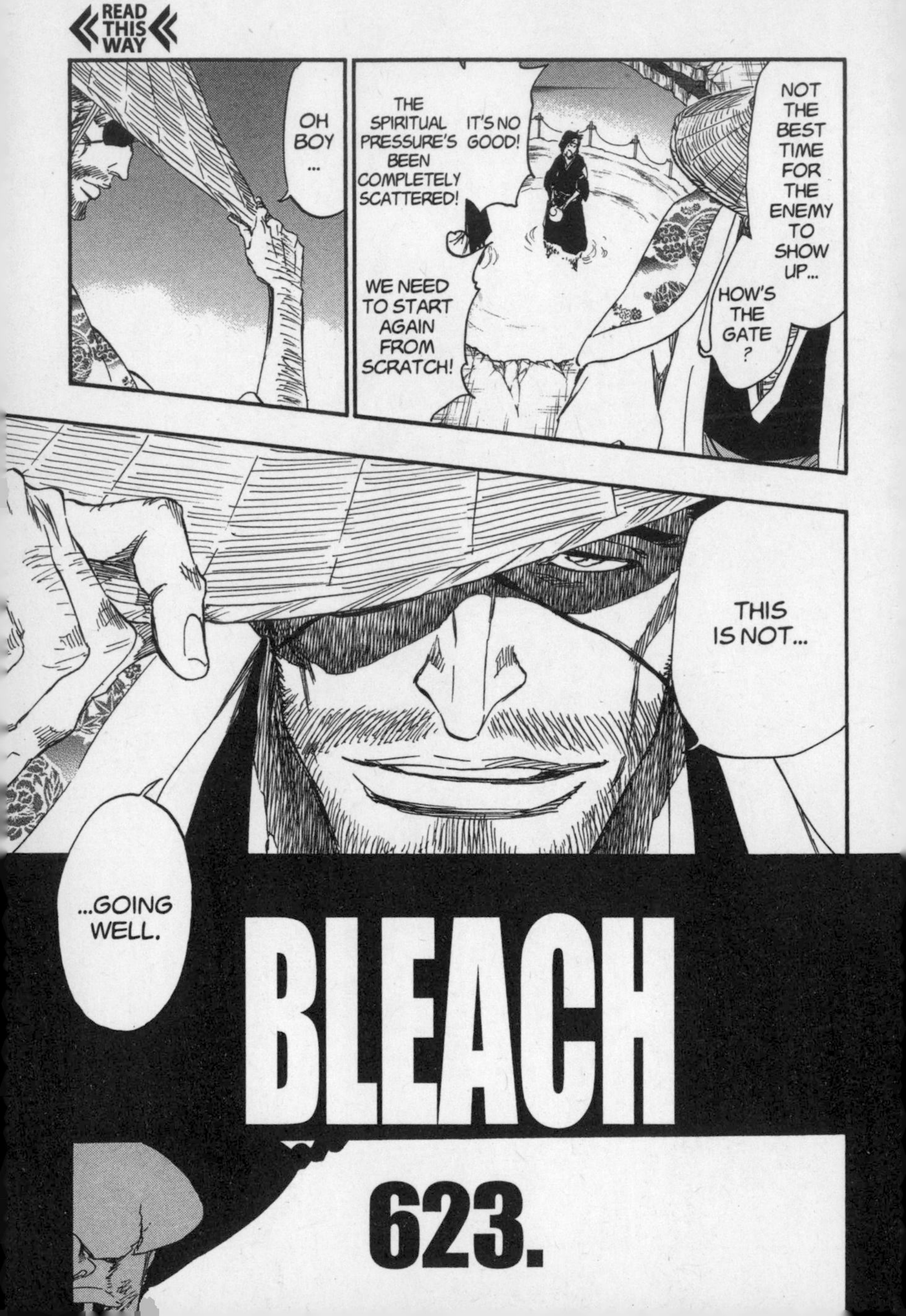
READ THIS WAY
NOT THE BEST TIME FOR THE ENEMY TO SHOW UP...
HOW'S THE GATE?
IT'S NO GOOD!
THE SPIRITUAL PRESSURE'S BEEN COMPLETELY SCATTERED!
WE NEED TO START AGAIN FROM SCRATCH!
OH BOY...
THIS IS NOT...
...GOING WELL.
BLEACH
623.

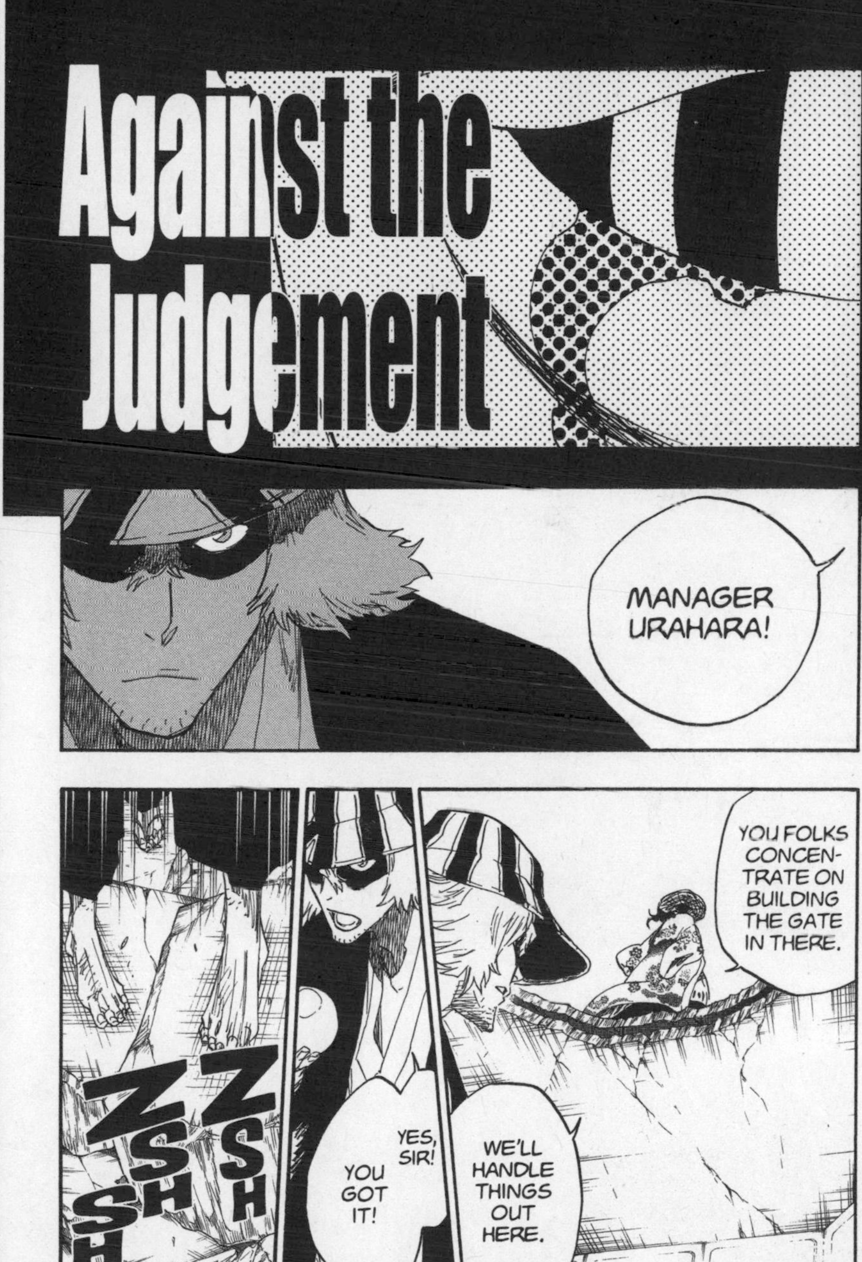
Against the Judgement
MANAGER URAHARA!
YOU FOLKS CONCENTRATE ON BUILDING THE GATE IN THERE.
WE'LL HANDLE THINGS OUT HERE.
YES, SIR!
YOU GOT IT!
ZSH
ZSH
ZSH

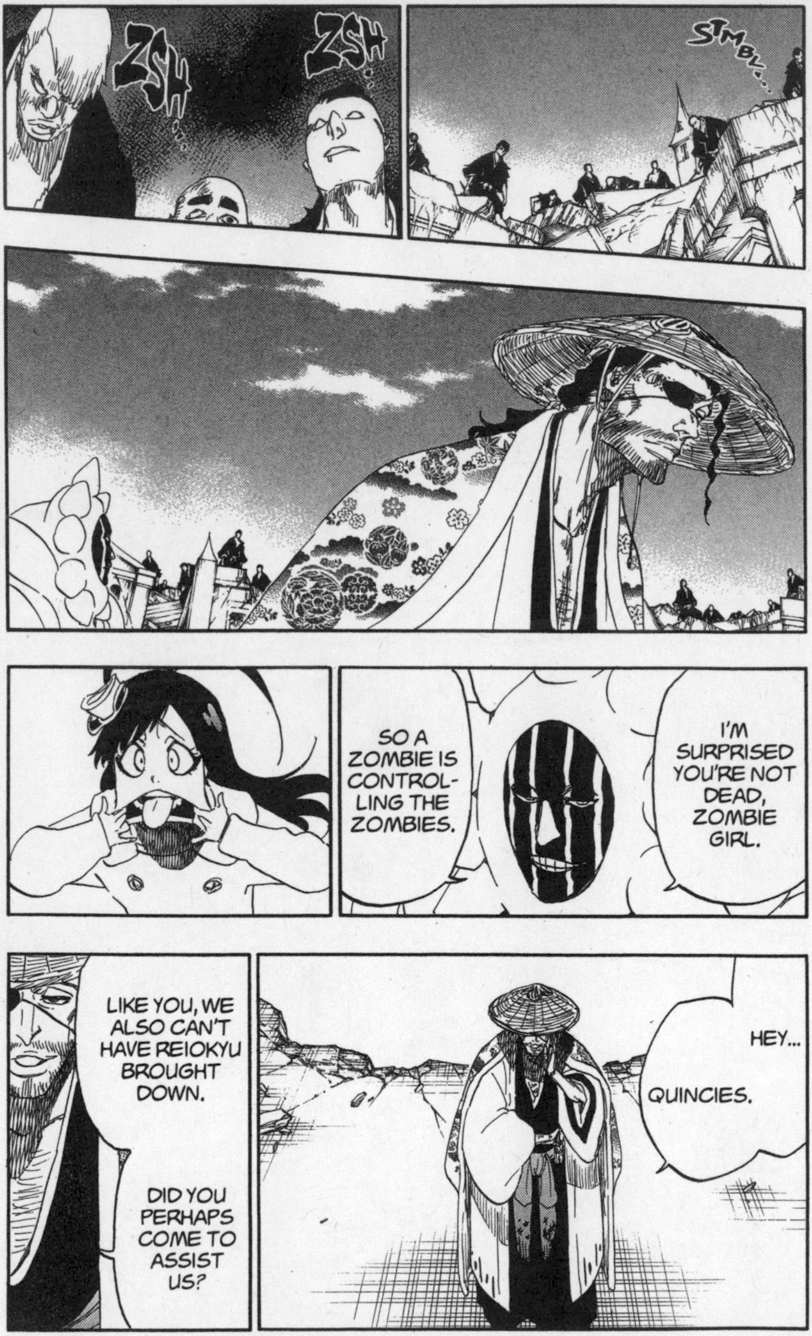
STMBL...
ZSH
ZSH
I'M SURPRISED YOU'RE NOT DEAD, ZOMBIE GIRL.
SO A ZOMBIE IS CONTROL-LING THE ZOMBIES.
HEY...
QUINCIES.
LIKE YOU, WE ALSO CAN'T HAVE REIOKYU BROUGHT DOWN.
DID YOU PERHAPS COME TO ASSIST US?

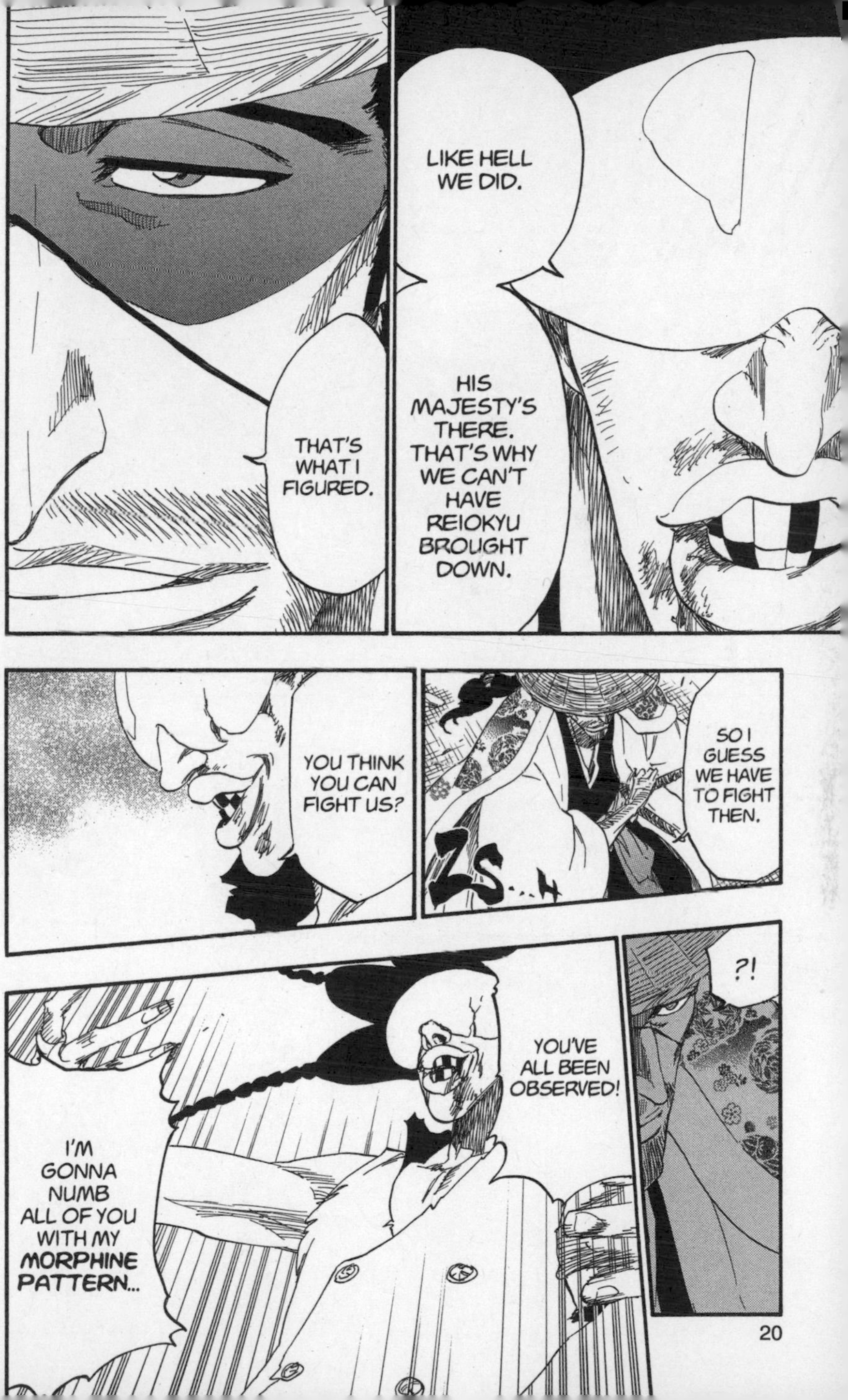
LIKE HELL WE DID.
HIS MAJESTY'S THERE. THAT'S WHY WE CAN'T HAVE REIOKYU BROUGHT DOWN.
THAT'S WHAT I FIGURED.
SO I GUESS WE HAVE TO FIGHT THEN.
ZS...H
YOU THINK YOU CAN FIGHT US?
?!
YOU'VE ALL BEEN OBSERVED!
I'M GONNA NUMB ALL OF YOU WITH MY **MORPHINE PATTERN**...

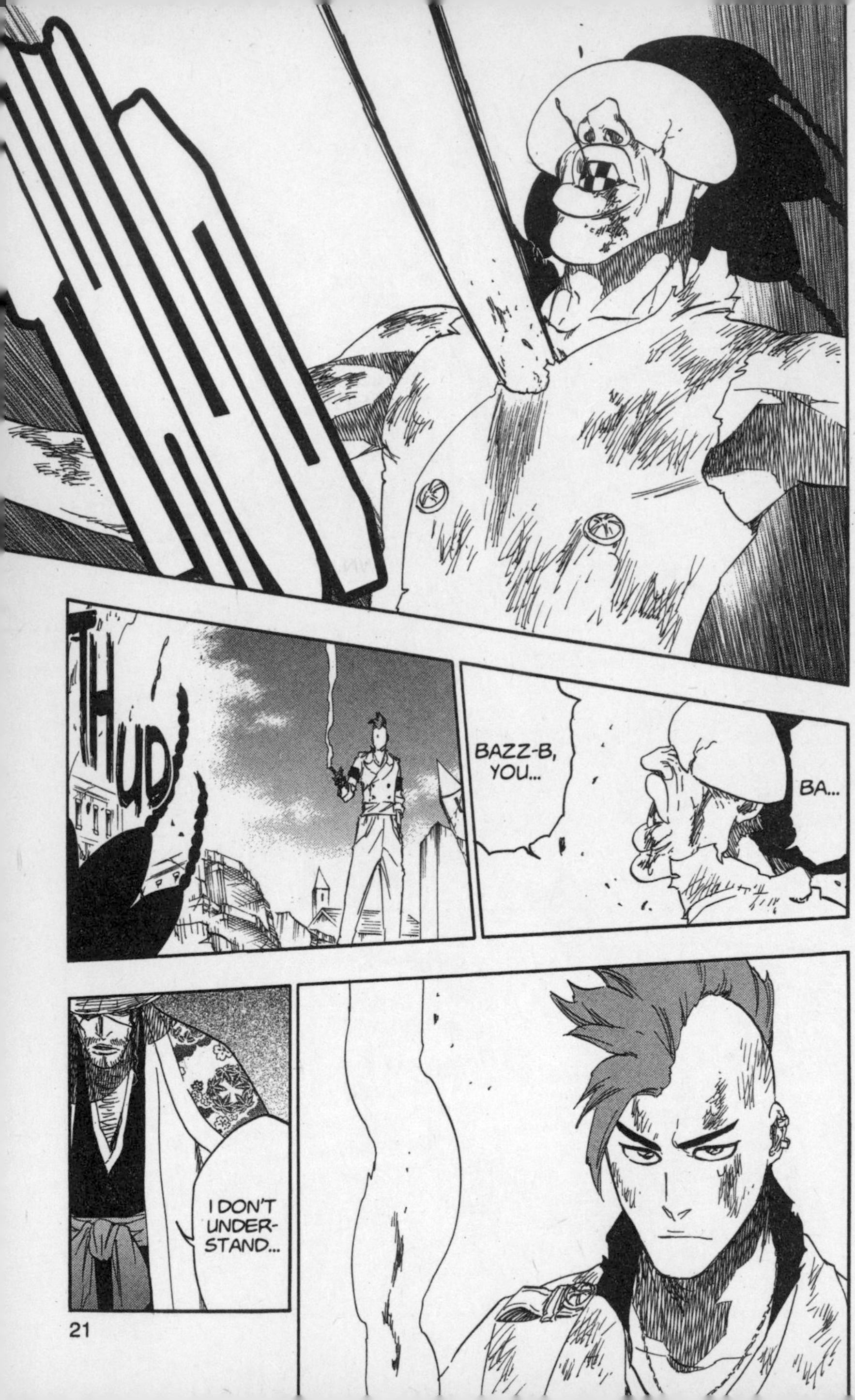
BAZZ-B, YOU...
BA...
THUD
I DON'T UNDER- STAND...

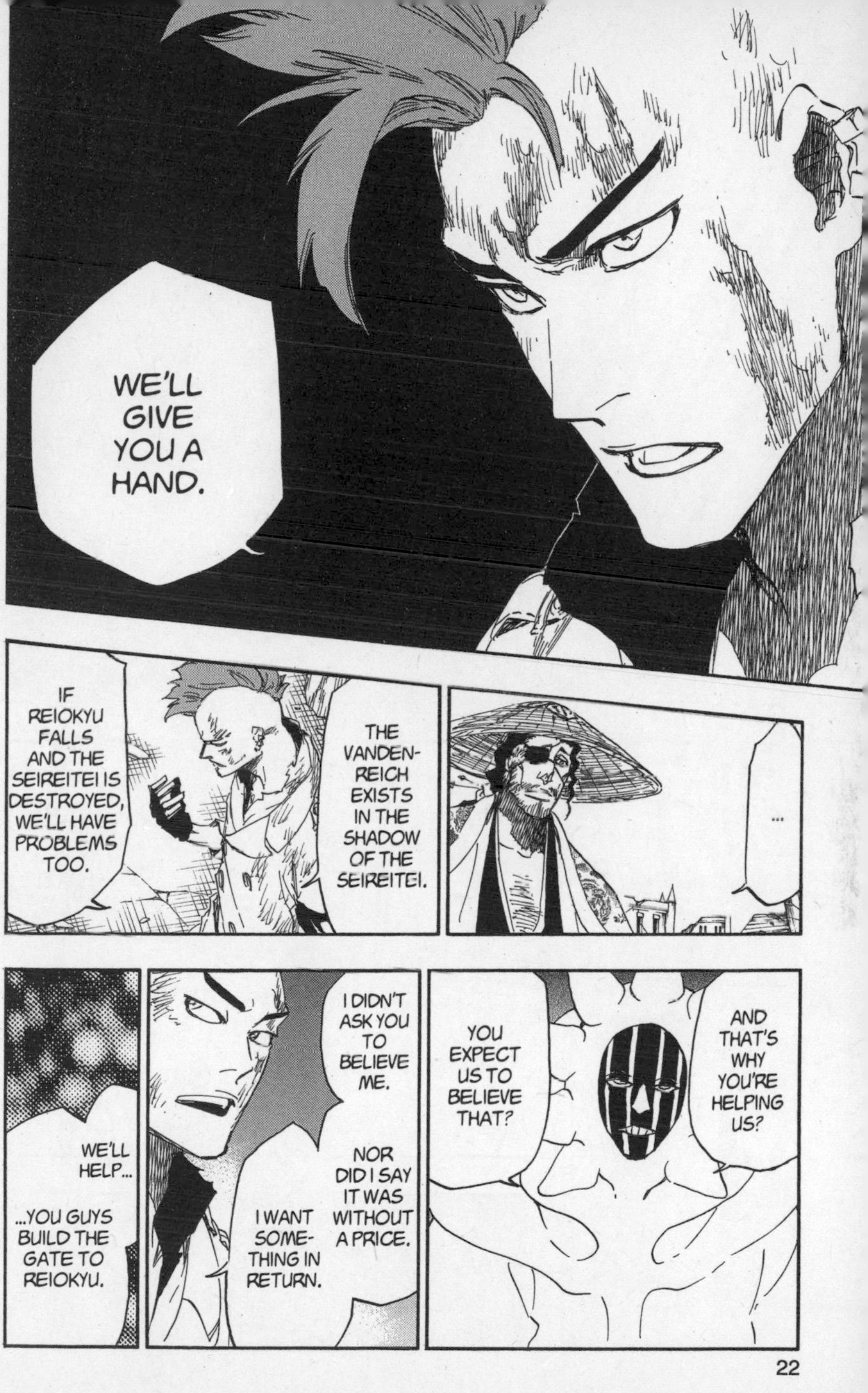
WE'LL GIVE YOU A HAND.
...
THE VANDENREICH EXISTS IN THE SHADOW OF THE SEIREITEI.
IF REIOKYU FALLS AND THE SEIREITEI IS DESTROYED, WE'LL HAVE PROBLEMS TOO.
AND THAT'S WHY YOU'RE HELPING US?
YOU EXPECT US TO BELIEVE THAT?
I DIDN'T ASK YOU TO BELIEVE ME.
NOR DID I SAY IT WAS WITHOUT A PRICE.
I WANT SOMETHING IN RETURN.
WE'LL HELP...
...YOU GUYS BUILD THE GATE TO REIOKYU.

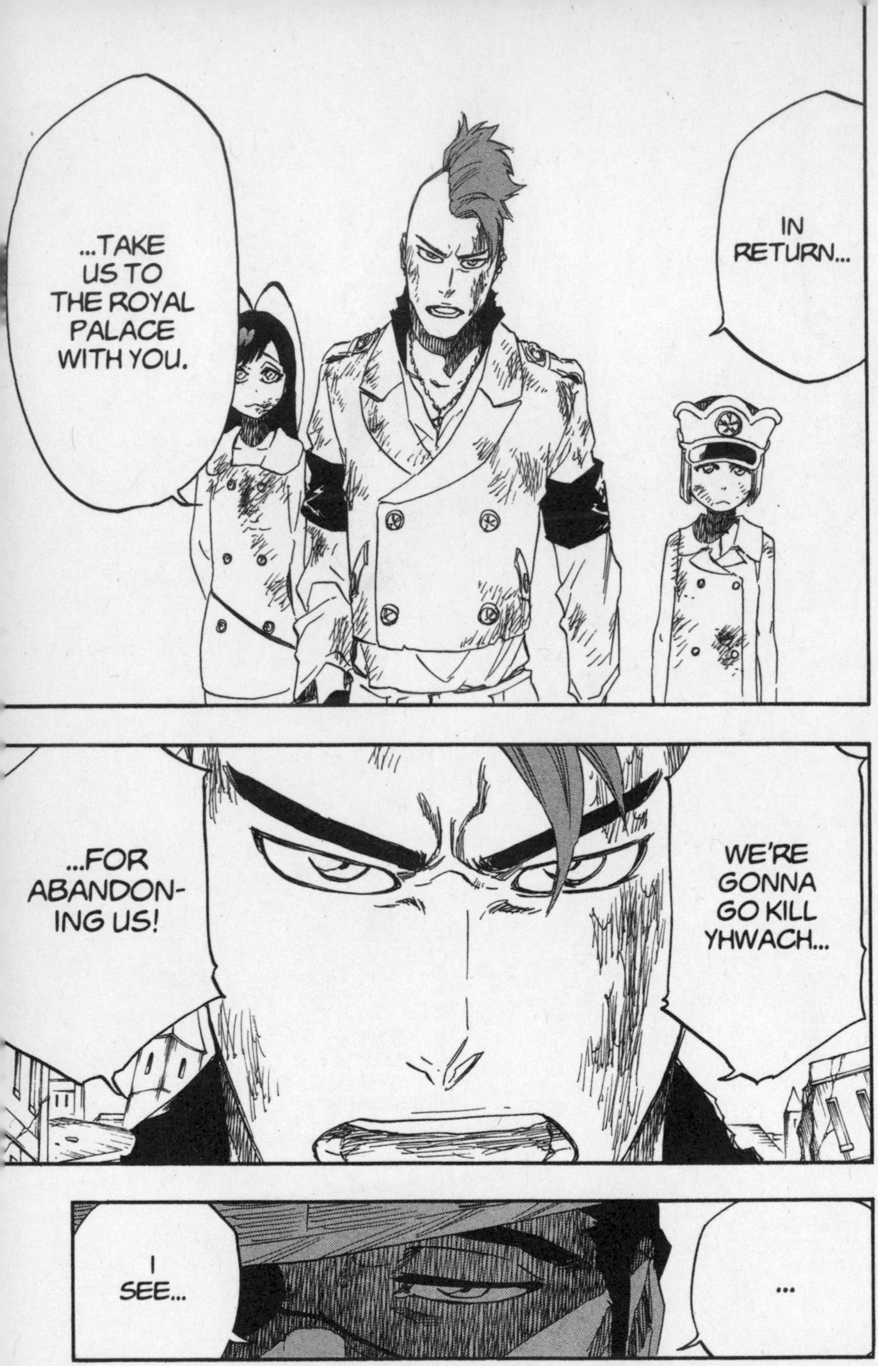
IN RETURN...
...TAKE US TO THE ROYAL PALACE WITH YOU.
WE'RE GONNA GO KILL YHWACH...
...FOR ABANDONING US!
...
I SEE...

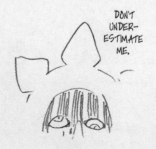

DON'T
UNDER-
ESTIMATE
ME.

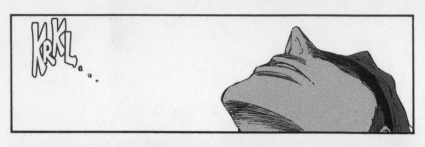

KRKL...

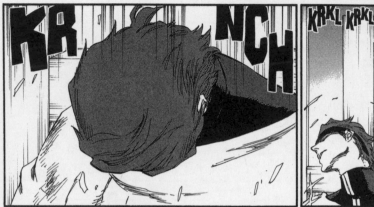

KR NCH

KRKL KRKL
KRKL...
KRKL...

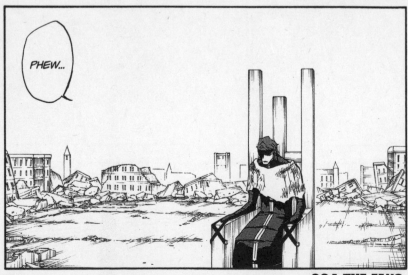

PHEW...

624. THE FANG

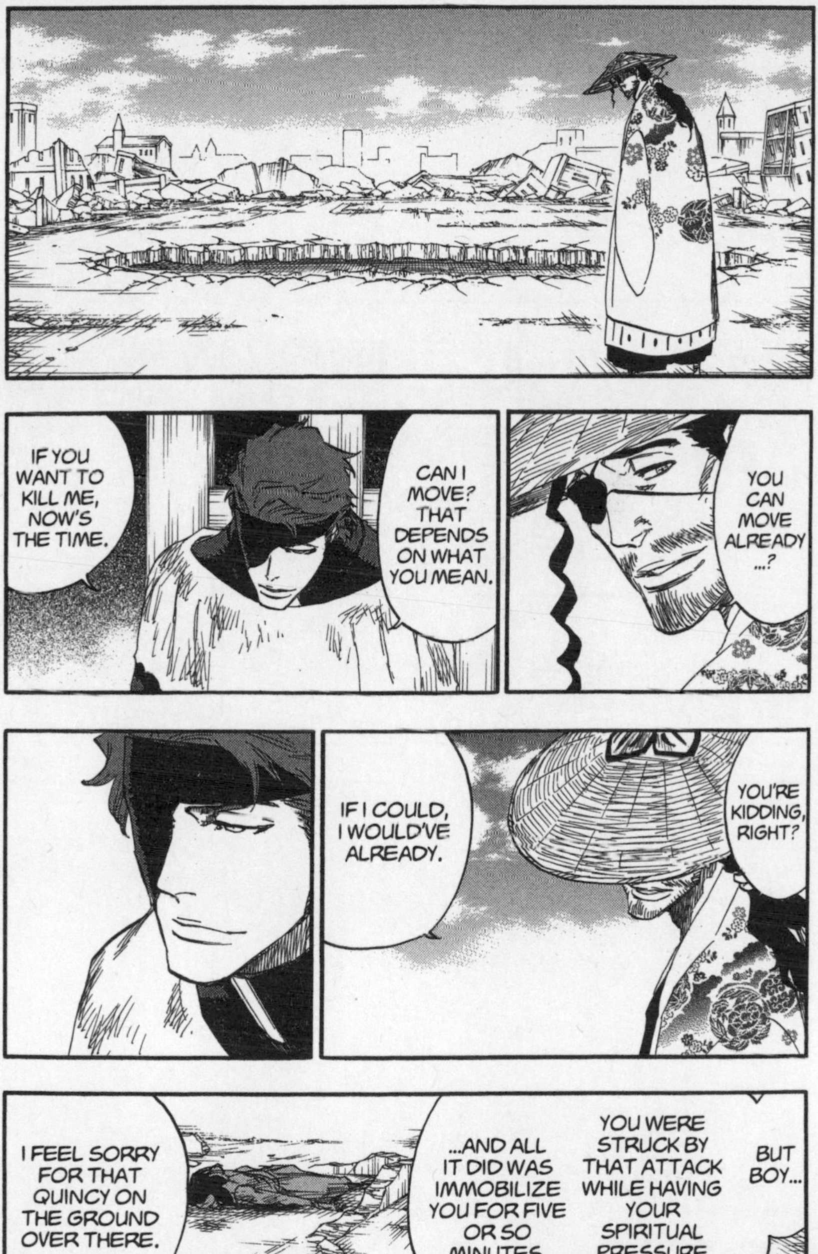
YOU CAN MOVE ALREADY ...?
CAN I MOVE? THAT DEPENDS ON WHAT YOU MEAN.
IF YOU WANT TO KILL ME, NOW'S THE TIME.
YOU'RE KIDDING, RIGHT?
IF I COULD, I WOULD'VE ALREADY.
BUT BOY...
YOU WERE STRUCK BY THAT ATTACK WHILE HAVING YOUR SPIRITUAL PRESSURE SUPPRESSED...
...AND ALL IT DID WAS IMMOBILIZE YOU FOR FIVE OR SO MINUTES.
I FEEL SORRY FOR THAT QUINCY ON THE GROUND OVER THERE.

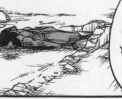

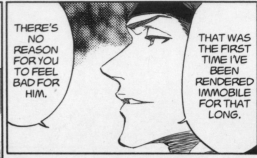

THAT WAS THE FIRST TIME I'VE BEEN RENDERED IMMOBILE FOR THAT LONG.

THERE'S NO REASON FOR YOU TO FEEL BAD FOR HIM.

WELL THEN. IF YOU AREN'T UP TO SPEED YET...

...DO YOU MIND WAITING HERE QUIETLY?

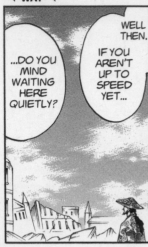

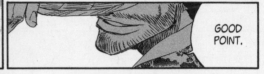

GOOD POINT.

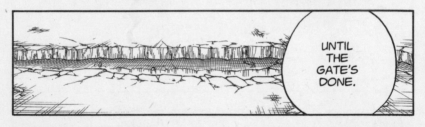

UNTIL THE GATE'S DONE.

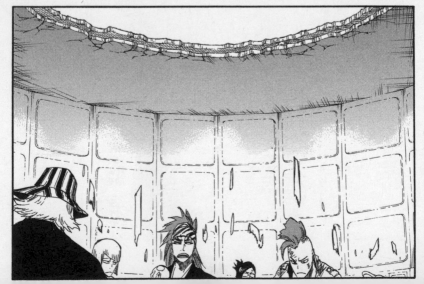

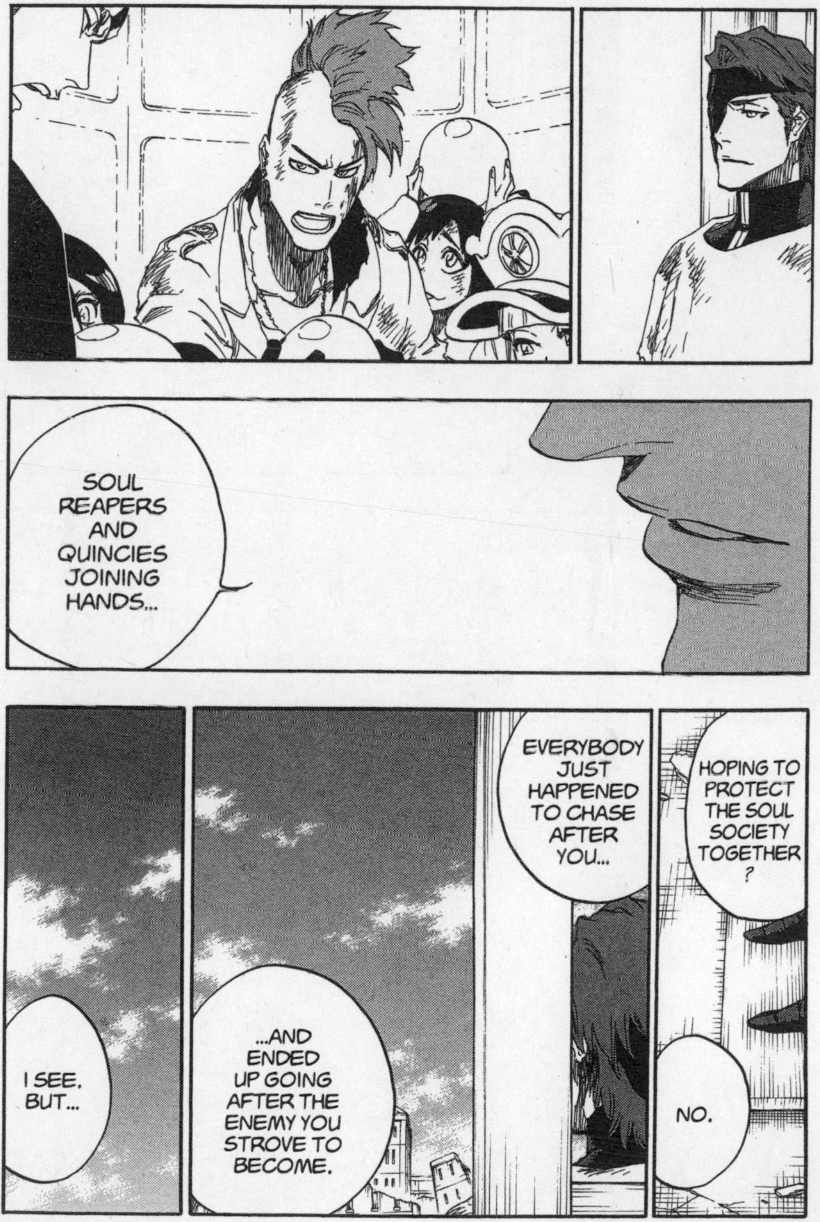
SOUL REAPERS AND QUINCIES JOINING HANDS...
HOPING TO PROTECT THE SOUL SOCIETY TOGETHER?
NO.
EVERYBODY JUST HAPPENED TO CHASE AFTER YOU...
...AND ENDED UP GOING AFTER THE ENEMY YOU STROVE TO BECOME.
I SEE. BUT...

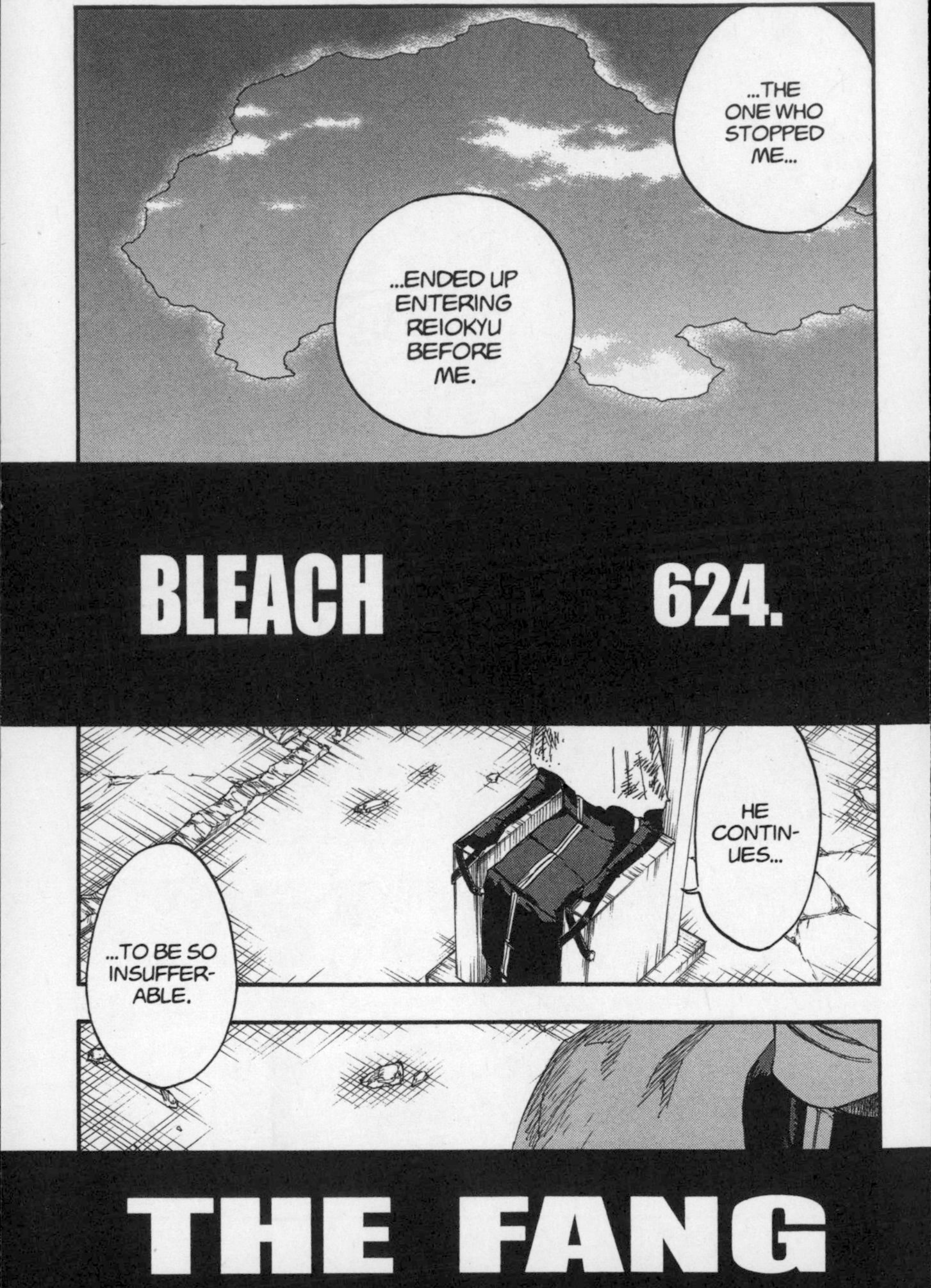
...THE ONE WHO STOPPED ME...
...ENDED UP ENTERING REIOKYU BEFORE ME.
BLEACH 624.
HE CONTIN-UES...
...TO BE SO INSUFFER-ABLE.
THE FANG

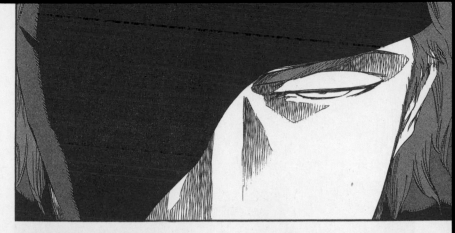

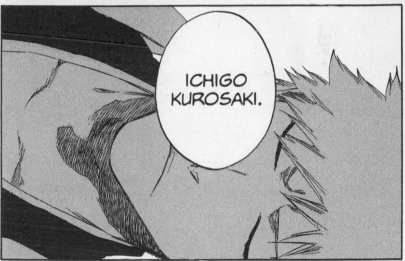

ICHIGO KUROSAKI.

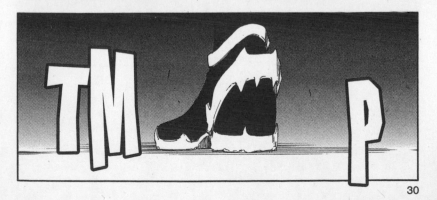

TM P

READ THIS WAY

TMP
TMP
TMP

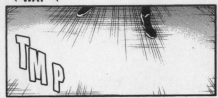

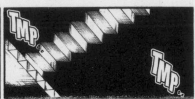

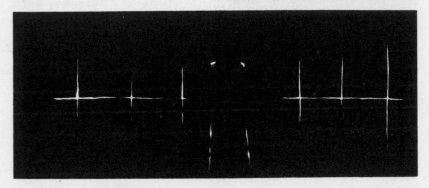

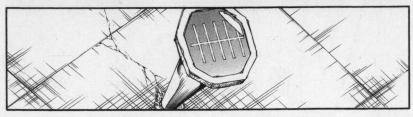

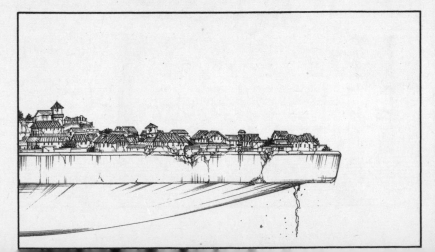

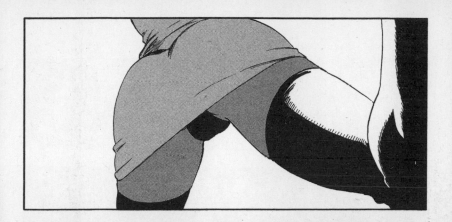

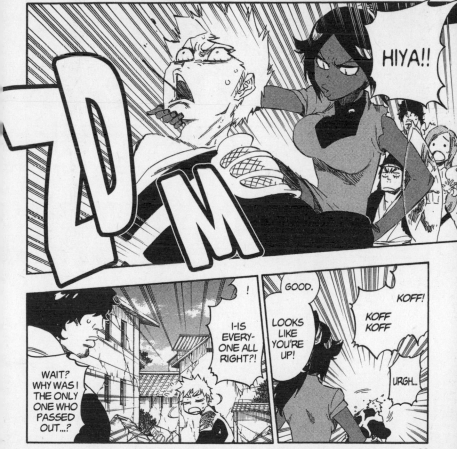

HIYA!!

!

GOOD.

KOFF!

KOFF
KOFF

LOOKS
LIKE
YOU'RE
UP!

I-IS
EVERY-
ONE ALL
RIGHT?!

URGH...

WAIT?
WHY WAS I
THE ONLY
ONE WHO
PASSED
OUT....?

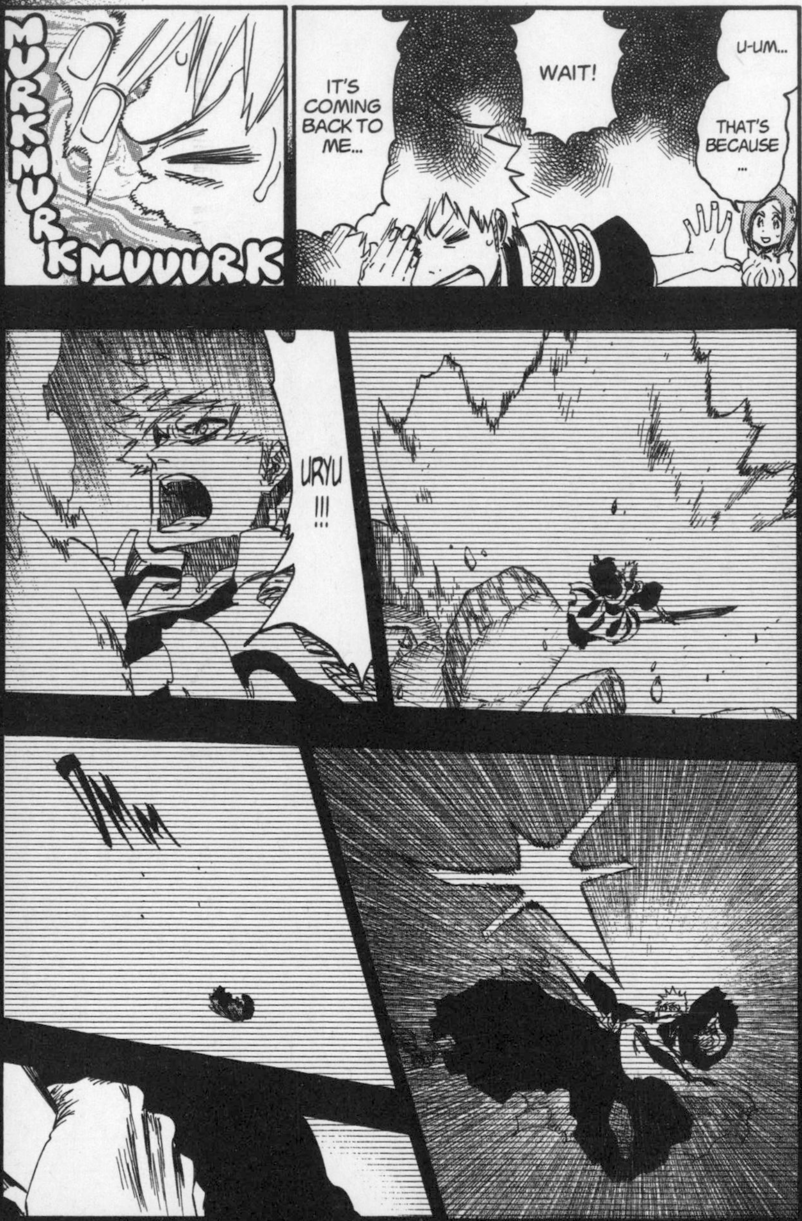
U-UM...
THAT'S BECAUSE ...
WAIT!
IT'S COMING BACK TO ME...
MURKMURK MUUUURK
URYU !!!

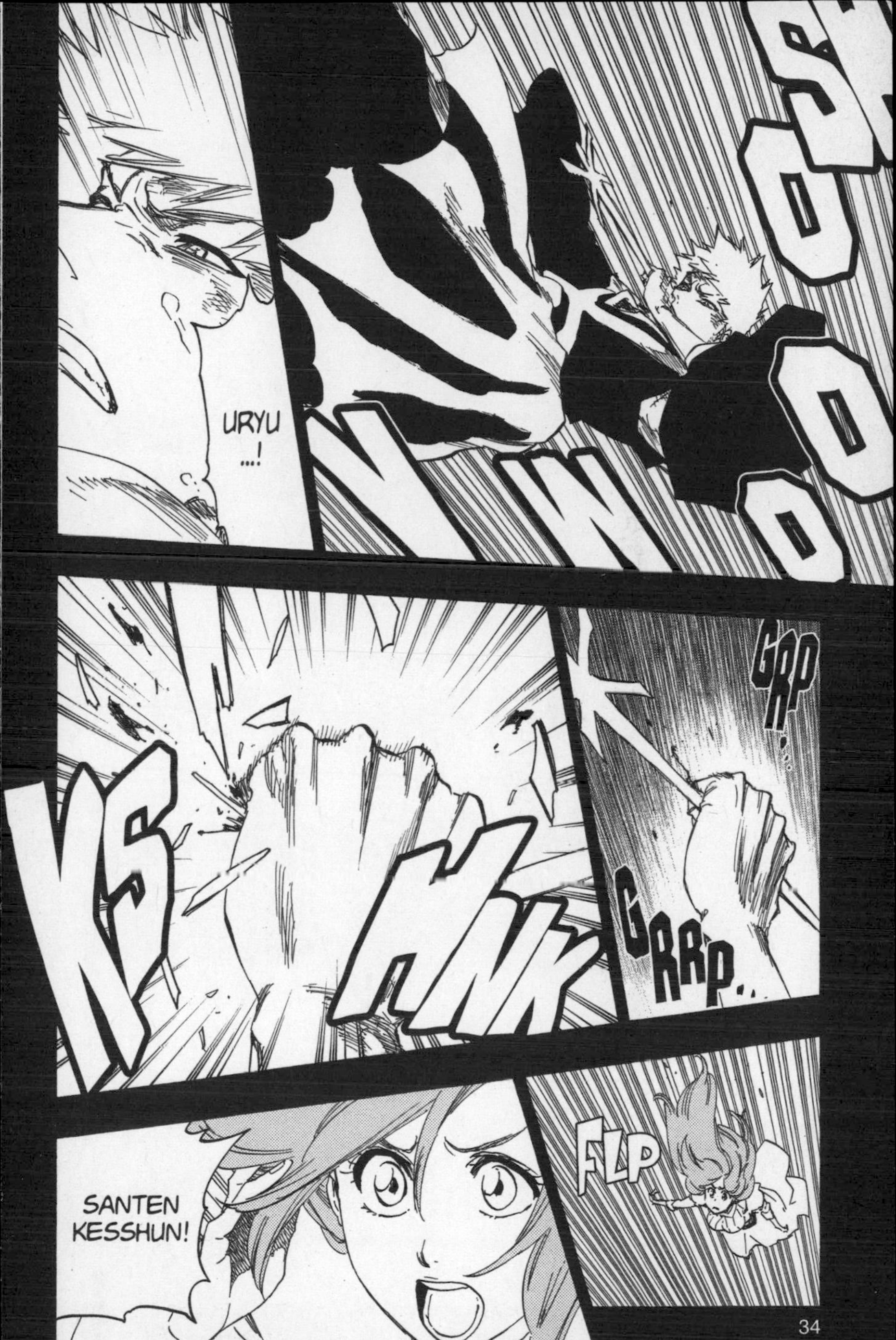
SGOOOO
VWN
URYU ...!
GRP
GRRP...
HNK
KS
FLP
SANTEN KESSHUN!

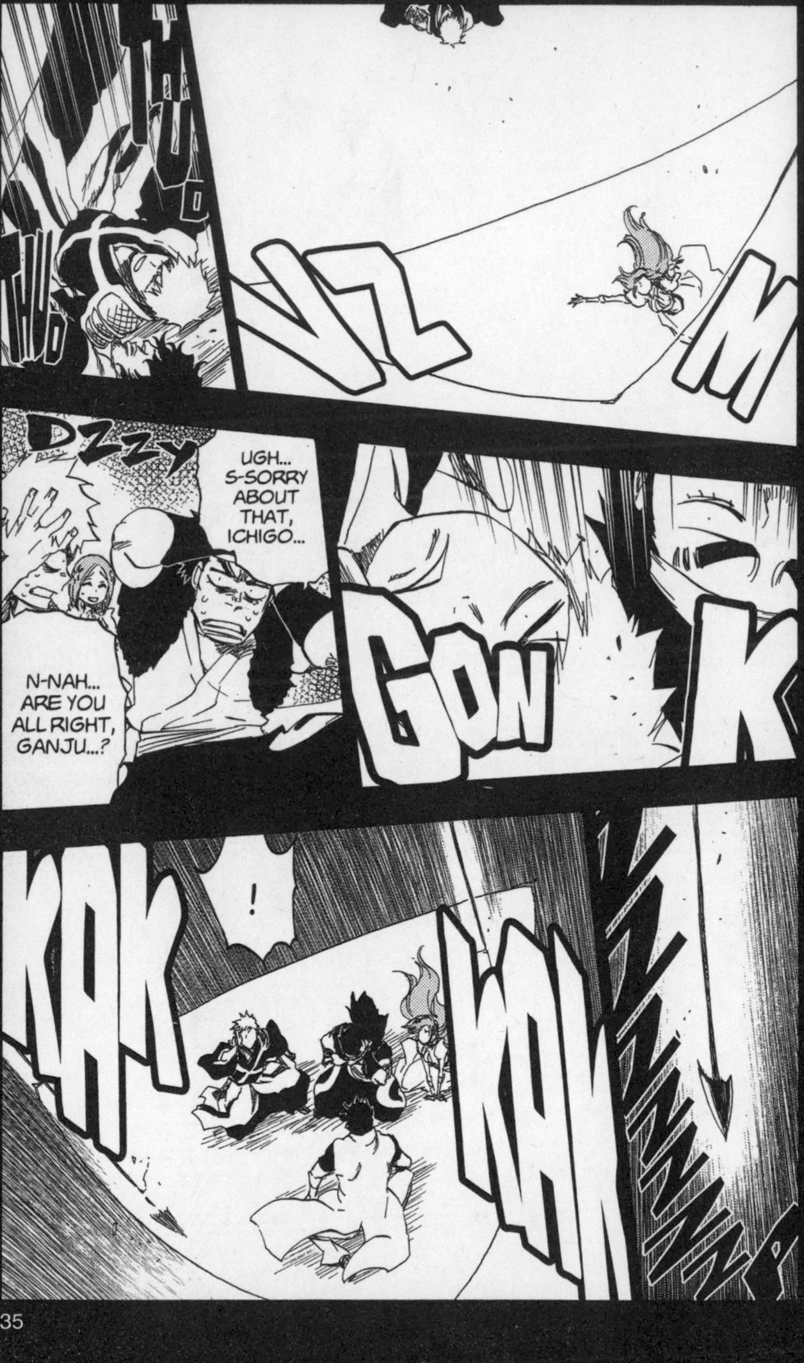
THUD
THUD
GONK
DZZY
UGH... S-SORRY ABOUT THAT, ICHIGO...
N-NAH... ARE YOU ALL RIGHT, GANJU...?
!
KAK
KAK

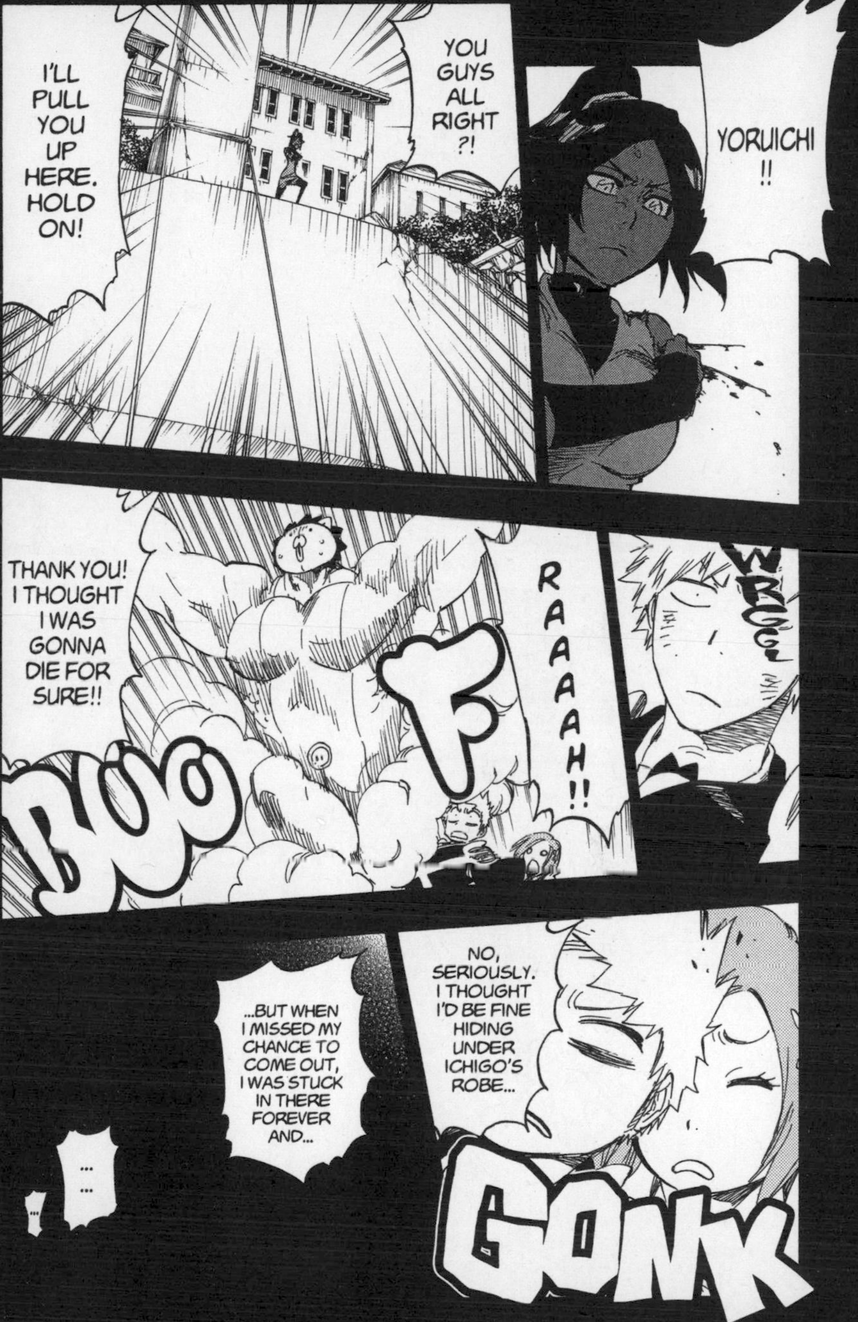
YORUICHI!!
YOU GUYS ALL RIGHT?!
I'LL PULL YOU UP HERE. HOLD ON!
WRGGL
RAAAAAH!!
THANK YOU! I THOUGHT I WAS GONNA DIE FOR SURE!!
BOOF
NO, SERIOUSLY. I THOUGHT I'D BE FINE HIDING UNDER ICHIGO'S ROBE...
GONK
...BUT WHEN I MISSED MY CHANCE TO COME OUT, I WAS STUCK IN THERE FOREVER AND...
......
...

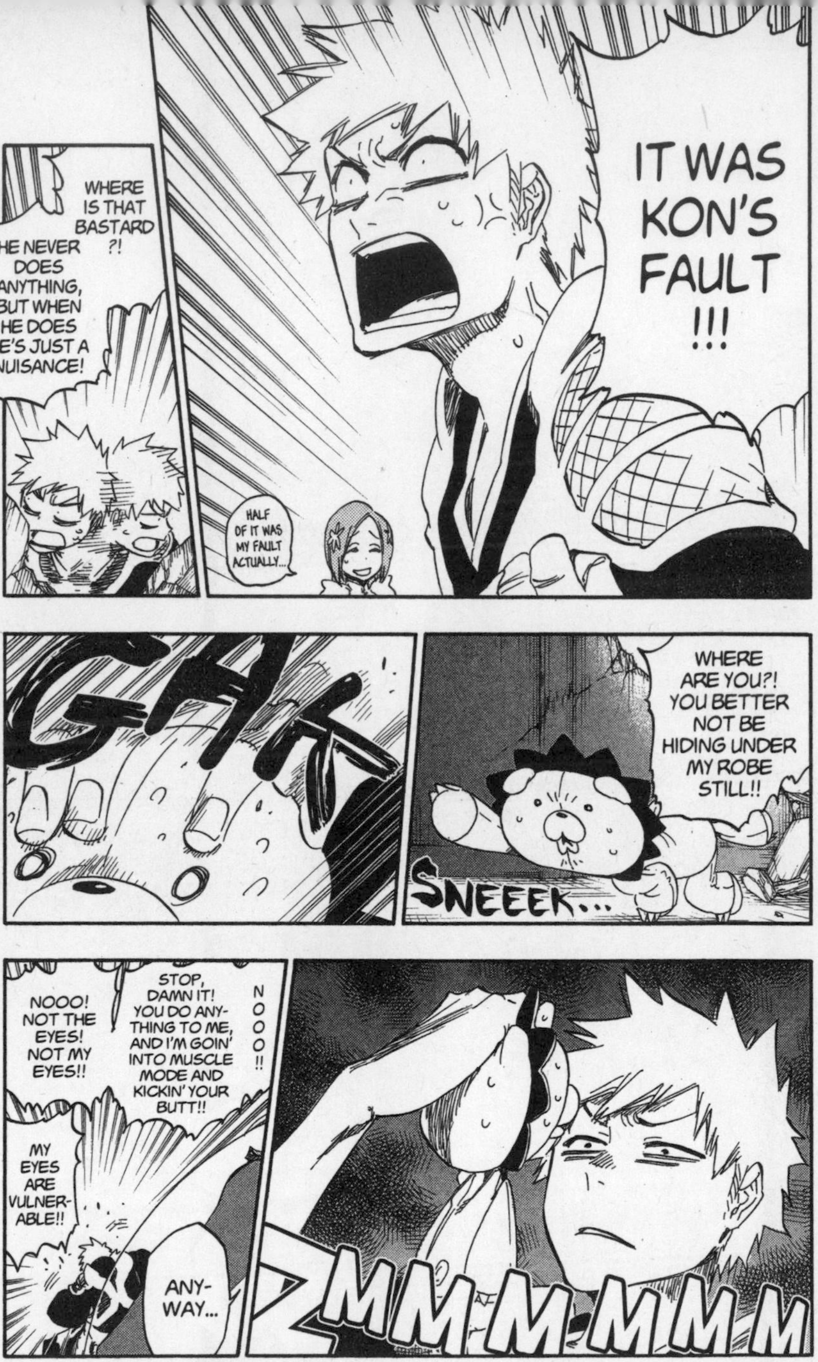
IT WAS KON'S FAULT!!!
HALF OF IT WAS MY FAULT ACTUALLY...
WHERE IS THAT BASTARD ?!
HE NEVER DOES ANYTHING, BUT WHEN HE DOES HE'S JUST A NUISANCE!
WHERE ARE YOU?! YOU BETTER NOT BE HIDING UNDER MY ROBE STILL!!
SNEEEK...
GHK
ZMMMMMMMM
NOOOO!!
STOP, DAMN IT! YOU DO ANYTHING TO ME, AND I'M GOIN' INTO MUSCLE MODE AND KICKIN' YOUR BUTT!!
NOOO! NOT THE EYES! NOT MY EYES!!
MY EYES ARE VULNERABLE!!
ANYWAY...

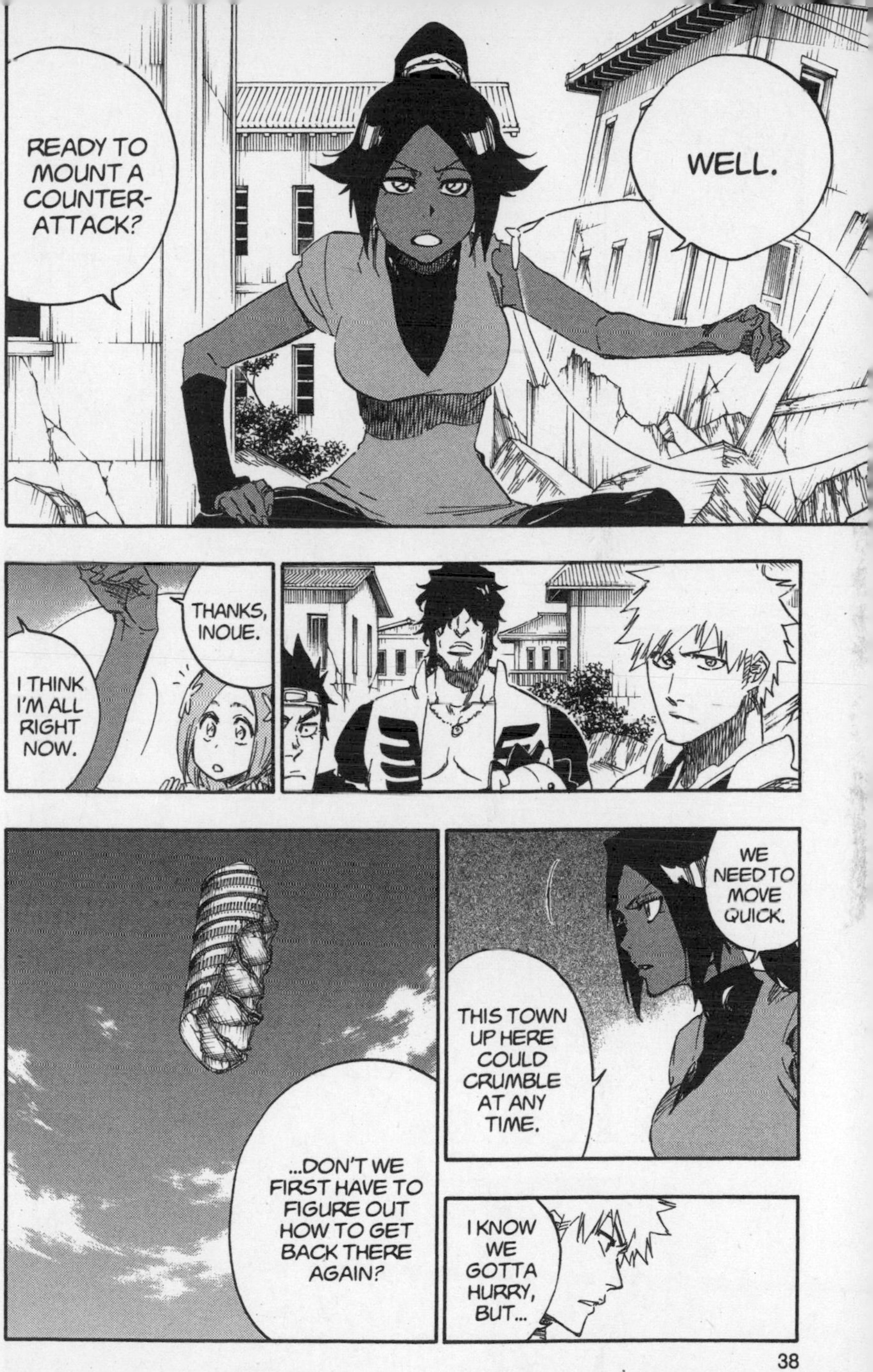
WELL.
READY TO MOUNT A COUNTER-ATTACK?
THANKS, INOUE.
I THINK I'M ALL RIGHT NOW.
WE NEED TO MOVE QUICK.
THIS TOWN UP HERE COULD CRUMBLE AT ANY TIME.
I KNOW WE GOTTA HURRY, BUT...
...DON'T WE FIRST HAVE TO FIGURE OUT HOW TO GET BACK THERE AGAIN?

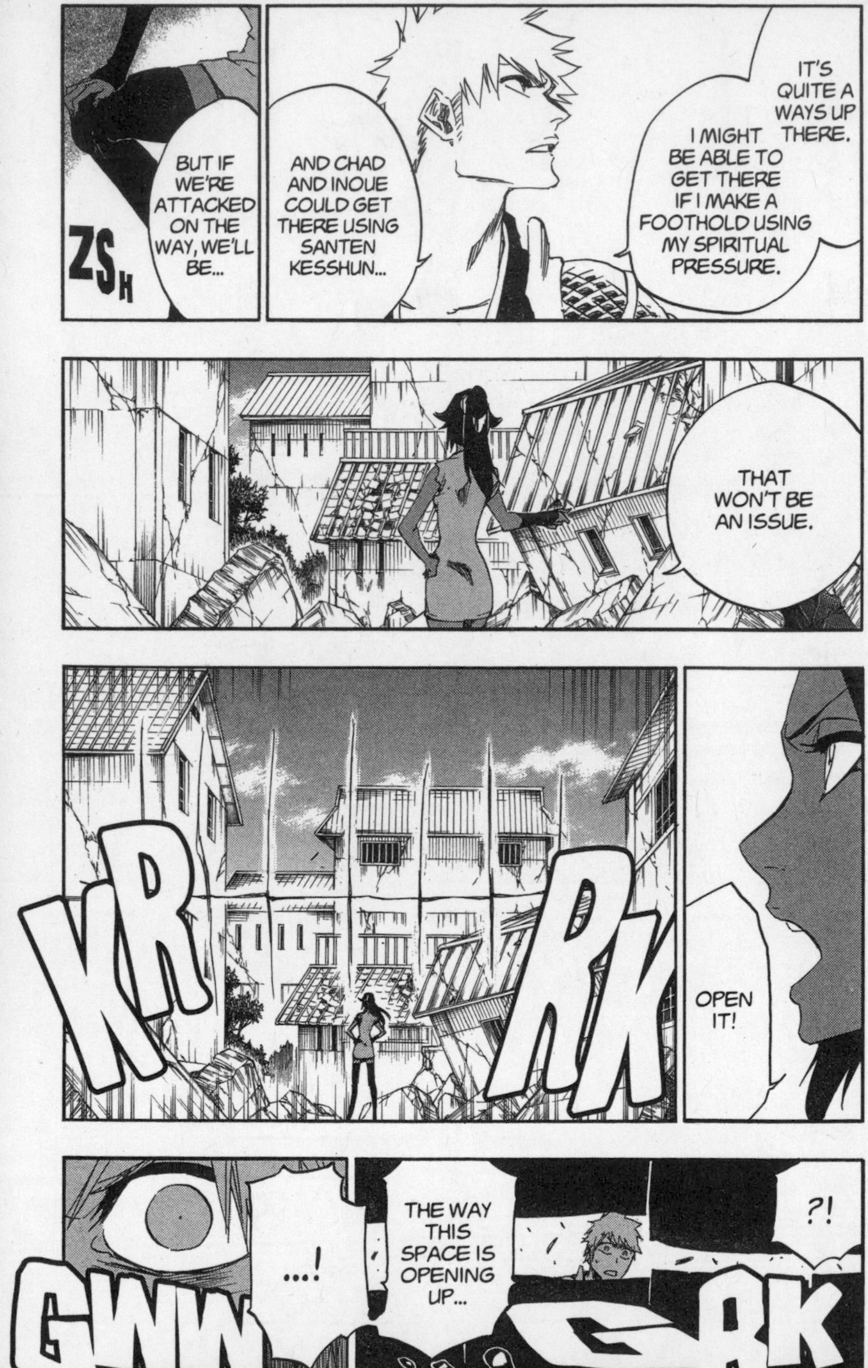
IT'S QUITE A WAYS UP THERE.
I MIGHT BE ABLE TO GET THERE IF I MAKE A FOOTHOLD USING MY SPIRITUAL PRESSURE.
AND CHAD AND INOUE COULD GET THERE USING SANTEN KESSHUN...
BUT IF WE'RE ATTACKED ON THE WAY, WE'LL BE...
ZSH
THAT WON'T BE AN ISSUE.
OPEN IT!
KRRK
?!
THE WAY THIS SPACE IS OPENING UP...
GRK
...!
GWN

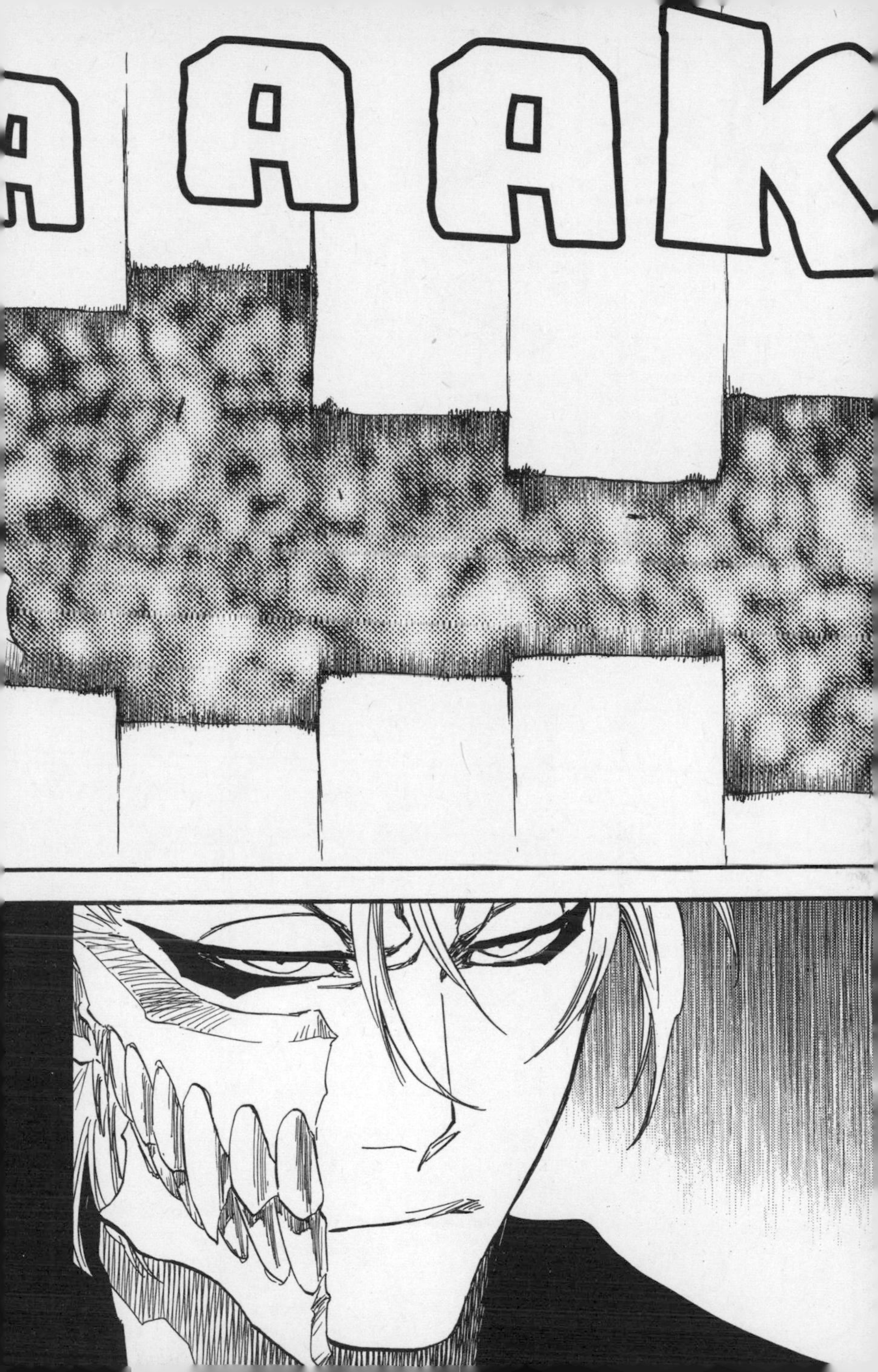
AAAK

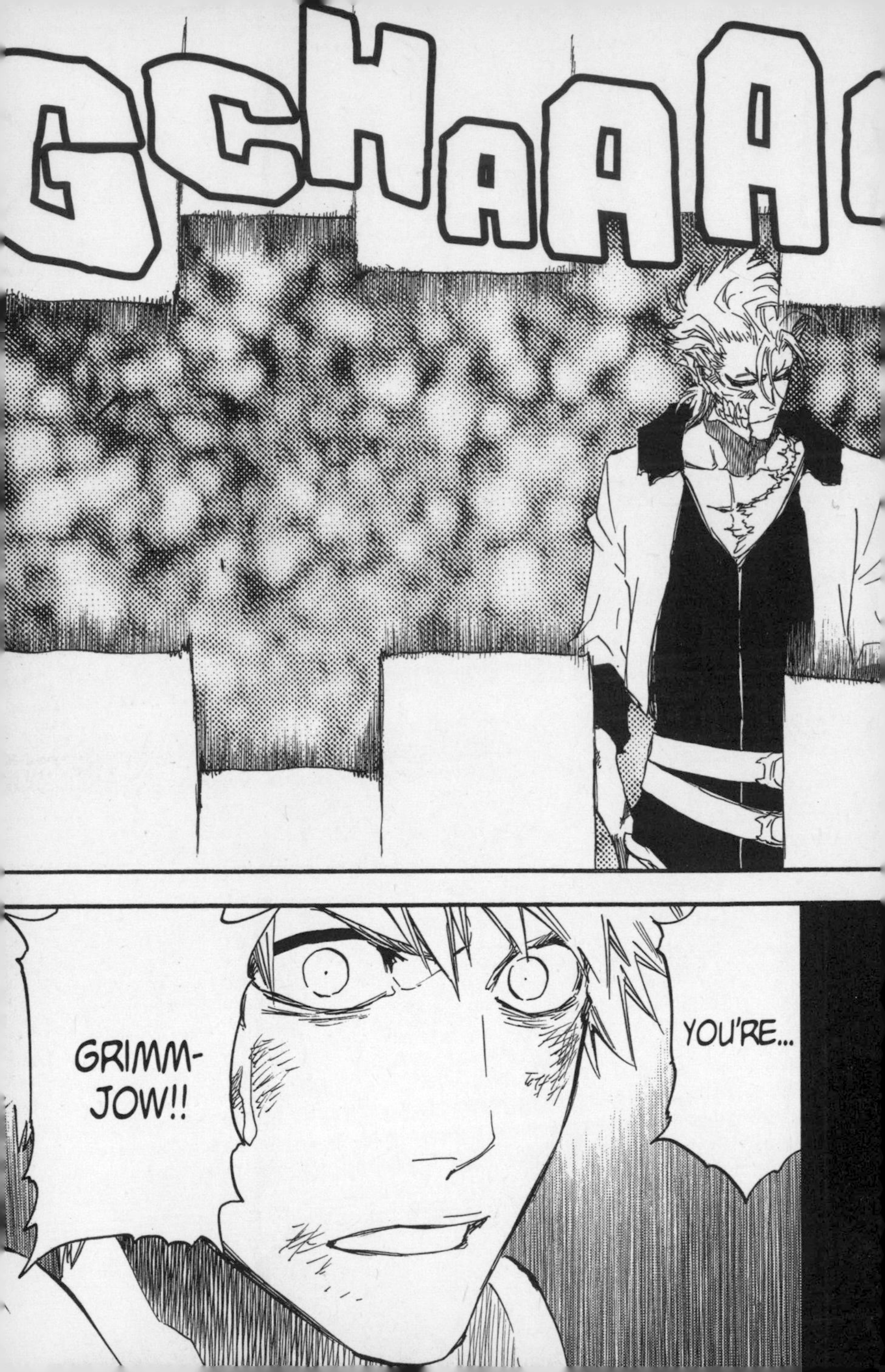
GCHAAA
YOU'RE...
GRIMM-
JOW!!

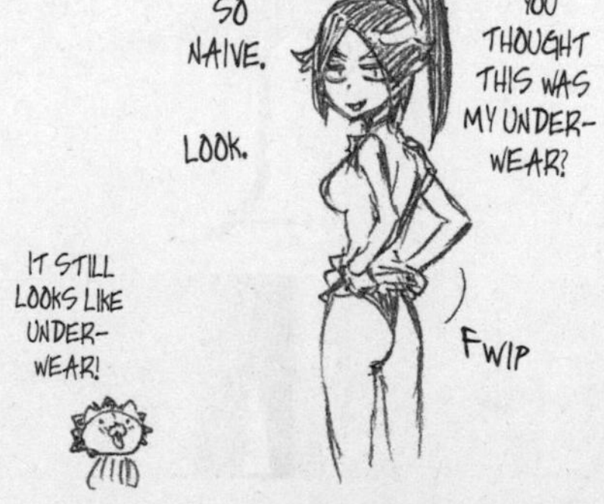
YOU THOUGHT THIS WAS MY UNDER-WEAR?
SO NAIVE.
LOOK.
FWIP
IT STILL LOOKS LIKE UNDER-WEAR!

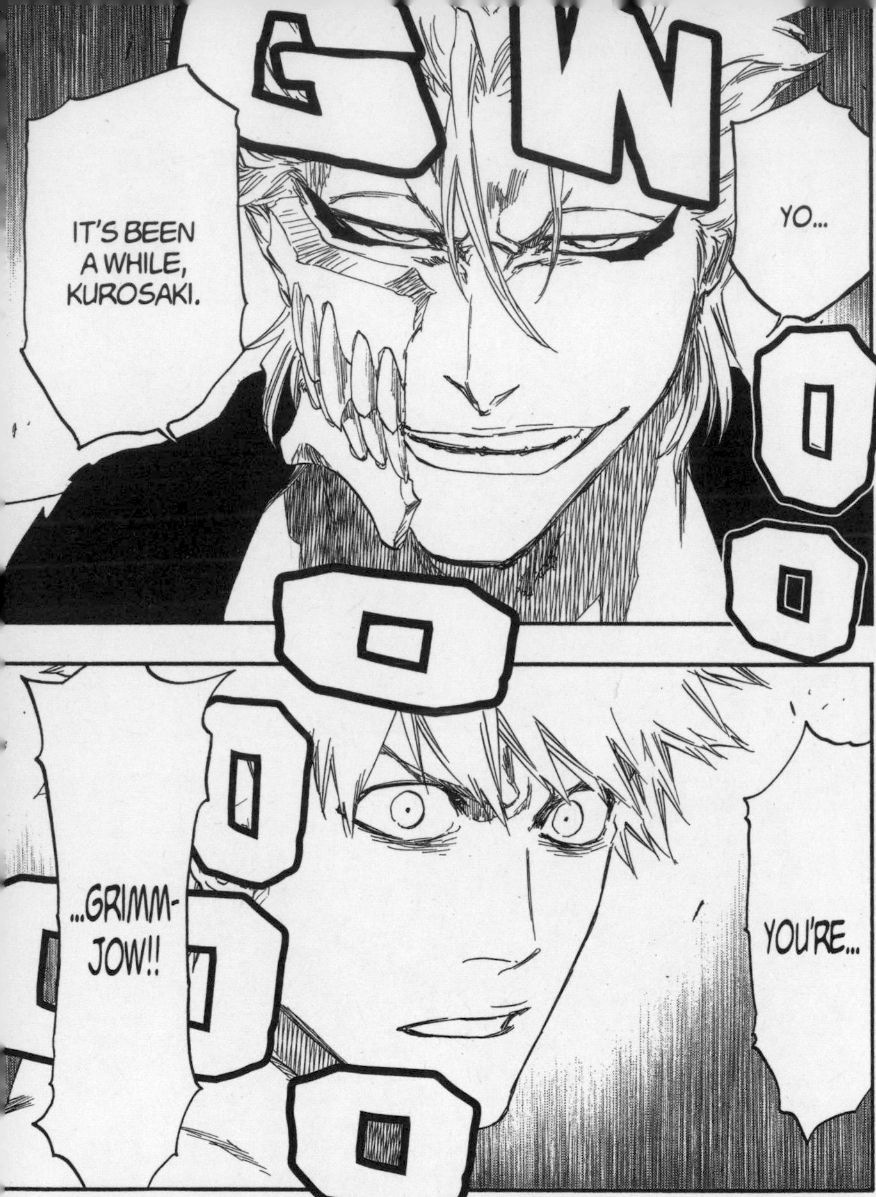
YO...
IT'S BEEN A WHILE, KUROSAKI.
YOU'RE...
...GRIMM-JOW!!

625.LIVING JAGUAR

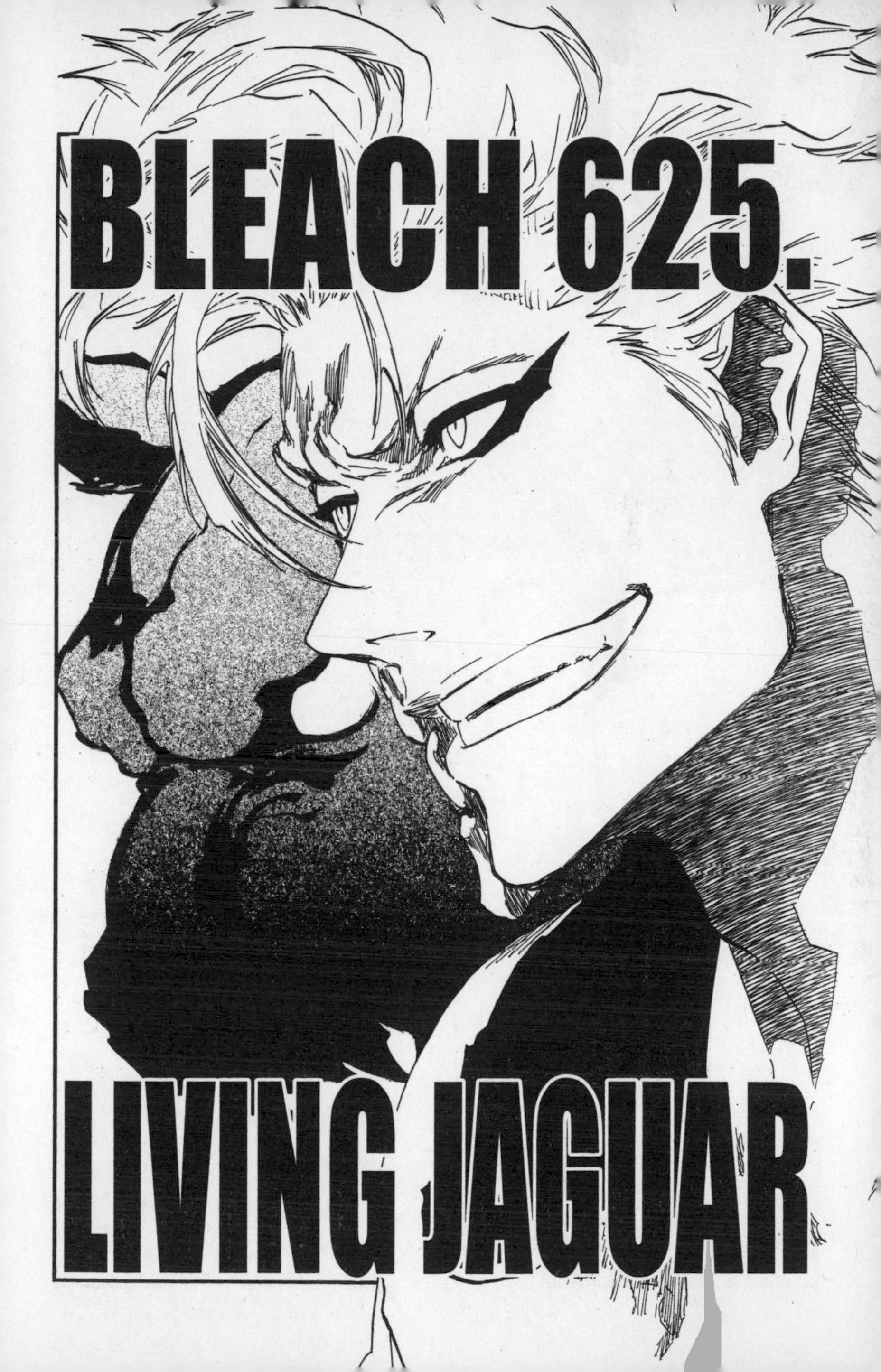
BLEACH 625.
LIVING JAGUAR

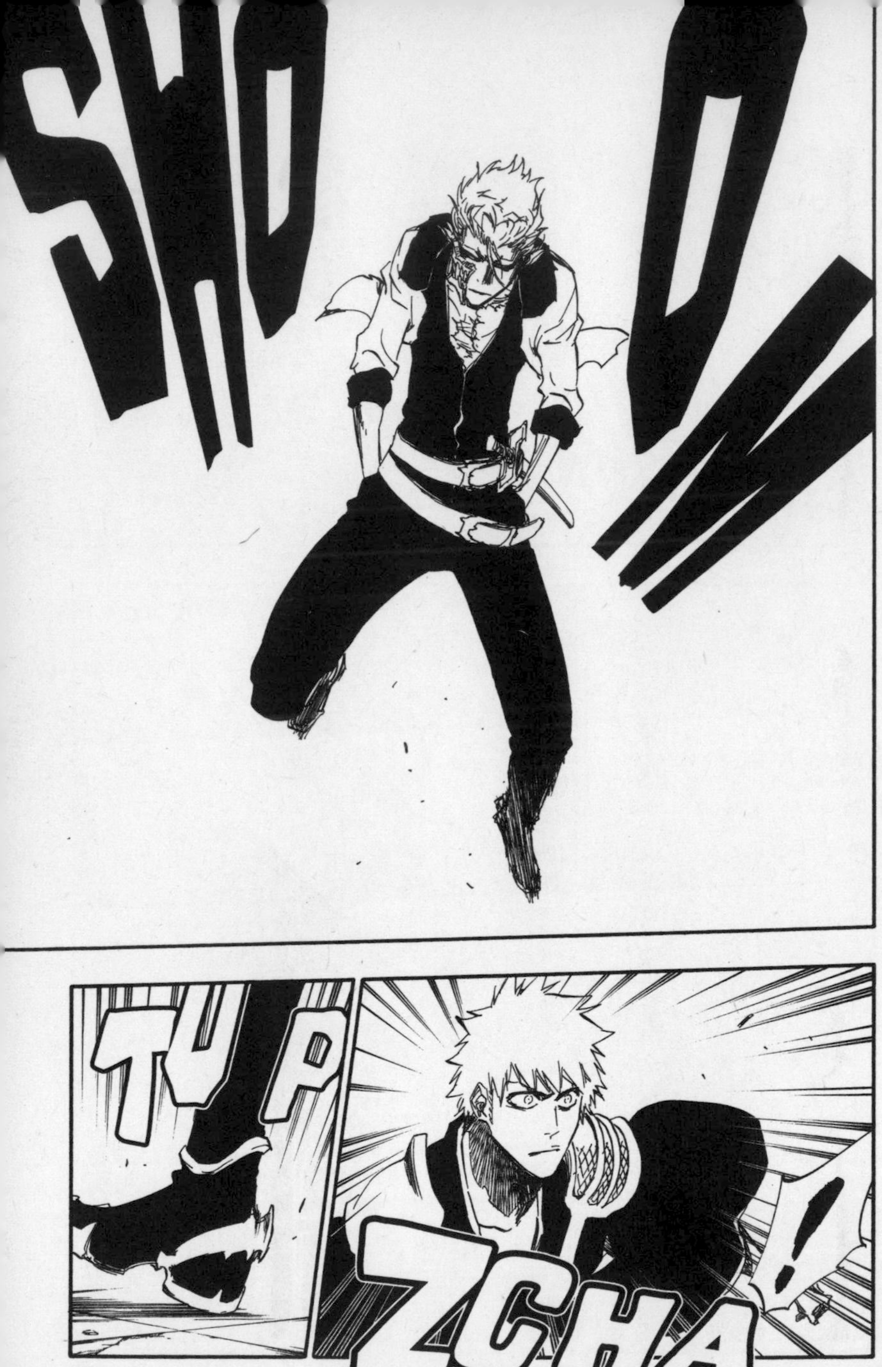
SHOOM
ZCHA!
TUP

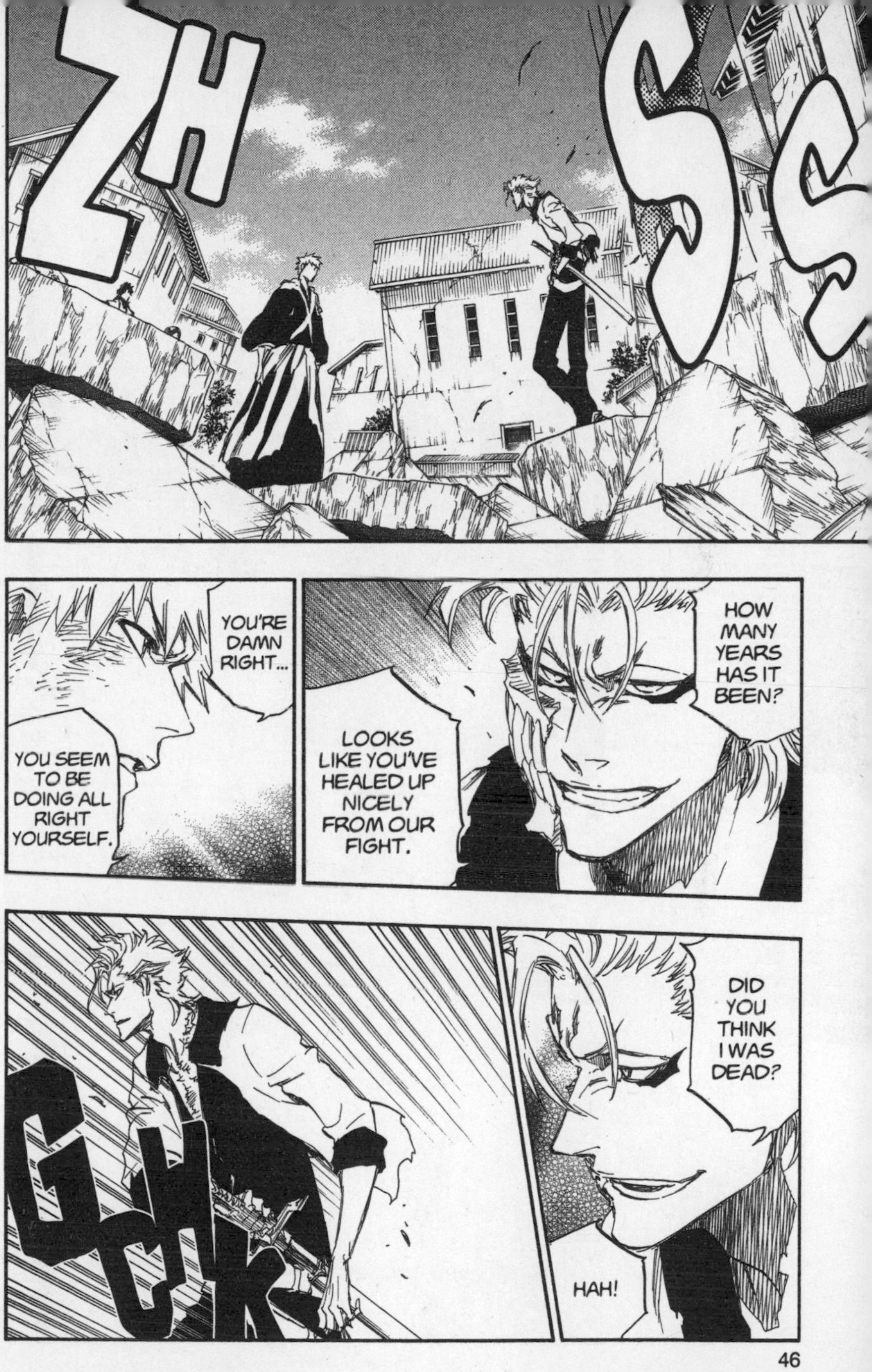
SS
ZH
HOW MANY YEARS HAS IT BEEN?
LOOKS LIKE YOU'VE HEALED UP NICELY FROM OUR FIGHT.
YOU'RE DAMN RIGHT...
YOU SEEM TO BE DOING ALL RIGHT YOURSELF.
DID YOU THINK I WAS DEAD?
HAH!
GCHK

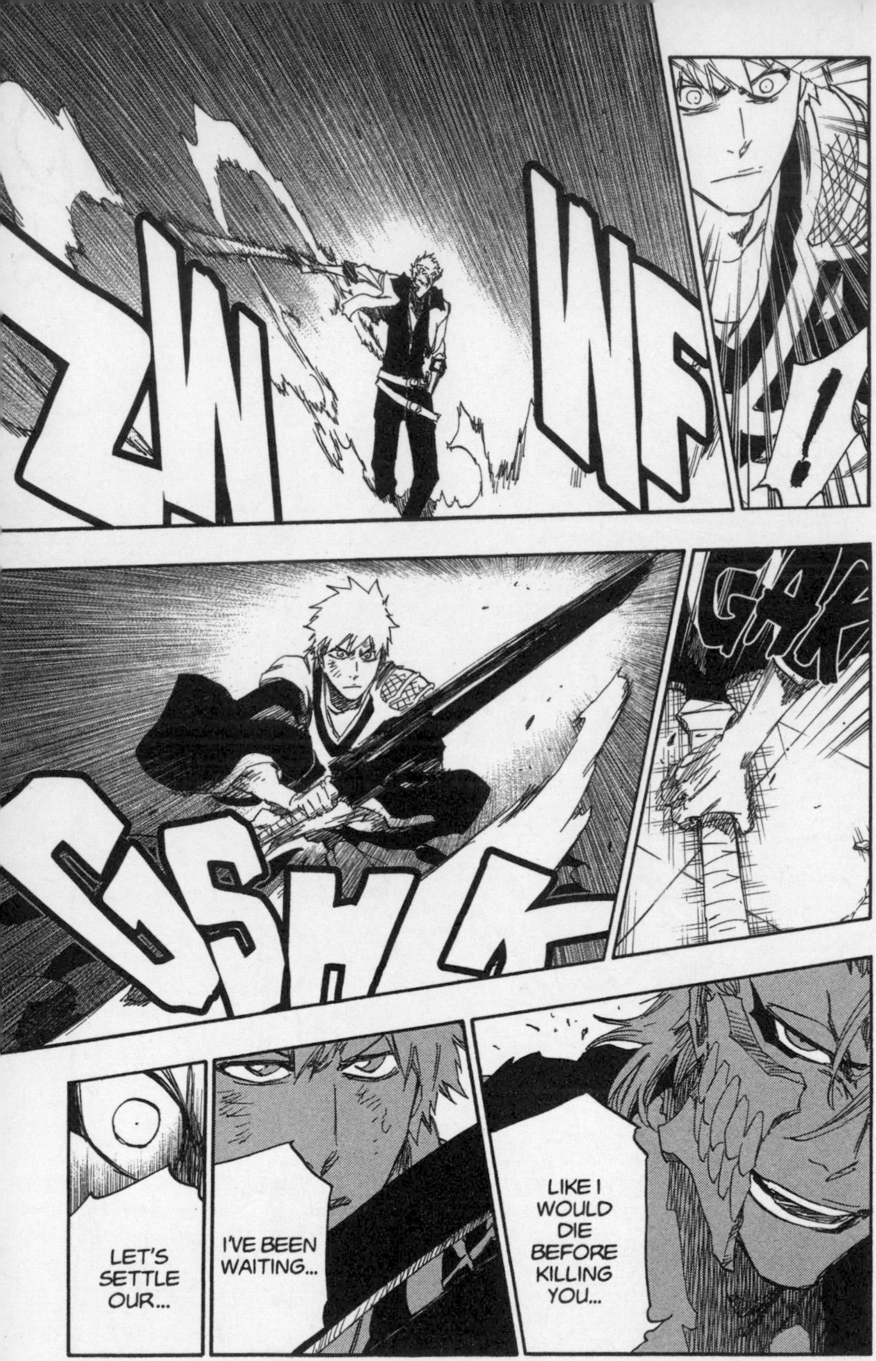
LIKE I WOULD DIE BEFORE KILLING YOU...
I'VE BEEN WAITING...
LET'S SETTLE OUR...

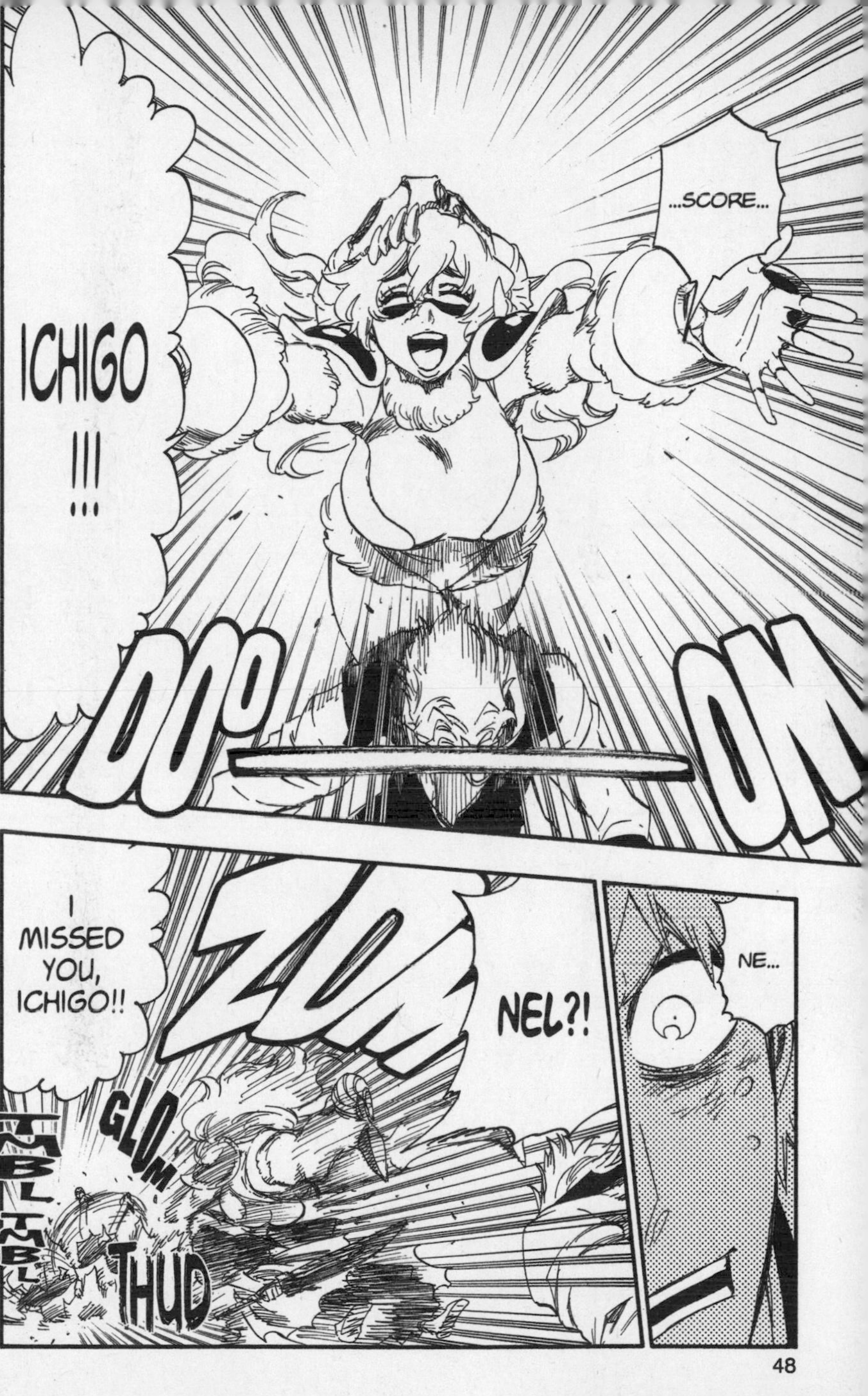
...SCORE...
ICHIGO !!!
DOO
OM
NE...
NEL?!
I MISSED YOU, ICHIGO!!
GLOM
TMBL TMBL
THUD

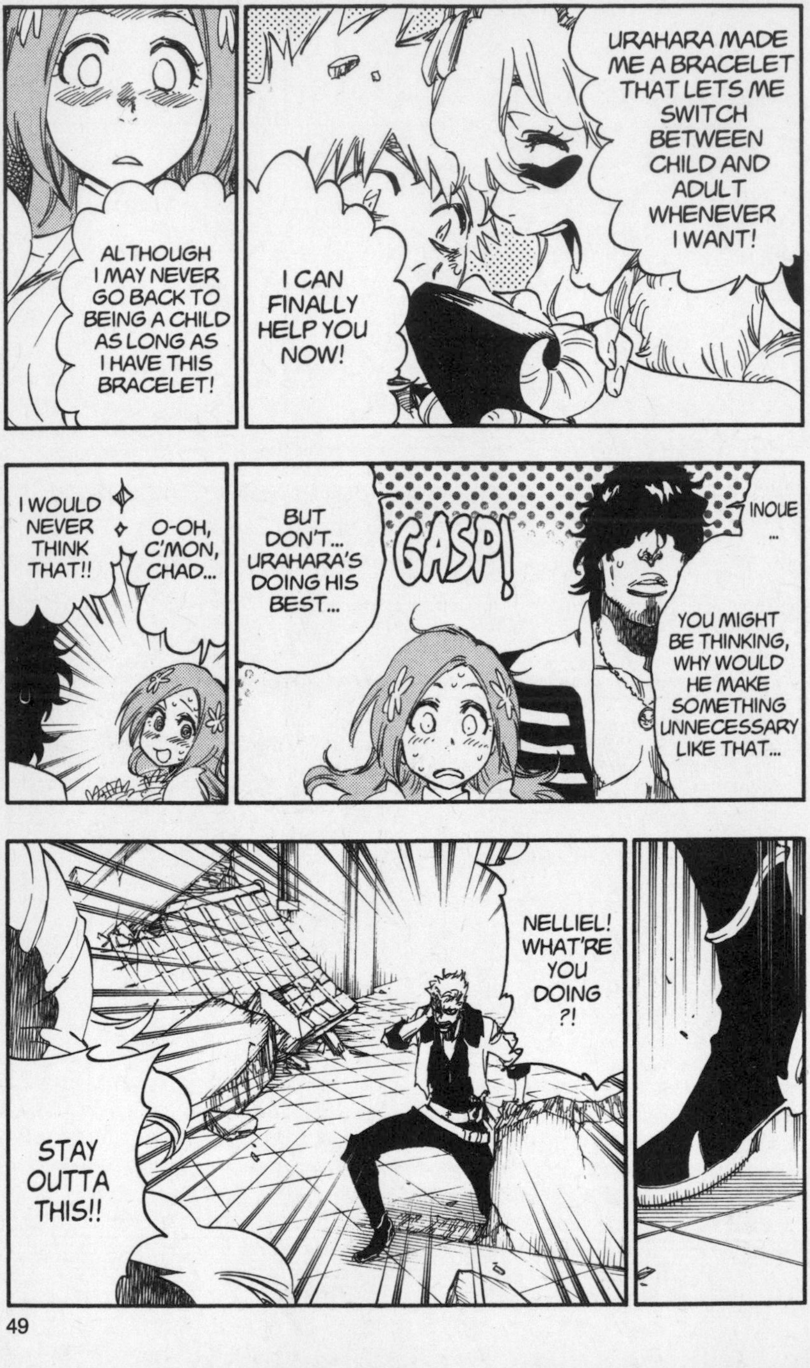
URAHARA MADE ME A BRACELET THAT LETS ME SWITCH BETWEEN CHILD AND ADULT WHENEVER I WANT!
I CAN FINALLY HELP YOU NOW!
ALTHOUGH I MAY NEVER GO BACK TO BEING A CHILD AS LONG AS I HAVE THIS BRACELET!
INOUE ...
YOU MIGHT BE THINKING, WHY WOULD HE MAKE SOMETHING UNNECESSARY LIKE THAT...
GASP!
BUT DON'T... URAHARA'S DOING HIS BEST...
O-OH, C'MON, CHAD...
I WOULD NEVER THINK THAT!!
NELLIEL! WHAT'RE YOU DOING ?!
STAY OUTTA THIS!!

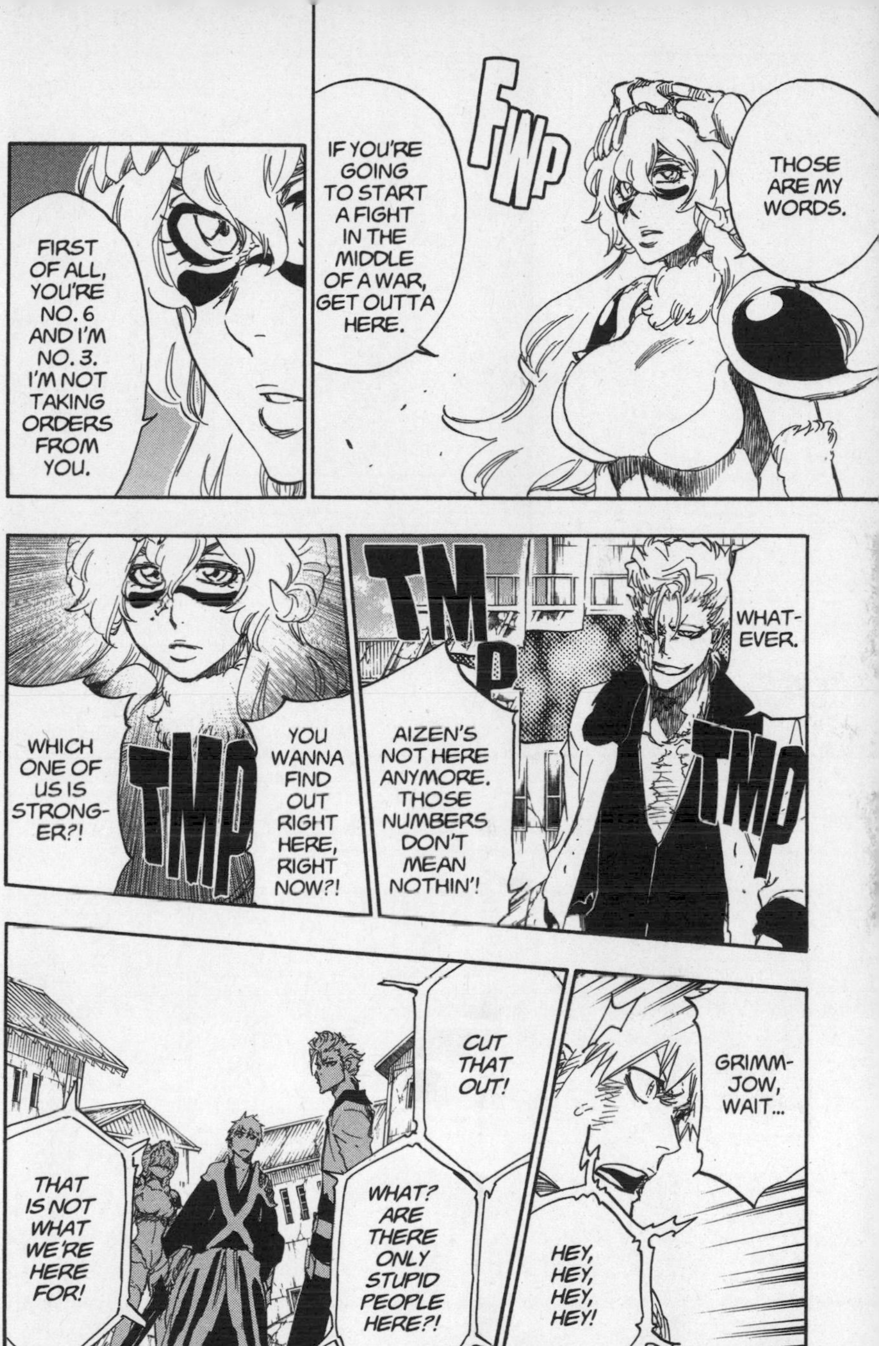

THOSE ARE MY WORDS.
FWP
IF YOU'RE GOING TO START A FIGHT IN THE MIDDLE OF A WAR, GET OUTTA HERE.
FIRST OF ALL, YOU'RE NO. 6 AND I'M NO. 3. I'M NOT TAKING ORDERS FROM YOU.
WHAT-EVER.
TMP
TMP
AIZEN'S NOT HERE ANYMORE. THOSE NUMBERS DON'T MEAN NOTHIN'!
YOU WANNA FIND OUT RIGHT HERE, RIGHT NOW?!
TMP
WHICH ONE OF US IS STRONG-ER?!
GRIMM-JOW, WAIT...
HEY, HEY, HEY, HEY!
CUT THAT OUT!
WHAT? ARE THERE ONLY STUPID PEOPLE HERE?!
THAT IS NOT WHAT WE'RE HERE FOR!

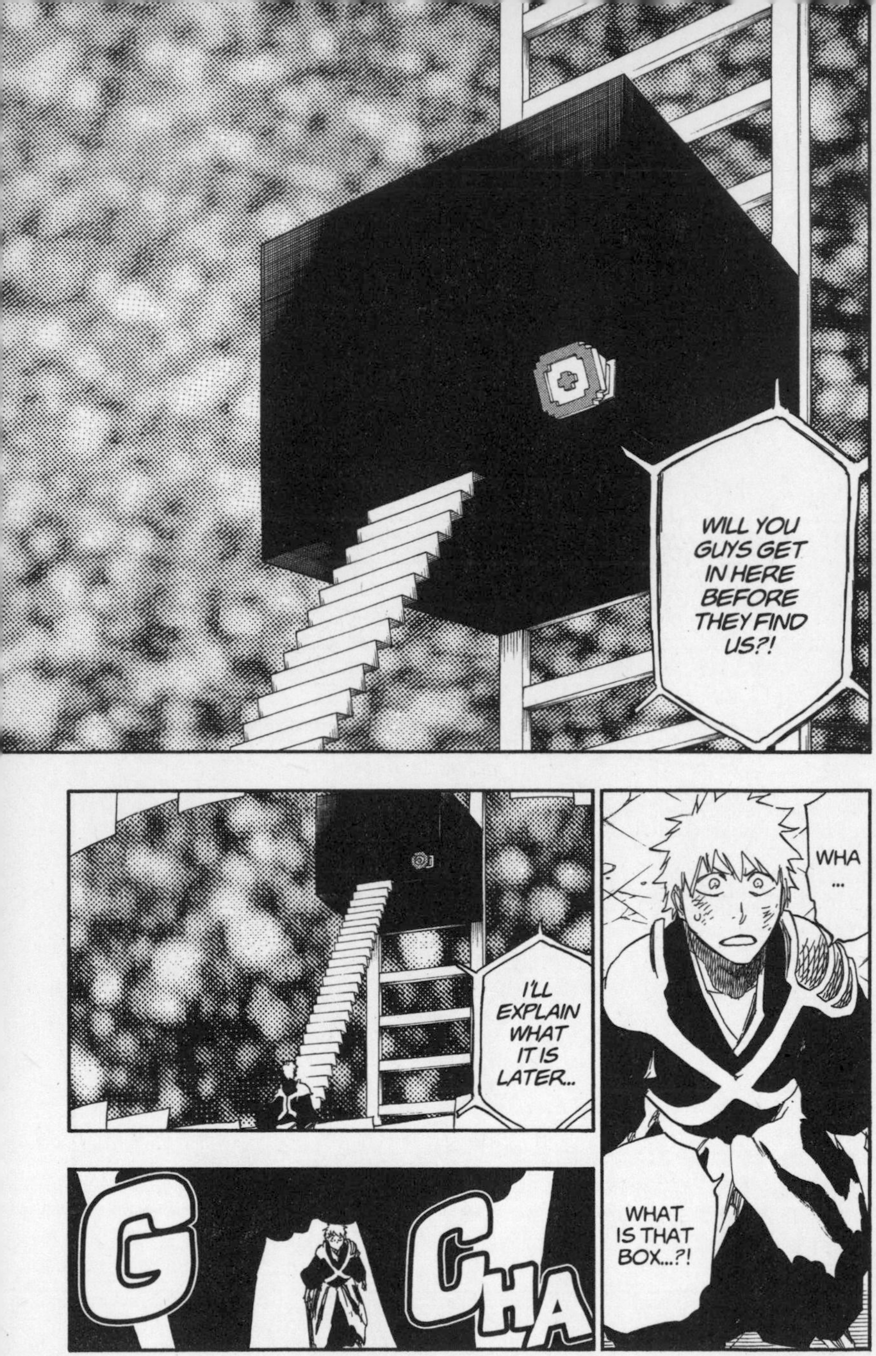
WILL YOU GUYS GET IN HERE BEFORE THEY FIND US?!
WHA ...
WHAT IS THAT BOX...?!
I'LL EXPLAIN WHAT IT IS LATER...
G CHA

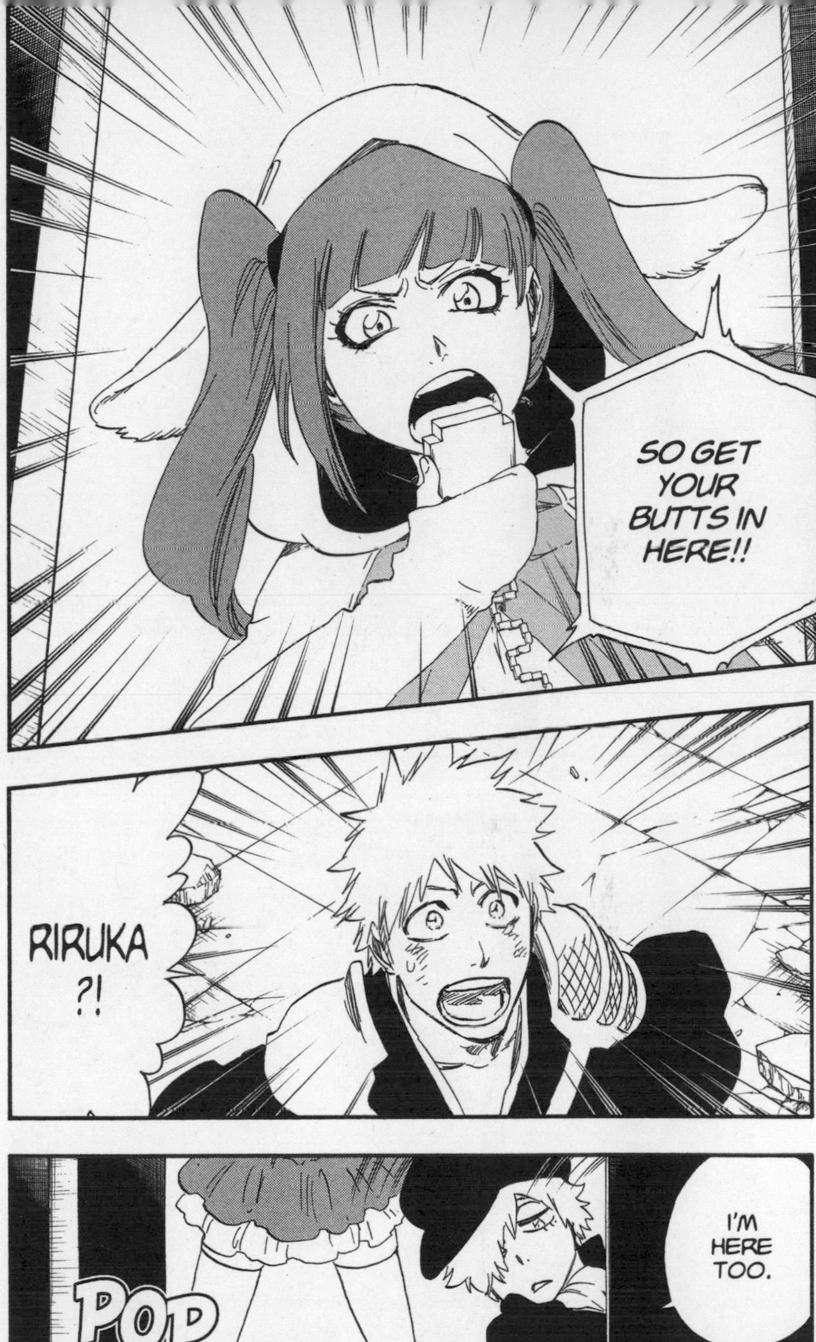
SO GET YOUR BUTTS IN HERE!!
RIRUKA ?!
I'M HERE TOO.
POP

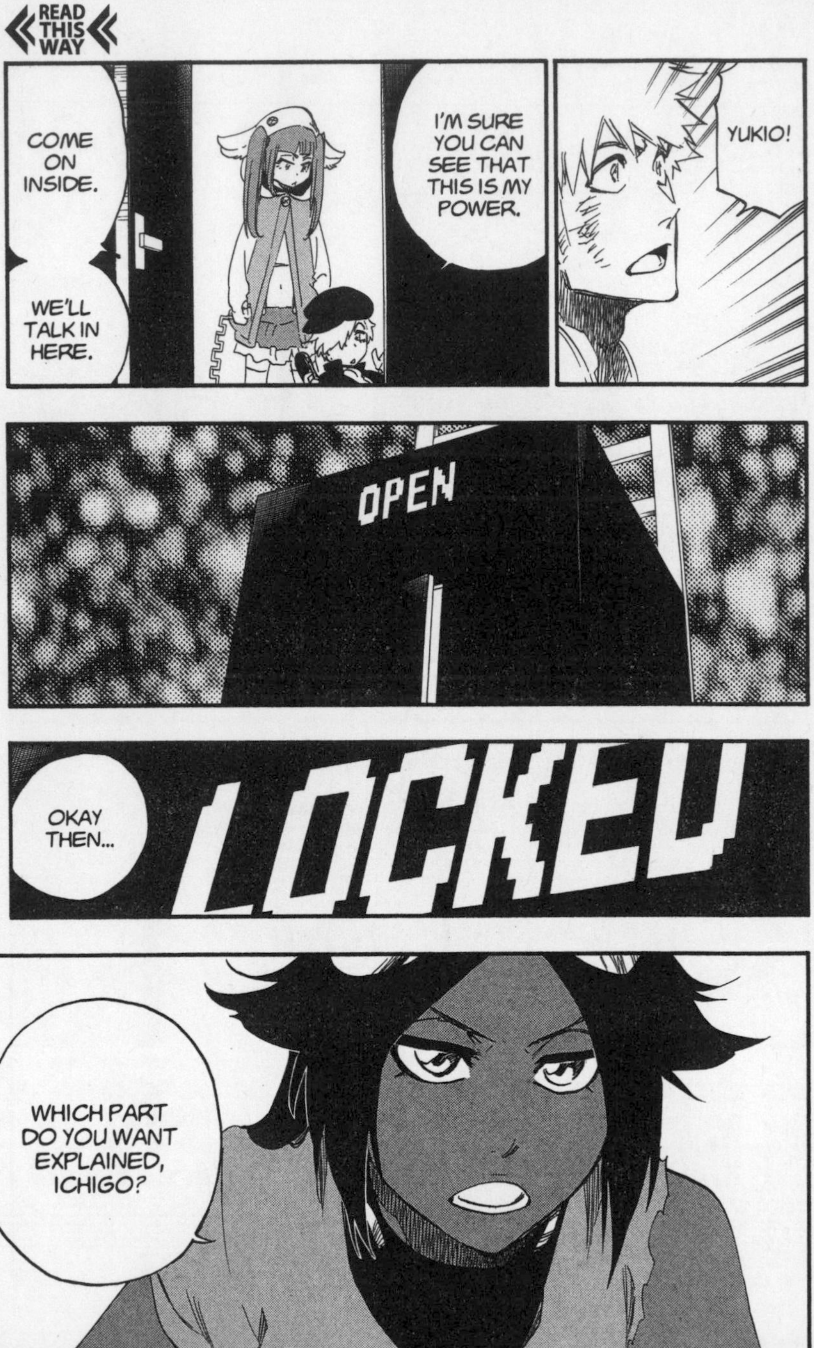
READ THIS WAY
YUKIO!
I'M SURE YOU CAN SEE THAT THIS IS MY POWER.
COME ON INSIDE.
WE'LL TALK IN HERE.
OPEN
LOCKED
OKAY THEN...
WHICH PART DO YOU WANT EXPLAINED, ICHIGO?

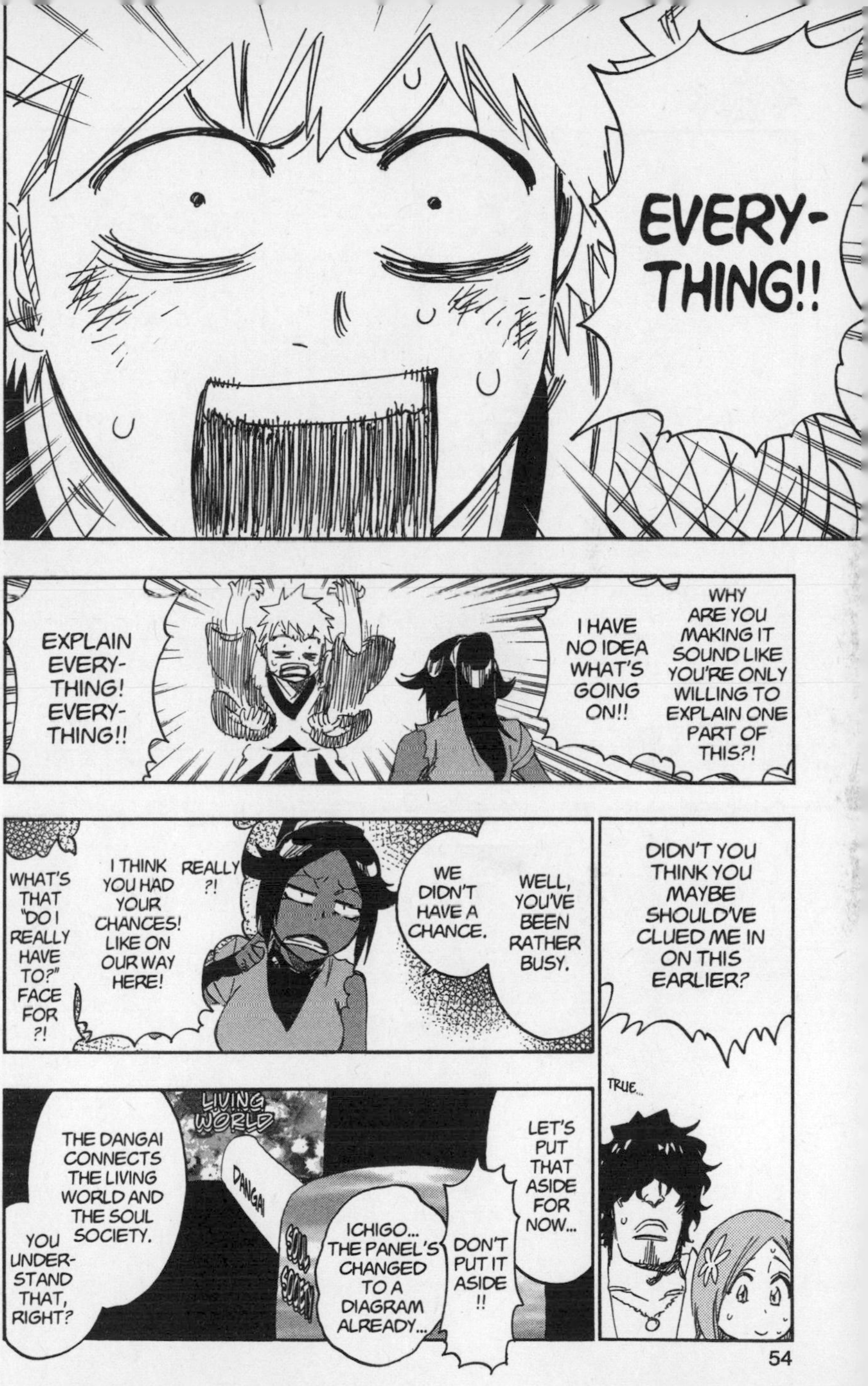
EVERY-THING!!
WHY ARE YOU MAKING IT SOUND LIKE YOU'RE ONLY WILLING TO EXPLAIN ONE PART OF THIS?!
I HAVE NO IDEA WHAT'S GOING ON!!
EXPLAIN EVERY-THING! EVERY-THING!!
DIDN'T YOU THINK YOU MAYBE SHOULD'VE CLUED ME IN ON THIS EARLIER?
TRUE...
WELL, YOU'VE BEEN RATHER BUSY.
WE DIDN'T HAVE A CHANCE.
REALLY?!
I THINK YOU HAD YOUR CHANCES! LIKE ON OUR WAY HERE!
WHAT'S THAT "DO I REALLY HAVE TO?" FACE FOR?!
LET'S PUT THAT ASIDE FOR NOW...
DON'T PUT IT ASIDE!!
ICHIGO... THE PANEL'S CHANGED TO A DIAGRAM ALREADY...
LIVING WORLD
DANGAI
SOUL SOCIETY
THE DANGAI CONNECTS THE LIVING WORLD AND THE SOUL SOCIETY.
YOU UNDERSTAND THAT, RIGHT?

READ THIS WAY

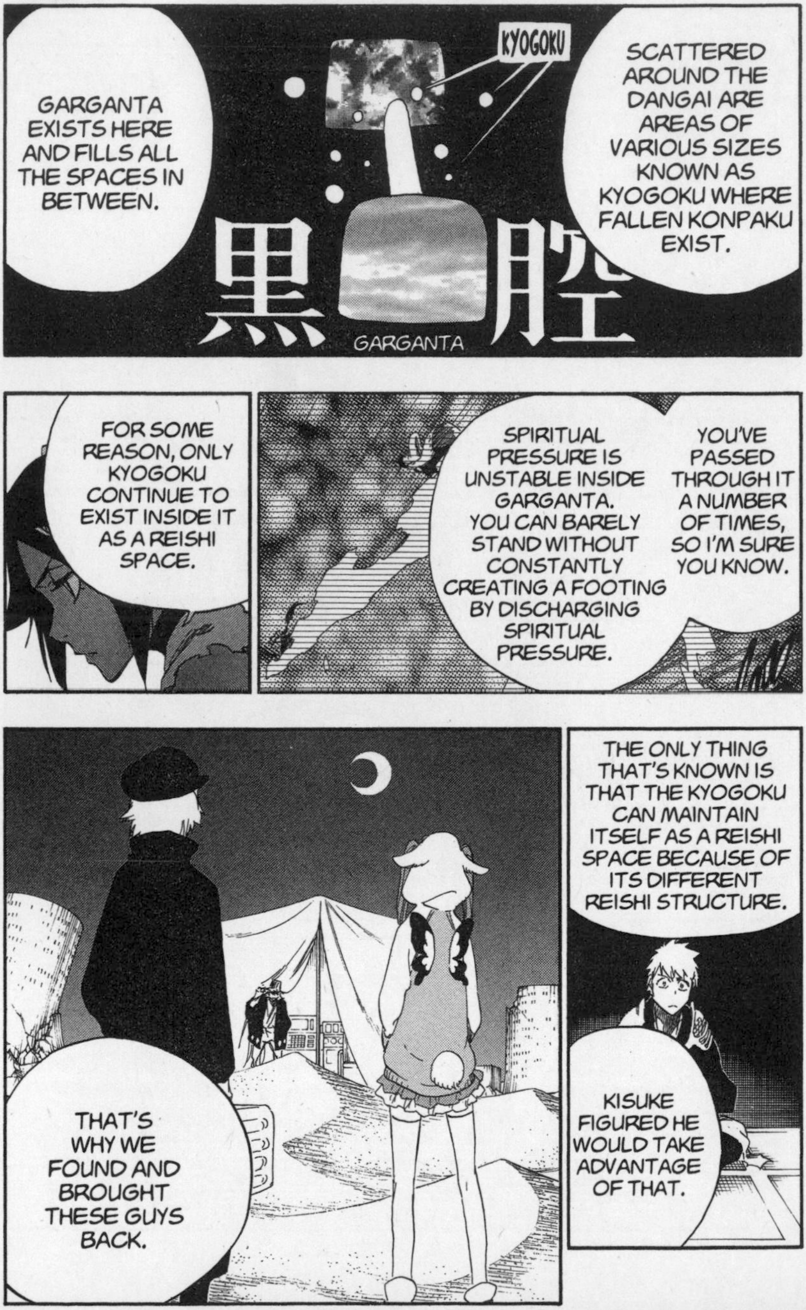
KYOGOKU
SCATTERED AROUND THE DANGAI ARE AREAS OF VARIOUS SIZES KNOWN AS KYOGOKU WHERE FALLEN KONPAKU EXIST.
GARGANTA EXISTS HERE AND FILLS ALL THE SPACES IN BETWEEN.
黒腔
GARGANTA
YOU'VE PASSED THROUGH IT A NUMBER OF TIMES, SO I'M SURE YOU KNOW.
SPIRITUAL PRESSURE IS UNSTABLE INSIDE GARGANTA. YOU CAN BARELY STAND WITHOUT CONSTANTLY CREATING A FOOTING BY DISCHARGING SPIRITUAL PRESSURE.
FOR SOME REASON, ONLY KYOGOKU CONTINUE TO EXIST INSIDE IT AS A REISHI SPACE.
THE ONLY THING THAT'S KNOWN IS THAT THE KYOGOKU CAN MAINTAIN ITSELF AS A REISHI SPACE BECAUSE OF ITS DIFFERENT REISHI STRUCTURE.
KISUKE FIGURED HE WOULD TAKE ADVANTAGE OF THAT.
THAT'S WHY WE FOUND AND BROUGHT THESE GUYS BACK.

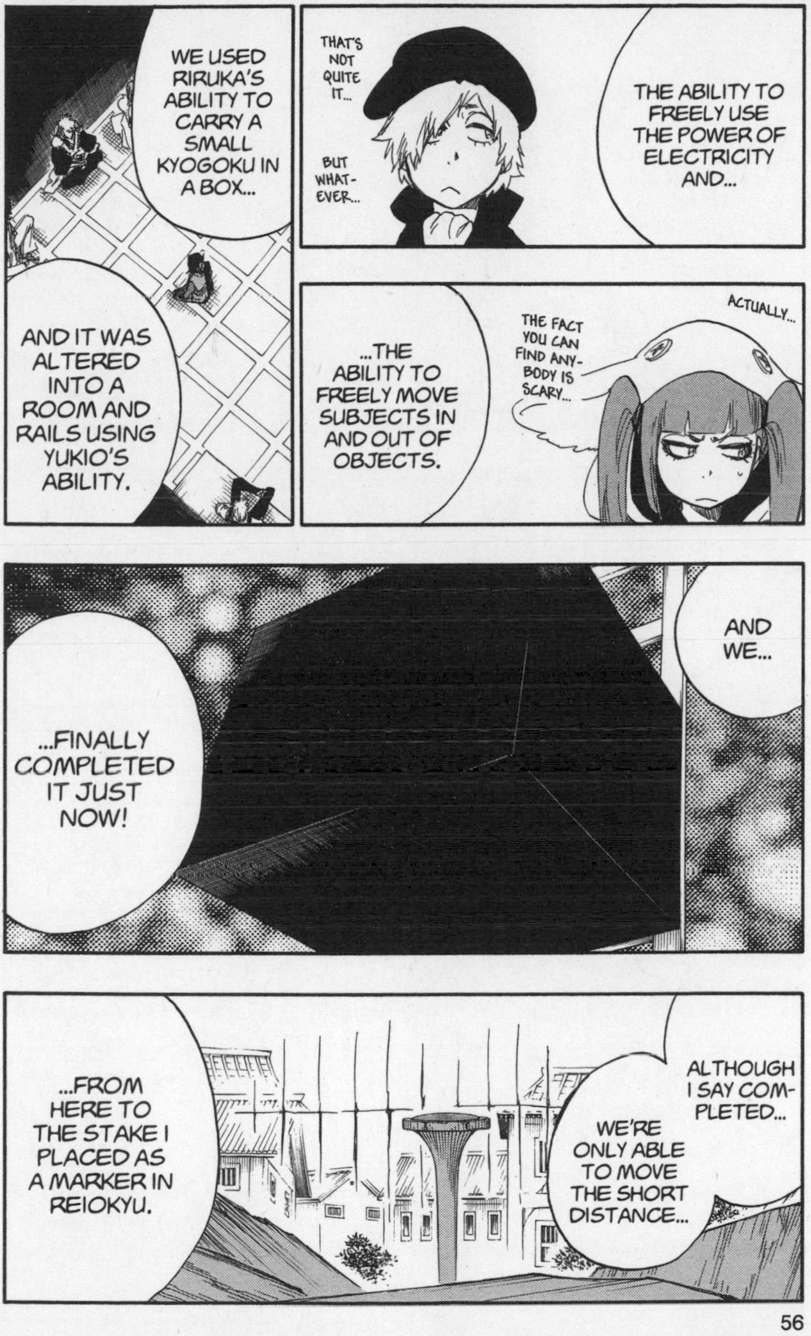
THE ABILITY TO FREELY USE THE POWER OF ELECTRICITY AND...
THAT'S NOT QUITE IT...
BUT WHATEVER...
...THE ABILITY TO FREELY MOVE SUBJECTS IN AND OUT OF OBJECTS.
ACTUALLY...
THE FACT YOU CAN FIND ANYBODY IS SCARY...
WE USED RIRUKA'S ABILITY TO CARRY A SMALL KYOGOKU IN A BOX...
AND IT WAS ALTERED INTO A ROOM AND RAILS USING YUKIO'S ABILITY.
AND WE...
...FINALLY COMPLETED IT JUST NOW!
ALTHOUGH I SAY COMPLETED...
WE'RE ONLY ABLE TO MOVE THE SHORT DISTANCE...
...FROM HERE TO THE STAKE I PLACED AS A MARKER IN REIOKYU.

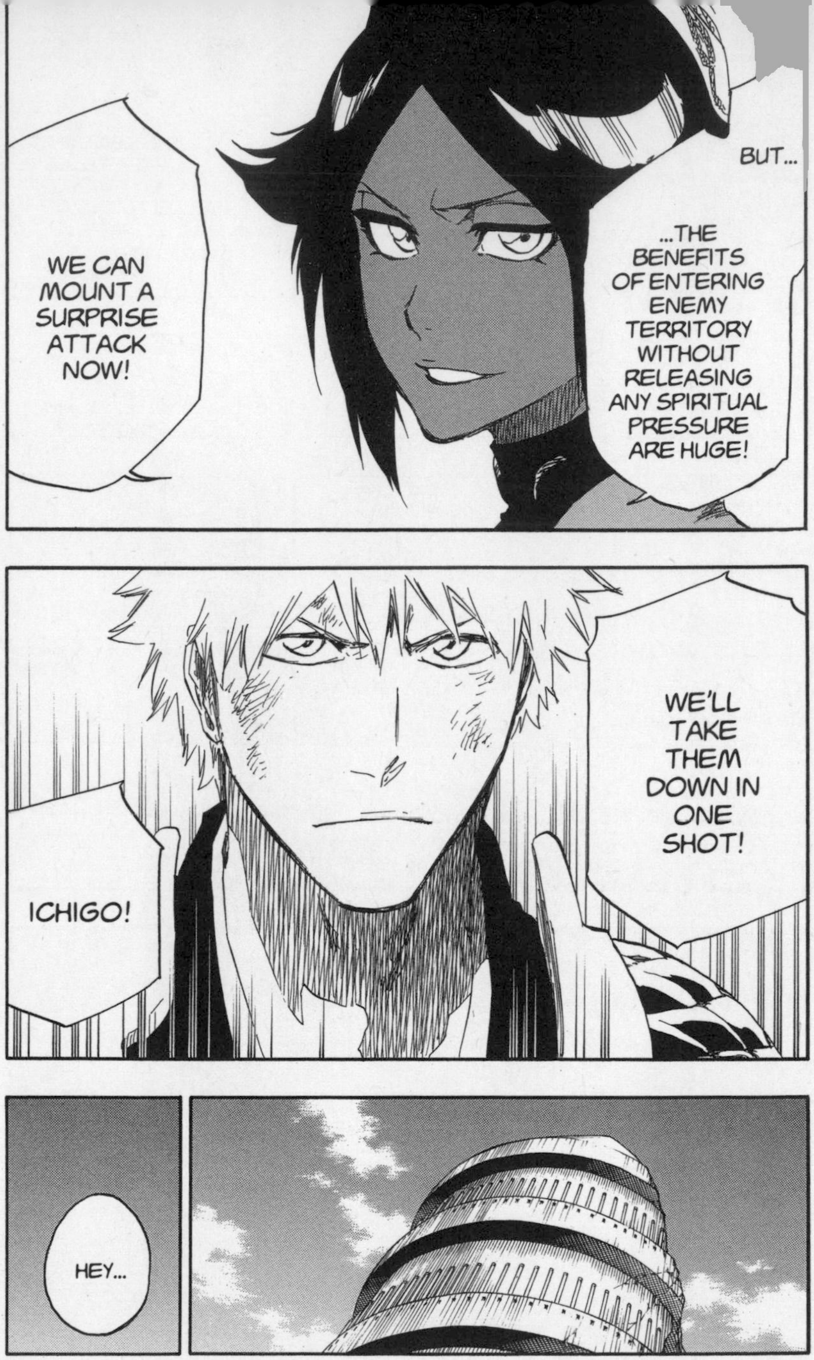
BUT...
...THE BENEFITS OF ENTERING ENEMY TERRITORY WITHOUT RELEASING ANY SPIRITUAL PRESSURE ARE HUGE!
WE CAN MOUNT A SURPRISE ATTACK NOW!
WE'LL TAKE THEM DOWN IN ONE SHOT!
ICHIGO!
HEY...

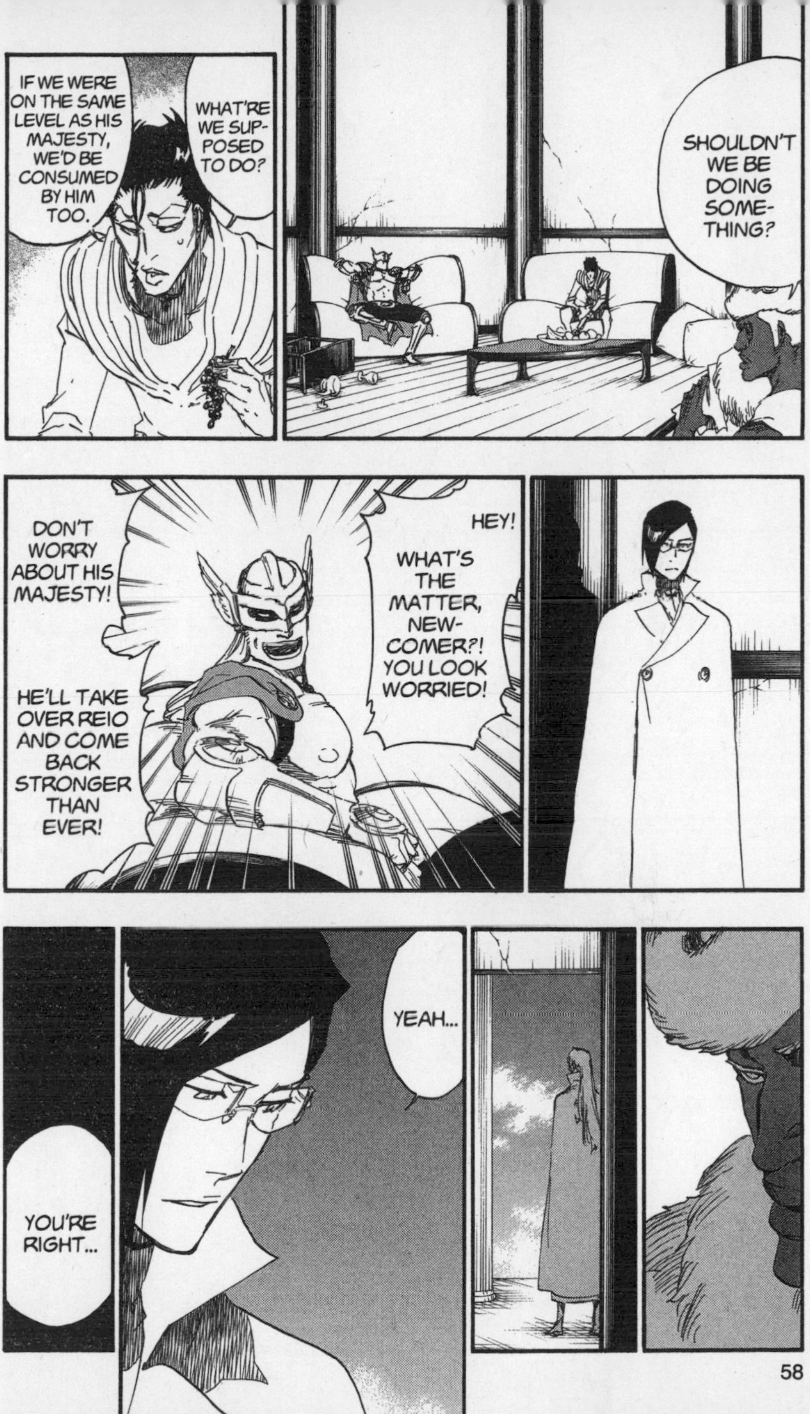
SHOULDN'T WE BE DOING SOME-THING?
WHAT'RE WE SUP-POSED TO DO?
IF WE WERE ON THE SAME LEVEL AS HIS MAJESTY, WE'D BE CONSUMED BY HIM TOO.
HEY!
WHAT'S THE MATTER, NEW-COMER?! YOU LOOK WORRIED!
DON'T WORRY ABOUT HIS MAJESTY!
HE'LL TAKE OVER REIO AND COME BACK STRONGER THAN EVER!
YEAH...
YOU'RE RIGHT...

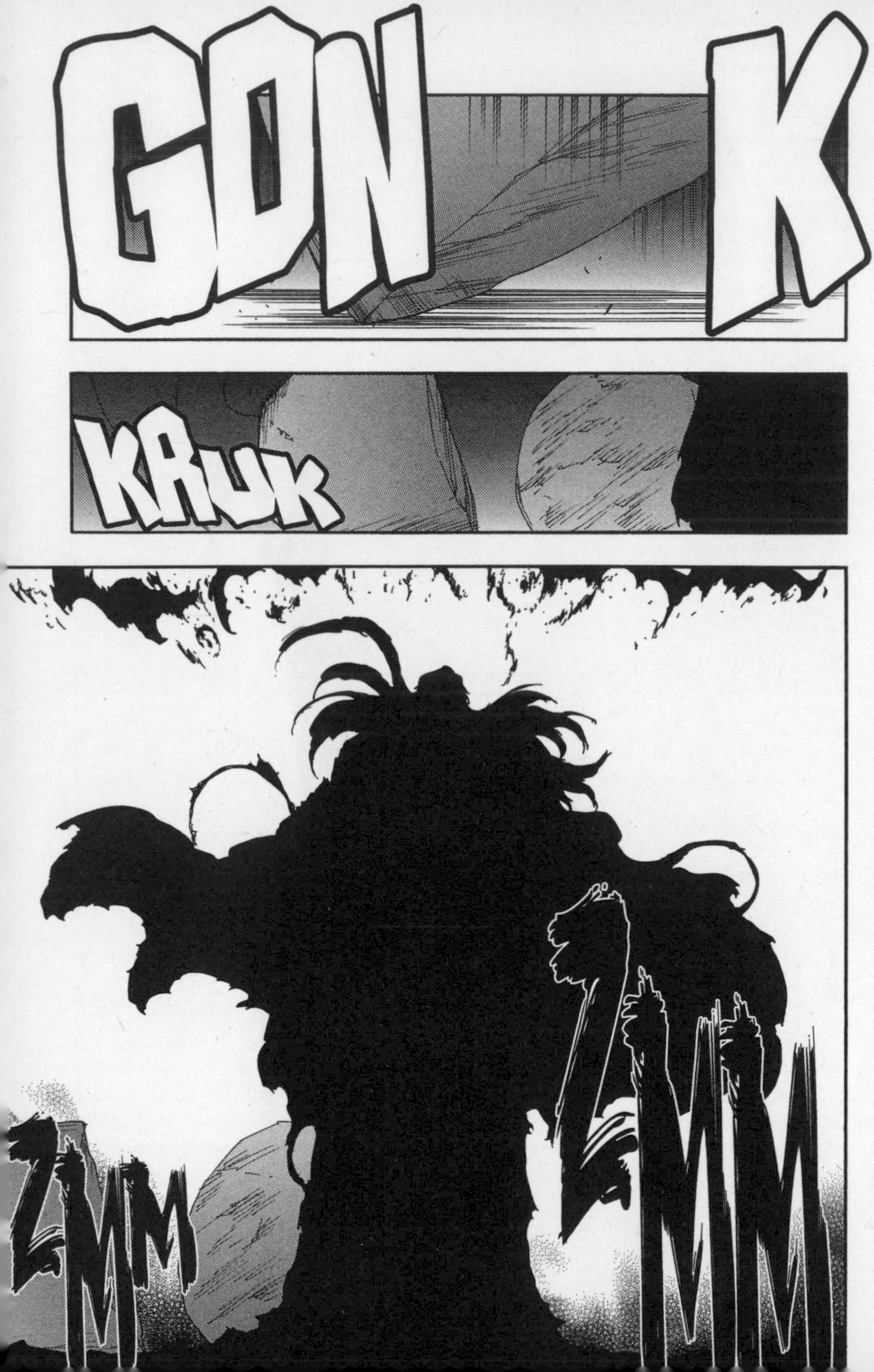
GONK
KRUK
ZMM
ZMM

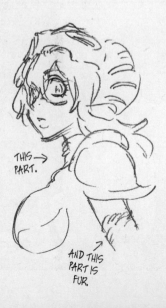

THIS →
PART.

AND THIS
PART IS
FUR.

626.THE HOLY NEWBORN

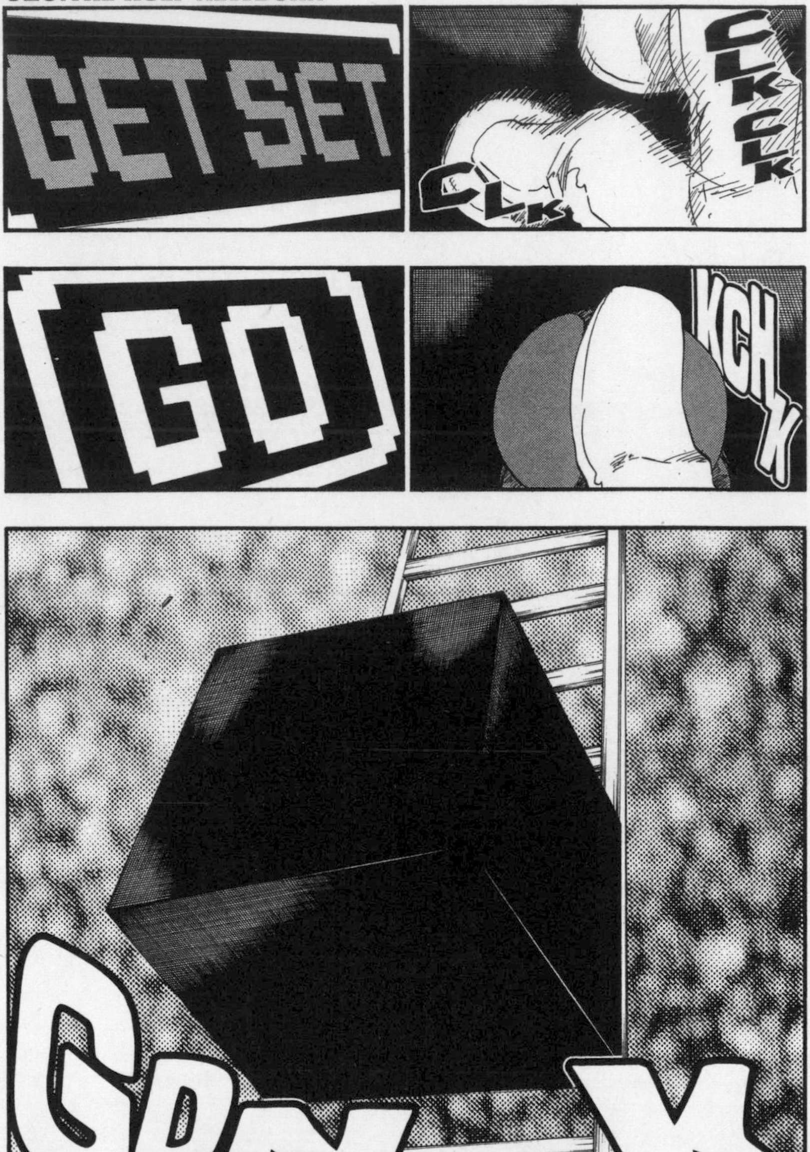
CLK CLK CLK
CLK
GET SET
KCHK
GO
GDNK

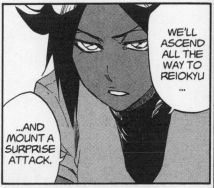

WE'LL ASCEND ALL THE WAY TO REIOKYU...

...AND MOUNT A SURPRISE ATTACK.

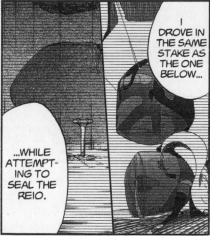

I DROVE IN THE SAME STAKE AS THE ONE BELOW...

...WHILE ATTEMPTING TO SEAL THE REIO.

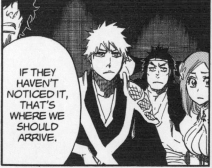

IF THEY HAVEN'T NOTICED IT, THAT'S WHERE WE SHOULD ARRIVE.

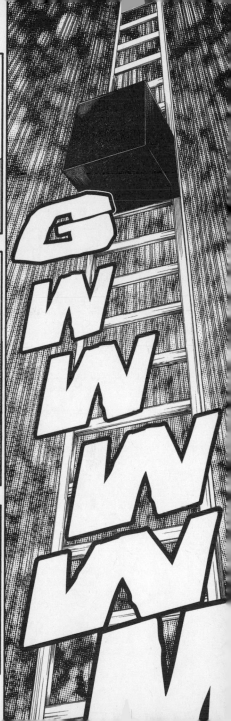

GWWWWWM

READ THIS WAY

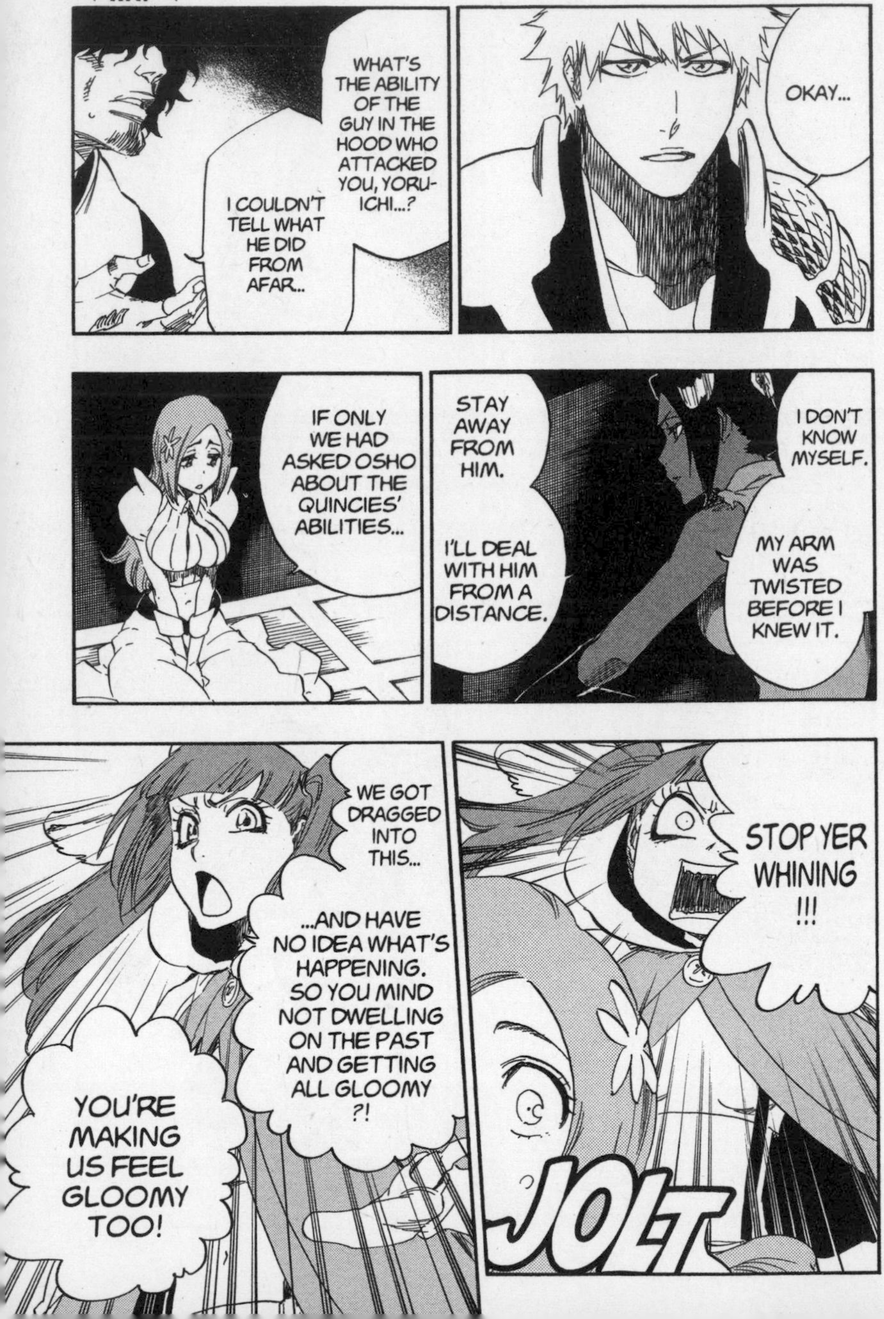
OKAY...
WHAT'S THE ABILITY OF THE GUY IN THE HOOD WHO ATTACKED YOU, YORU-ICHI...?
I COULDN'T TELL WHAT HE DID FROM AFAR...
I DON'T KNOW MYSELF.
MY ARM WAS TWISTED BEFORE I KNEW IT.
STAY AWAY FROM HIM.
I'LL DEAL WITH HIM FROM A DISTANCE.
IF ONLY WE HAD ASKED OSHO ABOUT THE QUINCIES' ABILITIES...
STOP YER WHINING !!!
JOLT
WE GOT DRAGGED INTO THIS...
...AND HAVE NO IDEA WHAT'S HAPPENING. SO YOU MIND NOT DWELLING ON THE PAST AND GETTING ALL GLOOMY ?!
YOU'RE MAKING US FEEL GLOOMY TOO!

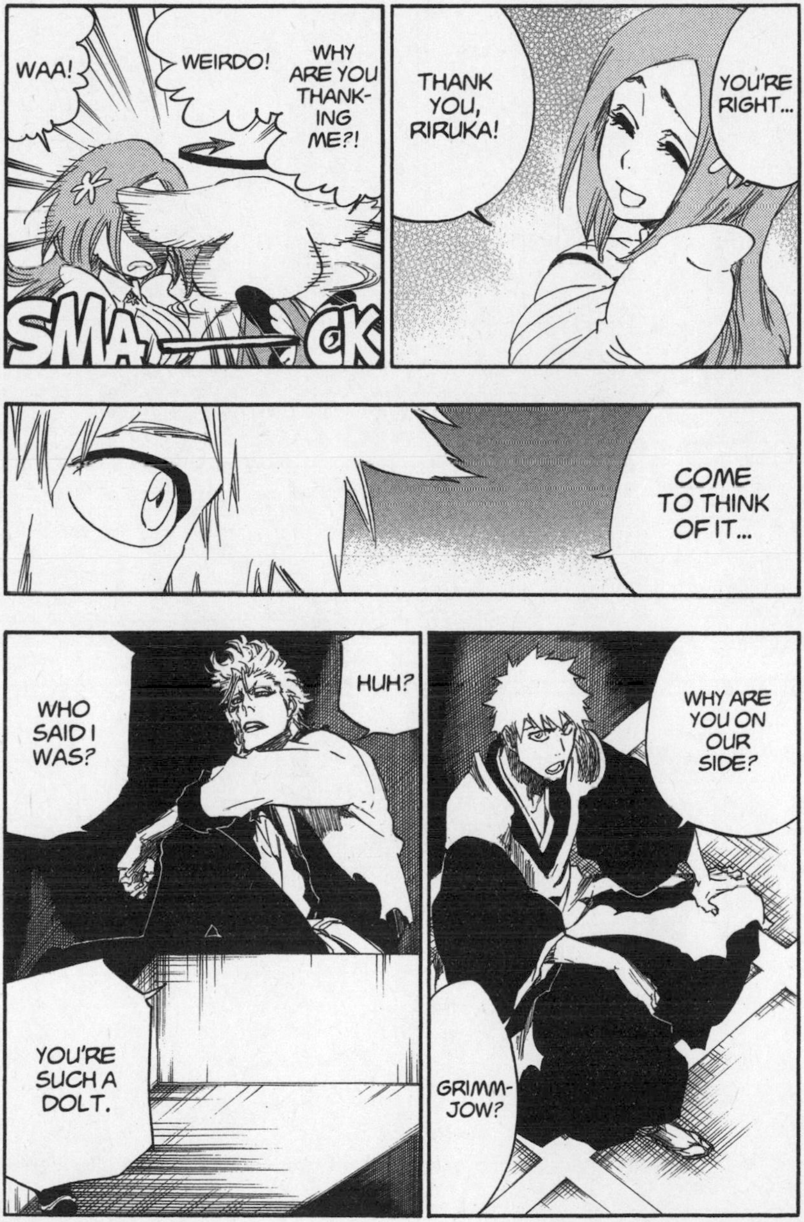
YOU'RE RIGHT...
THANK YOU, RIRUKA!
WHY ARE YOU THANKING ME?!
WEIRDO!
WAA!
SMA—CK
COME TO THINK OF IT...
WHY ARE YOU ON OUR SIDE?
GRIMMJOW?
HUH?
WHO SAID I WAS?
YOU'RE SUCH A DOLT.

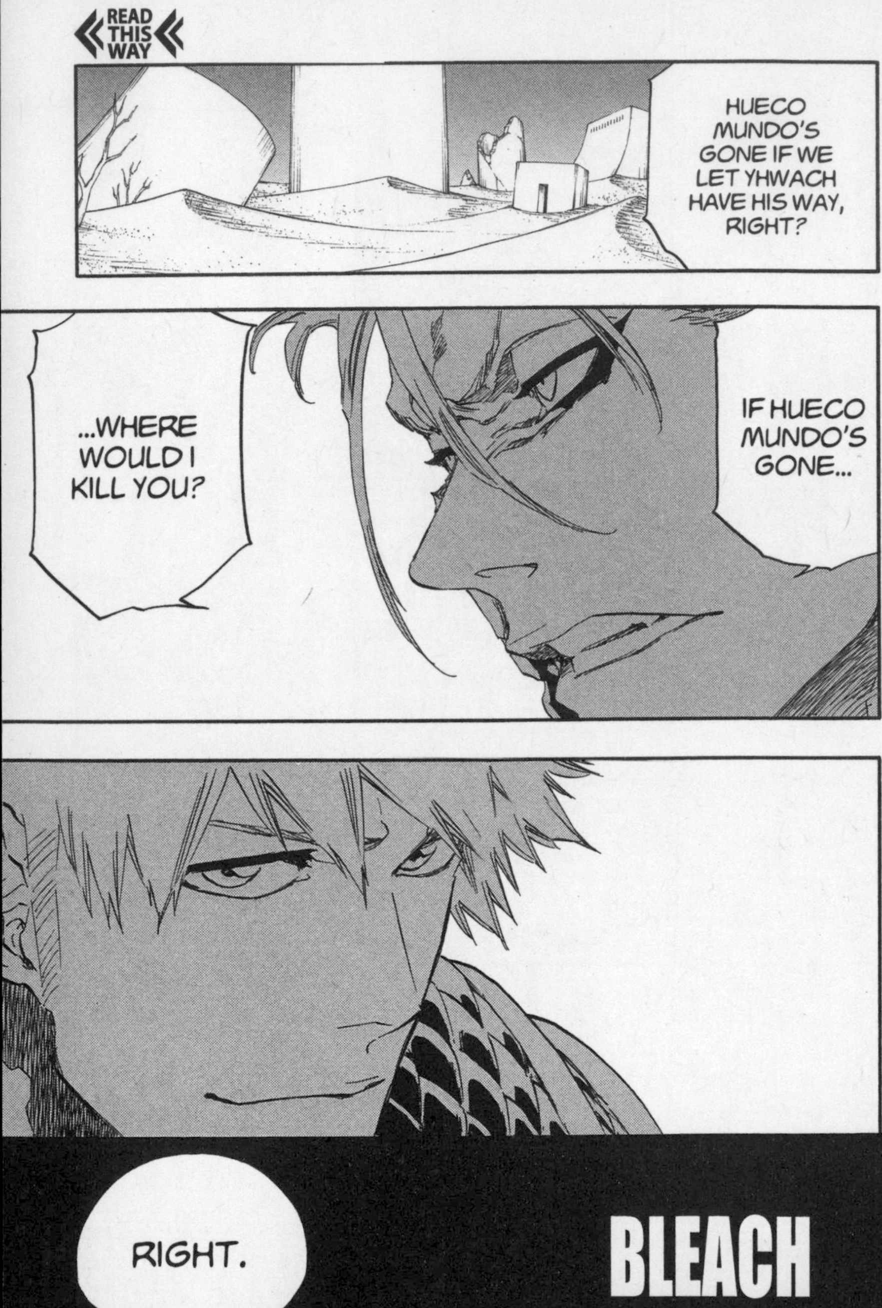
READ THIS WAY
HUECO MUNDO'S GONE IF WE LET YHWACH HAVE HIS WAY, RIGHT?
IF HUECO MUNDO'S GONE...
...WHERE WOULD I KILL YOU?
RIGHT.
BLEACH

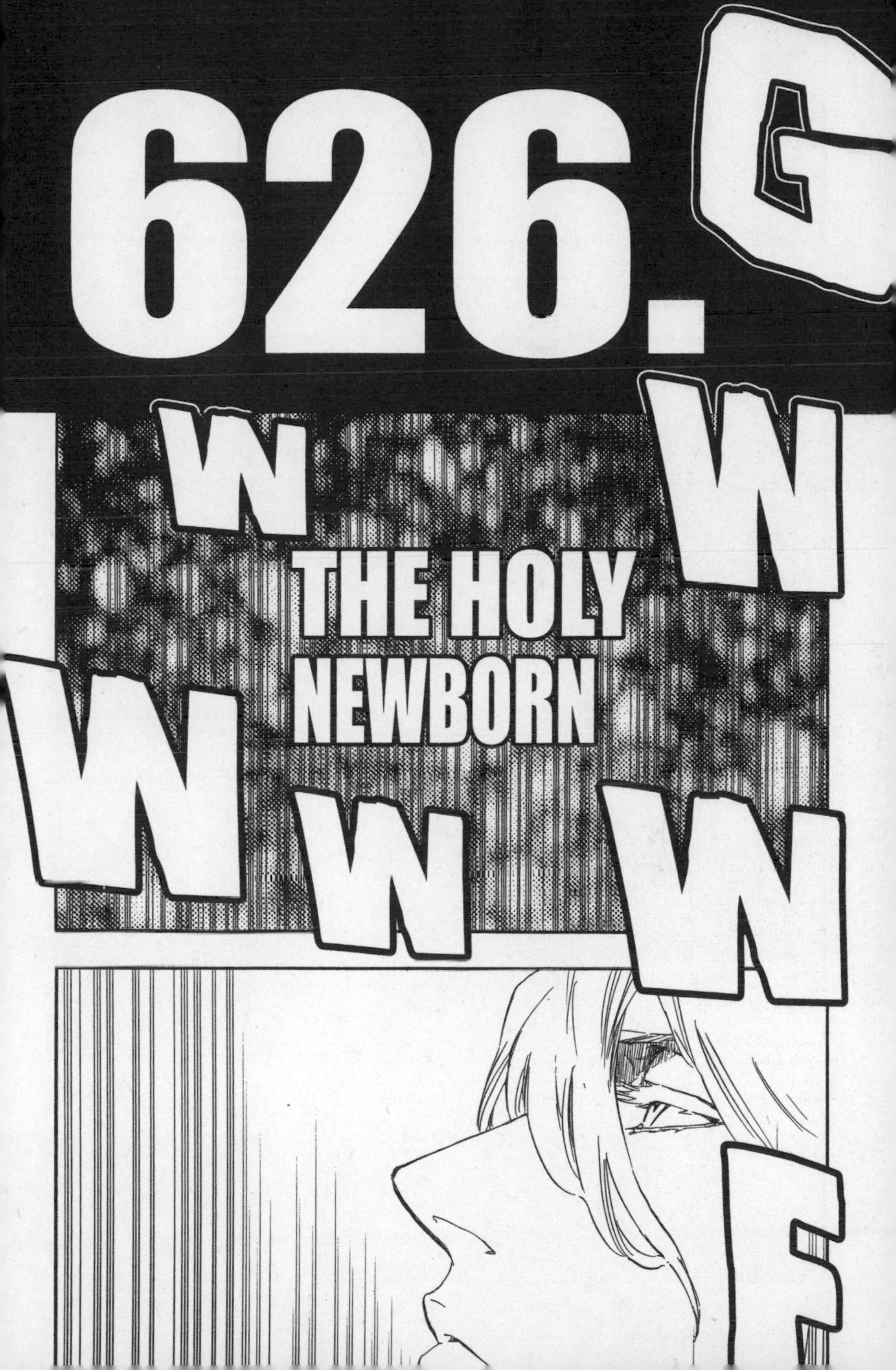
626. THE HOLY NEWBORN

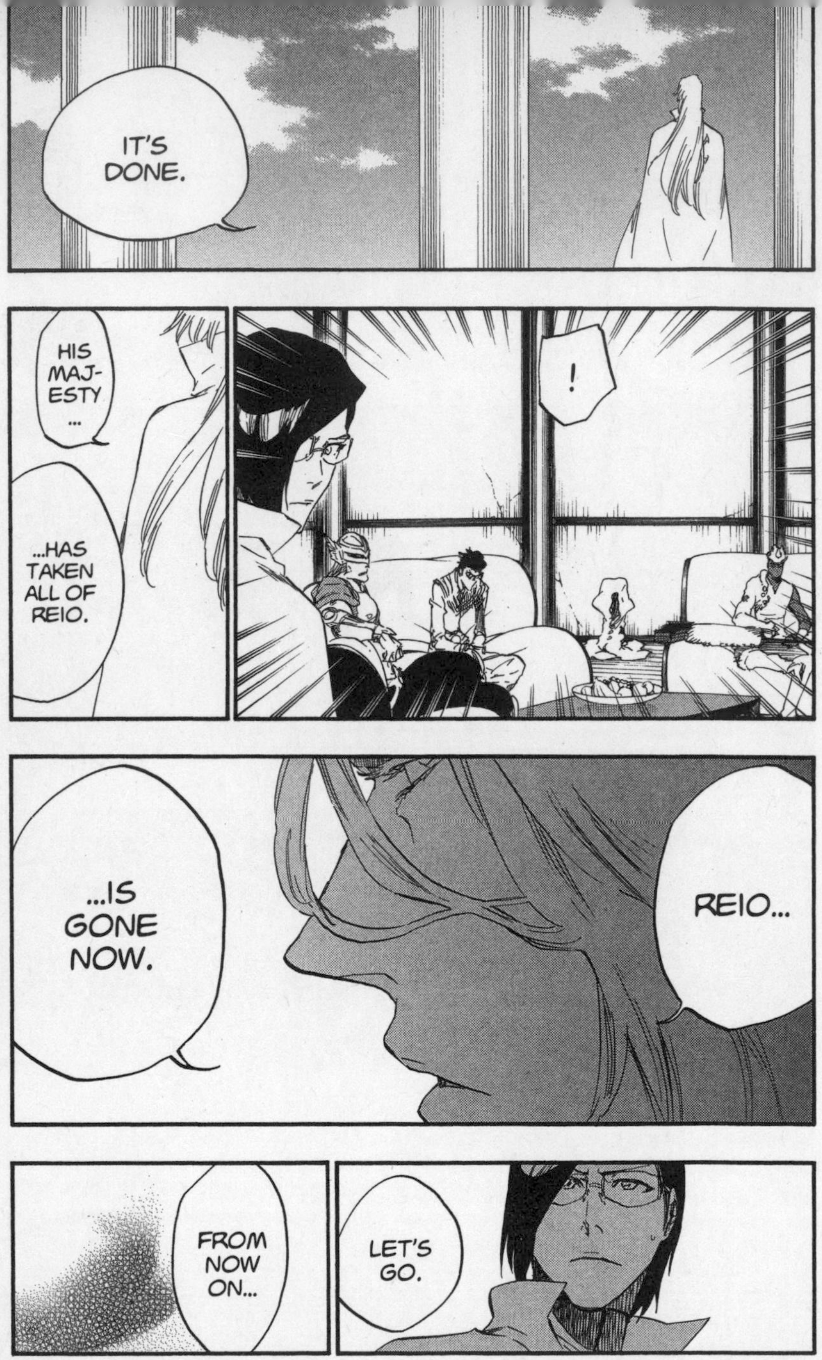
IT'S DONE.
!
HIS MAJ-ESTY...
...HAS TAKEN ALL OF REIO.
REIO...
...IS GONE NOW.
LET'S GO.
FROM NOW ON...

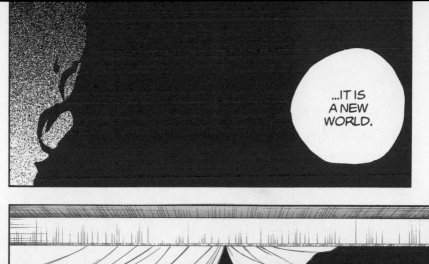

...IT IS
A NEW
WORLD.

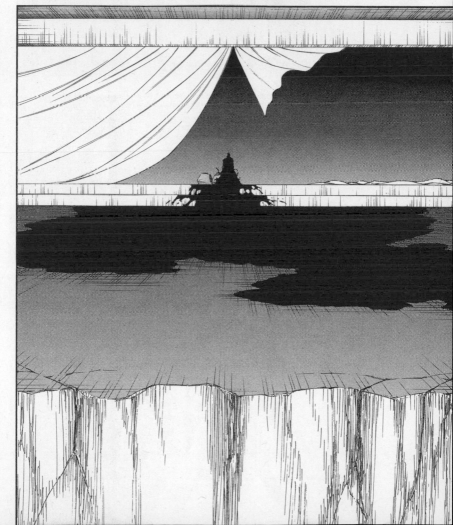

READ THIS WAY

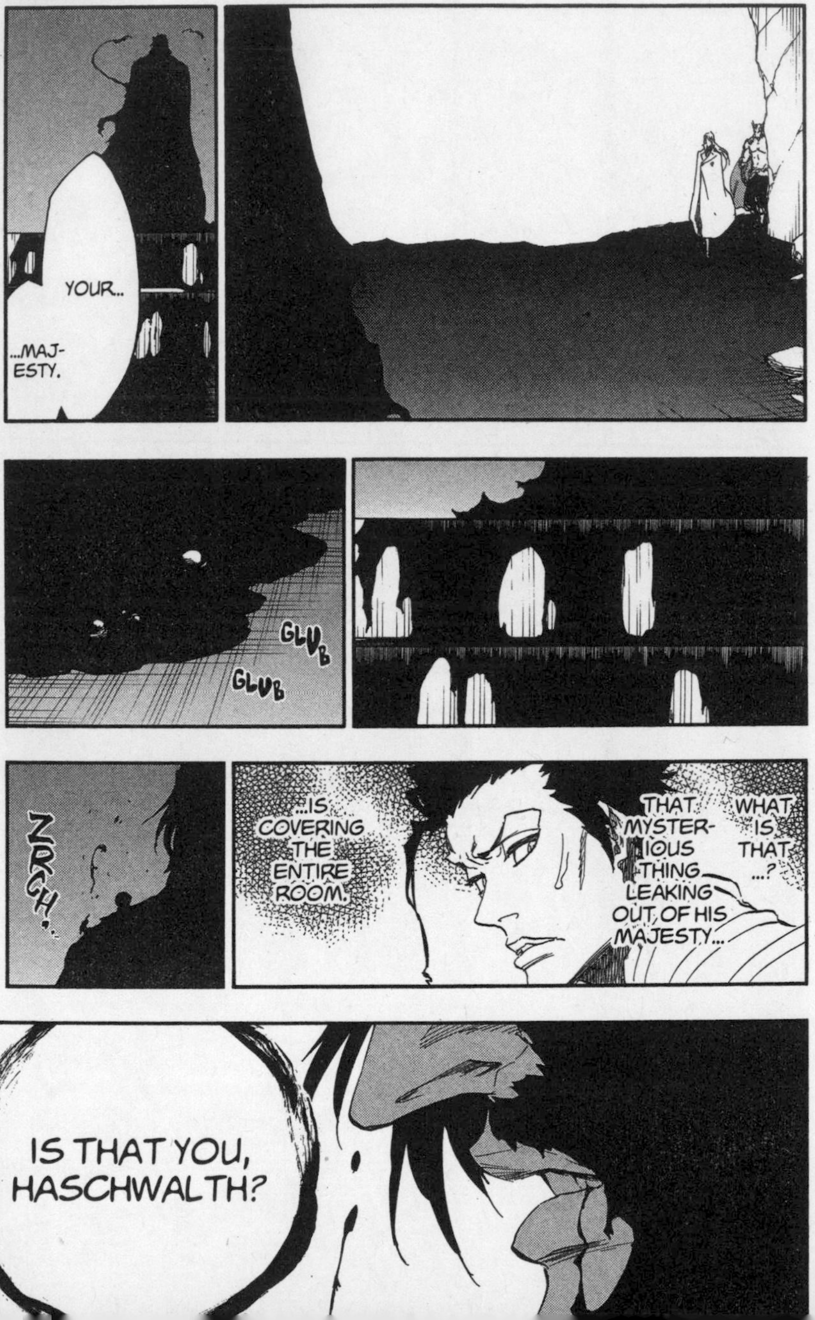
YOUR..
...MAJ-ESTY.
GLUB
GLUB
WHAT IS THAT...?
THAT MYSTER-IOUS THING LEAKING OUT OF HIS MAJESTY...
...IS COVERING THE ENTIRE ROOM.
ZRRGH...
IS THAT YOU, HASCHWALTH?

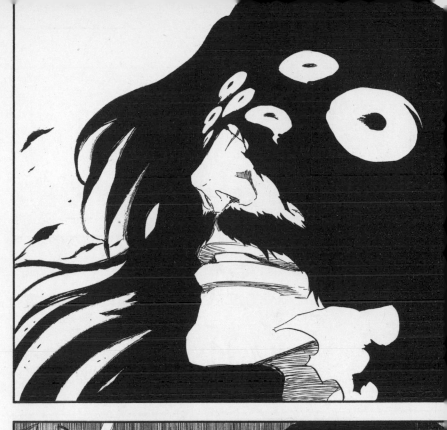

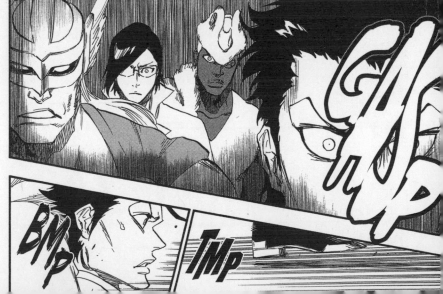

GASP

BMP

TMP

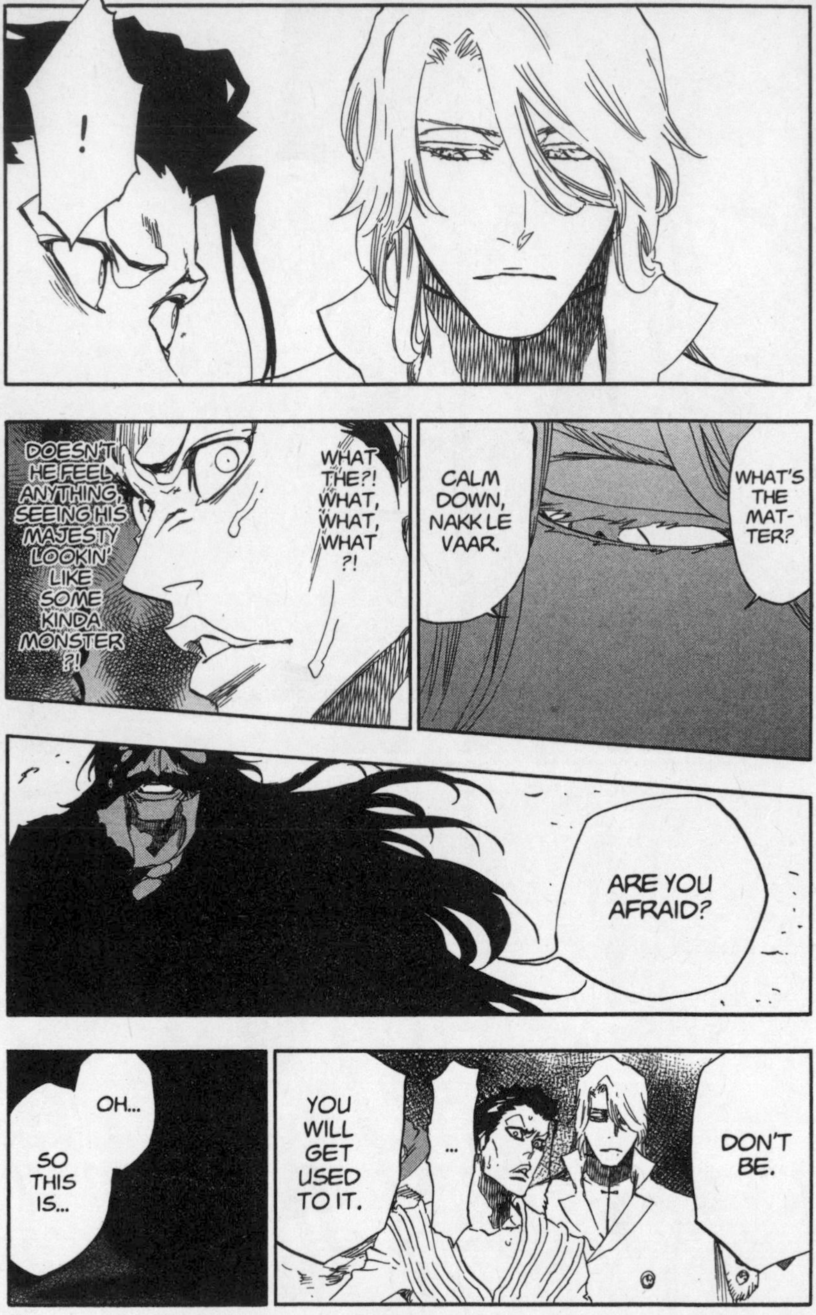
!
WHAT'S THE MATTER?
CALM DOWN, NAKK LE VAAR.
WHAT THE?! WHAT, WHAT, WHAT?!
DOESN'T HE FEEL ANYTHING, SEEING HIS MAJESTY LOOKIN' LIKE SOME KINDA MONSTER?!
ARE YOU AFRAID?
DON'T BE.
...
YOU WILL GET USED TO IT.
OH...
SO THIS IS...

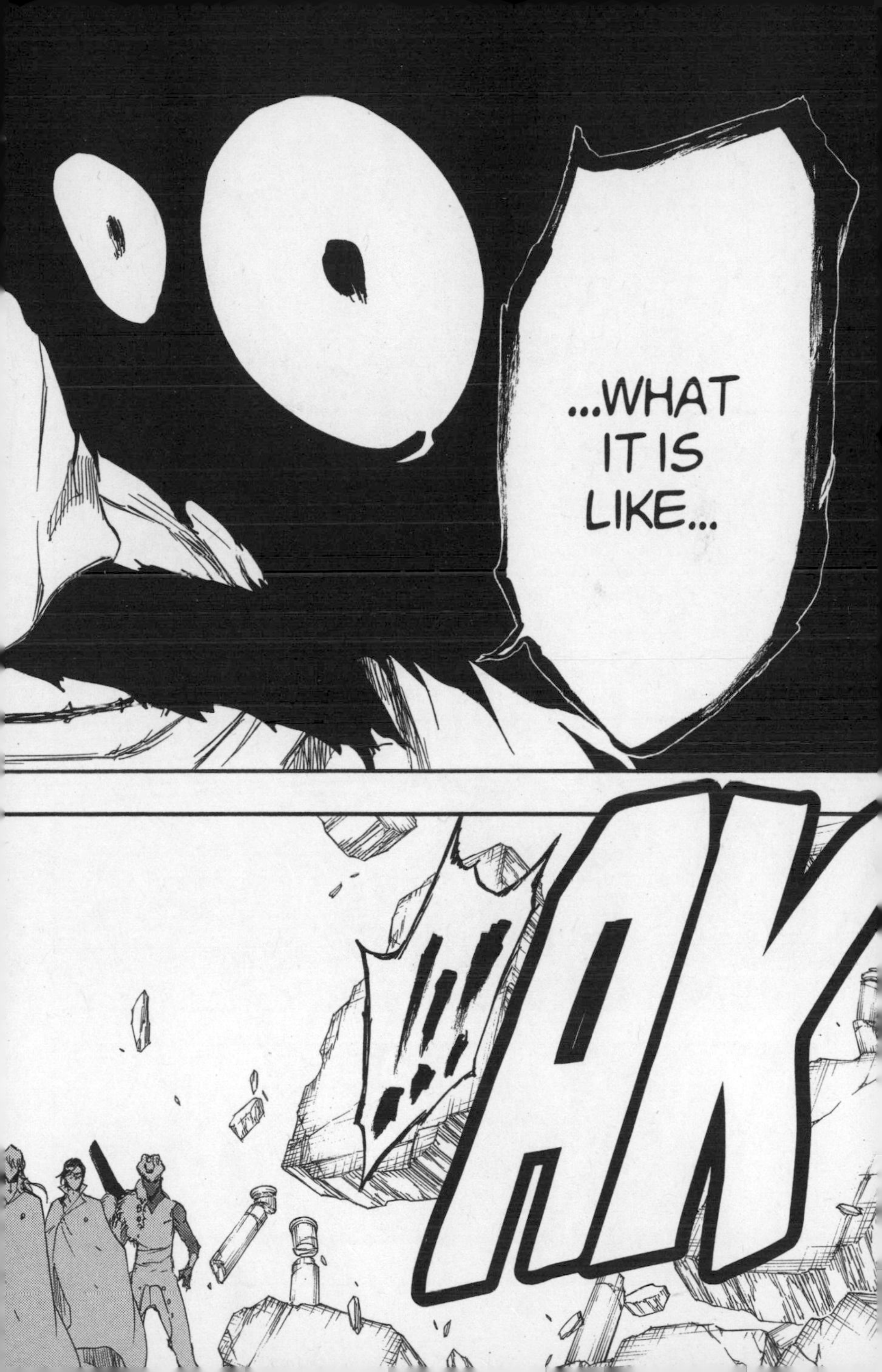
...WHAT IT IS LIKE...
HAK

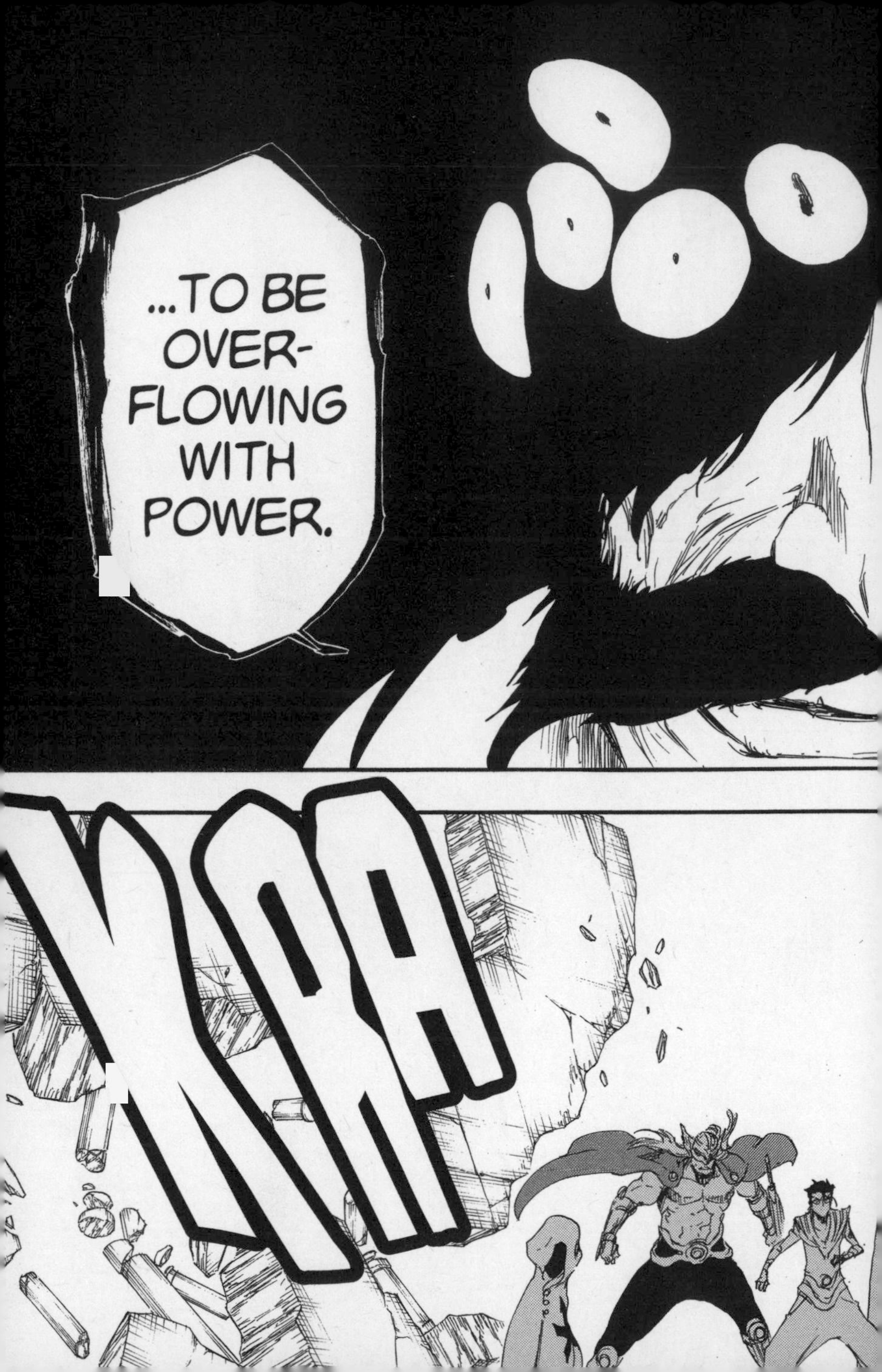
...TO BE OVER-FLOWING WITH POWER.

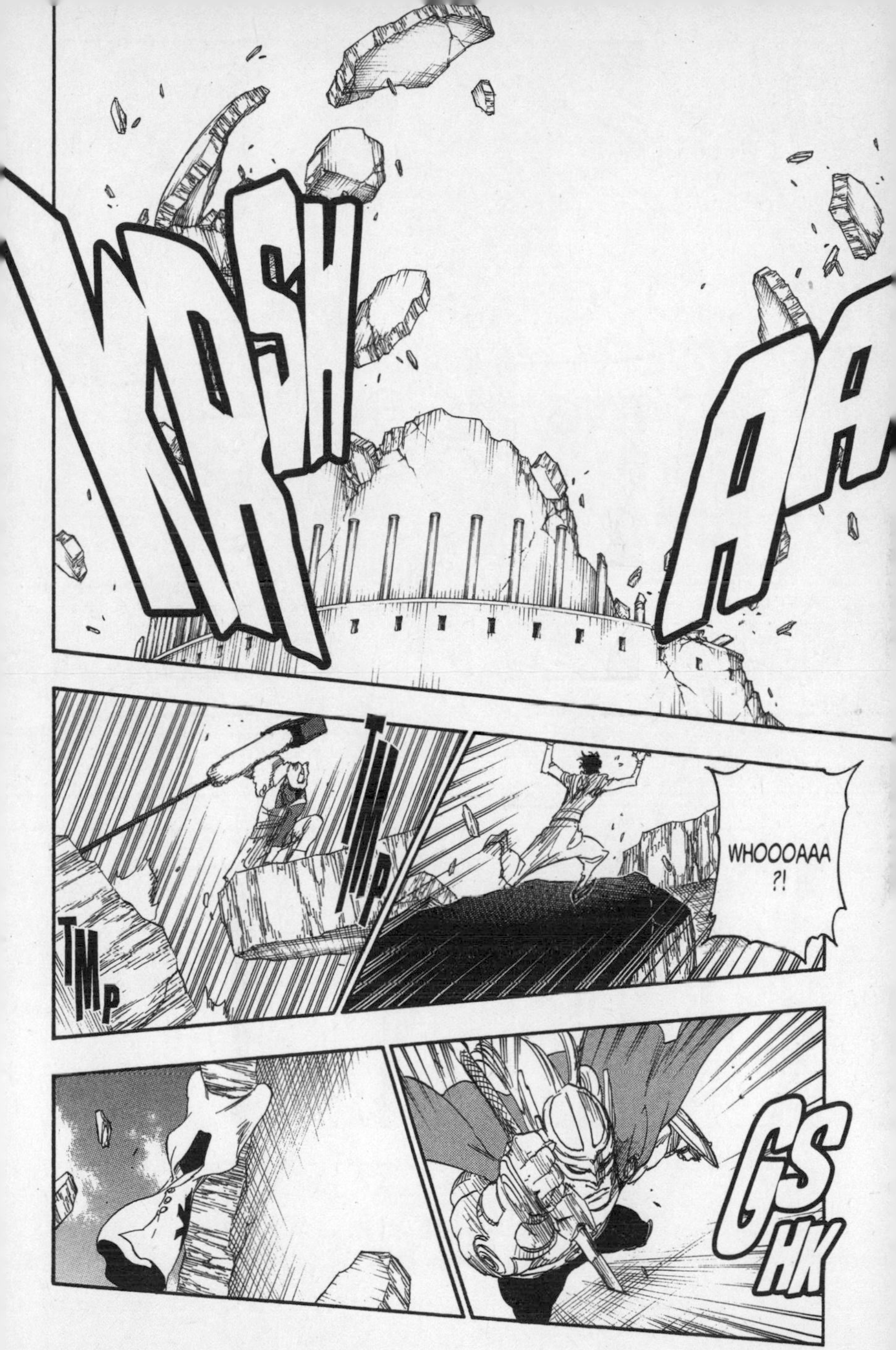
VRASH
AA
WHOOOAAA ?!
TMP
TMP
GSHK

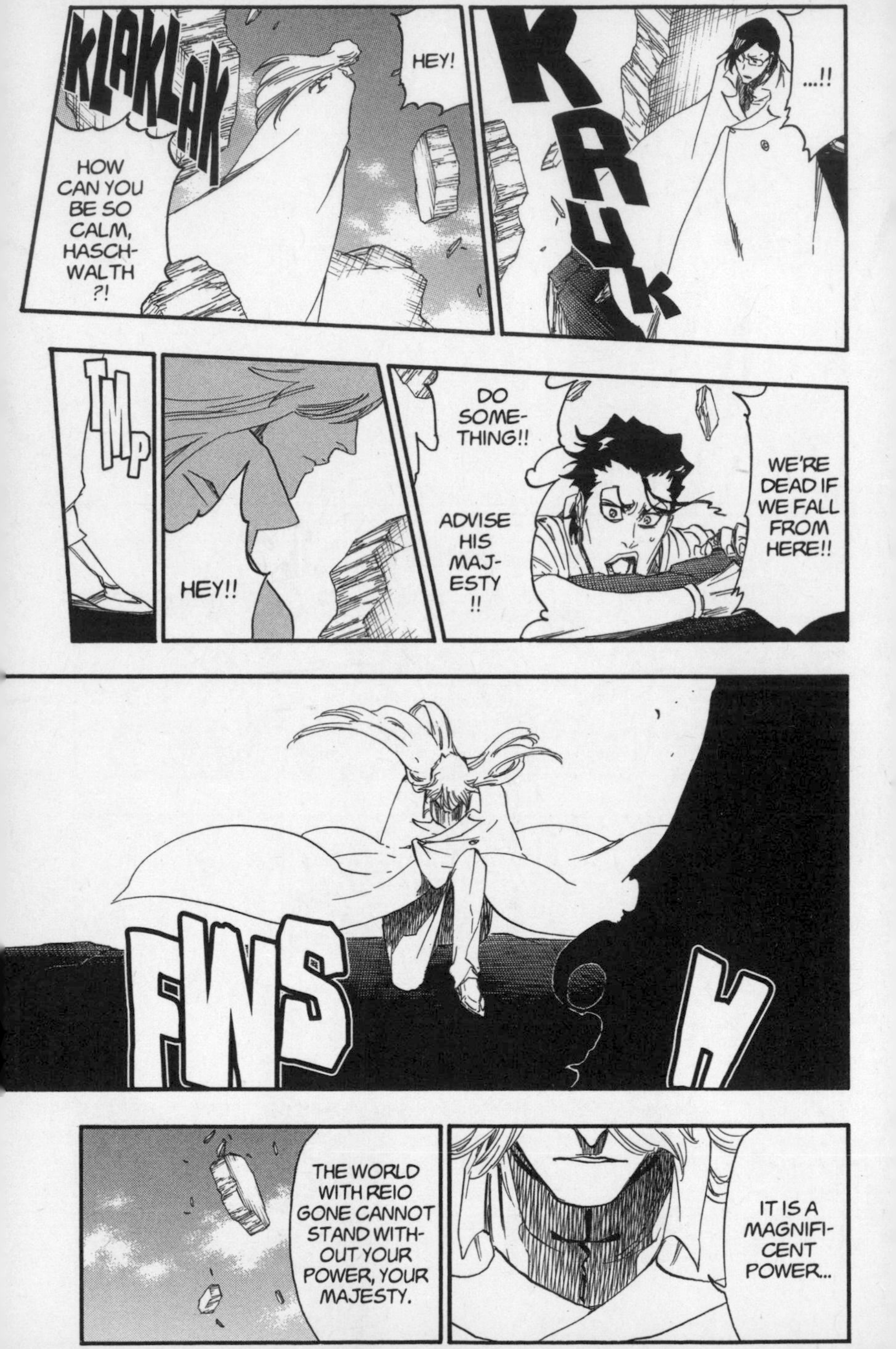
KRUK
...!!
HEY!
KLAKLAK
HOW CAN YOU BE SO CALM, HASCHWALTH?!
DO SOMETHING!!
WE'RE DEAD IF WE FALL FROM HERE!!
ADVISE HIS MAJESTY!!
HEY!!
TMP
FWSH
IT IS A MAGNIFICENT POWER...
THE WORLD WITH REIO GONE CANNOT STAND WITHOUT YOUR POWER, YOUR MAJESTY.

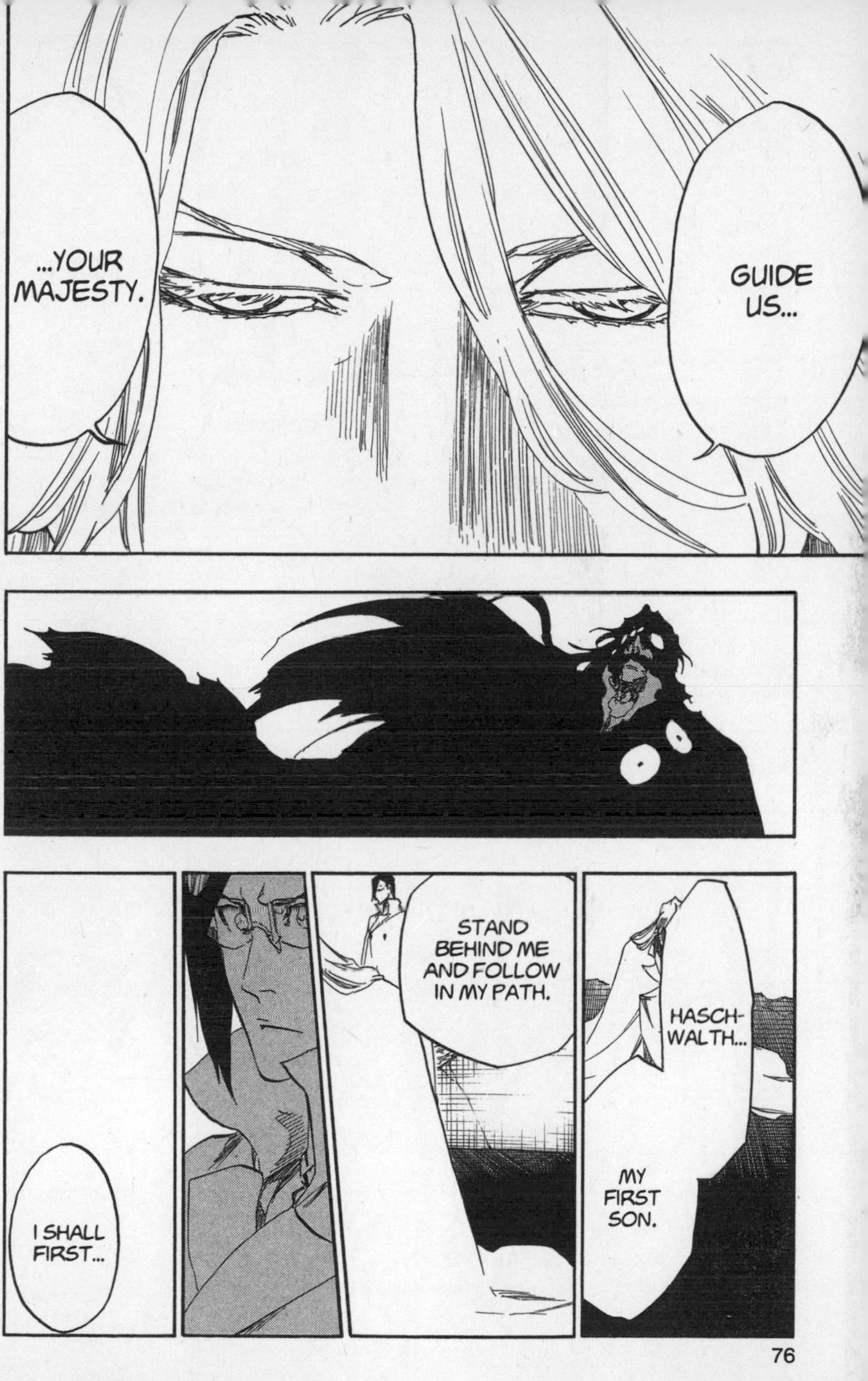
GUIDE US...
...YOUR MAJESTY.
HASCH-WALTH...
MY FIRST SON.
STAND BEHIND ME AND FOLLOW IN MY PATH.
I SHALL FIRST...

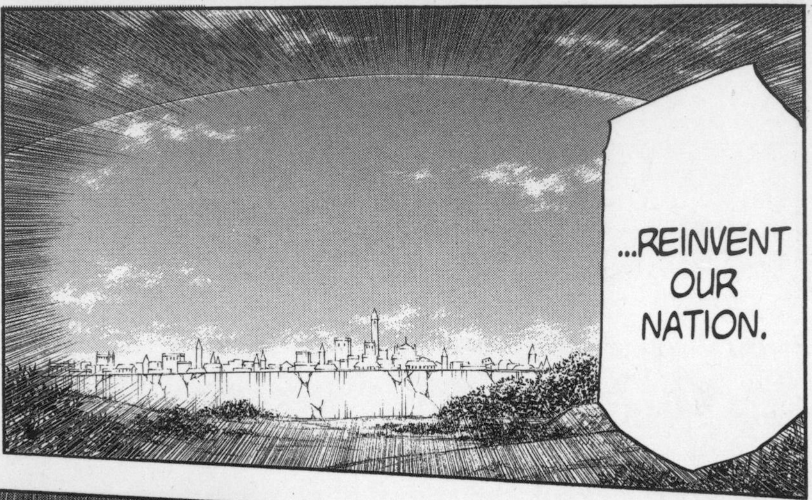
...REINVENT OUR NATION.
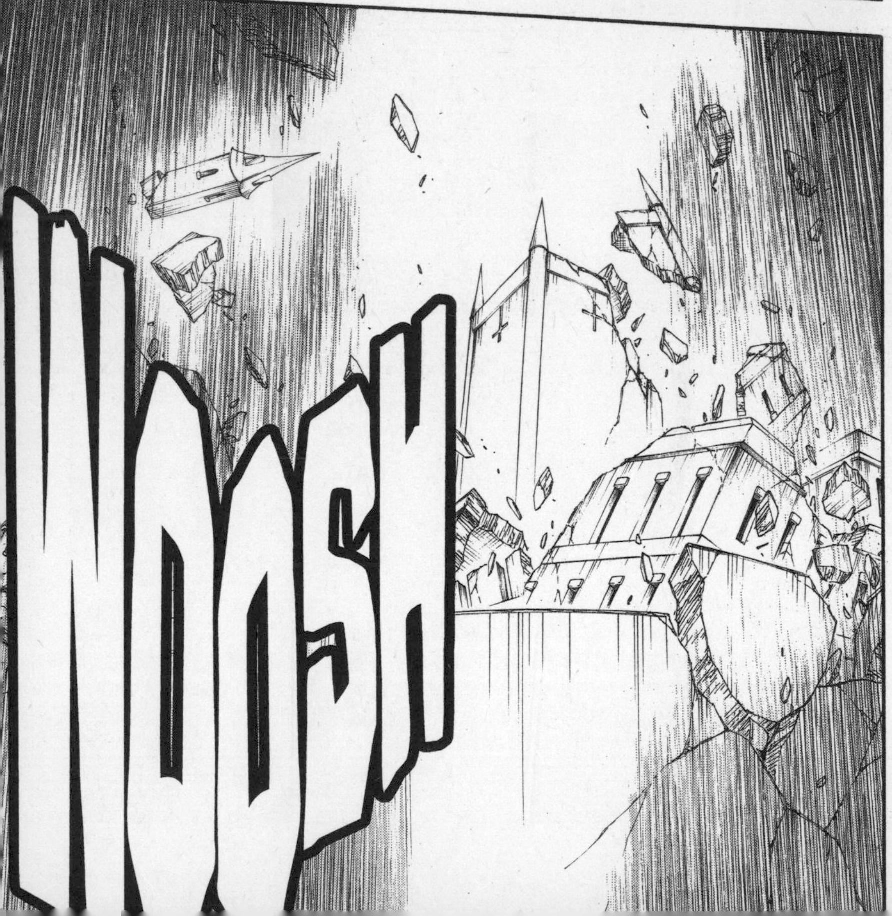
WOOSH

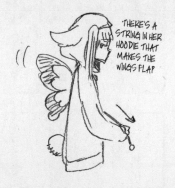

THERE'S A STRING IN HER HOODIE THAT MAKES THE WINGS FLAP

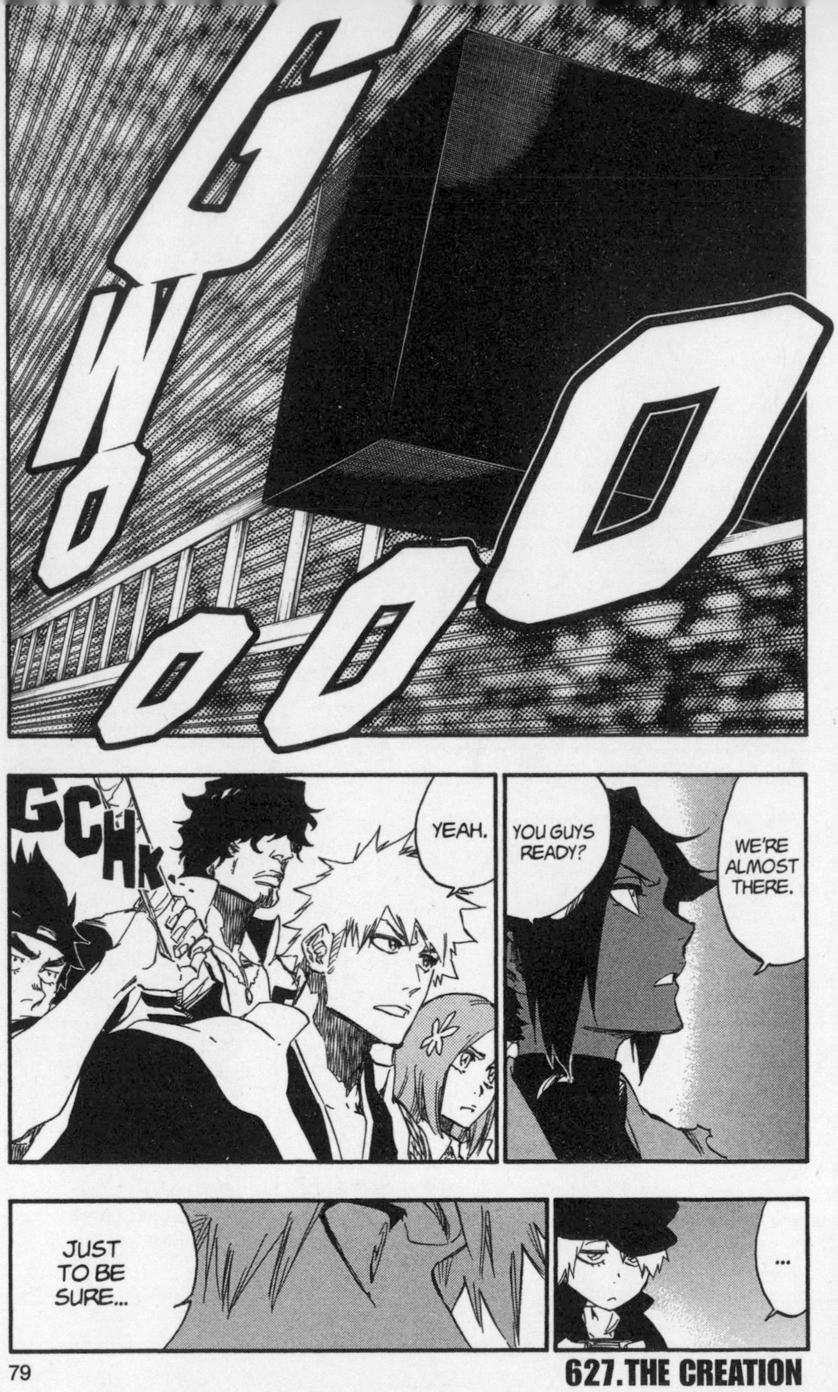

GWOOOO
WE'RE ALMOST THERE.
YOU GUYS READY?
YEAH.
GCHK
...
JUST TO BE SURE...

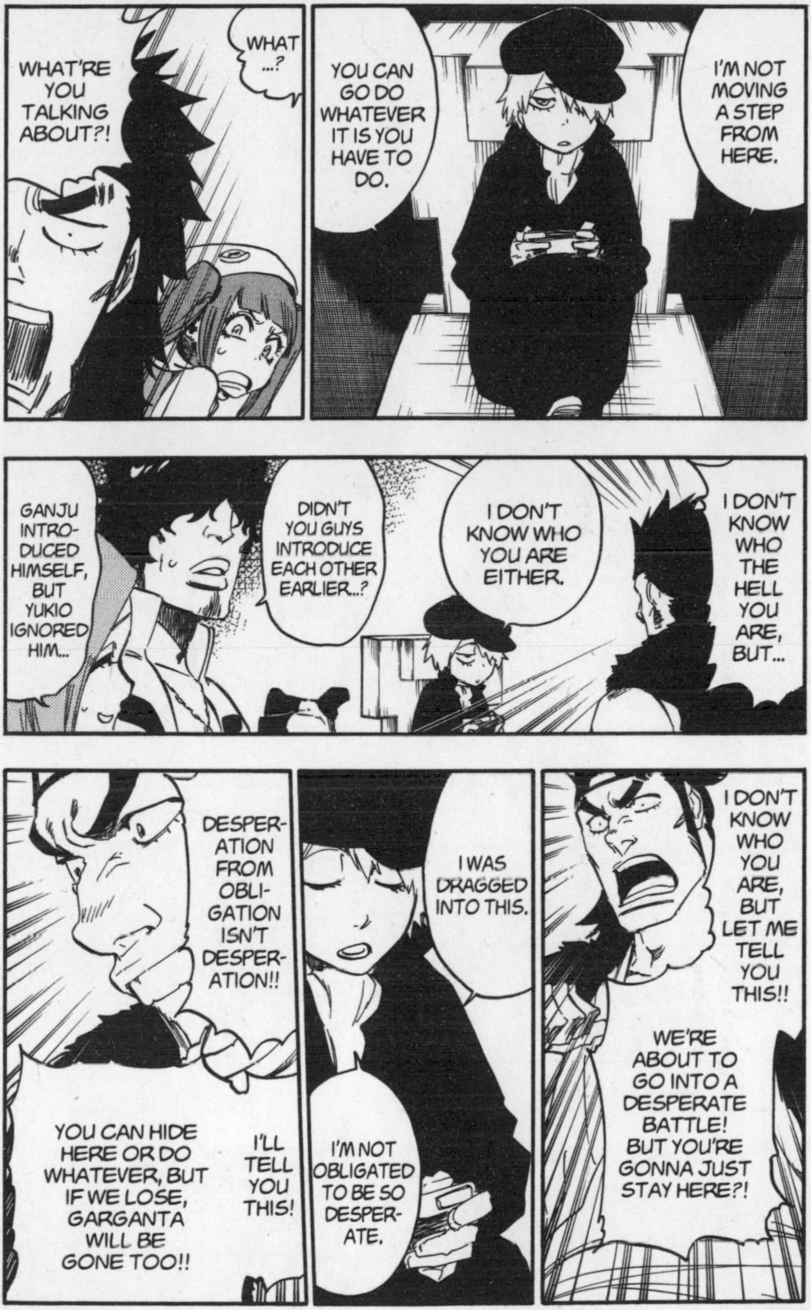
I'M NOT MOVING A STEP FROM HERE.
YOU CAN GO DO WHATEVER IT IS YOU HAVE TO DO.
WHAT ...?
WHAT'RE YOU TALKING ABOUT?!
I DON'T KNOW WHO THE HELL YOU ARE, BUT...
I DON'T KNOW WHO YOU ARE EITHER.
DIDN'T YOU GUYS INTRODUCE EACH OTHER EARLIER...?
GANJU INTRODUCED HIMSELF, BUT YUKIO IGNORED HIM...
I DON'T KNOW WHO YOU ARE, BUT LET ME TELL YOU THIS!!
WE'RE ABOUT TO GO INTO A DESPERATE BATTLE! BUT YOU'RE GONNA JUST STAY HERE?!
I WAS DRAGGED INTO THIS.
I'M NOT OBLIGATED TO BE SO DESPERATE.
DESPERATION FROM OBLIGATION ISN'T DESPERATION!!
I'LL TELL YOU THIS!
YOU CAN HIDE HERE OR DO WHATEVER, BUT IF WE LOSE, GARGANTA WILL BE GONE TOO!!

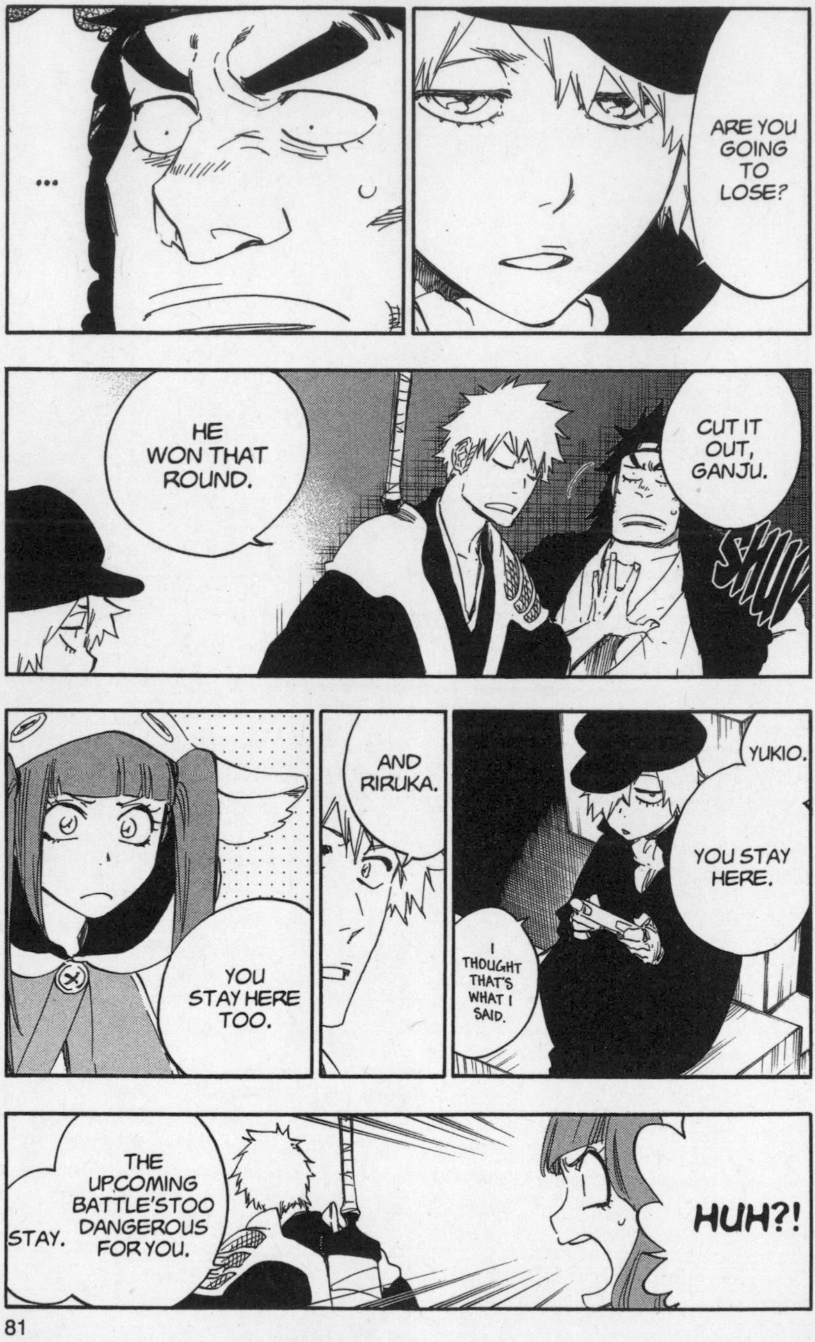
ARE YOU GOING TO LOSE?
...
CUT IT OUT, GANJU.
HE WON THAT ROUND.
YUKIO.
YOU STAY HERE.
I THOUGHT THAT'S WHAT I SAID.
AND RIRUKA.
YOU STAY HERE TOO.
HUH?!
THE UPCOMING BATTLE'S TOO DANGEROUS FOR YOU.
STAY.

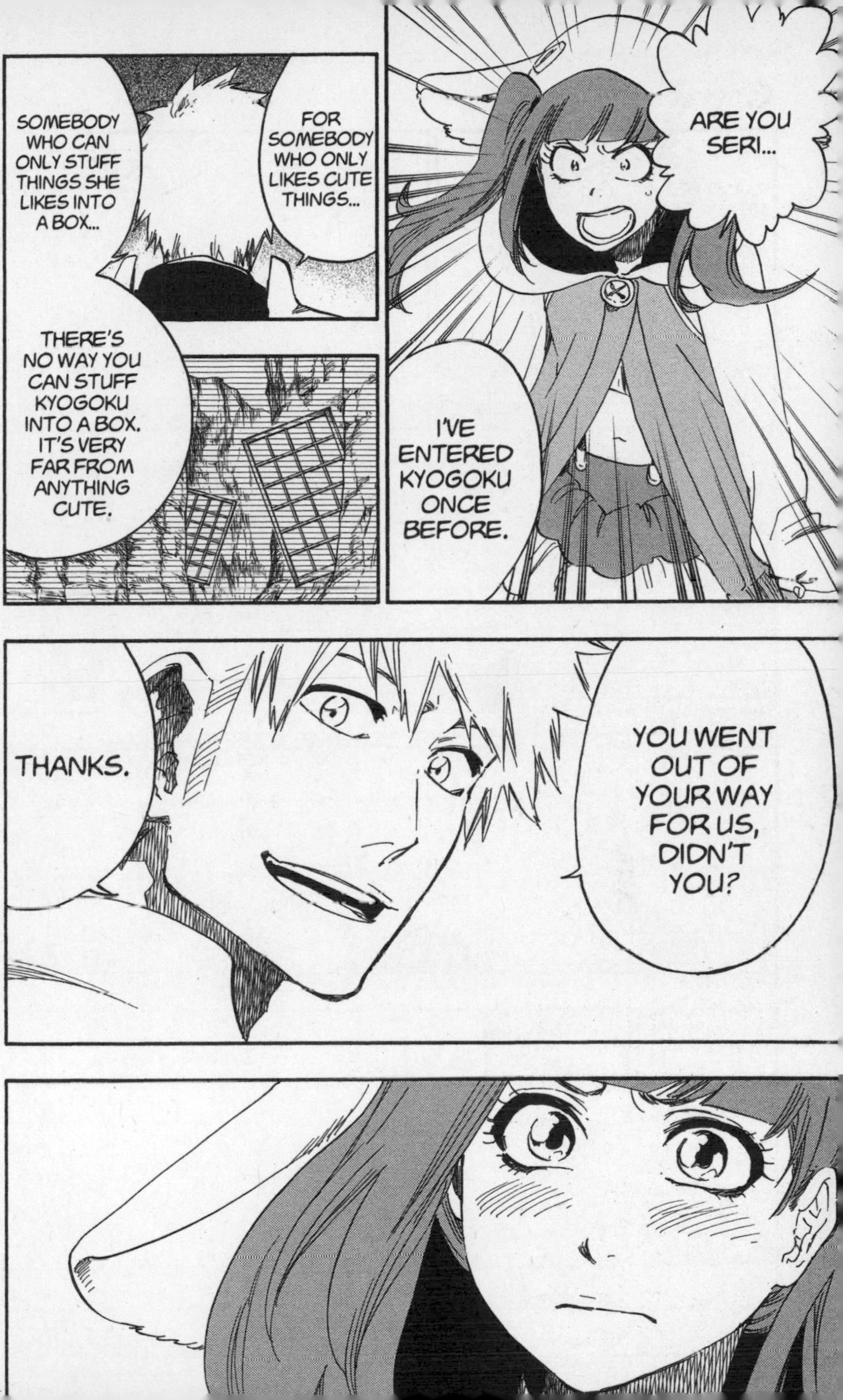
ARE YOU SERI...
I'VE ENTERED KYOGOKU ONCE BEFORE.
FOR SOMEBODY WHO ONLY LIKES CUTE THINGS...
SOMEBODY WHO CAN ONLY STUFF THINGS SHE LIKES INTO A BOX...
THERE'S NO WAY YOU CAN STUFF KYOGOKU INTO A BOX. IT'S VERY FAR FROM ANYTHING CUTE.
YOU WENT OUT OF YOUR WAY FOR US, DIDN'T YOU?
THANKS.

READ THIS WAY

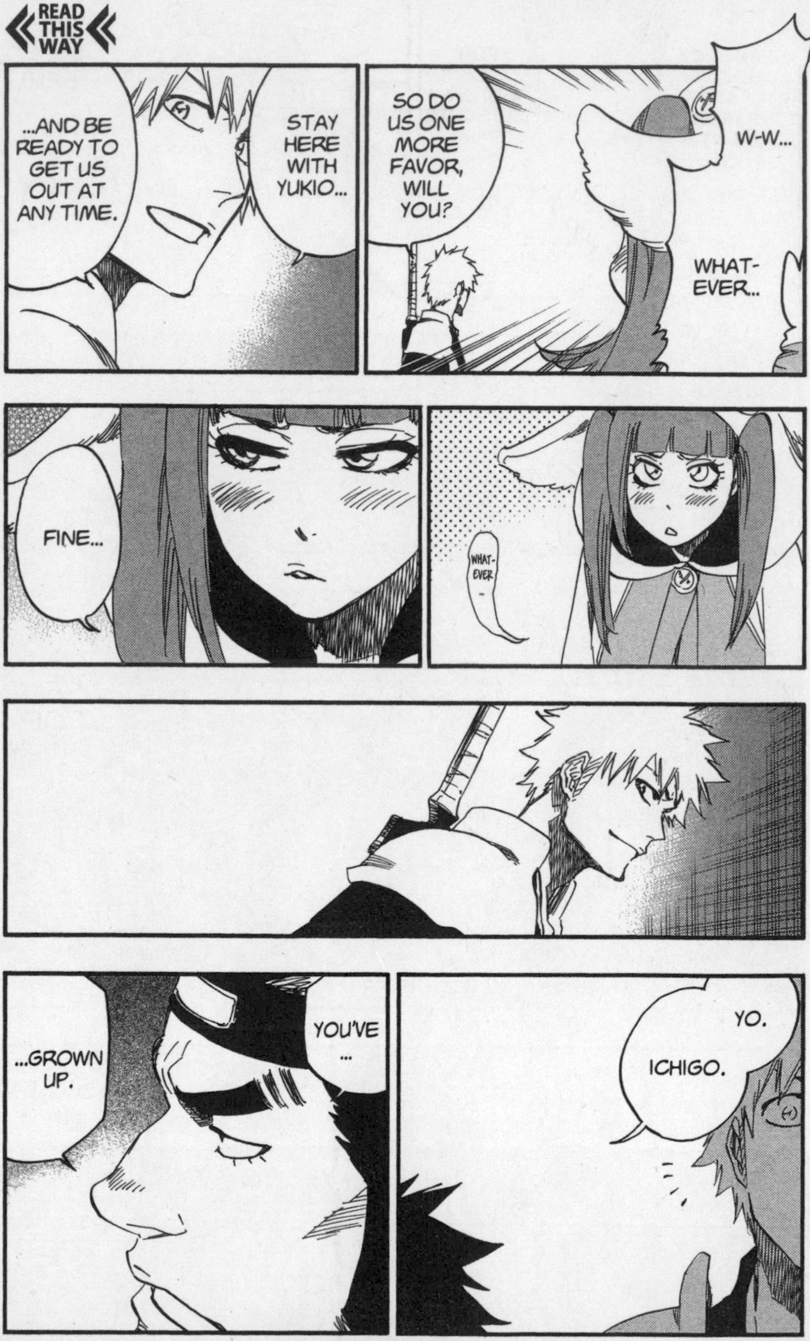
W-W...
WHAT-EVER...
SO DO US ONE MORE FAVOR, WILL YOU?
STAY HERE WITH YUKIO...
...AND BE READY TO GET US OUT AT ANY TIME.
WHAT-EVER...
FINE...
YO.
ICHIGO.
YOU'VE...
...GROWN UP.

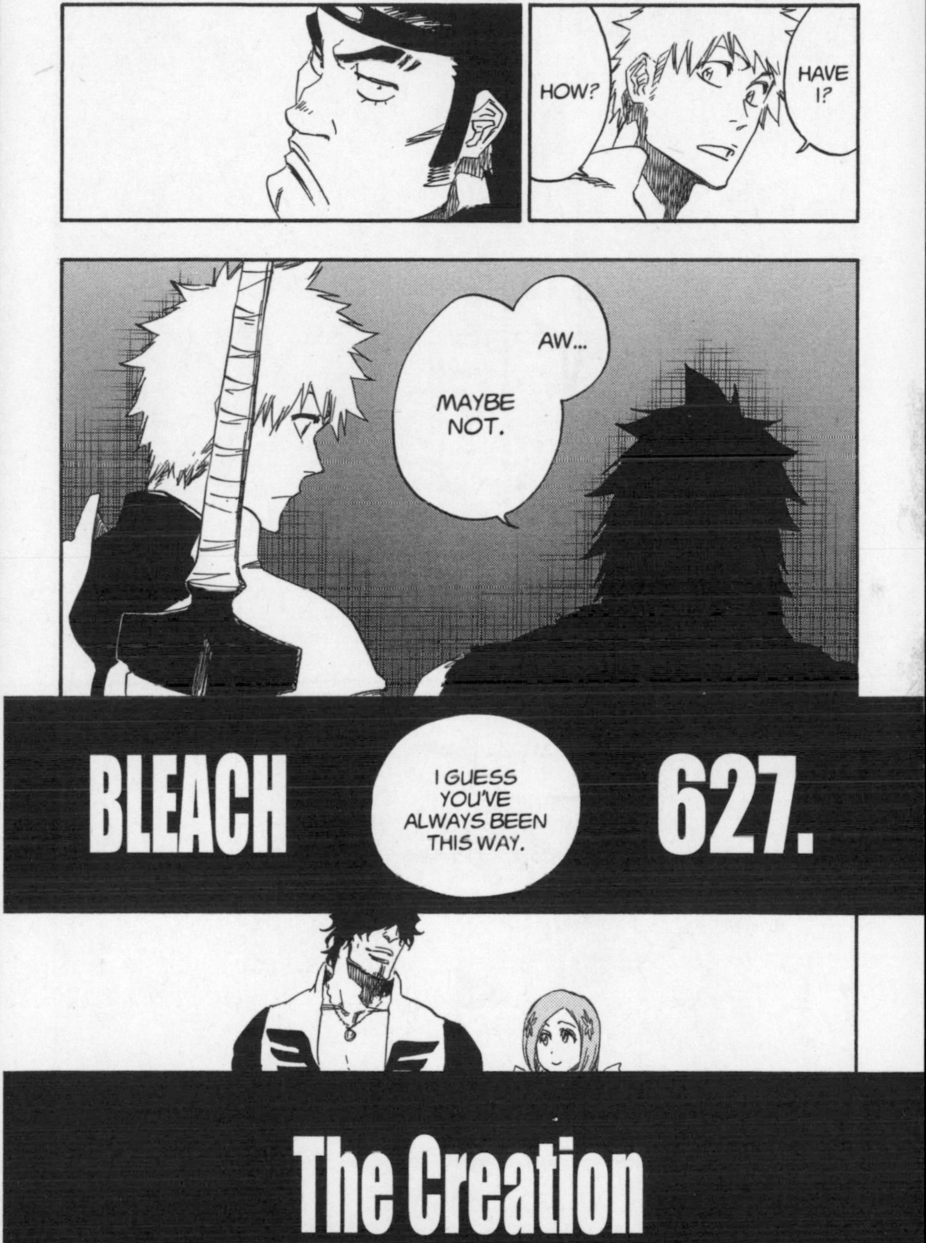
HAVE I?
HOW?
AW... MAYBE NOT.
BLEACH
627.
I GUESS YOU'VE ALWAYS BEEN THIS WAY.
The Creation

READ THIS WAY

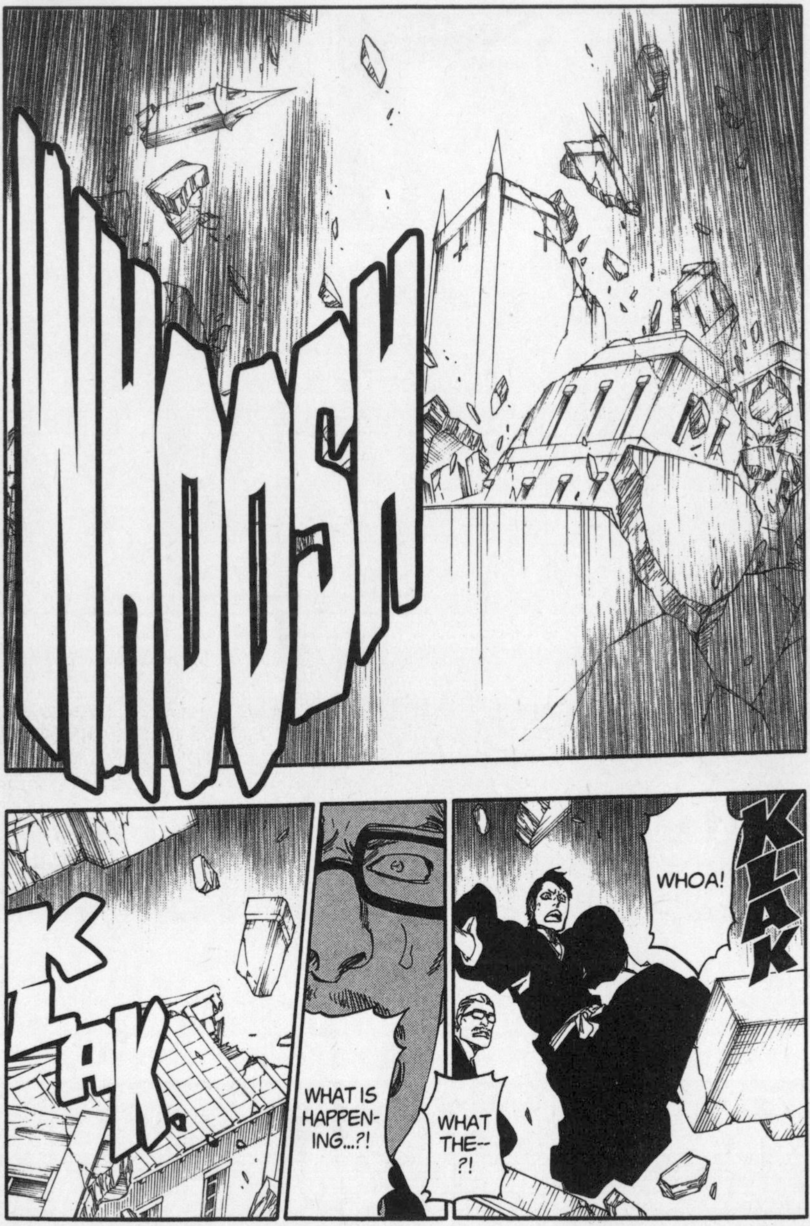
WHOOSH
KLAK
WHOA!
WHAT THE-- ?!
WHAT IS HAPPEN-ING...?!
KLAK

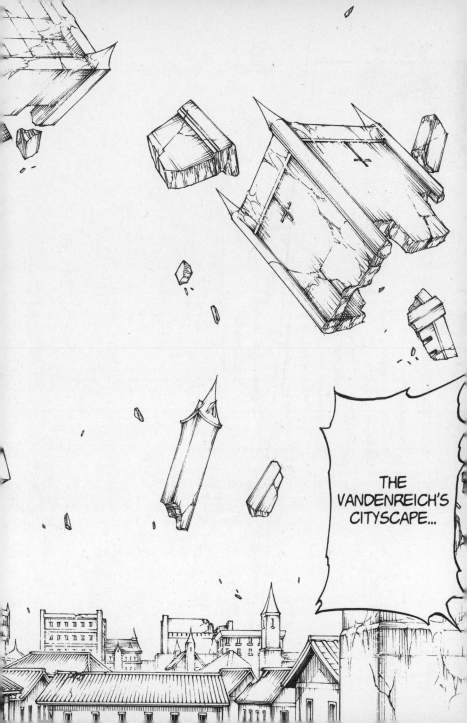

THE
VANDENREICH'S
CITYSCAPE...

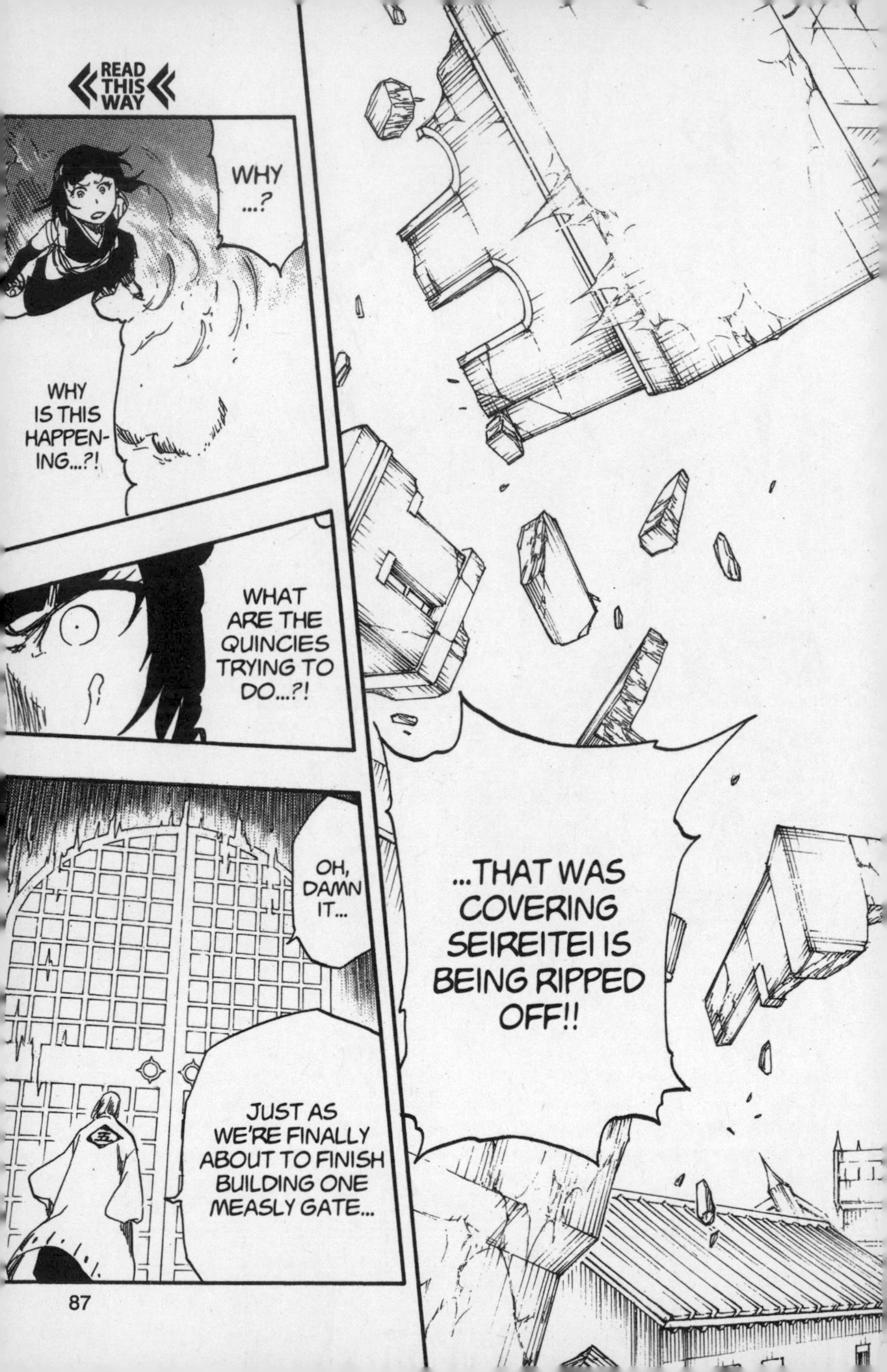
READ THIS WAY
...THAT WAS COVERING SEIREITEI IS BEING RIPPED OFF!!
WHY ...?
WHY IS THIS HAPPEN-ING...?!
WHAT ARE THE QUINCIES TRYING TO DO...?!
OH, DAMN IT...
JUST AS WE'RE FINALLY ABOUT TO FINISH BUILDING ONE MEASLY GATE...

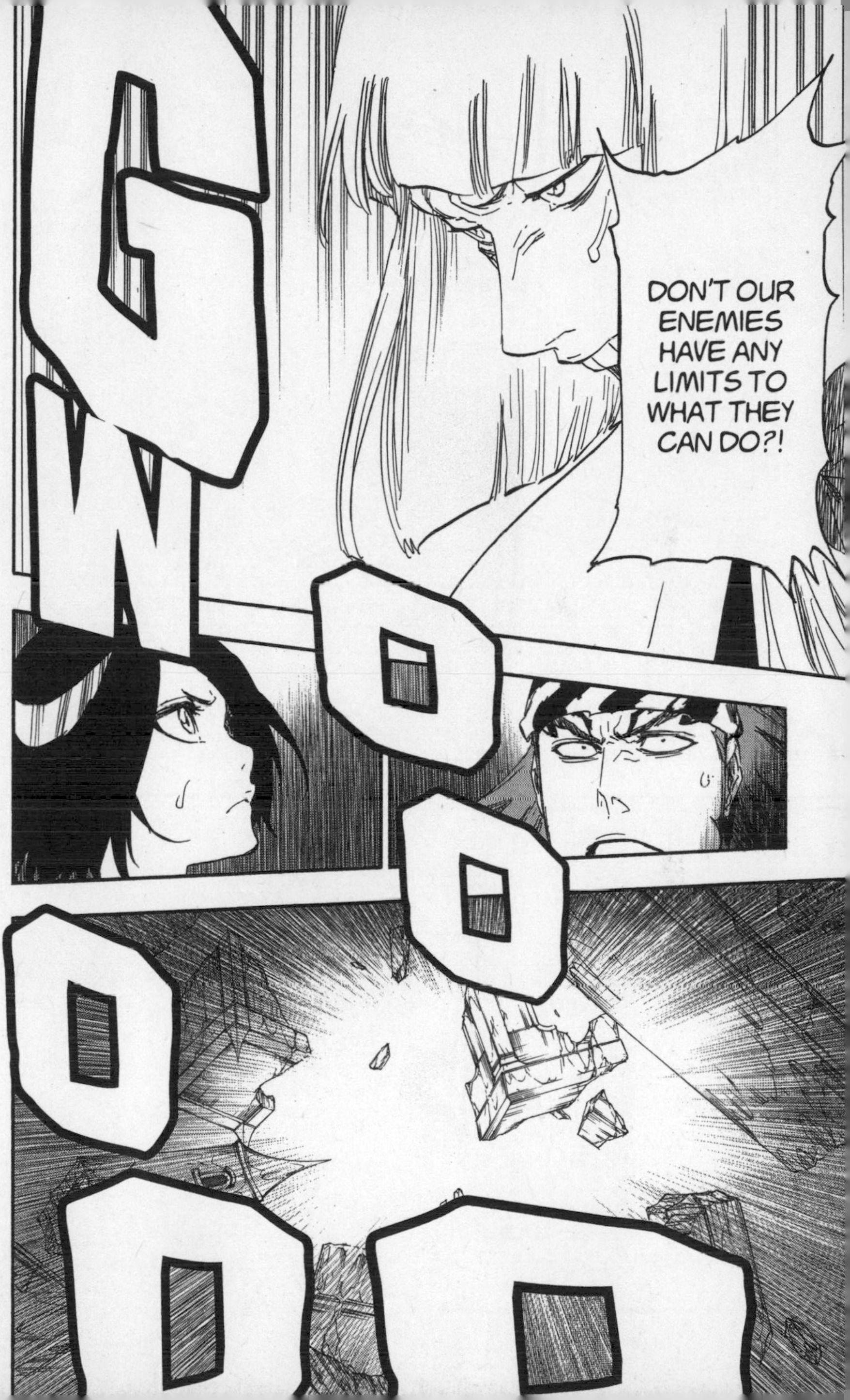
DON'T OUR ENEMIES HAVE ANY LIMITS TO WHAT THEY CAN DO?!
GWOOOOO

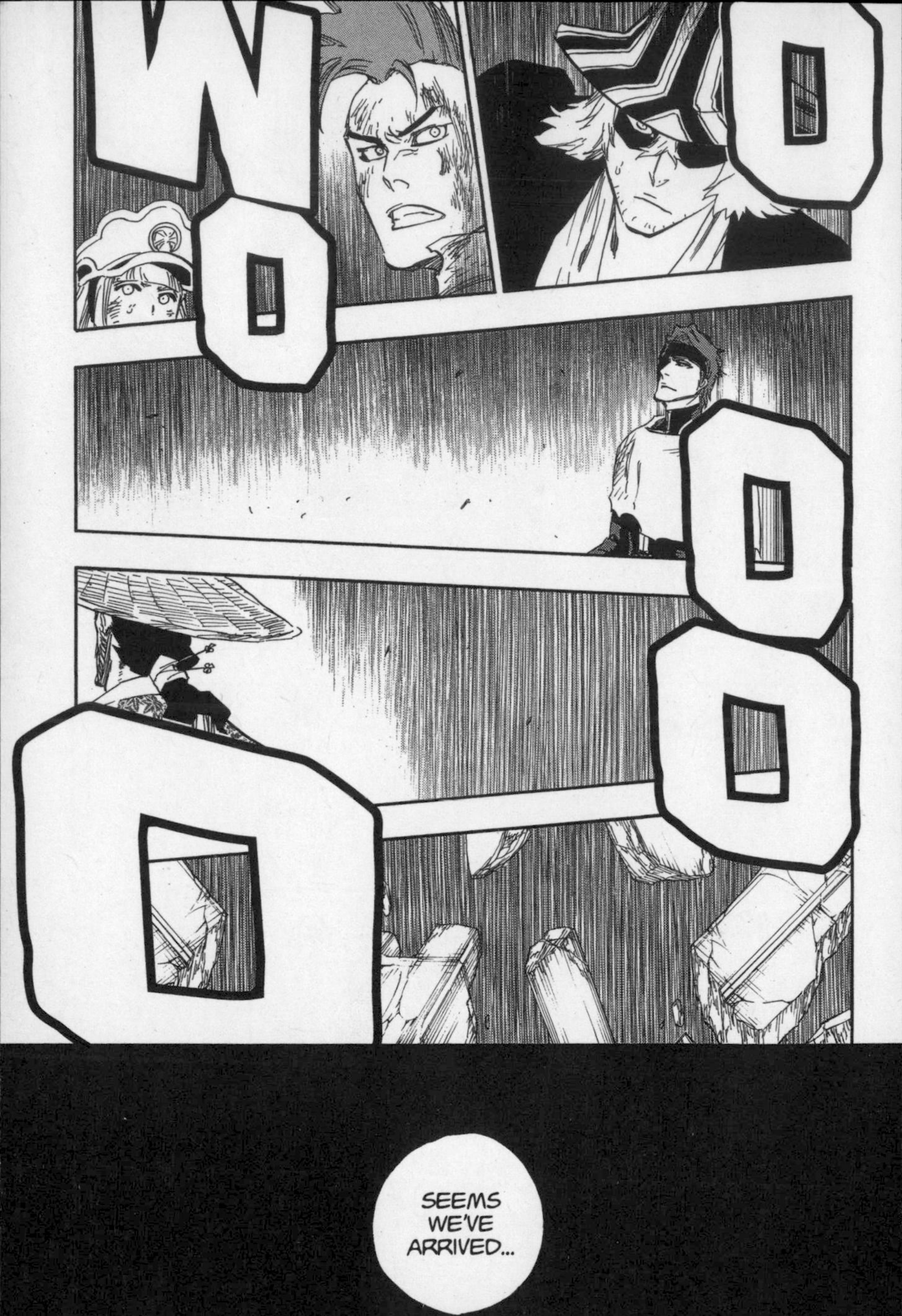
WOOOOO
SEEMS WE'VE ARRIVED...

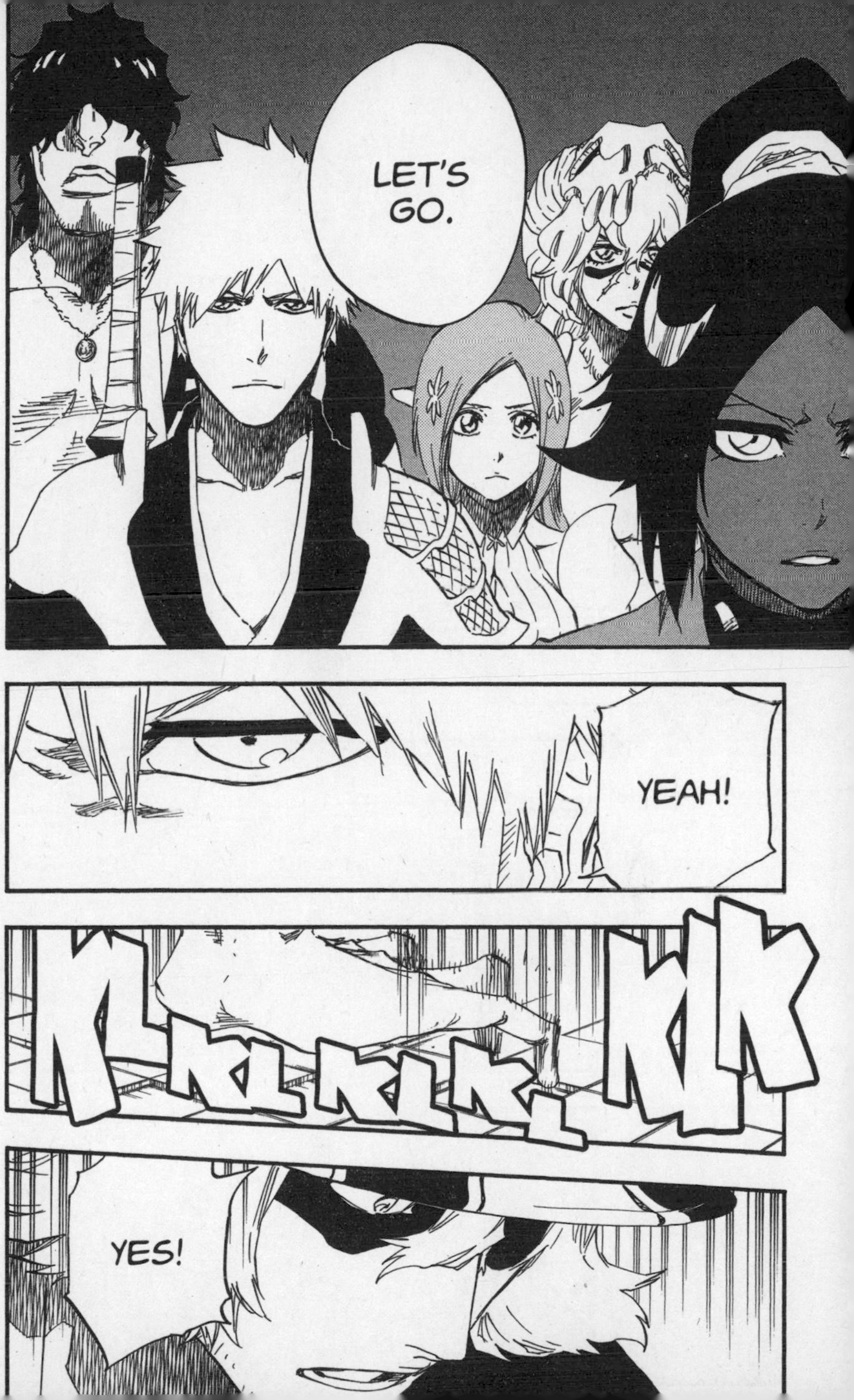
LET'S GO.
YEAH!
YES!

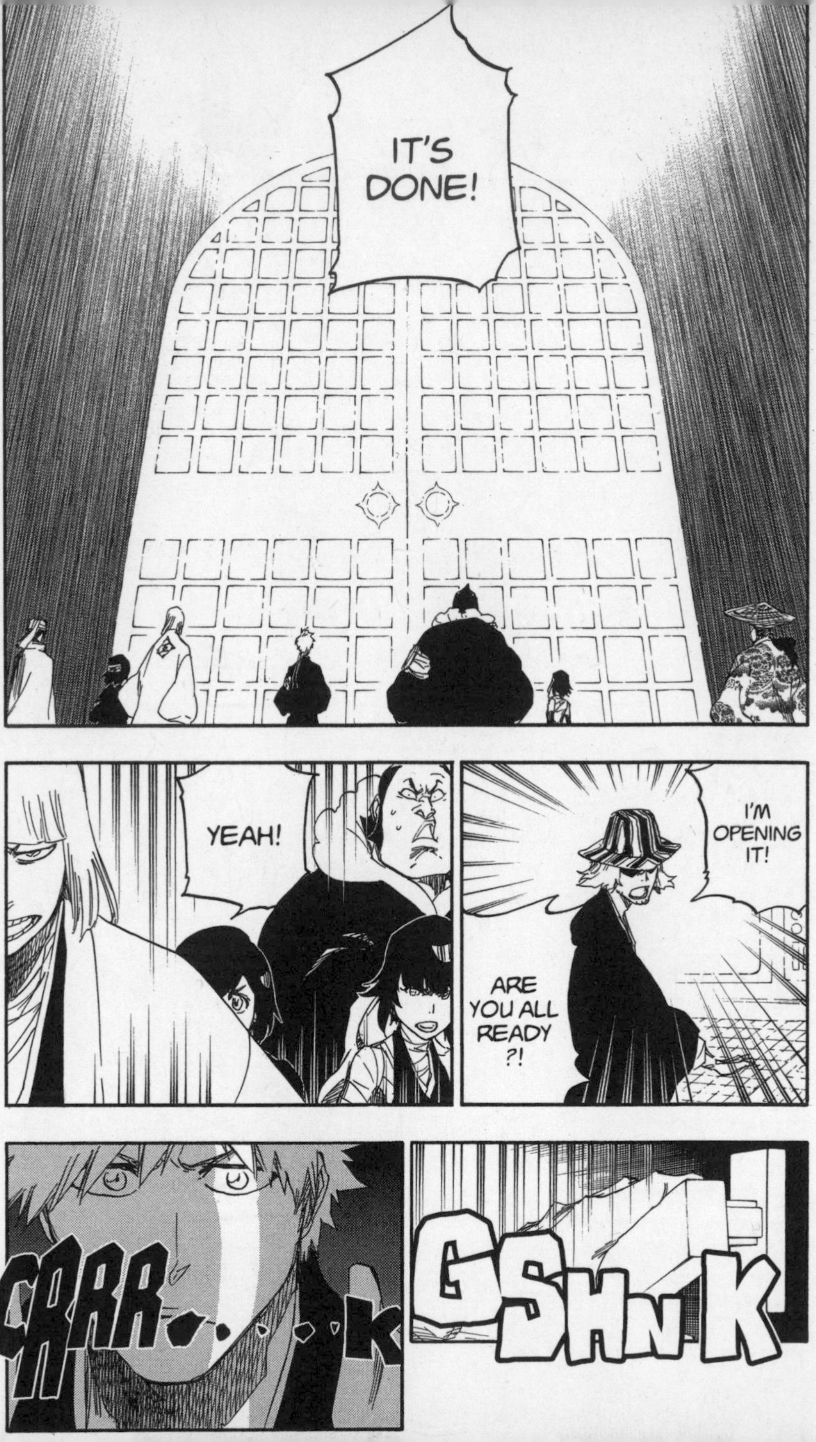
IT'S DONE!
I'M OPENING IT!
ARE YOU ALL READY ?!
YEAH!
GSHNK
CRR....K

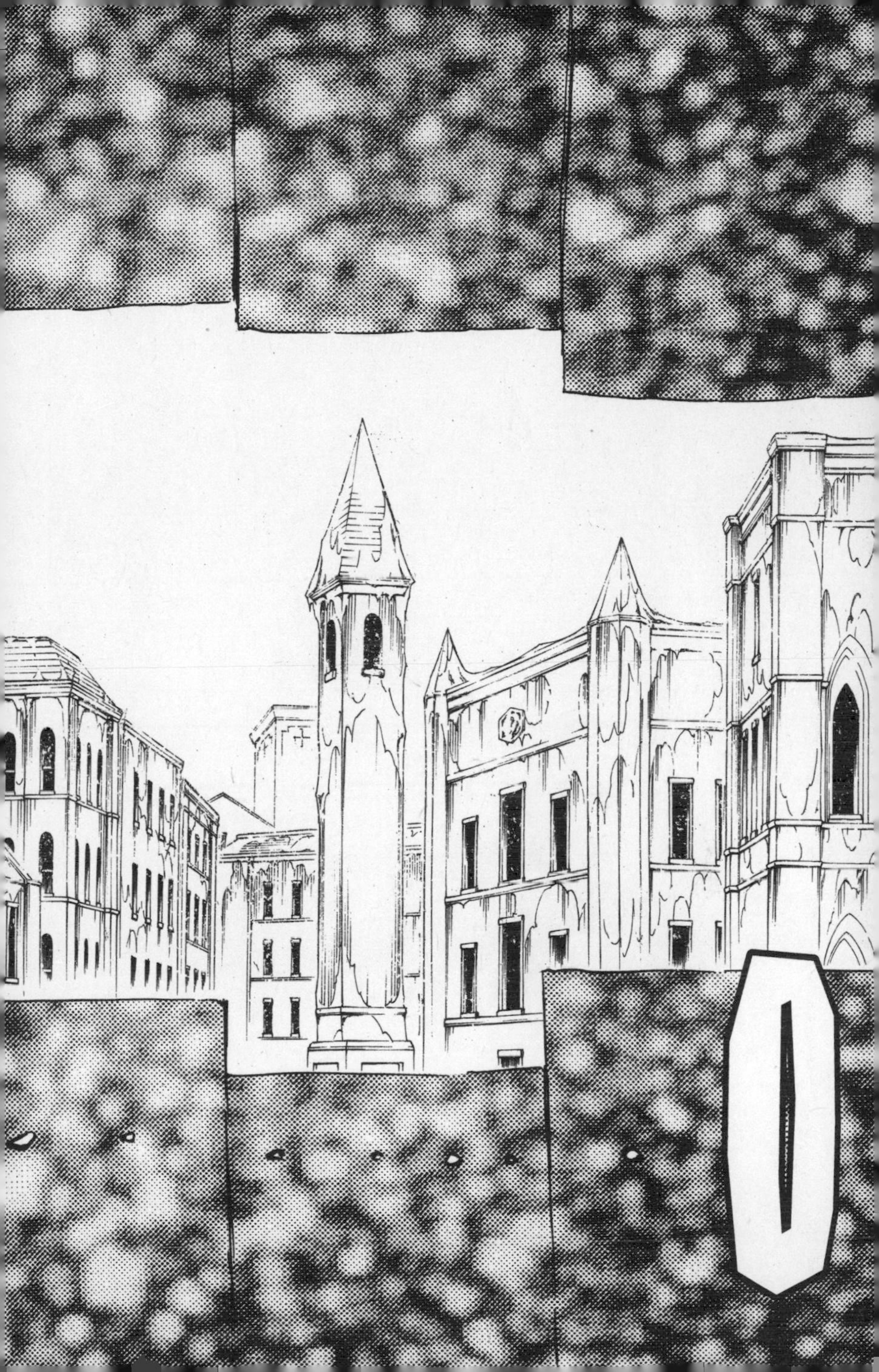
!

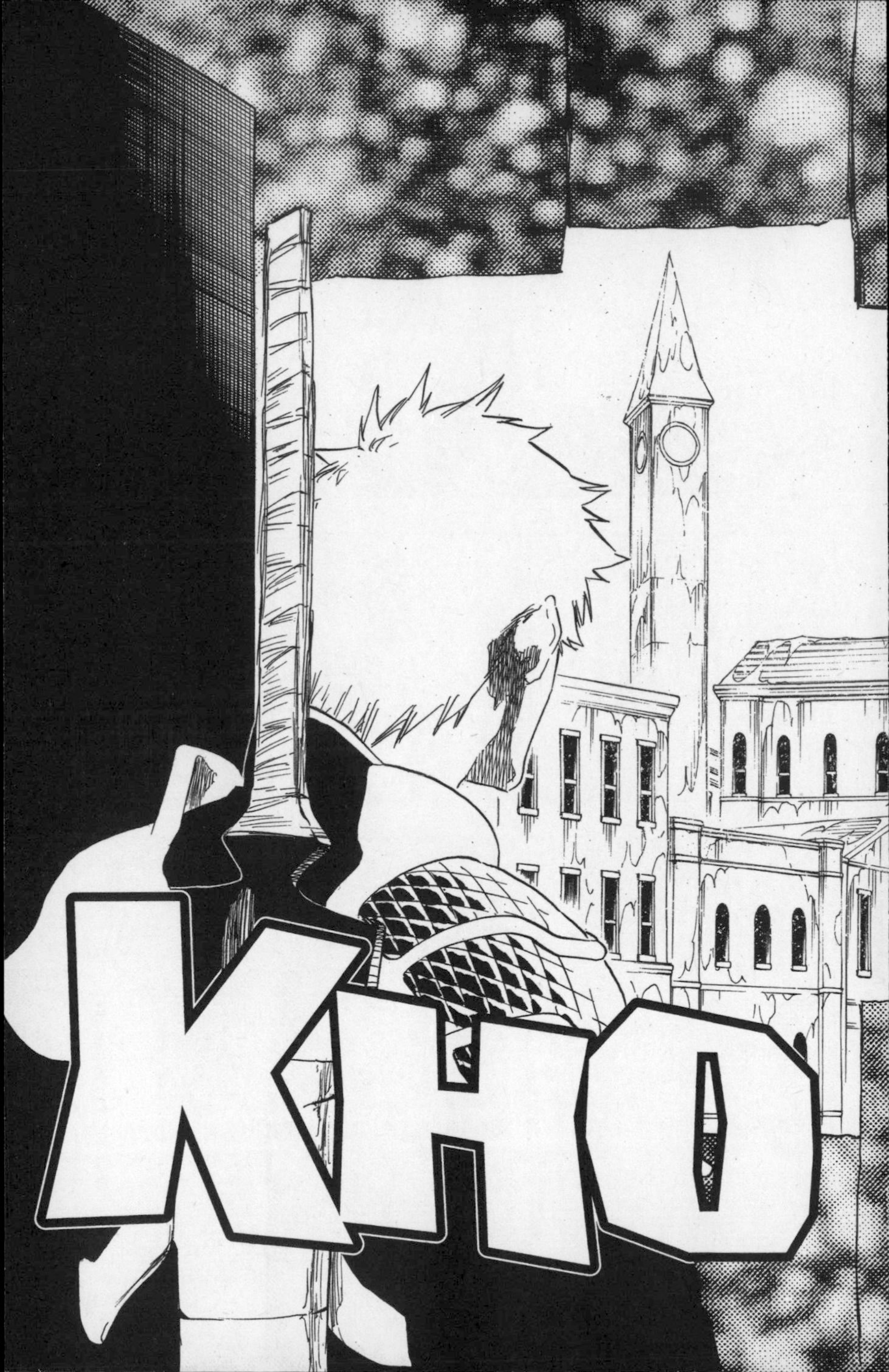
KHO

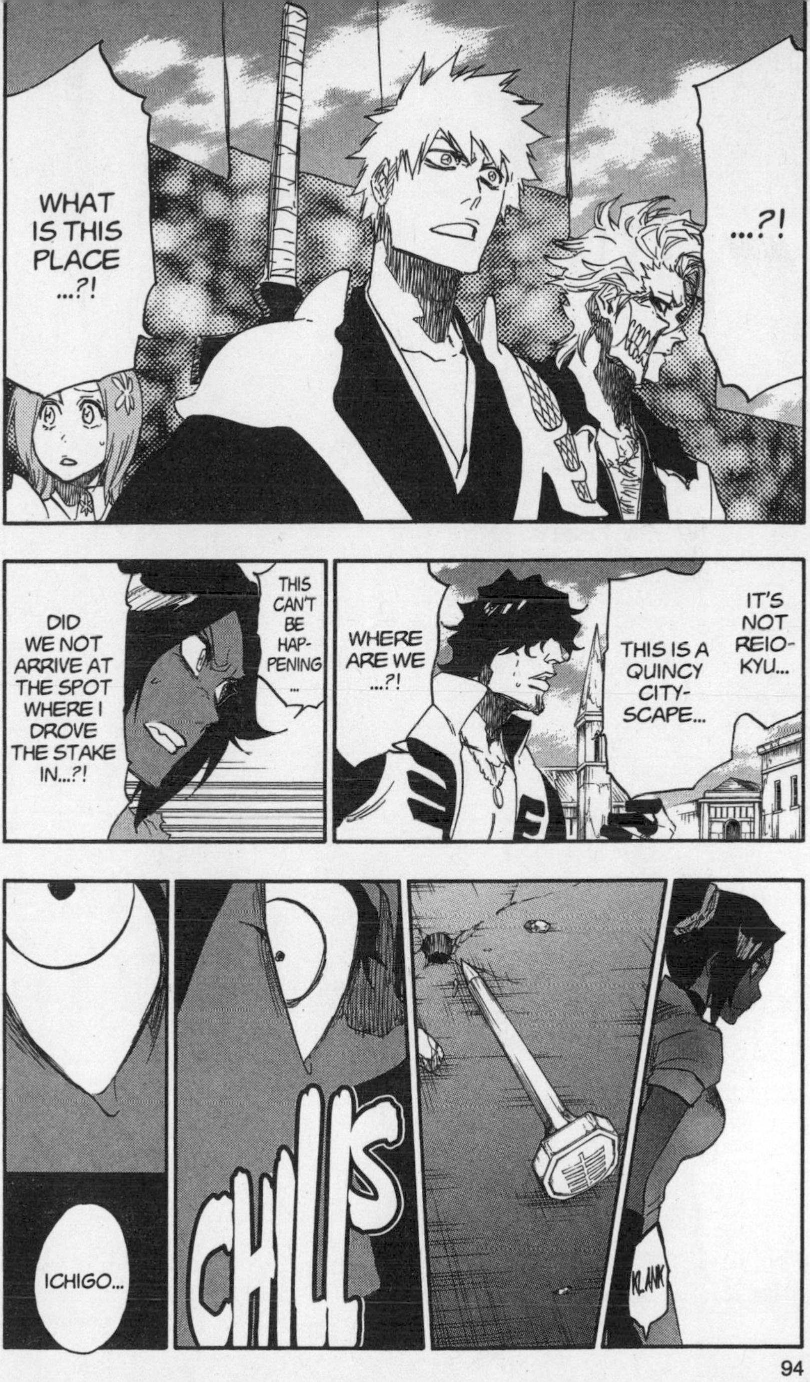
...?!
WHAT IS THIS PLACE ...?!
IT'S NOT REIO-KYU...
THIS IS A QUINCY CITY-SCAPE...
WHERE ARE WE ...?!
THIS CAN'T BE HAP-PENING ...
DID WE NOT ARRIVE AT THE SPOT WHERE I DROVE THE STAKE IN...?!
KLANK
CHILLS
ICHIGO...

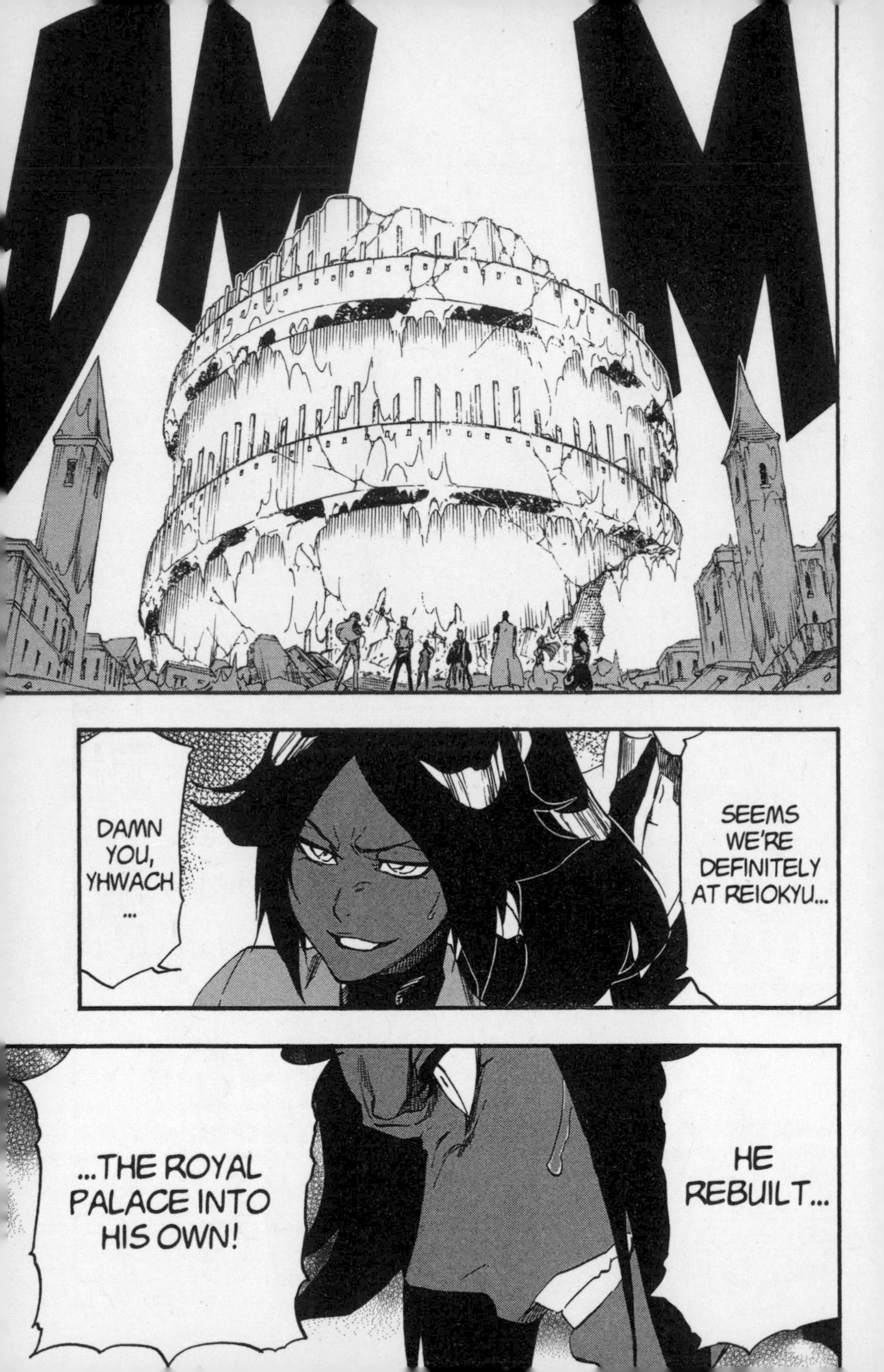
SEEMS WE'RE DEFINITELY AT REIOKYU...
DAMN YOU, YHWACH ...
HE REBUILT...
...THE ROYAL PALACE INTO HIS OWN!

SEE THE
FIRST MOVIE
FOR MORE
INFO ON
KYOGOKU.

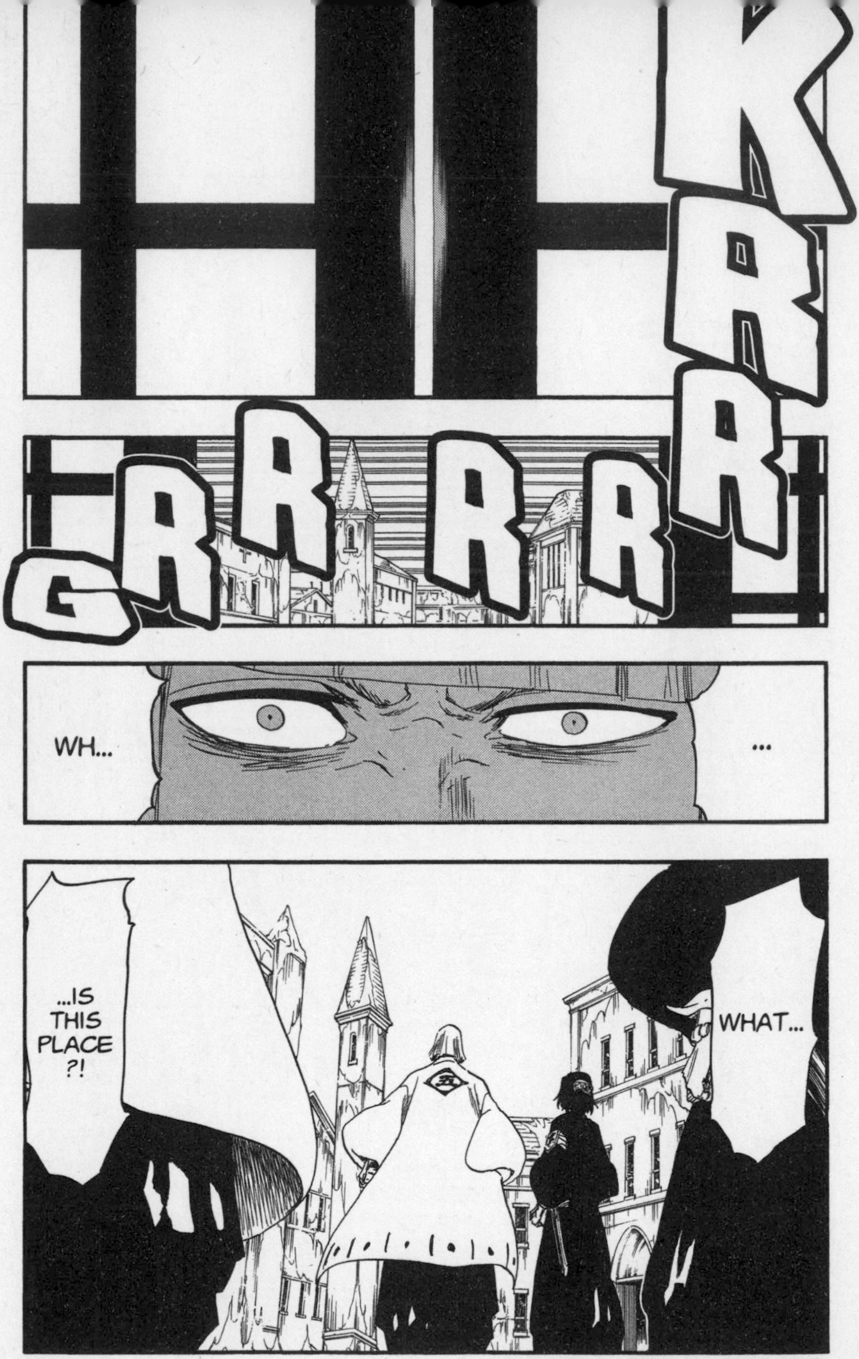
...
WH...
WHAT...
...IS THIS PLACE ?!

628.NEW WORLD ORDERS

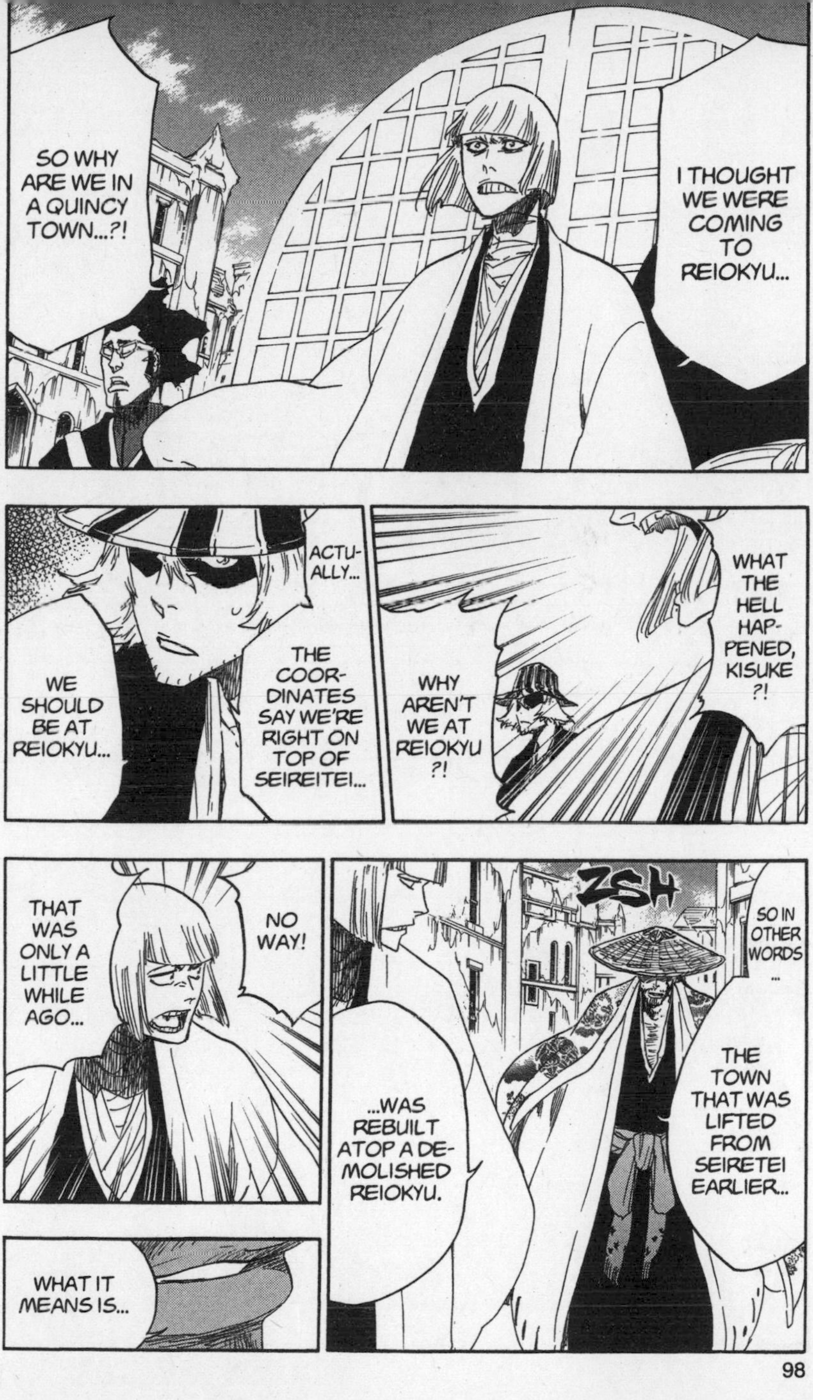
I THOUGHT WE WERE COMING TO REIOKYU...
SO WHY ARE WE IN A QUINCY TOWN...?!
WHAT THE HELL HAPPENED, KISUKE?!
WHY AREN'T WE AT REIOKYU?!
ACTU-ALLY...
THE COORD-INATES SAY WE'RE RIGHT ON TOP OF SEIREITEI...
WE SHOULD BE AT REIOKYU...
ZSH
SO IN OTHER WORDS...
THE TOWN THAT WAS LIFTED FROM SEIRETEI EARLIER...
...WAS REBUILT ATOP A DE-MOLISHED REIOKYU.
NO WAY!
THAT WAS ONLY A LITTLE WHILE AGO...
WHAT IT MEANS IS...

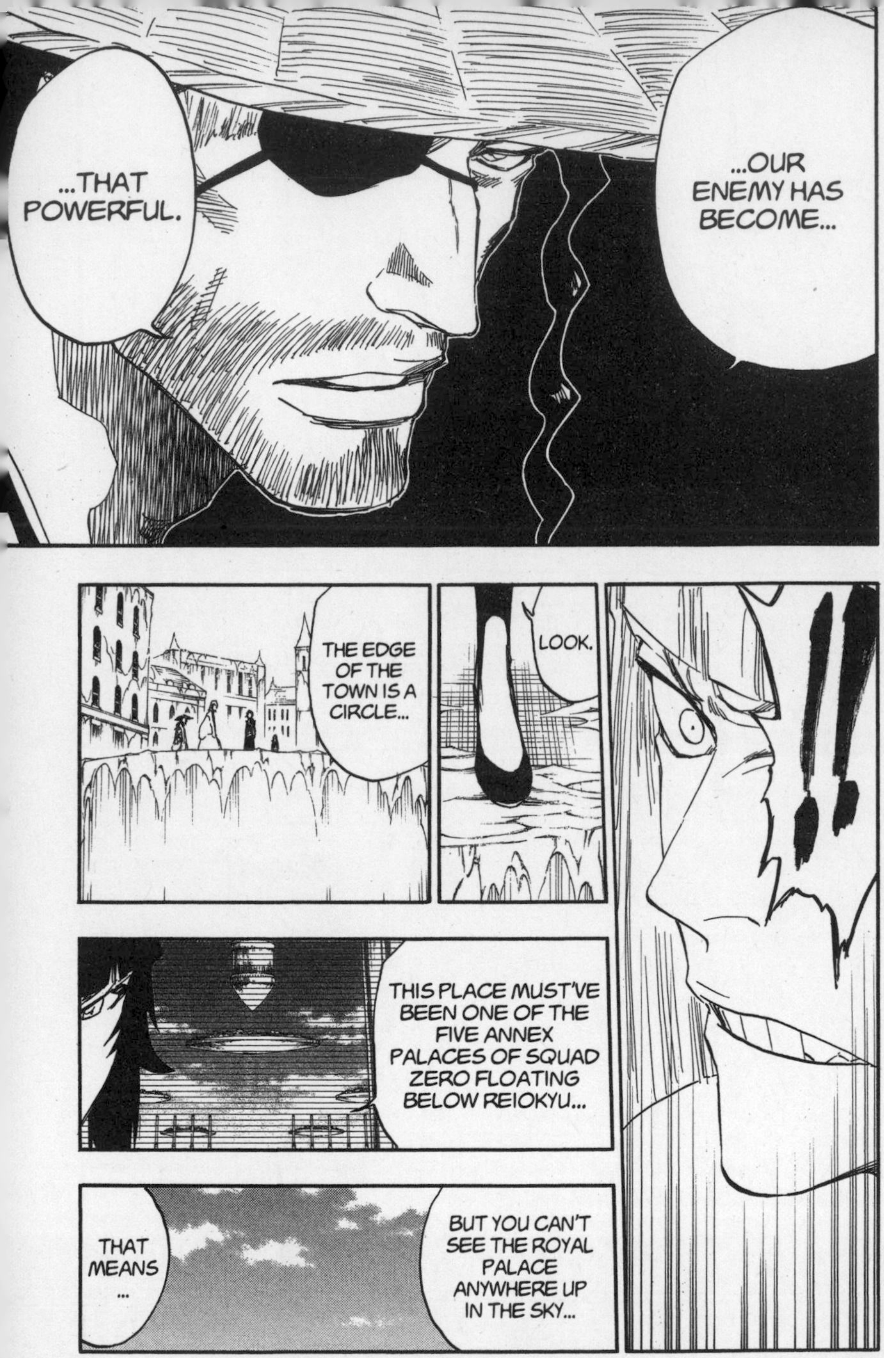
...OUR ENEMY HAS BECOME...
...THAT POWERFUL.
!!
LOOK.
THE EDGE OF THE TOWN IS A CIRCLE...
THIS PLACE MUST'VE BEEN ONE OF THE FIVE ANNEX PALACES OF SQUAD ZERO FLOATING BELOW REIOKYU...
BUT YOU CAN'T SEE THE ROYAL PALACE ANYWHERE UP IN THE SKY...
THAT MEANS ...

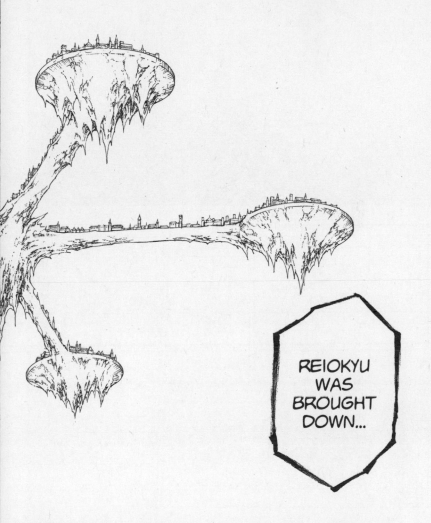

REIOKYU
WAS
BROUGHT
DOWN...

628.

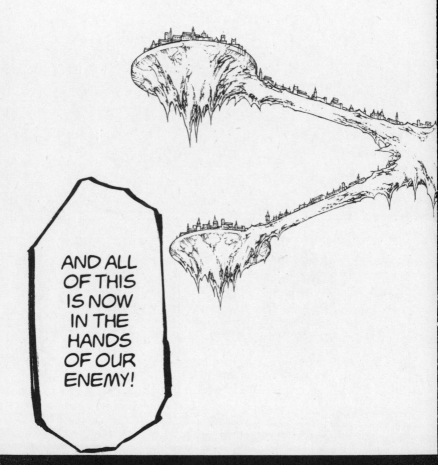

AND ALL OF THIS IS NOW IN THE HANDS OF OUR ENEMY!

BLEACH

New World Orders

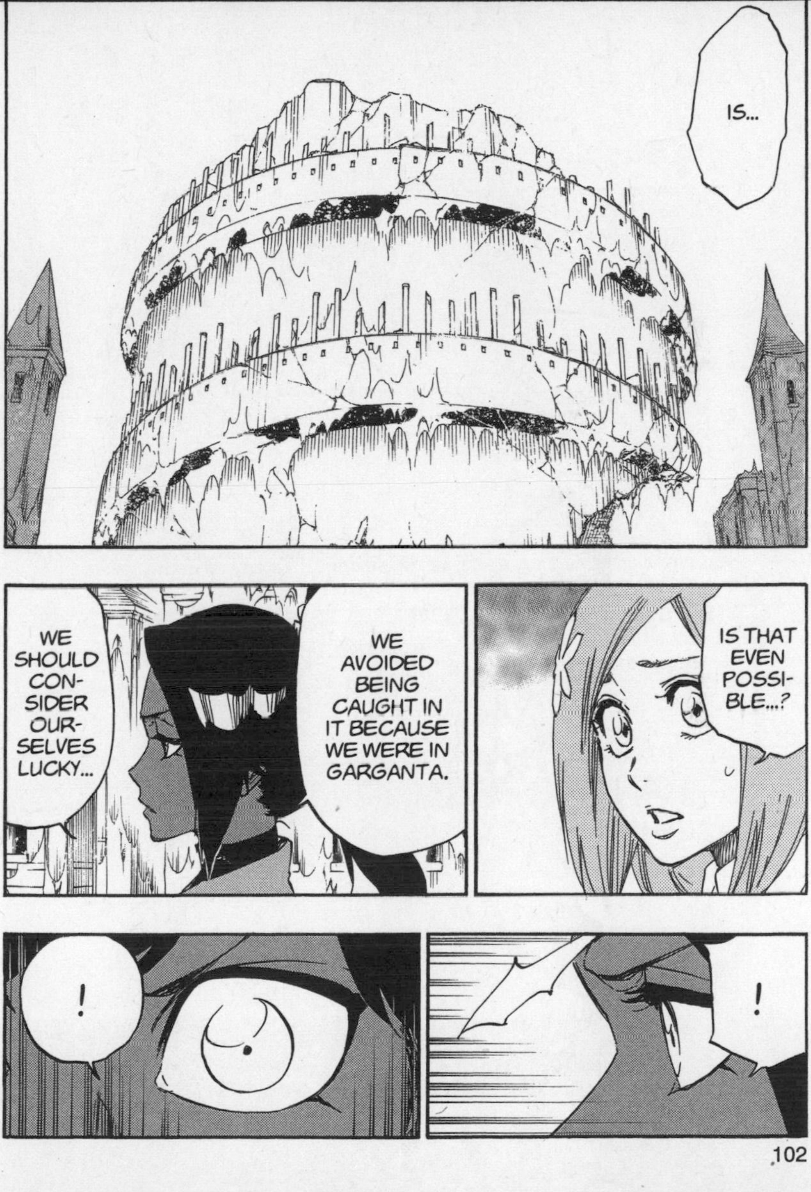
IS...
IS THAT EVEN POSSIBLE...?
WE AVOIDED BEING CAUGHT IN IT BECAUSE WE WERE IN GARGANTA.
WE SHOULD CONSIDER OURSELVES LUCKY...
!
!

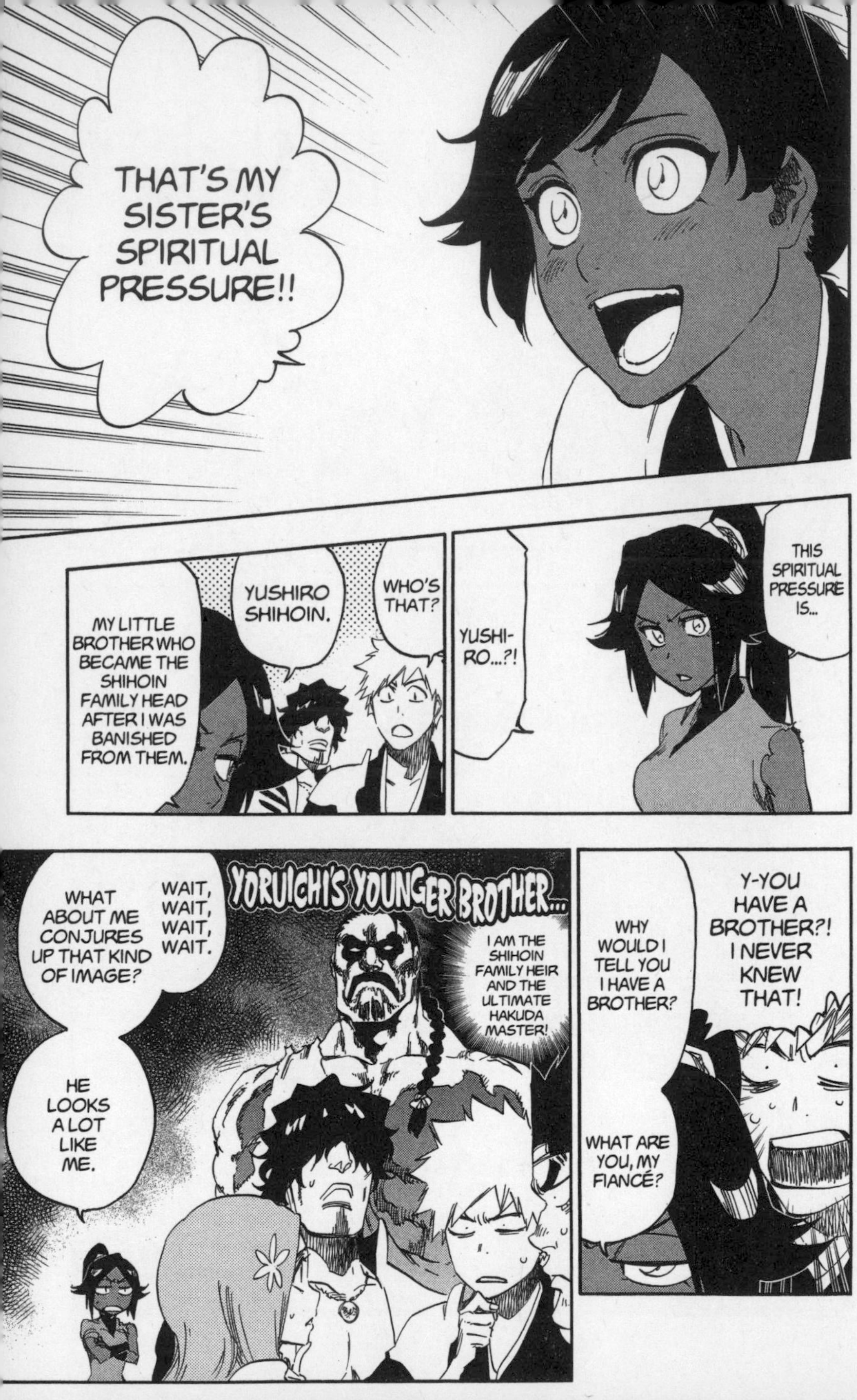
THAT'S MY SISTER'S SPIRITUAL PRESSURE!!
THIS SPIRITUAL PRESSURE IS...
YUSHI-RO...?!
WHO'S THAT?
YUSHIRO SHIHOIN.
MY LITTLE BROTHER WHO BECAME THE SHIHOIN FAMILY HEAD AFTER I WAS BANISHED FROM THEM.
Y-YOU HAVE A BROTHER?! I NEVER KNEW THAT!
WHY WOULD I TELL YOU I HAVE A BROTHER?
WHAT ARE YOU, MY FIANCÉ?
YORUICHI'S YOUNGER BROTHER...
I AM THE SHIHOIN FAMILY HEIR AND THE ULTIMATE HAKUDA MASTER!
WAIT, WAIT, WAIT, WAIT.
WHAT ABOUT ME CONJURES UP THAT KIND OF IMAGE?
HE LOOKS A LOT LIKE ME.

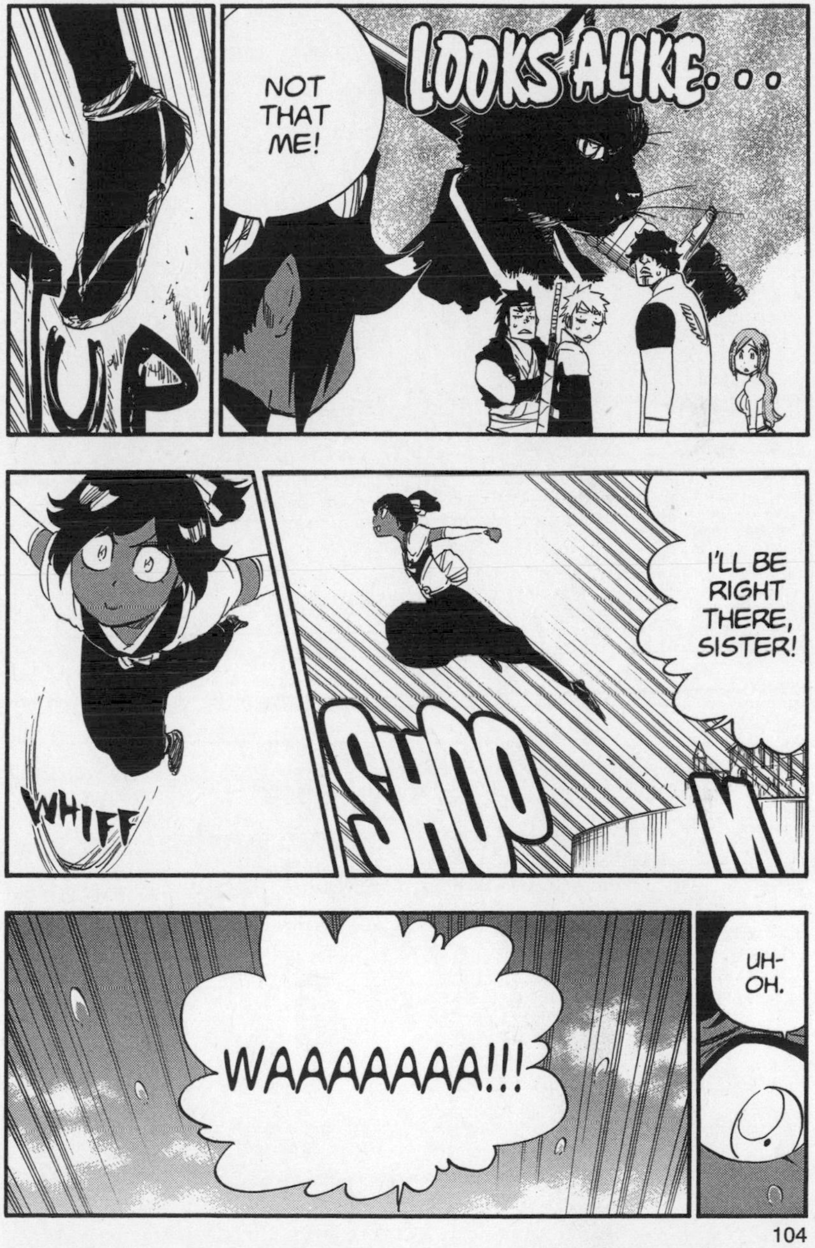
LOOKS ALIKE...
NOT THAT ME!
TUP
I'LL BE RIGHT THERE, SISTER!
SHOOM
WHIFF
UH-OH.
WAAAAAAA!!!

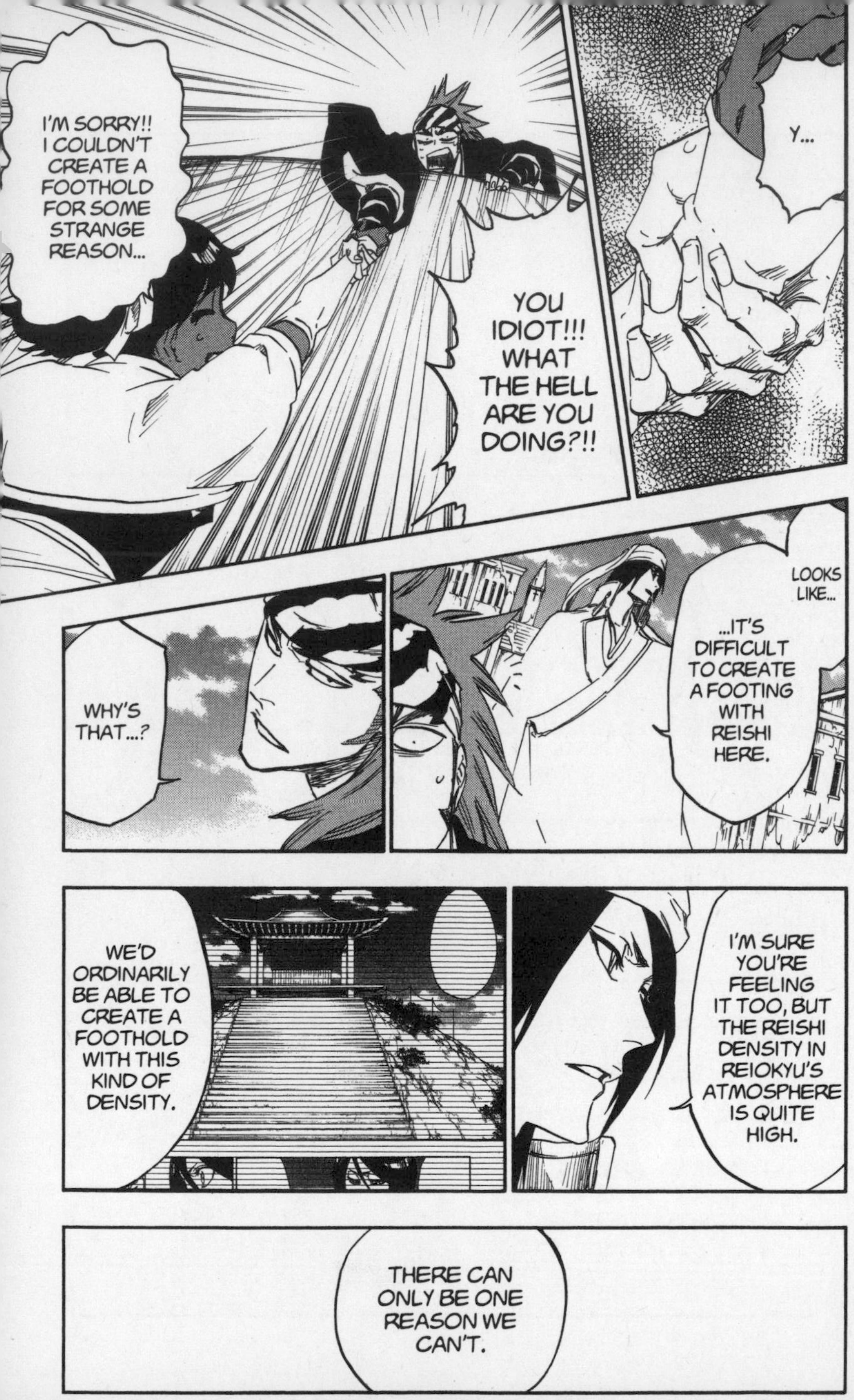
Y...
YOU IDIOT!!! WHAT THE HELL ARE YOU DOING?!!
I'M SORRY!! I COULDN'T CREATE A FOOTHOLD FOR SOME STRANGE REASON...
LOOKS LIKE...
...IT'S DIFFICULT TO CREATE A FOOTING WITH REISHI HERE.
WHY'S THAT...?
I'M SURE YOU'RE FEELING IT TOO, BUT THE REISHI DENSITY IN REIOKYU'S ATMOSPHERE IS QUITE HIGH.
WE'D ORDINARILY BE ABLE TO CREATE A FOOTHOLD WITH THIS KIND OF DENSITY.
THERE CAN ONLY BE ONE REASON WE CAN'T.

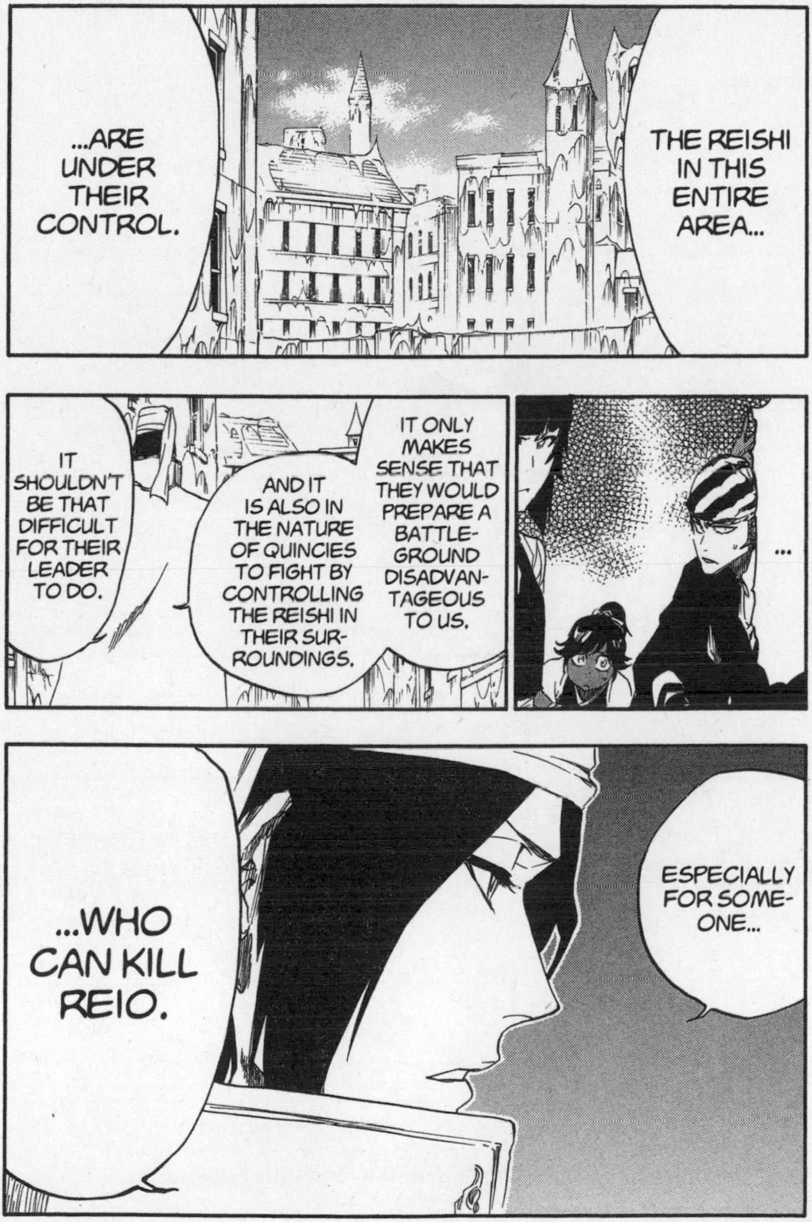
THE REISHI IN THIS ENTIRE AREA...
...ARE UNDER THEIR CONTROL.
...
IT ONLY MAKES SENSE THAT THEY WOULD PREPARE A BATTLE-GROUND DISADVAN-TAGEOUS TO US.
AND IT IS ALSO IN THE NATURE OF QUINCIES TO FIGHT BY CONTROLLING THE REISHI IN THEIR SUR-ROUNDINGS.
IT SHOULDN'T BE THAT DIFFICULT FOR THEIR LEADER TO DO.
ESPECIALLY FOR SOME-ONE...
...WHO CAN KILL REIO.

READ THIS WAY

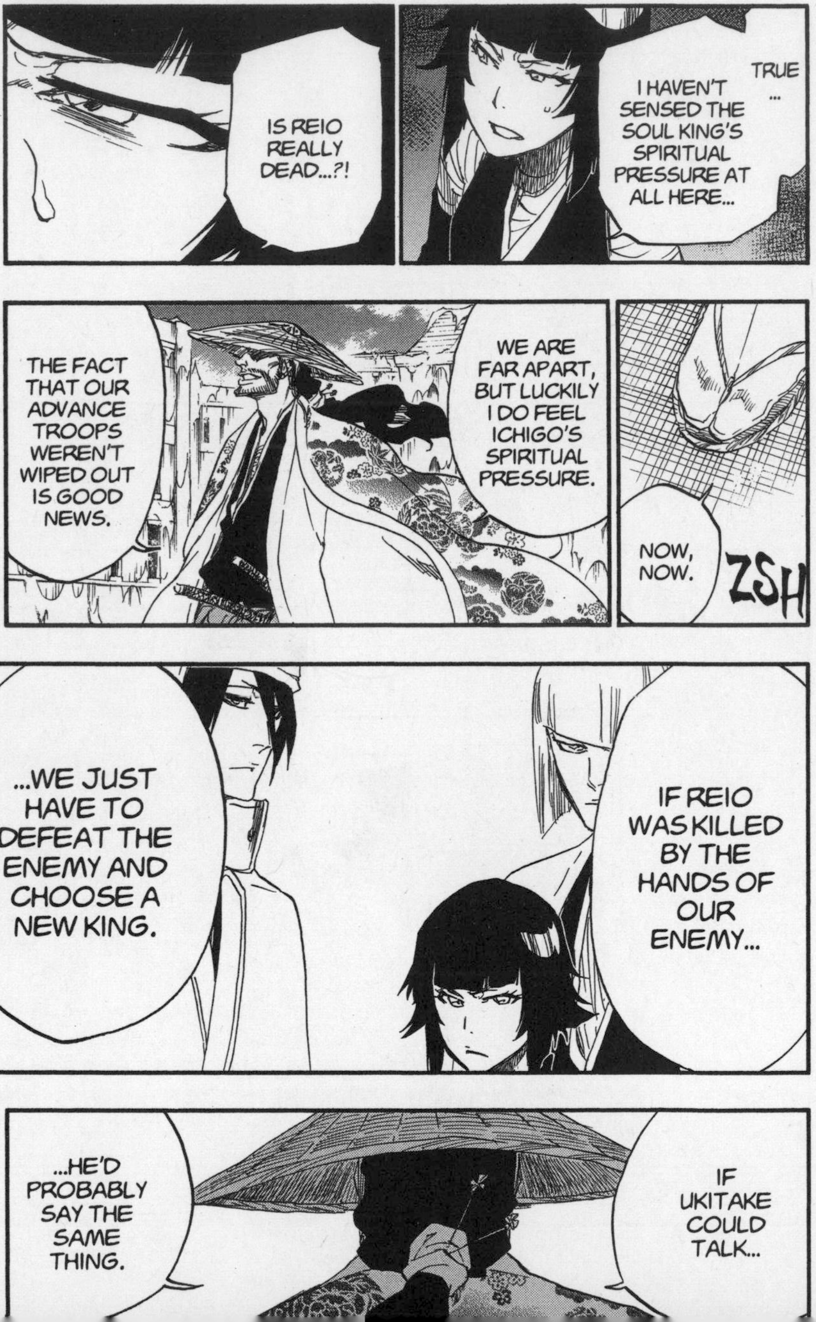

TRUE...
I HAVEN'T SENSED THE SOUL KING'S SPIRITUAL PRESSURE AT ALL HERE...
IS REIO REALLY DEAD...?!
NOW, NOW.
ZSH
WE ARE FAR APART, BUT LUCKILY I DO FEEL ICHIGO'S SPIRITUAL PRESSURE.
THE FACT THAT OUR ADVANCE TROOPS WEREN'T WIPED OUT IS GOOD NEWS.
IF REIO WAS KILLED BY THE HANDS OF OUR ENEMY...
...WE JUST HAVE TO DEFEAT THE ENEMY AND CHOOSE A NEW KING.
IF UKITAKE COULD TALK...
...HE'D PROBABLY SAY THE SAME THING.

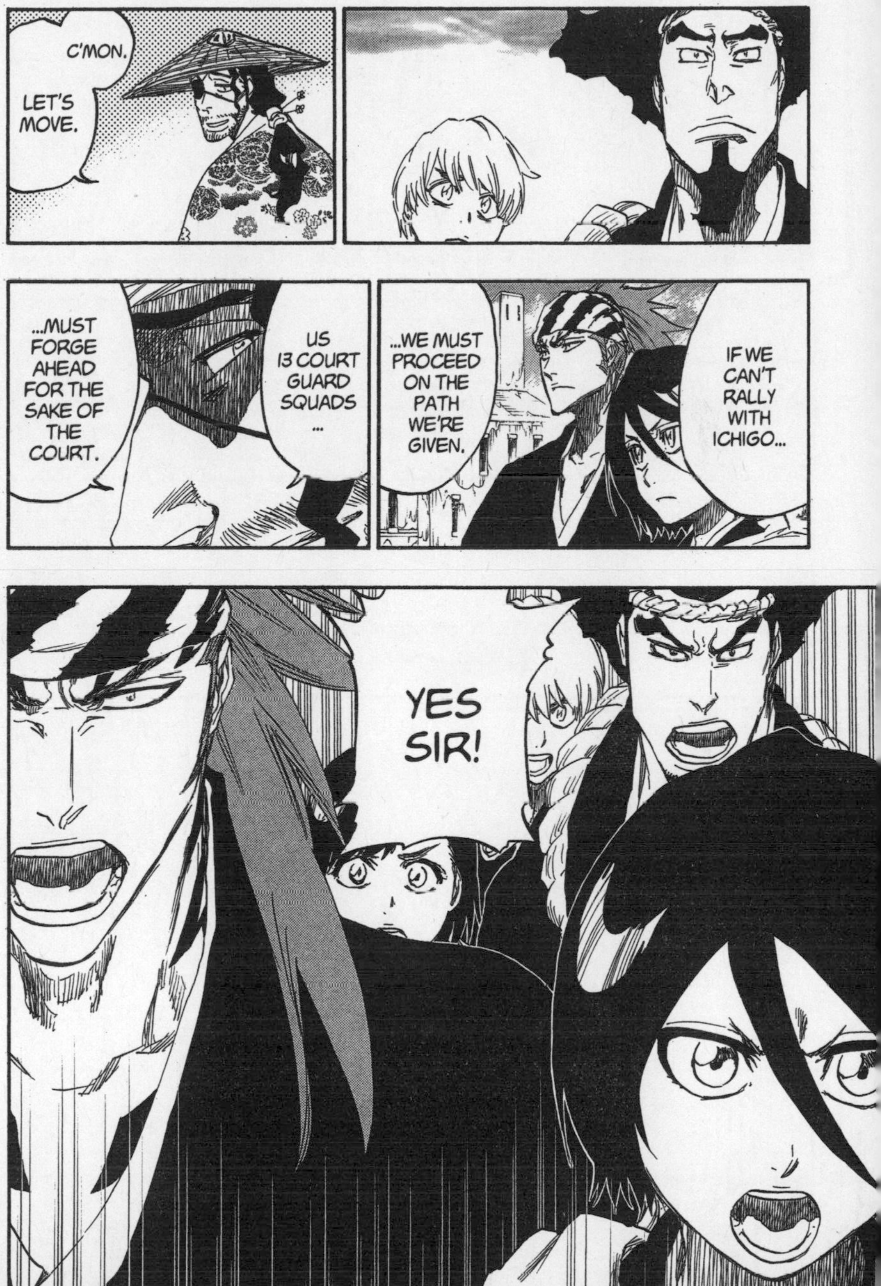
C'MON.
LET'S MOVE.
IF WE CAN'T RALLY WITH ICHIGO...
...WE MUST PROCEED ON THE PATH WE'RE GIVEN.
US 13 COURT GUARD SQUADS ...
...MUST FORGE AHEAD FOR THE SAKE OF THE COURT.
YES SIR!

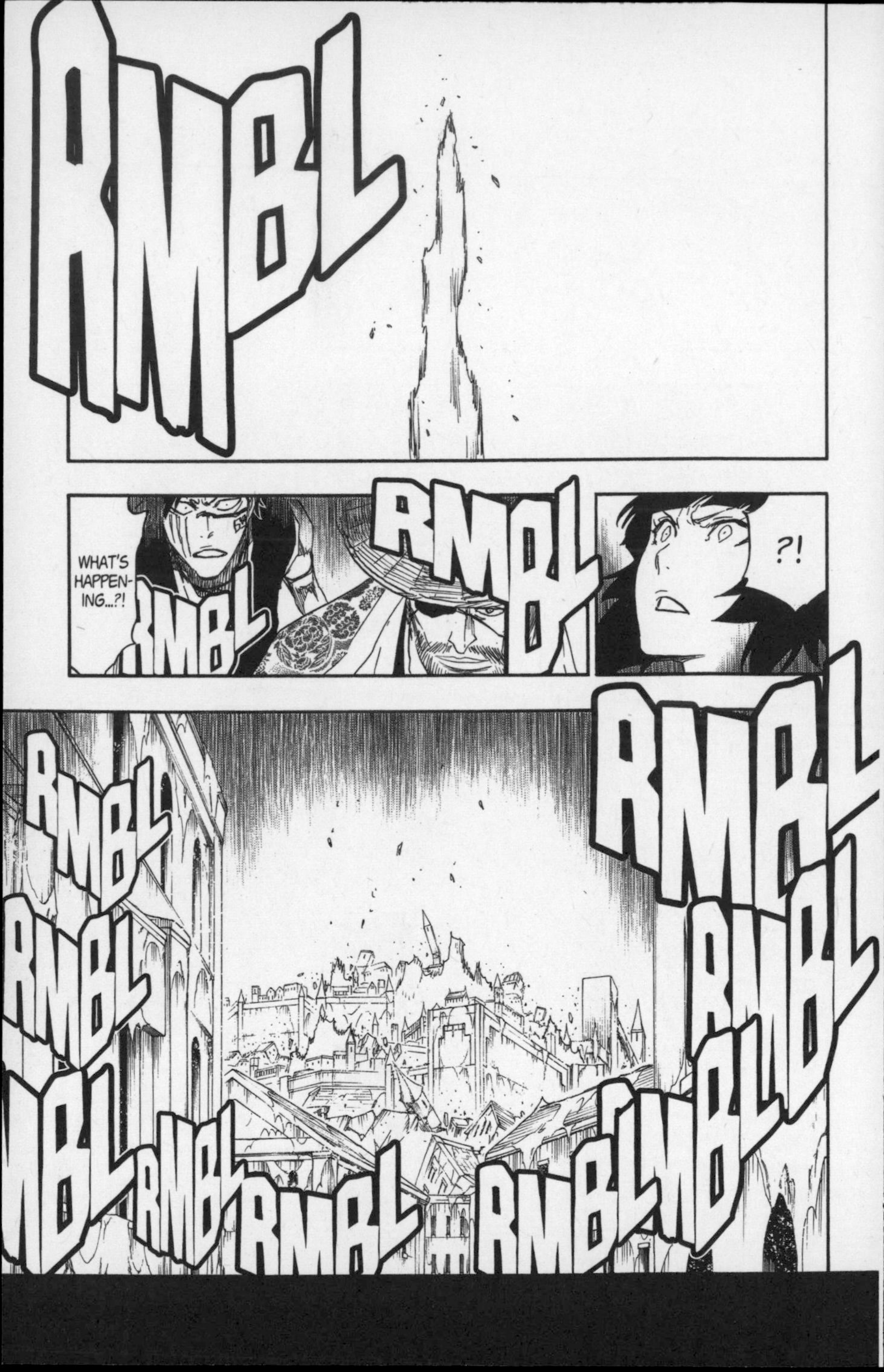
RMBL
?!
RMBL
WHAT'S HAPPEN-ING...?!
RMBL
RMBL
RMBL
RMBL
RMBL
RMBL
RMBL
RMBL
RMBL
RMBL

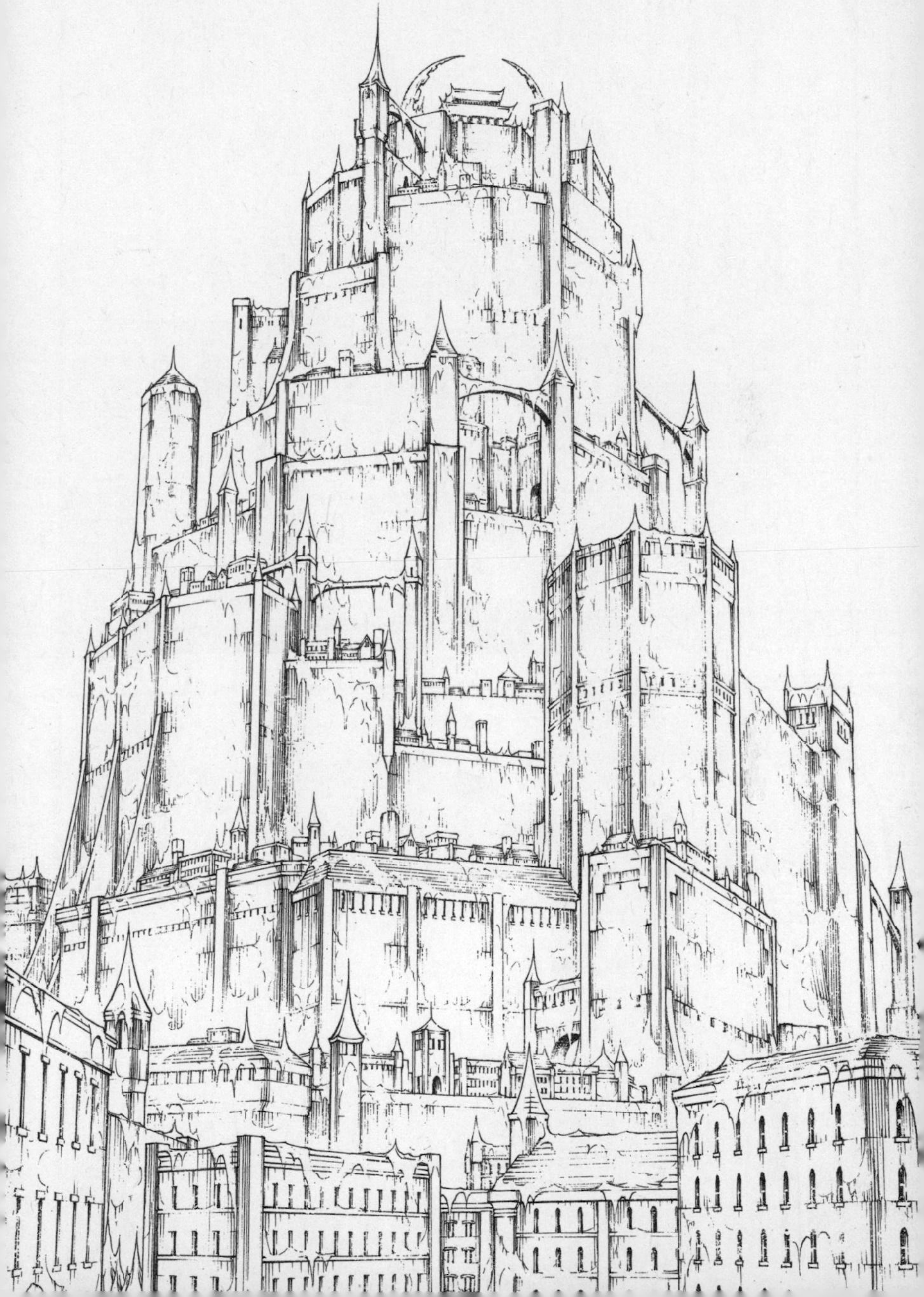

READ THIS WAY

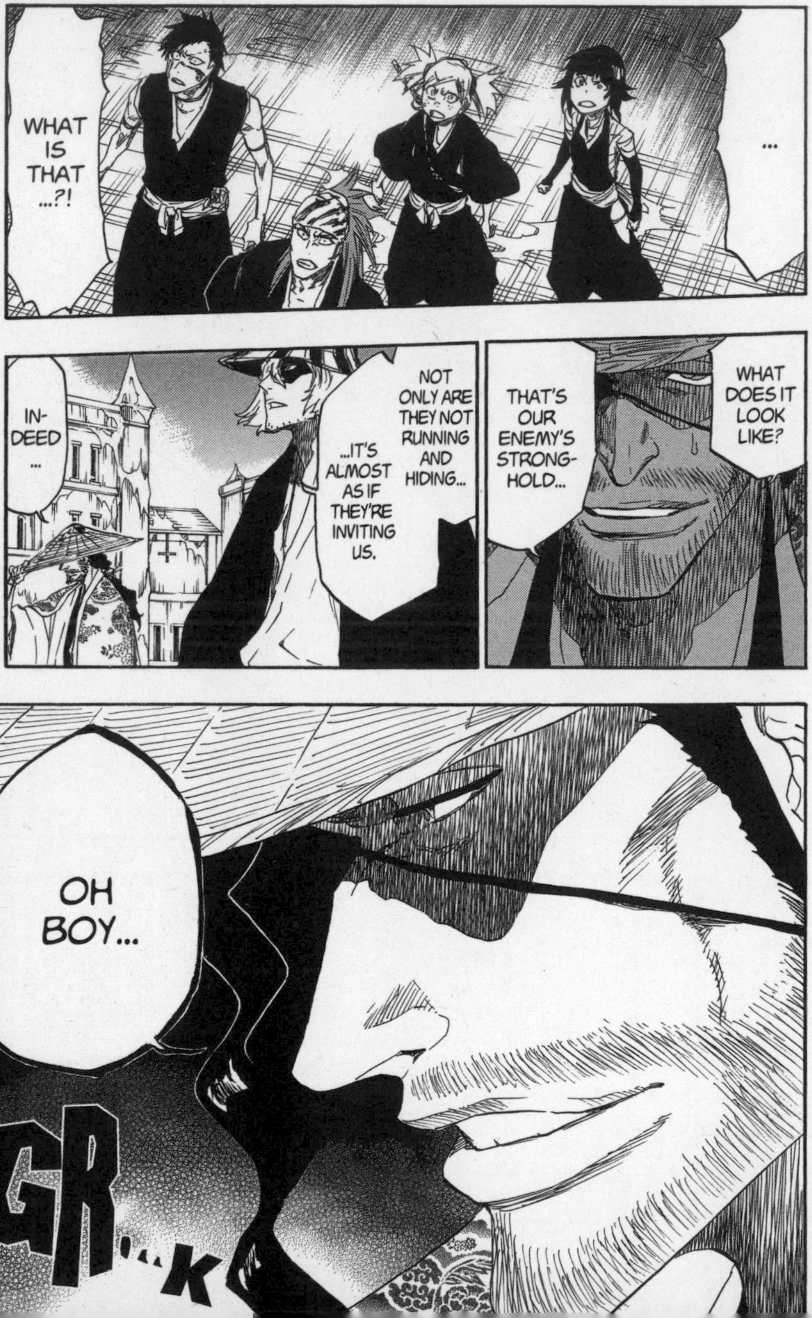
...
WHAT IS THAT ...?!
WHAT DOES IT LOOK LIKE?
THAT'S OUR ENEMY'S STRONGHOLD...
NOT ONLY ARE THEY NOT RUNNING AND HIDING...
...IT'S ALMOST AS IF THEY'RE INVITING US.
INDEED...
OH BOY...
GR...K

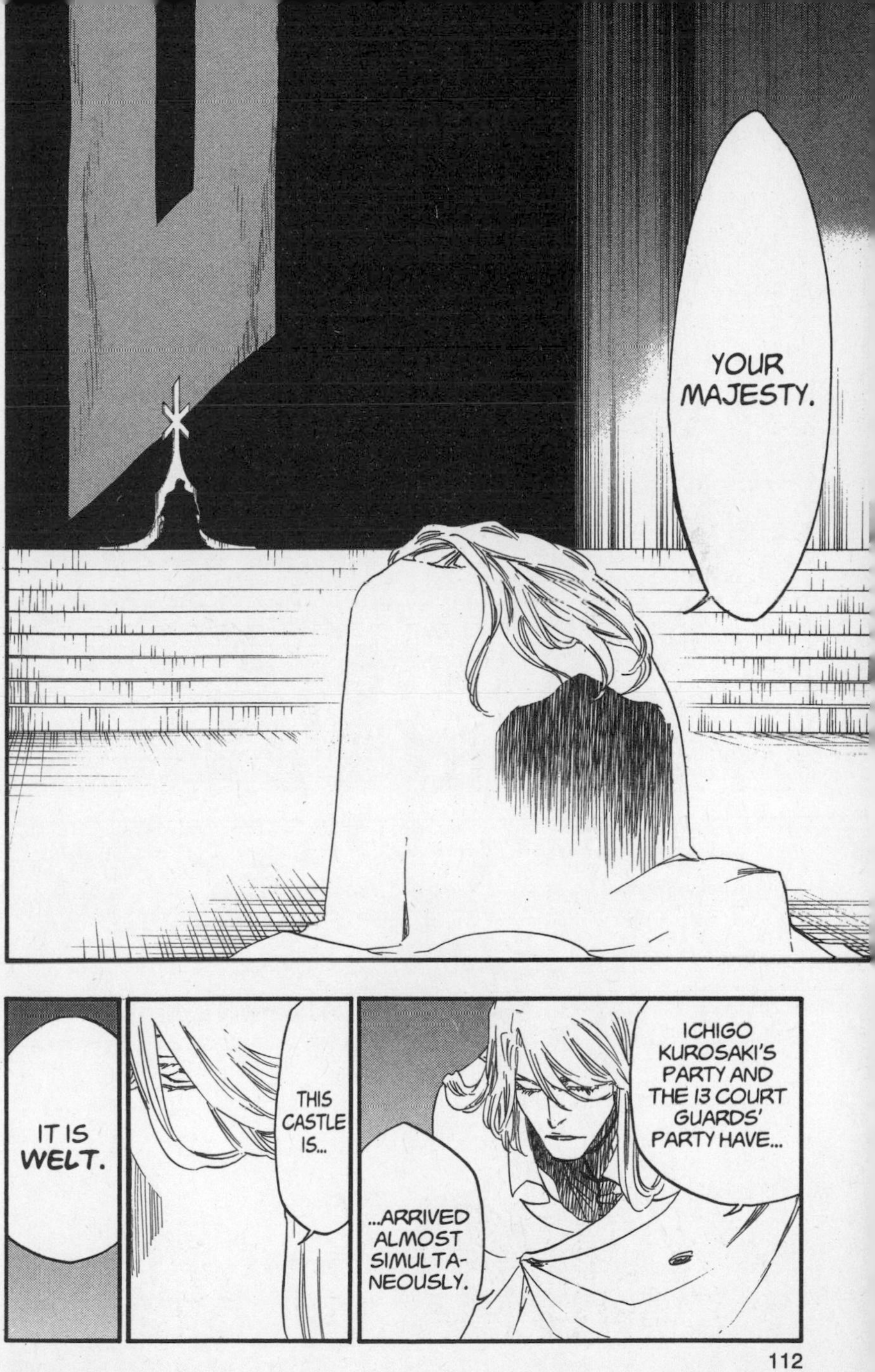
YOUR MAJESTY.
ICHIGO KUROSAKI'S PARTY AND THE 13 COURT GUARDS' PARTY HAVE...
...ARRIVED ALMOST SIMULTANEOUSLY.
THIS CASTLE IS...
IT IS WELT.

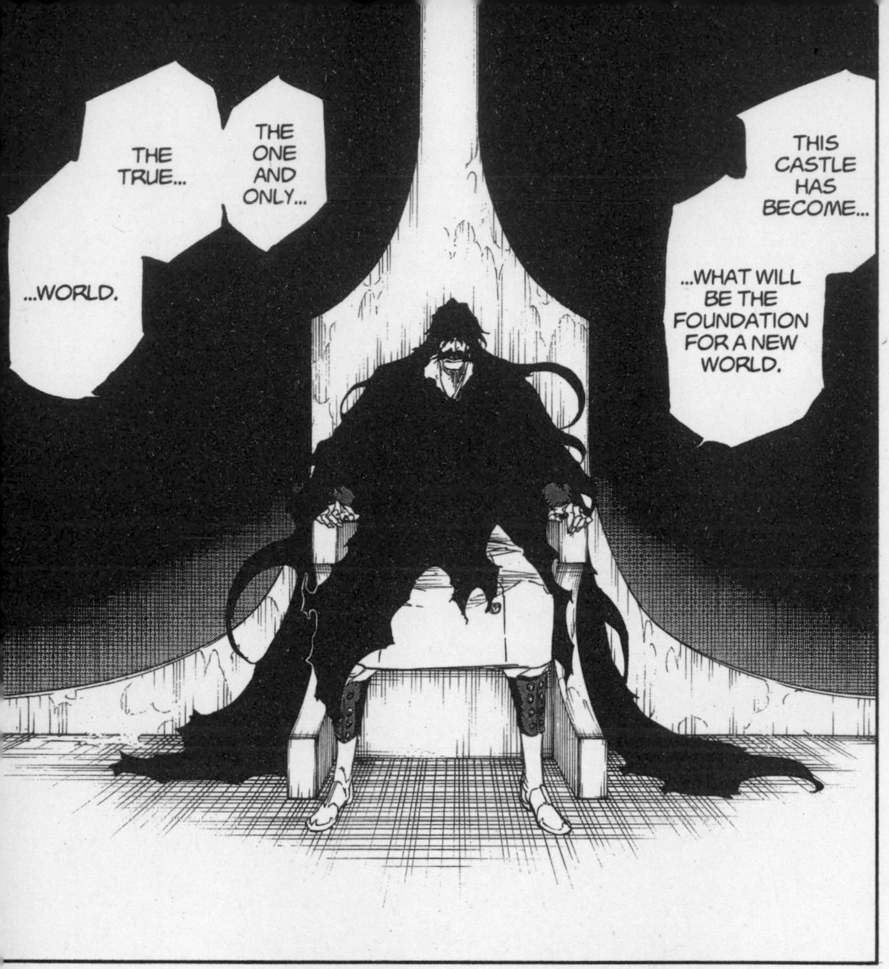
THIS CASTLE HAS BECOME...
...WHAT WILL BE THE FOUNDATION FOR A NEW WORLD.
THE ONE AND ONLY...
THE TRUE...
...WORLD.
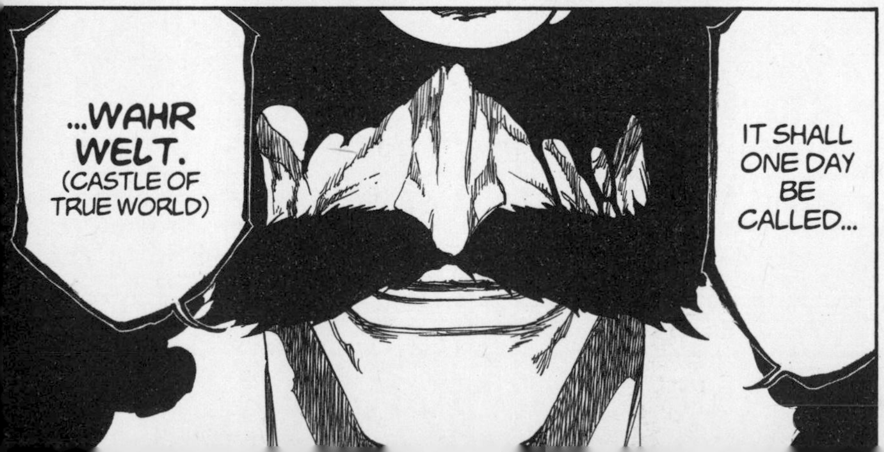
IT SHALL ONE DAY BE CALLED...
...WAHR WELT. (CASTLE OF TRUE WORLD)

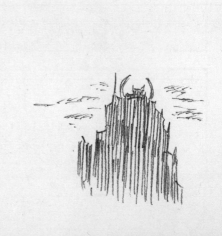

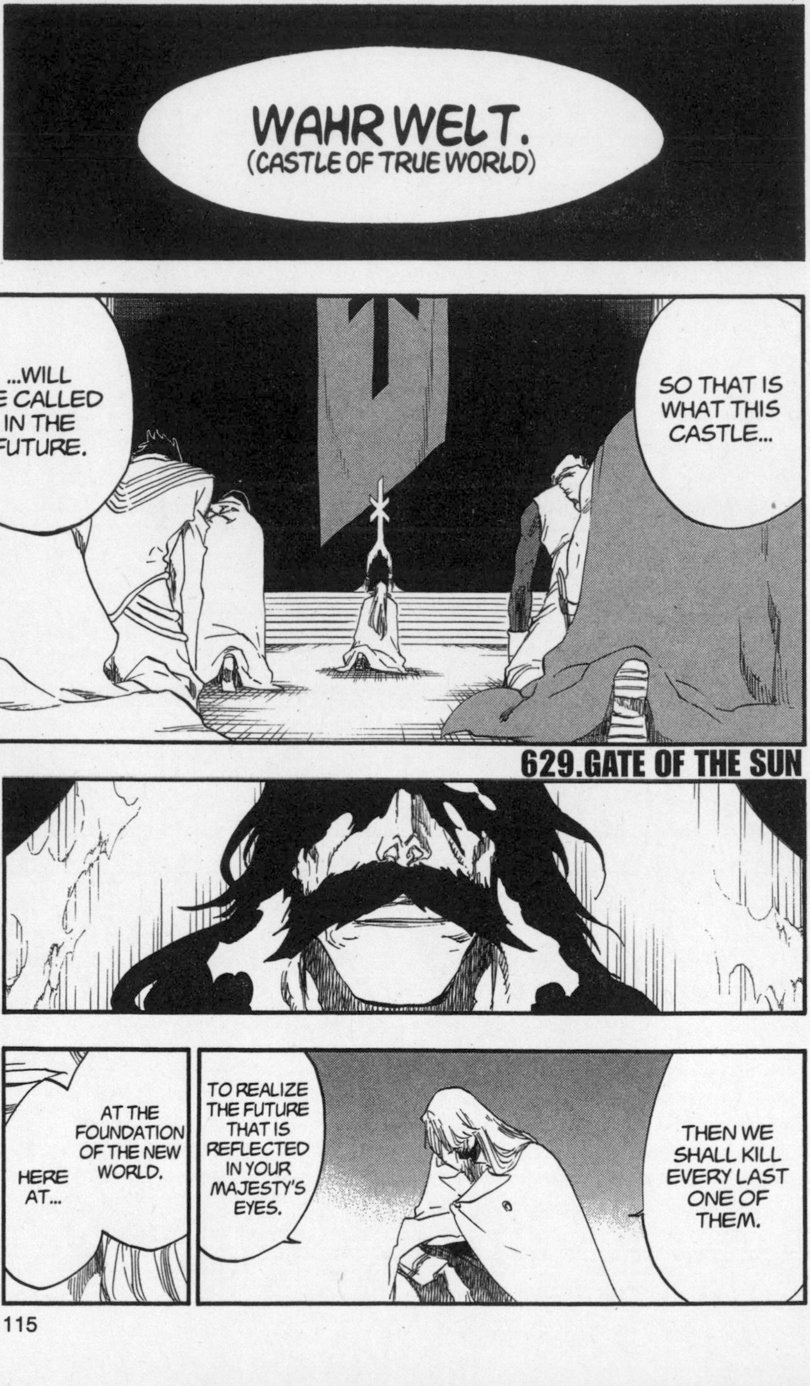
WAHR WELT.
(CASTLE OF TRUE WORLD)
SO THAT IS WHAT THIS CASTLE...
...WILL BE CALLED IN THE FUTURE.
629.GATE OF THE SUN
THEN WE SHALL KILL EVERY LAST ONE OF THEM.
TO REALIZE THE FUTURE THAT IS REFLECTED IN YOUR MAJESTY'S EYES.
HERE AT...
AT THE FOUNDATION OF THE NEW WORLD.

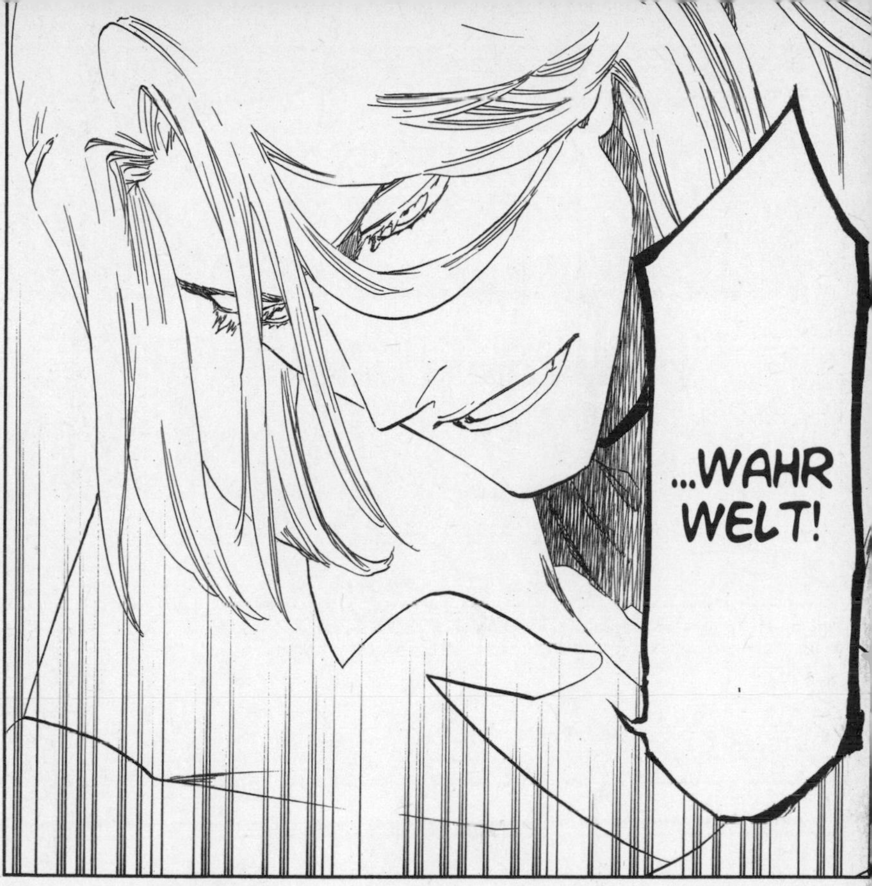
...WAHR
WELT!

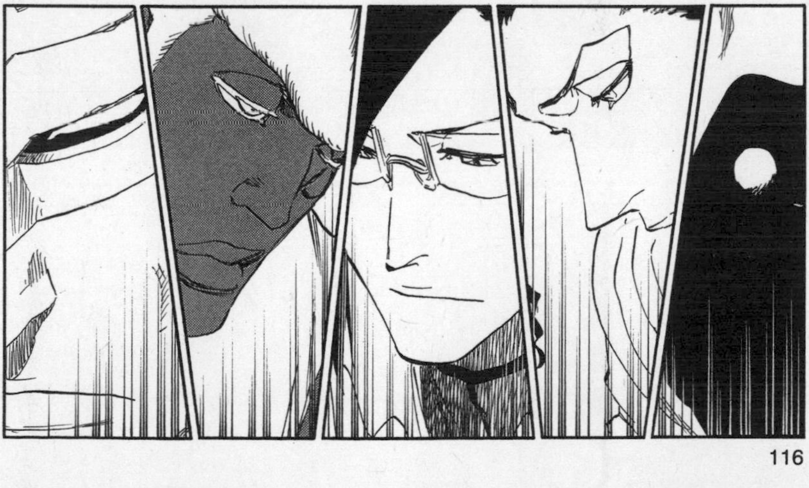

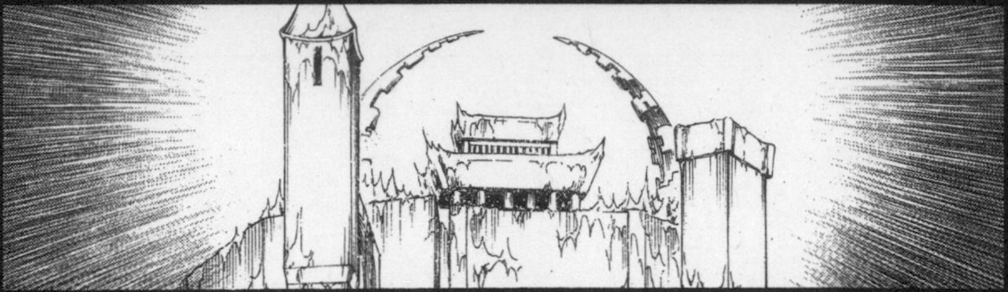

BLEACH 629.

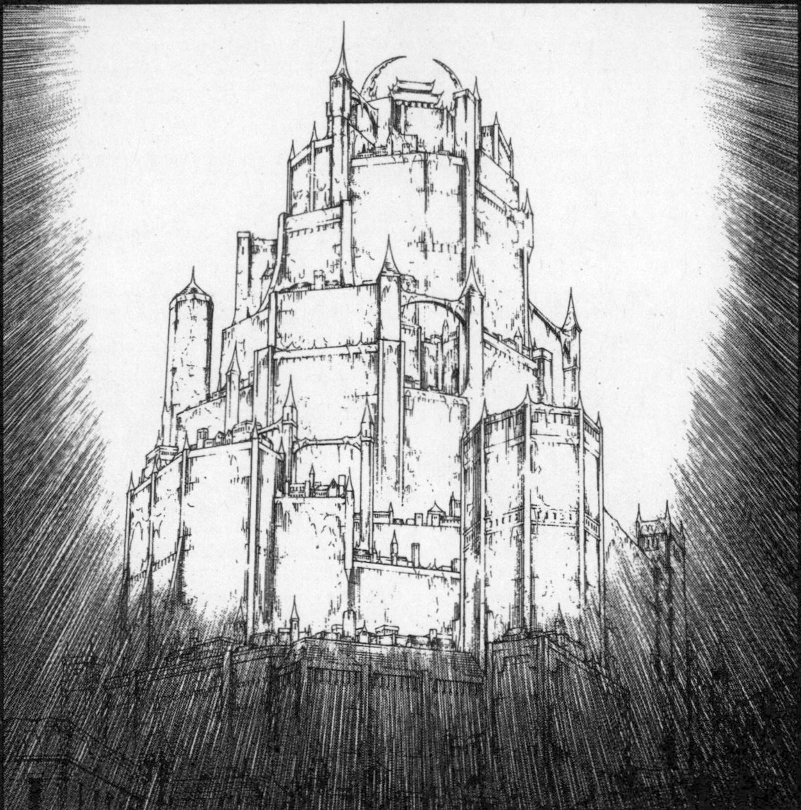

Gate of the Sun

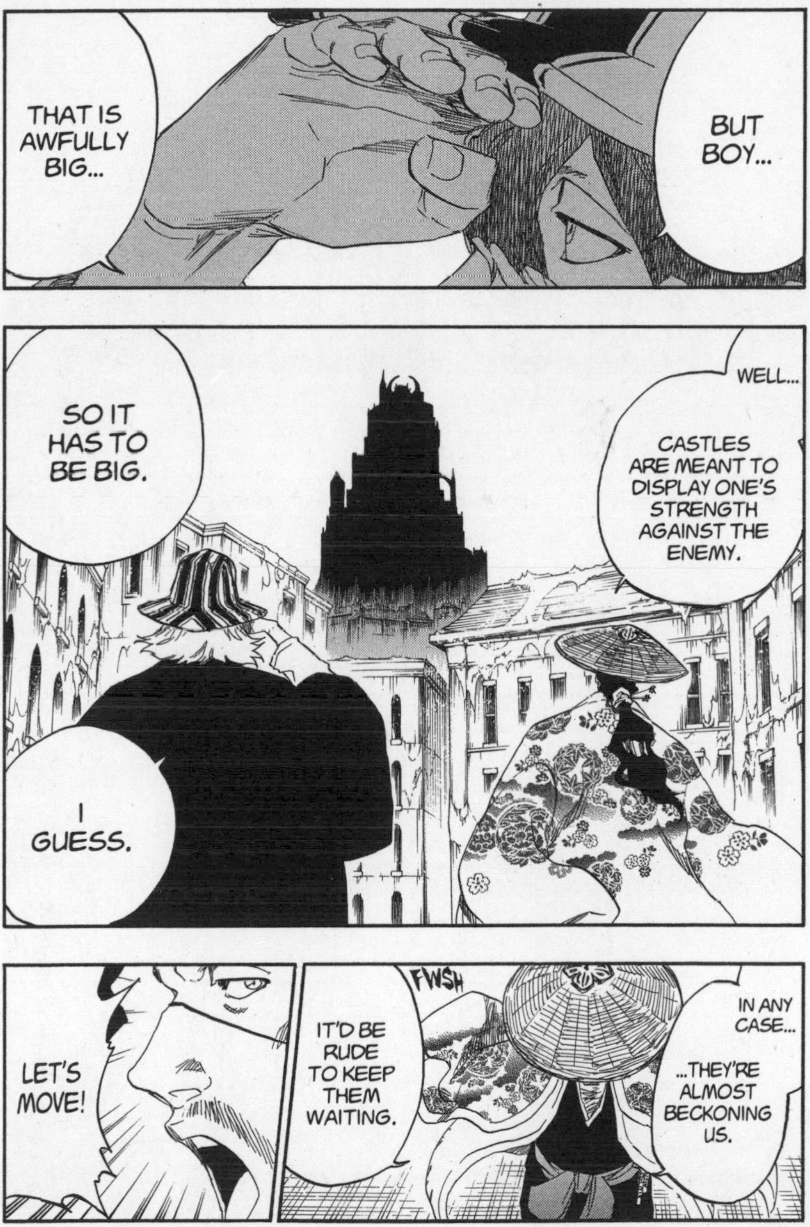
BUT BOY...
THAT IS AWFULLY BIG...
WELL...
CASTLES ARE MEANT TO DISPLAY ONE'S STRENGTH AGAINST THE ENEMY.
SO IT HAS TO BE BIG.
I GUESS.
IN ANY CASE...
...THEY'RE ALMOST BECKONING US.
FWSH
IT'D BE RUDE TO KEEP THEM WAITING.
LET'S MOVE!

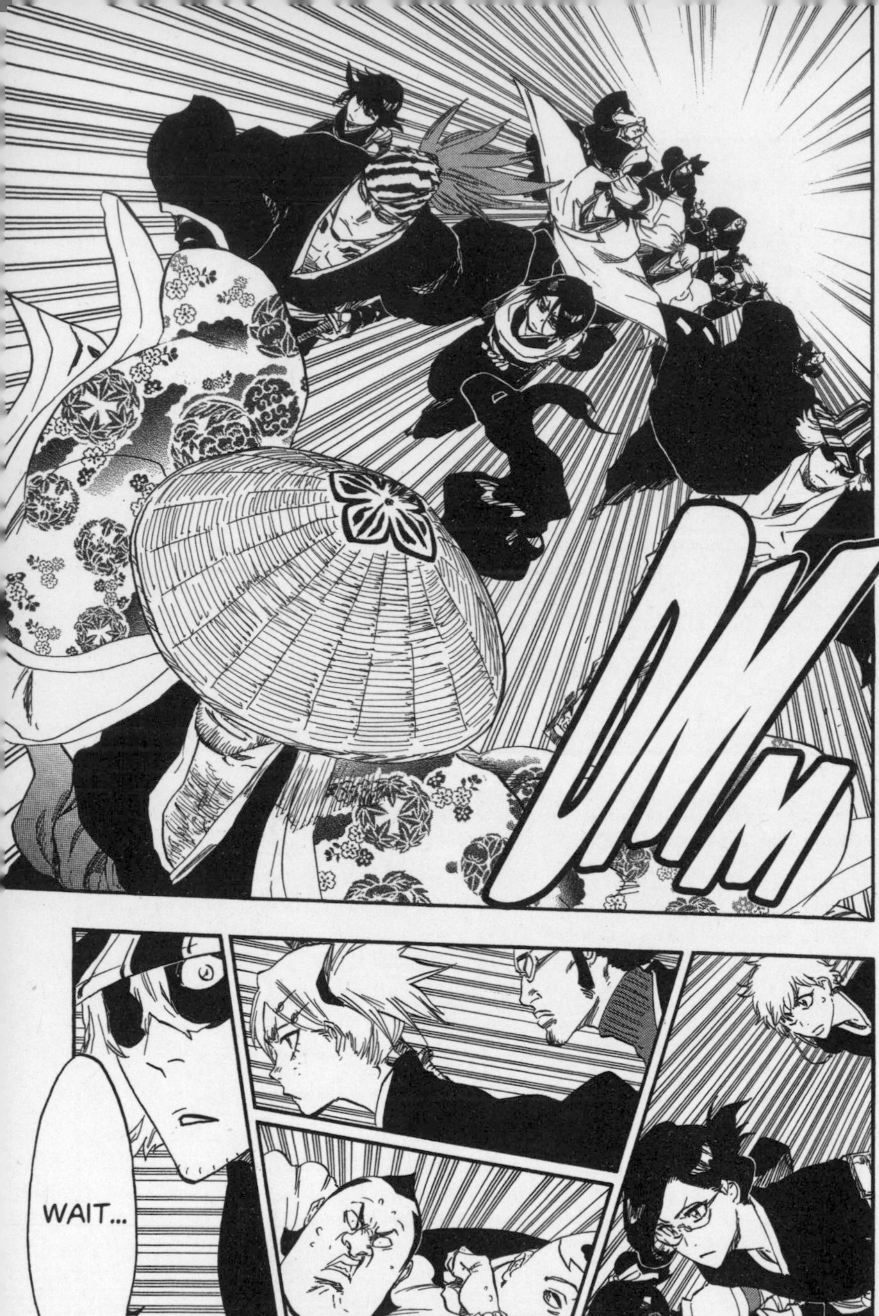
DMM
WAIT...

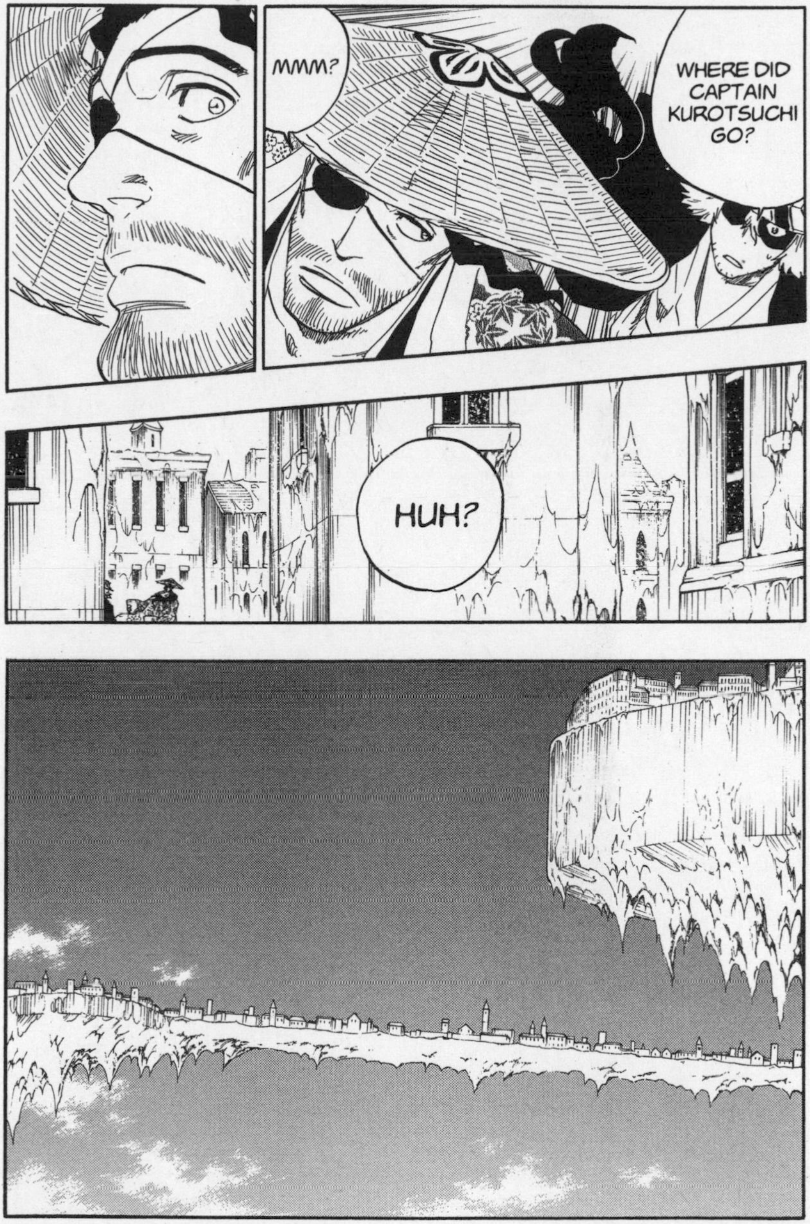
WHERE DID CAPTAIN KUROTSUCHI GO?
MMM?
HUH?

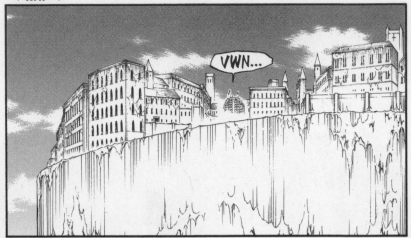

READ THIS WAY

VWN...
HEH HEH HEH...
ZHOOP
CLOSING THE GATE, THEN REOPENING IT AFTER TILTING THE AXIS...
...MAKES IT SO EASY TO GO OFF BY YOURSELF EVEN WITHIN REIOKYU.
TMP
THEY MUST BE FLUSTERED, REALIZING I'M MISSING RIGHT ABOUT NOW...
AT ANY RATE, I WON'T BE BOTHERED BY THOSE PHILISTINES. NOW I'LL BE FREE TO...

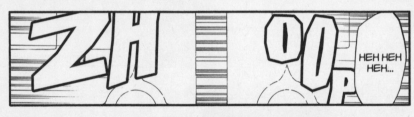

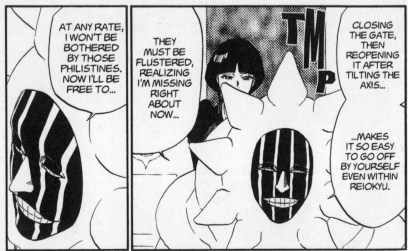

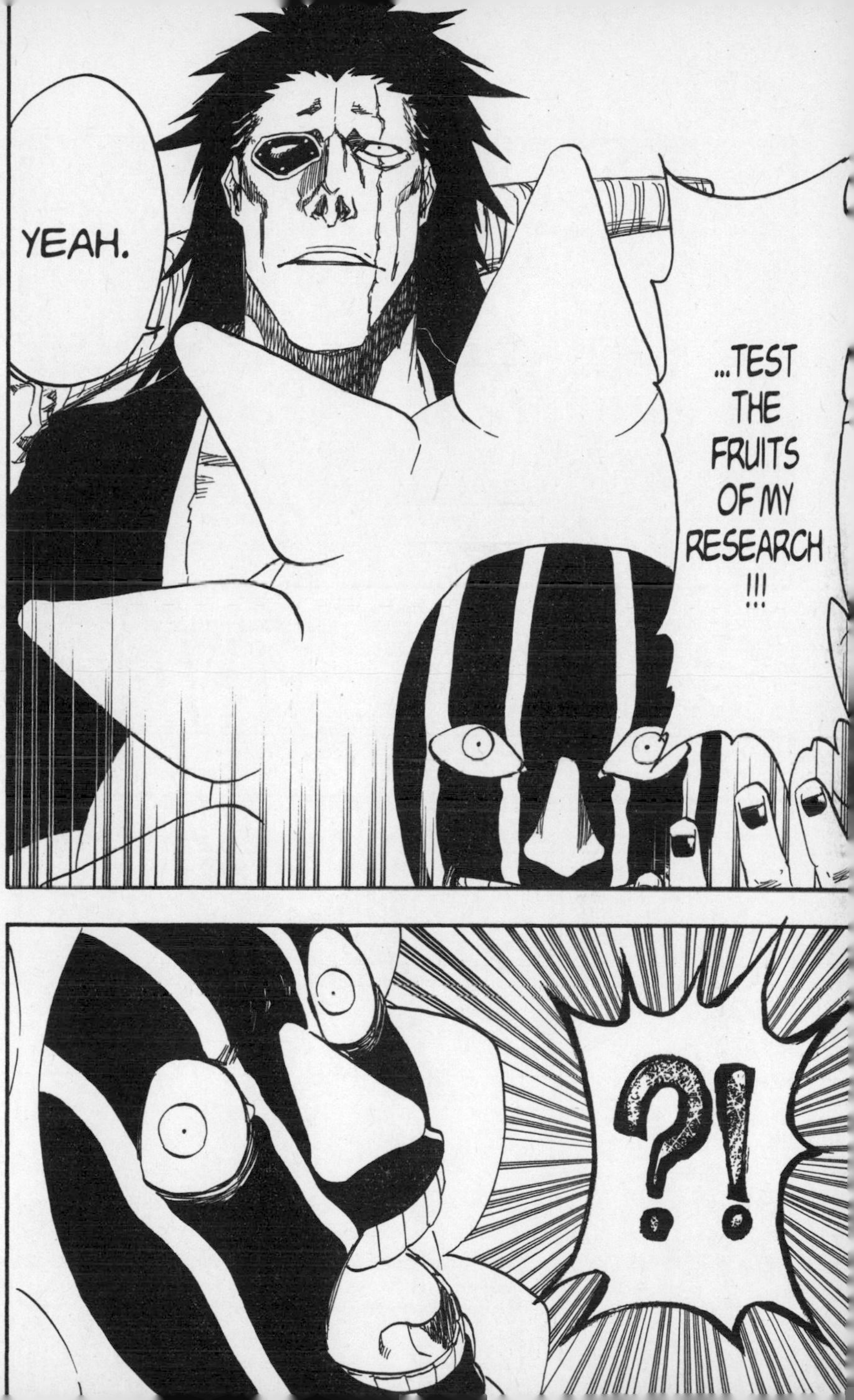
...TEST THE FRUITS OF MY RESEARCH !!!
YEAH.
?!

READ THIS WAY

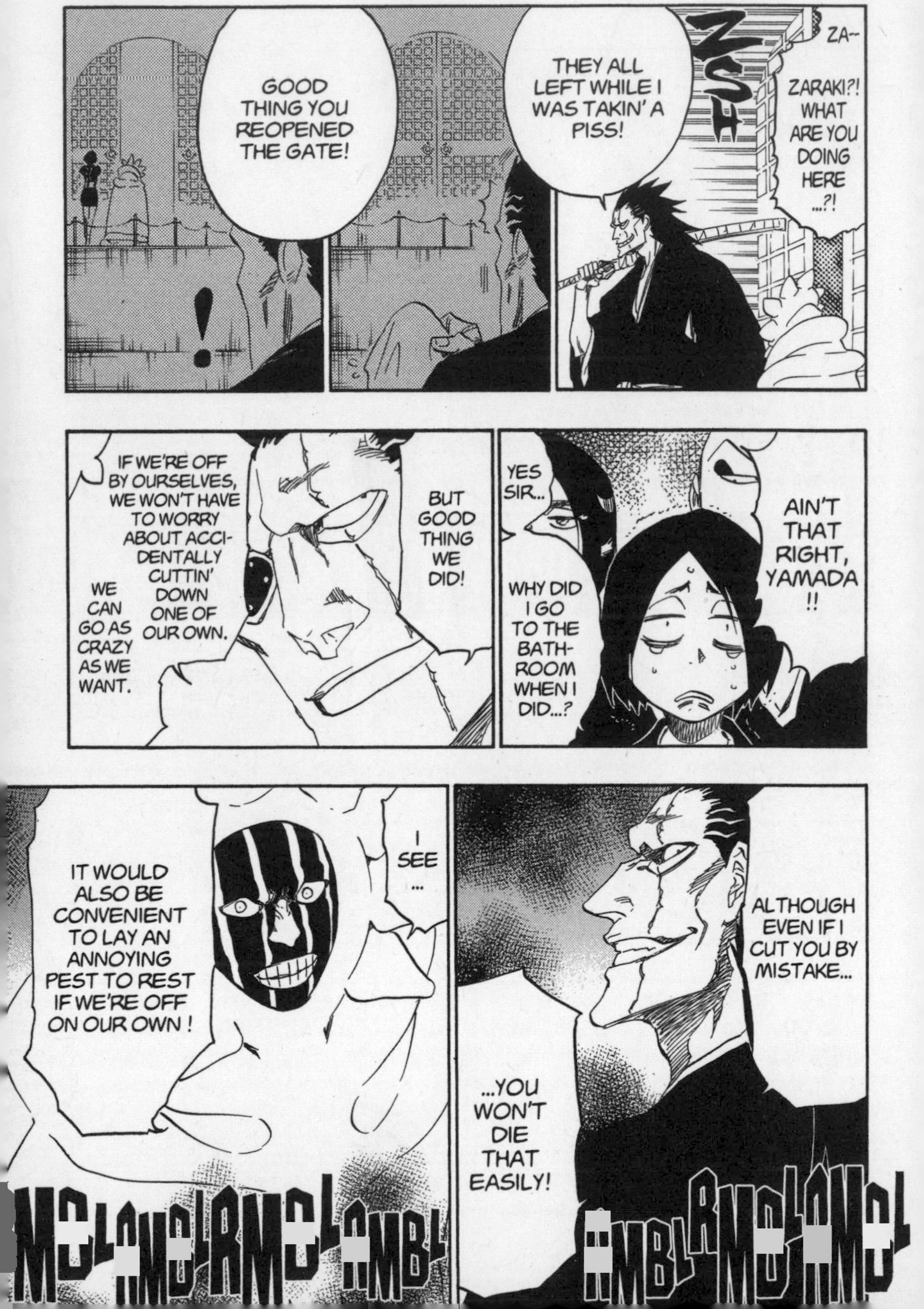
ZA--
ZARAKI?! WHAT ARE YOU DOING HERE ...?!
ZSH
THEY ALL LEFT WHILE I WAS TAKIN' A PISS!
GOOD THING YOU REOPENED THE GATE!
!
AIN'T THAT RIGHT, YAMADA!!
YES SIR...
WHY DID I GO TO THE BATHROOM WHEN I DID...?
BUT GOOD THING WE DID!
IF WE'RE OFF BY OURSELVES, WE WON'T HAVE TO WORRY ABOUT ACCIDENTALLY CUTTIN' DOWN ONE OF OUR OWN.
WE CAN GO AS CRAZY AS WE WANT.
ALTHOUGH EVEN IF I CUT YOU BY MISTAKE...
...YOU WON'T DIE THAT EASILY!
I SEE ...
IT WOULD ALSO BE CONVENIENT TO LAY AN ANNOYING PEST TO REST IF WE'RE OFF ON OUR OWN!

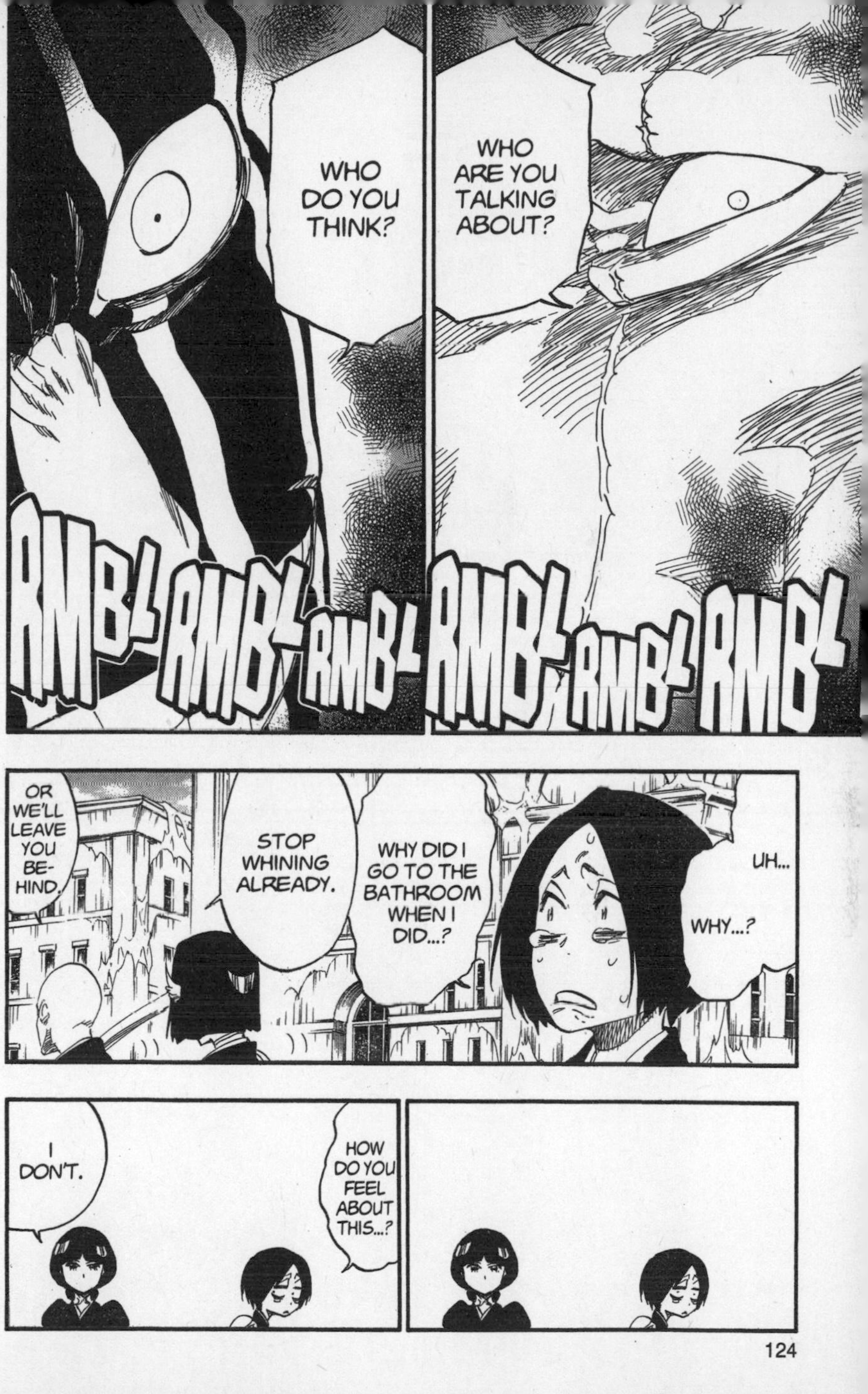
WHO ARE YOU TALKING ABOUT?
WHO DO YOU THINK?
RMBL RMBL RMBL RMBL RMBL RMBL
UH... WHY...?
WHY DID I GO TO THE BATHROOM WHEN I DID...?
STOP WHINING ALREADY.
OR WE'LL LEAVE YOU BE-HIND.
HOW DO YOU FEEL ABOUT THIS...?
I DON'T.

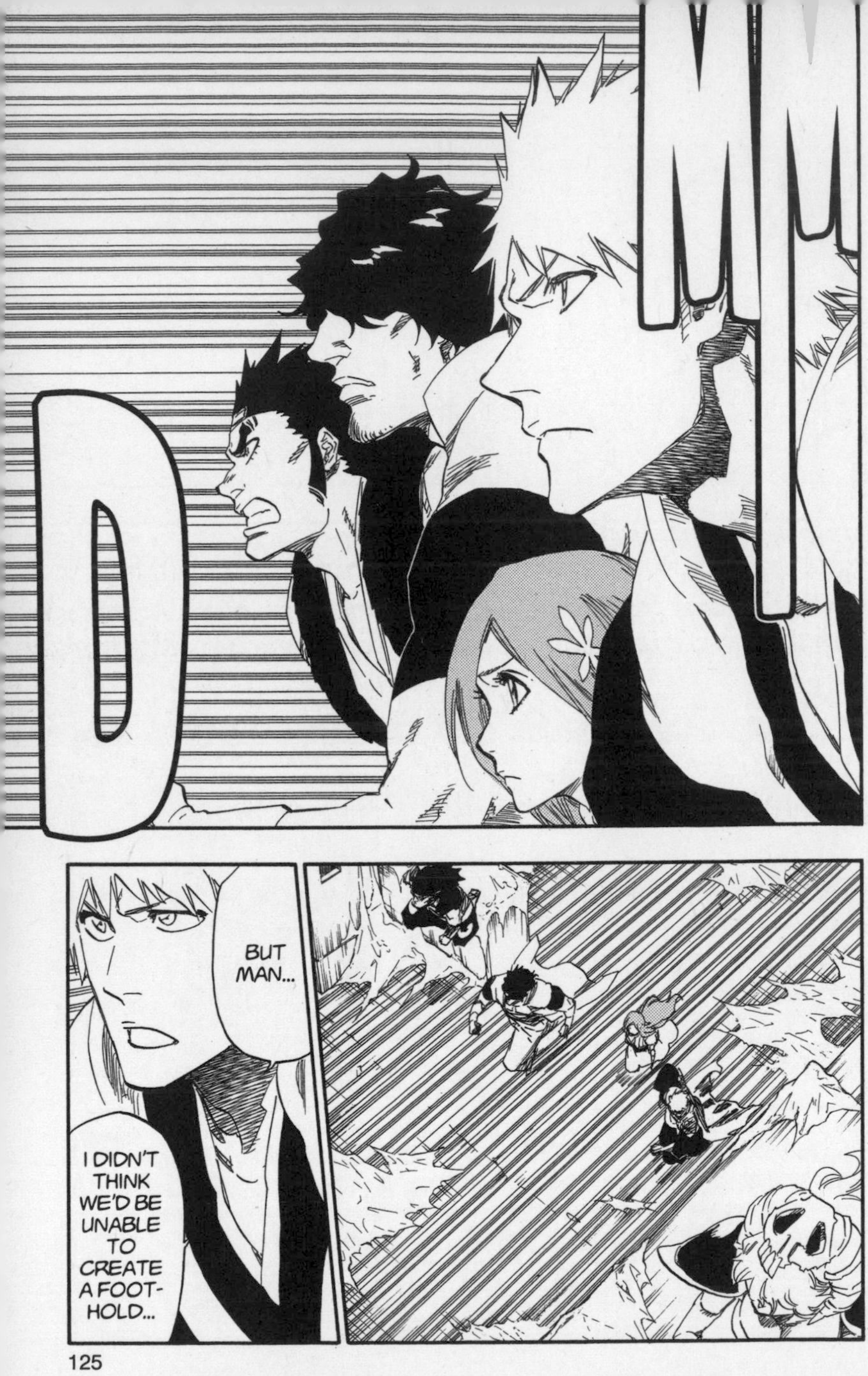
DMM
BUT MAN...
I DIDN'T THINK WE'D BE UNABLE TO CREATE A FOOT-HOLD...

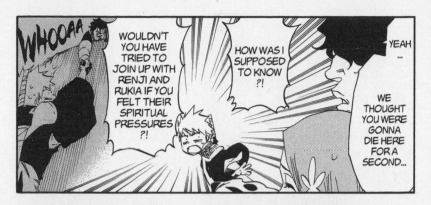

YEAH ...
WE THOUGHT YOU WERE GONNA DIE HERE FOR A SECOND...
WHOOAA
WOULDN'T YOU HAVE TRIED TO JOIN UP WITH RENJI AND RUKIA IF YOU FELT THEIR SPIRITUAL PRESSURES ?!
HOW WAS I SUPPOSED TO KNOW ?!
FROM THE SPIRITUAL PRESSURE I SENSED, SEEMS YUSHIRO DID THE SAME THING.
MEANS YOU TWO ARE ABOUT AS SMART AS EACH OTHER.
I CAN'T TELL IF THAT'S A COMPLIMENT OR NOT.
WHAT PART OF THAT MADE YOU THINK IT WAS A COMPLIMENT?
STOP THAT.
YEAH...
WOULDA BEEN NICE TO LINK UP WITH THEM.
IT'S BETTER NOT TO SPREAD OURSELVES THIN NOW THAT WE CAN'T FLANK THEM AND DON'T HAVE THE ELEMENT OF SURPRISE.
THAT'S EXACTLY RIGHT...

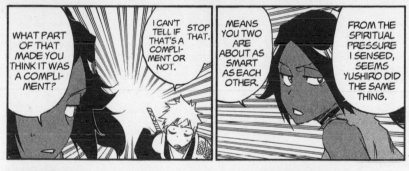

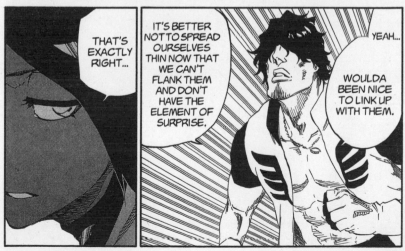

READ THIS WAY

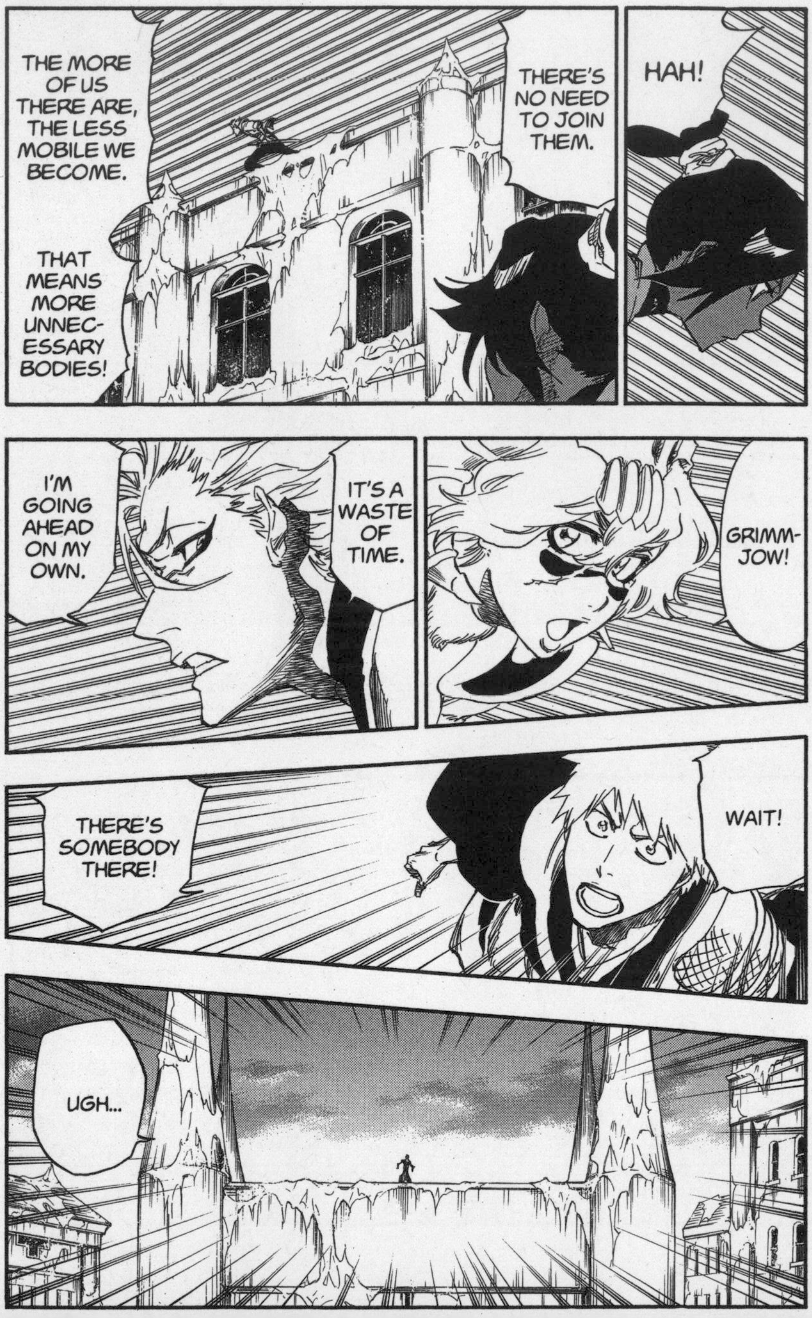
HAH!
THERE'S NO NEED TO JOIN THEM.
THE MORE OF US THERE ARE, THE LESS MOBILE WE BECOME.
THAT MEANS MORE UNNECESSARY BODIES!
GRIMMJOW!
IT'S A WASTE OF TIME.
I'M GOING AHEAD ON MY OWN.
WAIT!
THERE'S SOMEBODY THERE!
UGH...

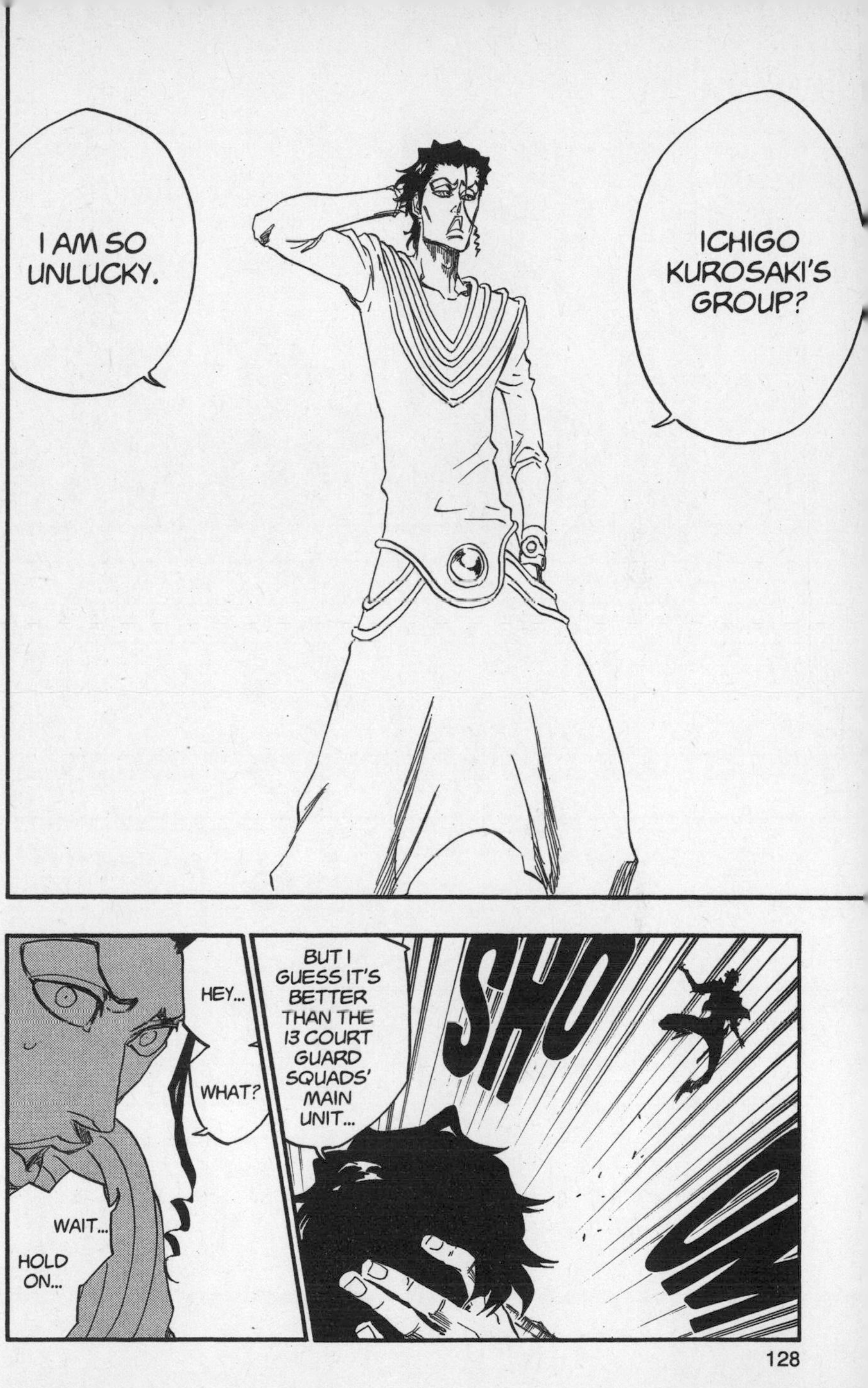
ICHIGO KUROSAKI'S GROUP?
I AM SO UNLUCKY.
BUT I GUESS IT'S BETTER THAN THE 13 COURT GUARD SQUADS' MAIN UNIT...
HEY...
WHAT?
WAIT...
HOLD ON...

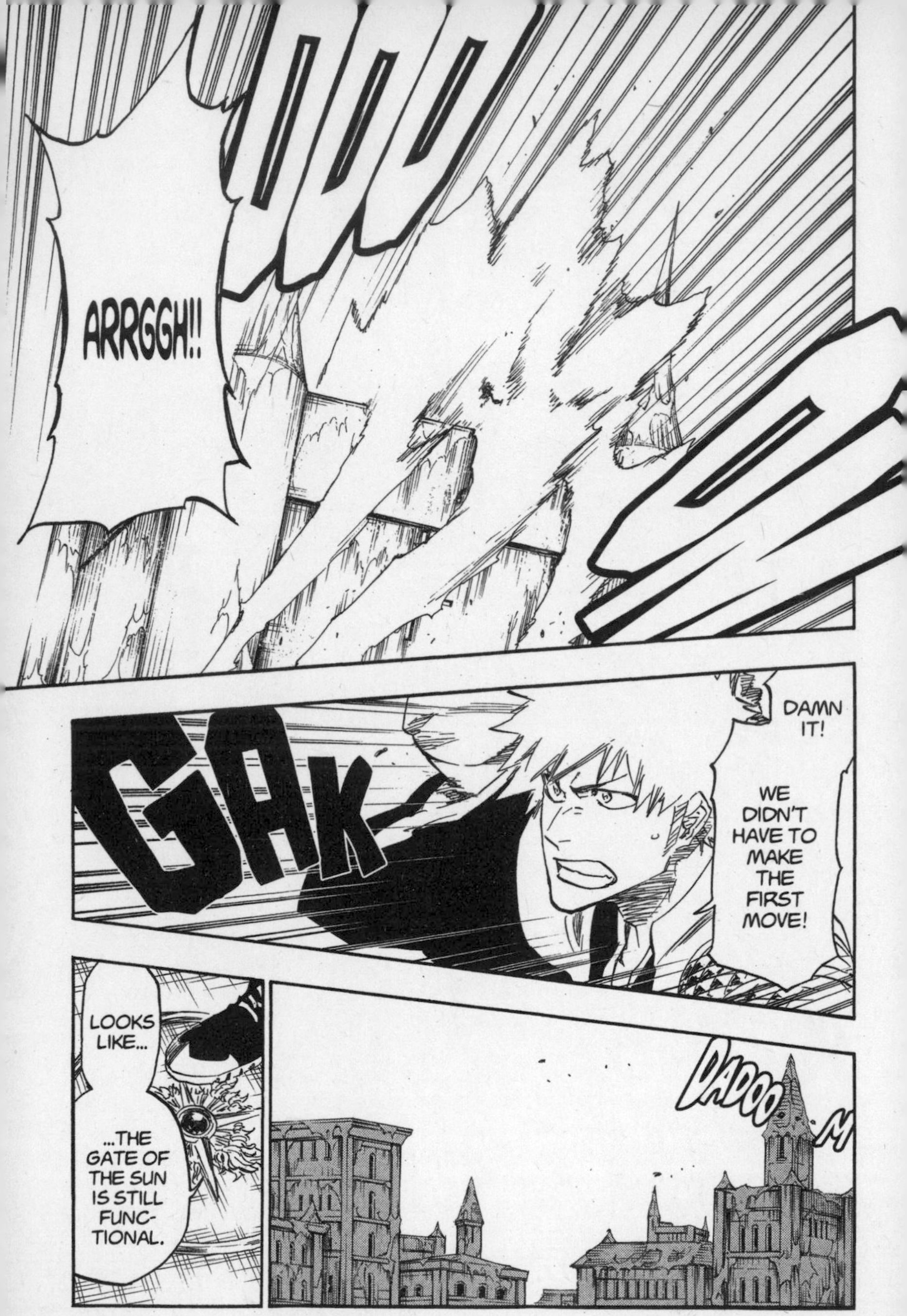
ARRGGH!!
GAK
DAMN IT!
WE DIDN'T HAVE TO MAKE THE FIRST MOVE!
DADOOM
LOOKS LIKE...
...THE GATE OF THE SUN IS STILL FUNCTIONAL.

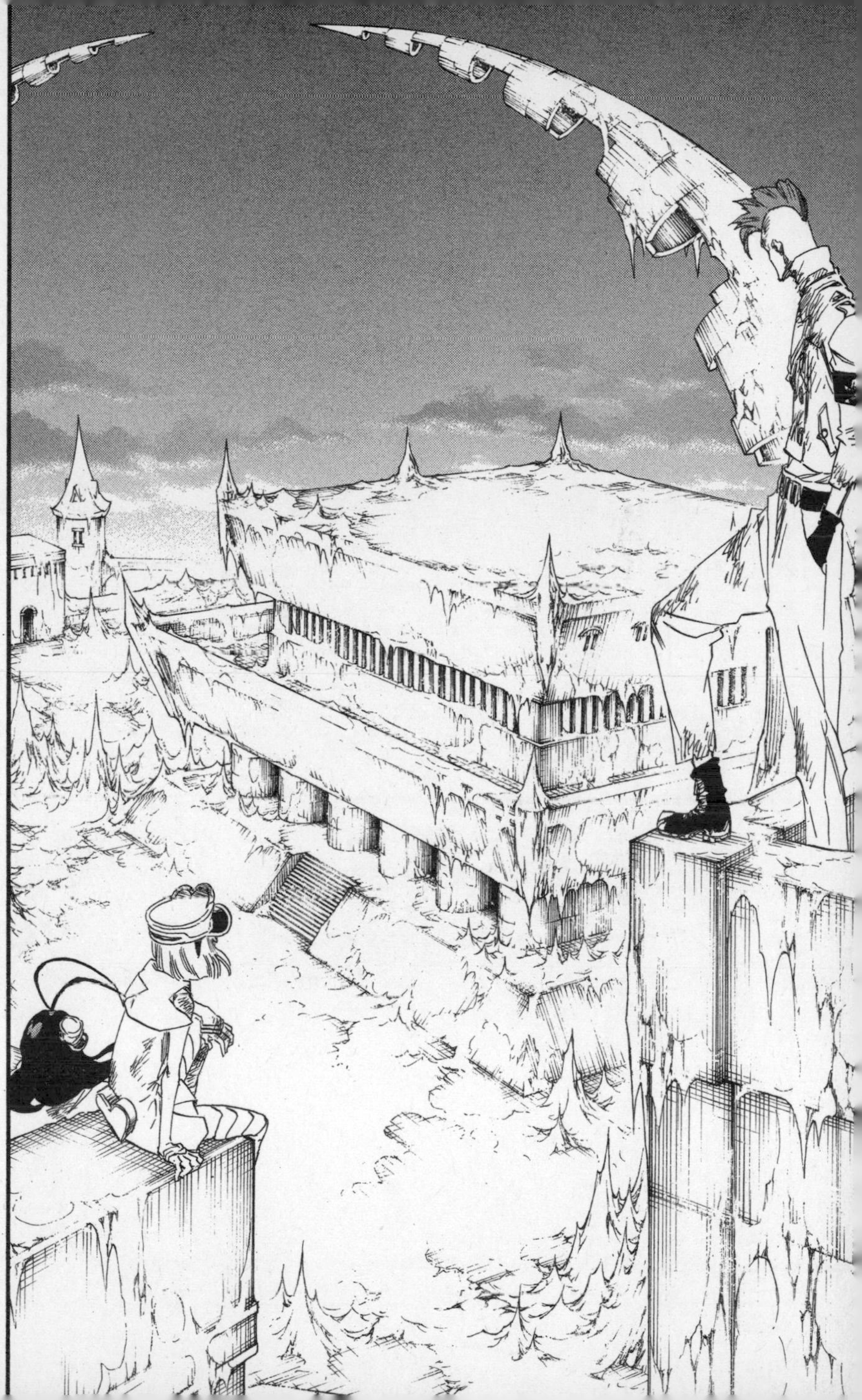

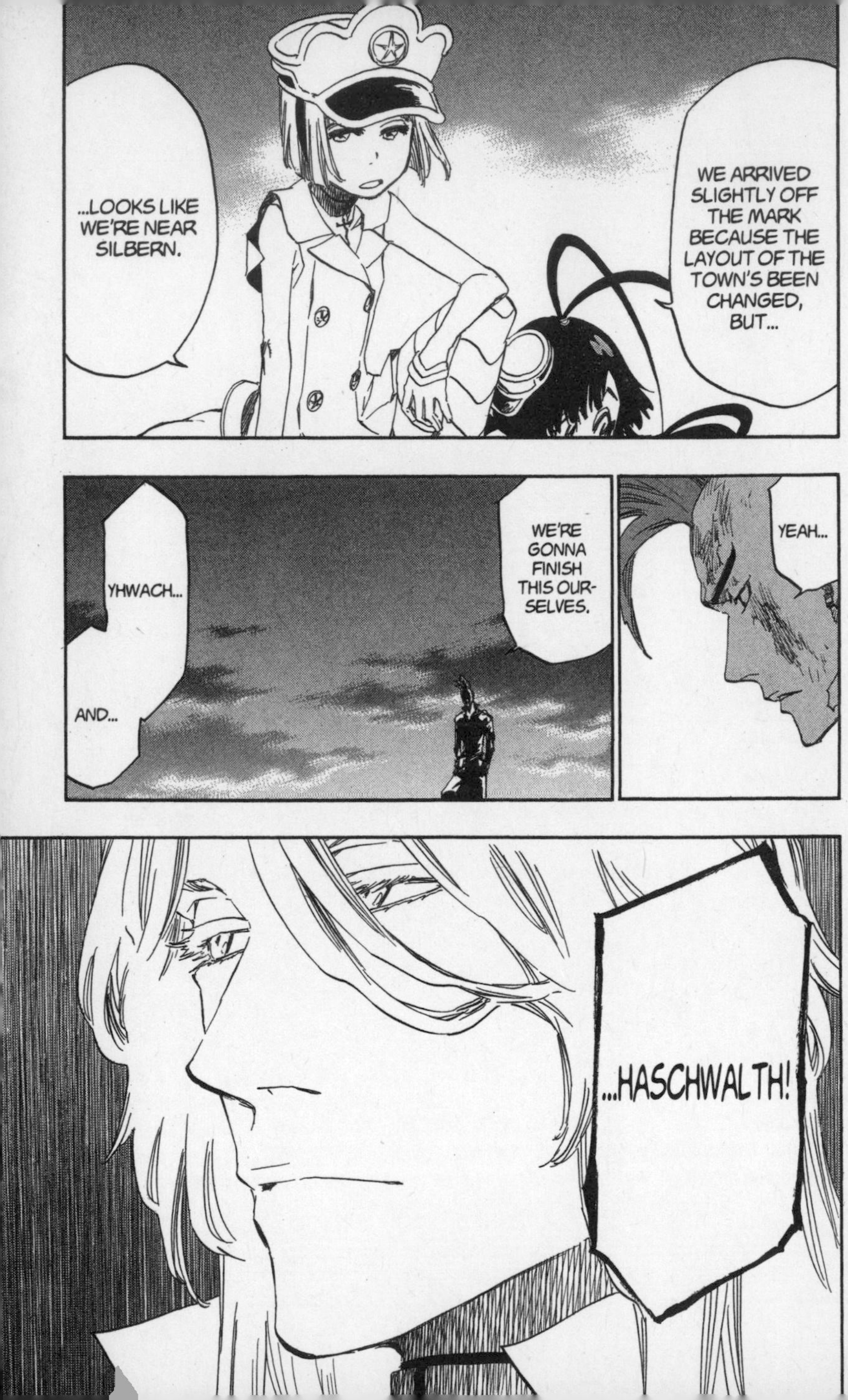
WE ARRIVED SLIGHTLY OFF THE MARK BECAUSE THE LAYOUT OF THE TOWN'S BEEN CHANGED, BUT...
...LOOKS LIKE WE'RE NEAR SILBERN.
YEAH...
WE'RE GONNA FINISH THIS OUR-SELVES.
YHWACH...
AND...
...HASCHWALTH!

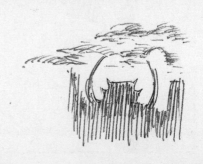

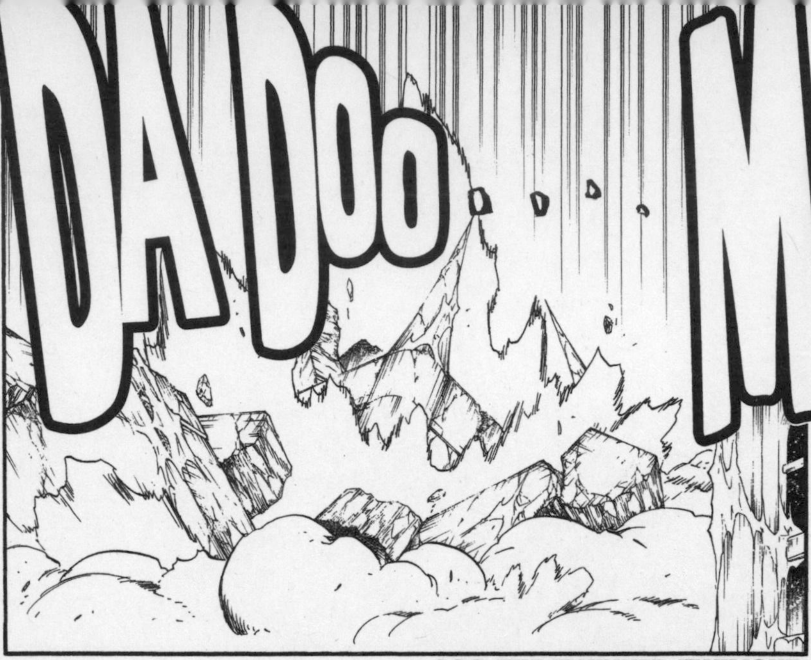
DADOO...M

630. THE TWINNED TWILIGHT

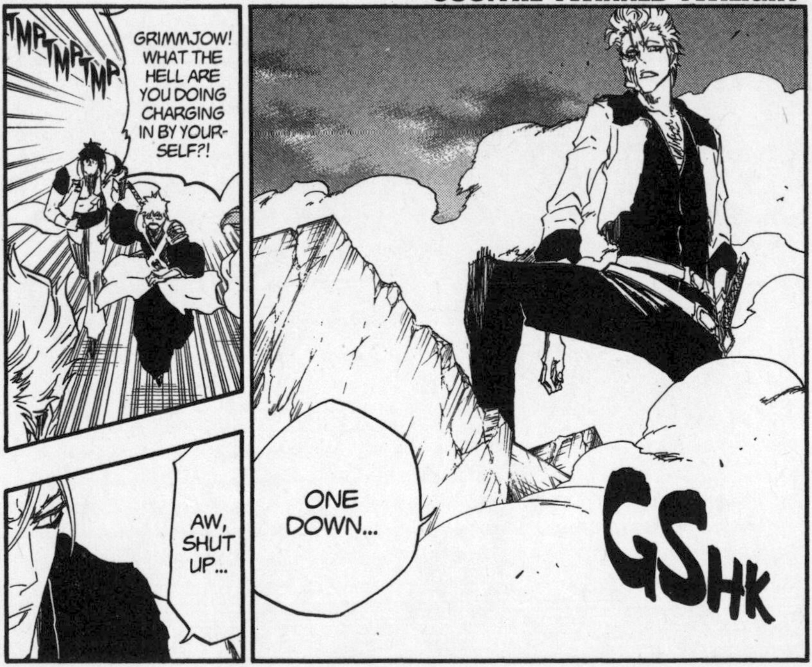
ONE DOWN...
GSHK
TMP TMP TMP TMP
GRIMMJOW! WHAT THE HELL ARE YOU DOING CHARGING IN BY YOURSELF?!
AW, SHUT UP...

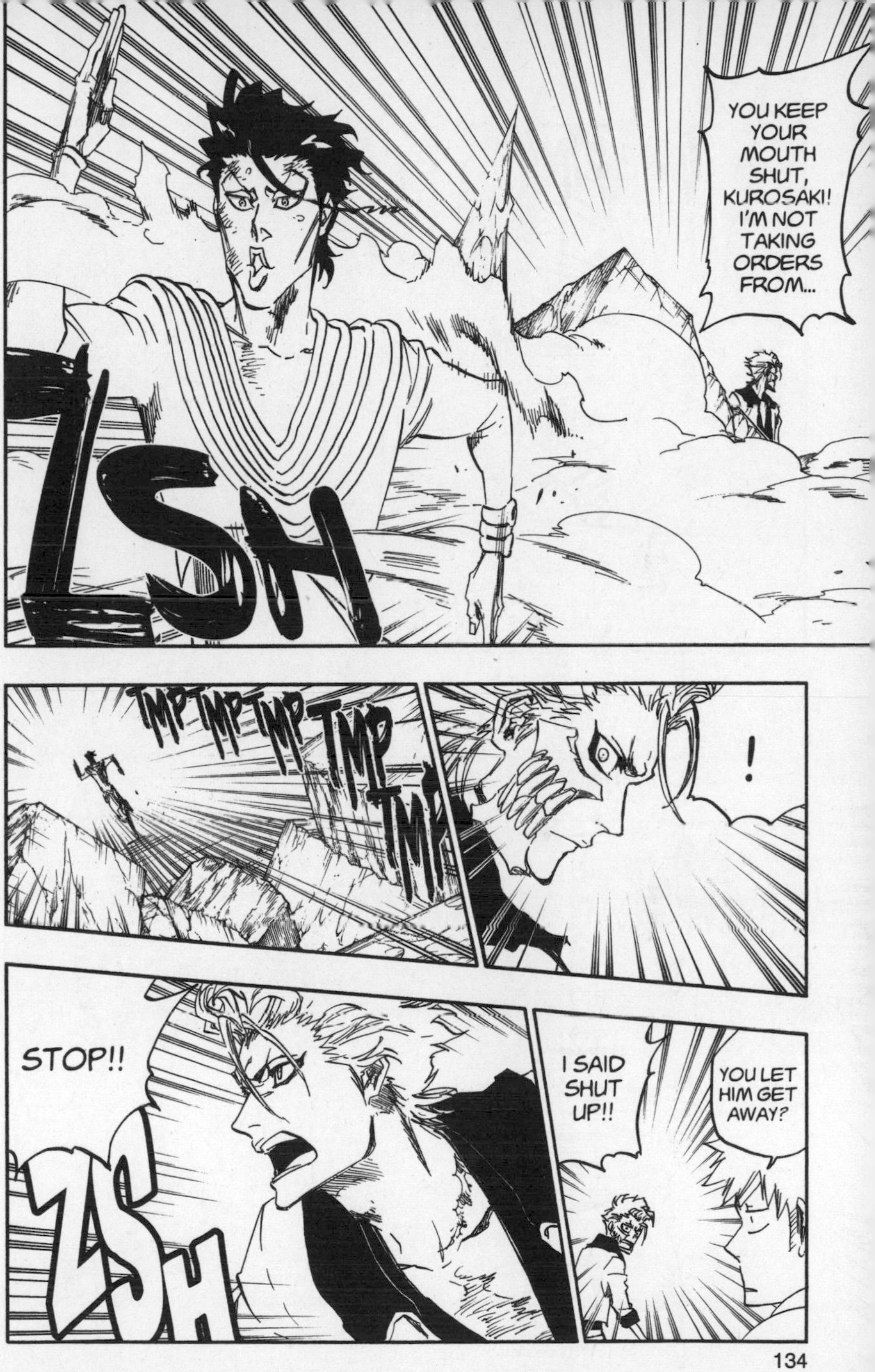
YOU KEEP YOUR MOUTH SHUT, KUROSAKI! I'M NOT TAKING ORDERS FROM...
TSH
!
TMP TMP TMP TMP TMP TMP
YOU LET HIM GET AWAY?
I SAID SHUT UP!!
STOP!!
ZSH

READ THIS WAY

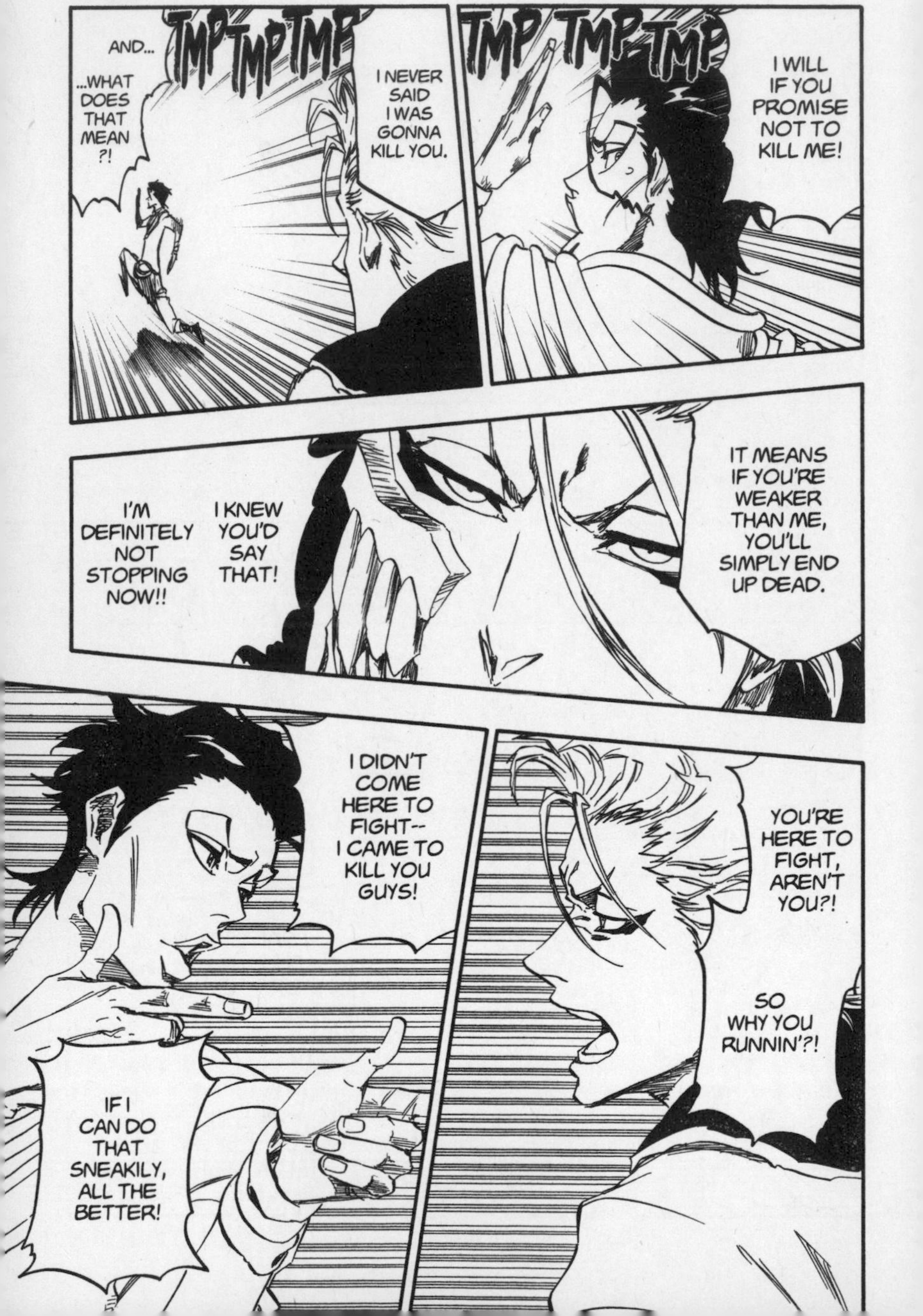
TMP TMP TMP TMP
I WILL IF YOU PROMISE NOT TO KILL ME!
I NEVER SAID I WAS GONNA KILL YOU.
TMP TMP TMP
AND...
...WHAT DOES THAT MEAN ?!
IT MEANS IF YOU'RE WEAKER THAN ME, YOU'LL SIMPLY END UP DEAD.
I KNEW YOU'D SAY THAT!
I'M DEFINITELY NOT STOPPING NOW!!
YOU'RE HERE TO FIGHT, AREN'T YOU?!
SO WHY YOU RUNNIN'?!
I DIDN'T COME HERE TO FIGHT-- I CAME TO KILL YOU GUYS!
IF I CAN DO THAT SNEAKILY, ALL THE BETTER!

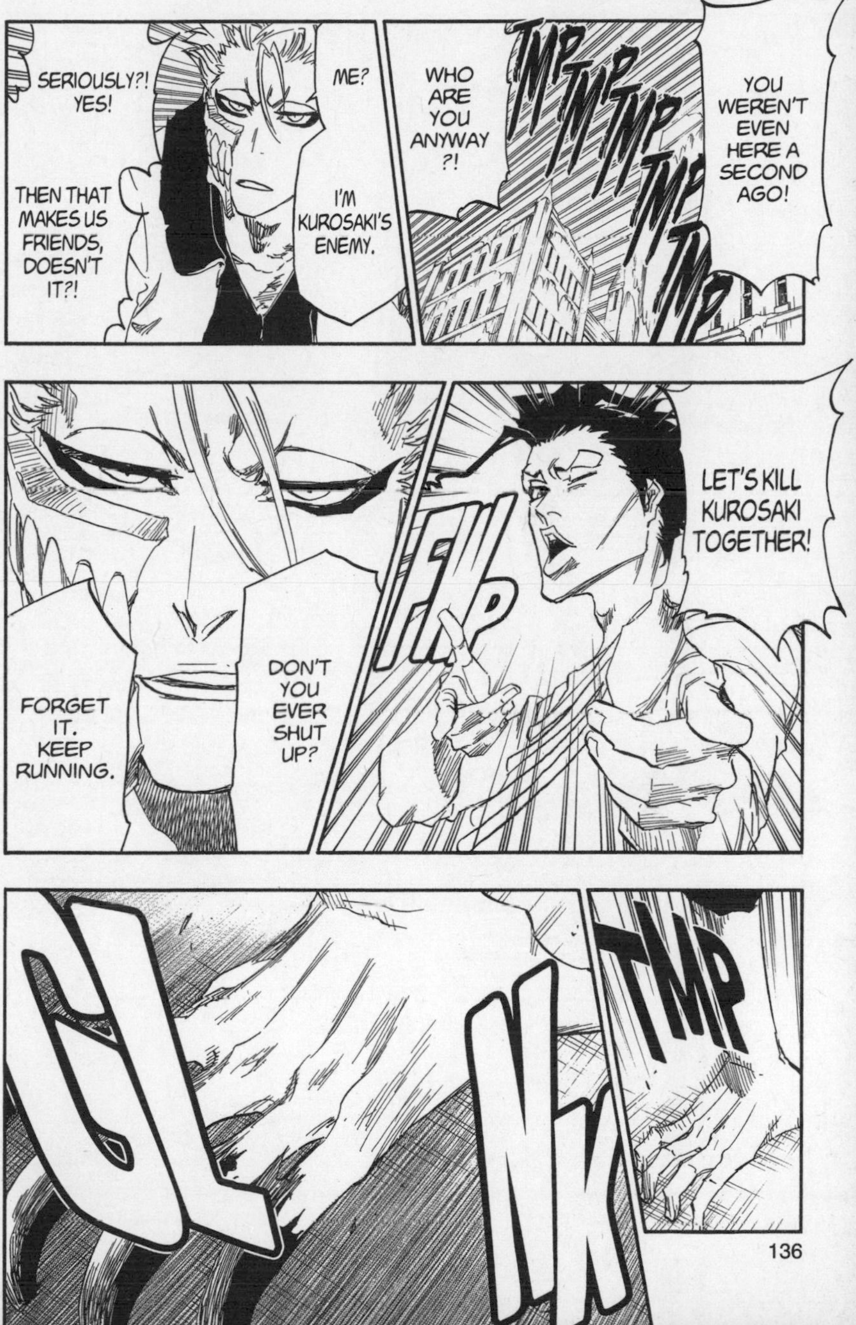
YOU WEREN'T EVEN HERE A SECOND AGO!
TMP TMP TMP TMP TMP
WHO ARE YOU ANYWAY ?!
ME?
I'M KUROSAKI'S ENEMY.
SERIOUSLY?! YES!
THEN THAT MAKES US FRIENDS, DOESN'T IT?!
LET'S KILL KUROSAKI TOGETHER!
FWP
DON'T YOU EVER SHUT UP?
FORGET IT. KEEP RUNNING.
TMP
CLNK

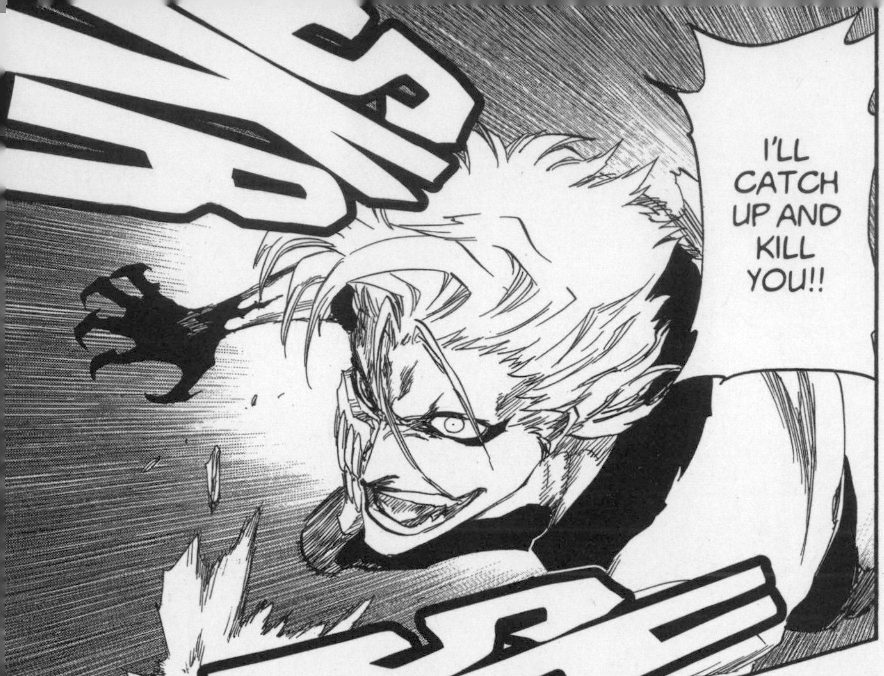
I'LL CATCH UP AND KILL YOU!!
WH...
WHOOAA?!

BLEACH 630.

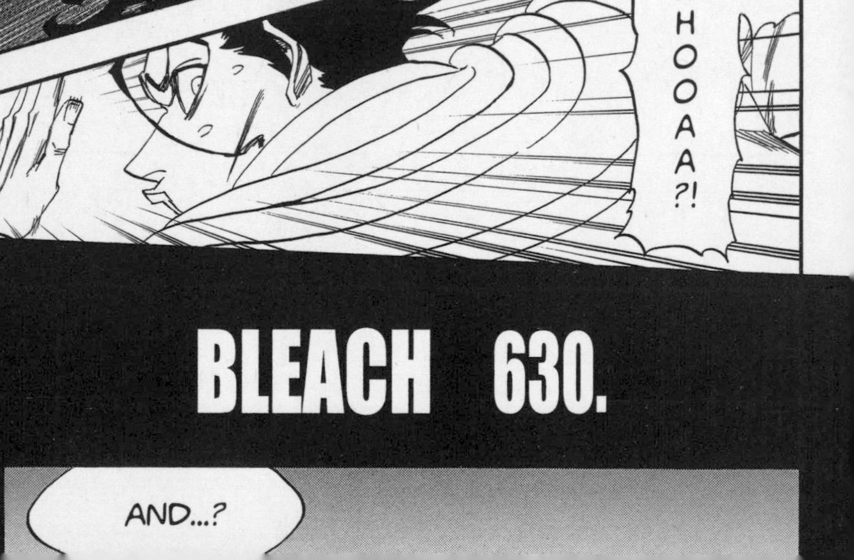
AND...?

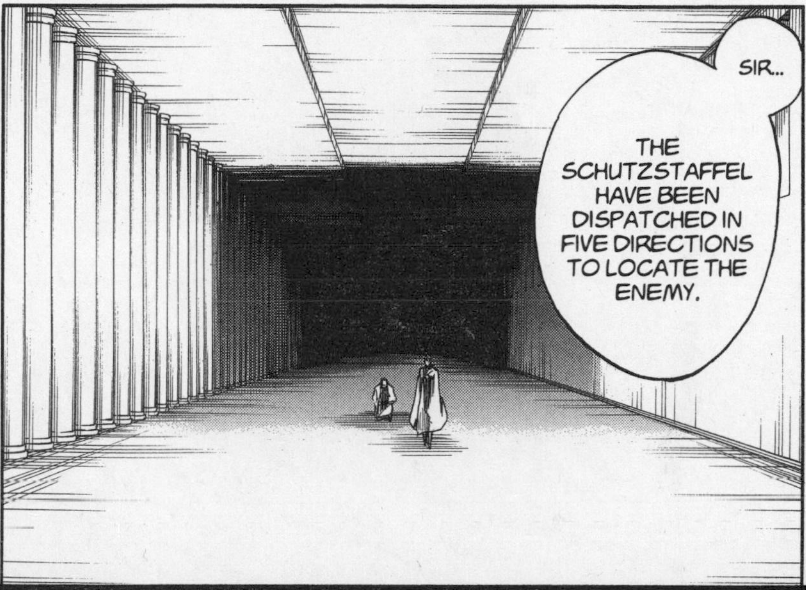
SIR...
THE SCHUTZSTAFFEL HAVE BEEN DISPATCHED IN FIVE DIRECTIONS TO LOCATE THE ENEMY.

The Twinned Twilight

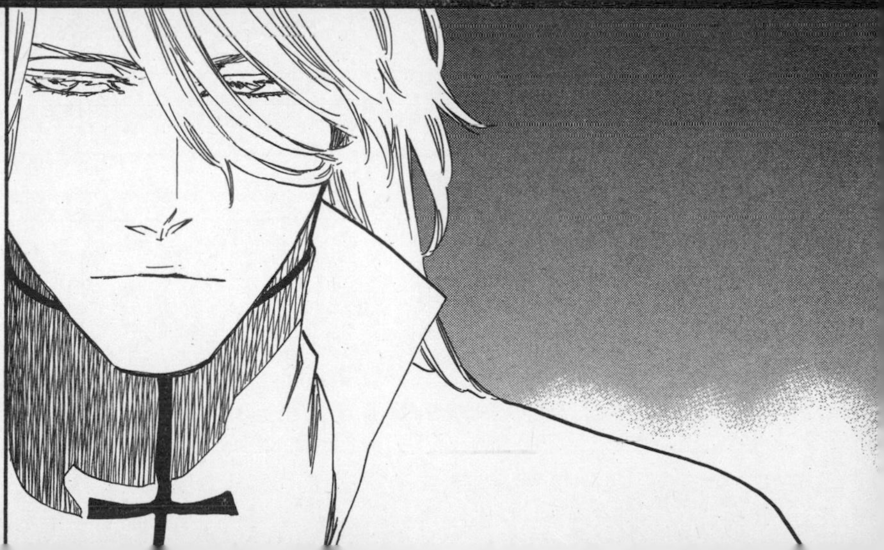

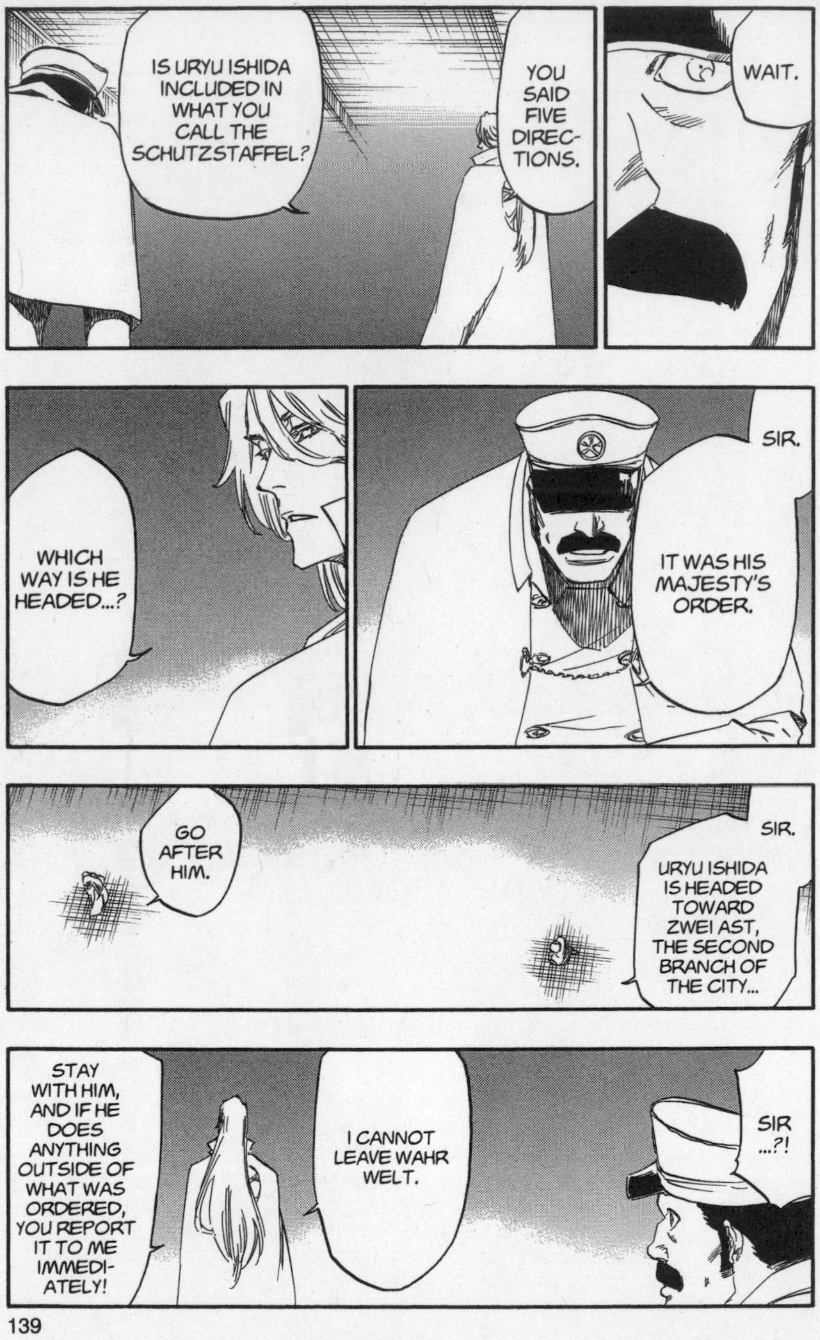
WAIT.
YOU SAID FIVE DIRECTIONS.
IS URYU ISHIDA INCLUDED IN WHAT YOU CALL THE SCHUTZSTAFFEL?
SIR.
IT WAS HIS MAJESTY'S ORDER.
WHICH WAY IS HE HEADED...?
SIR.
URYU ISHIDA IS HEADED TOWARD ZWEI AST, THE SECOND BRANCH OF THE CITY...
GO AFTER HIM.
SIR ...?!
I CANNOT LEAVE WAHR WELT.
STAY WITH HIM, AND IF HE DOES ANYTHING OUTSIDE OF WHAT WAS ORDERED, YOU REPORT IT TO ME IMMEDIATELY!

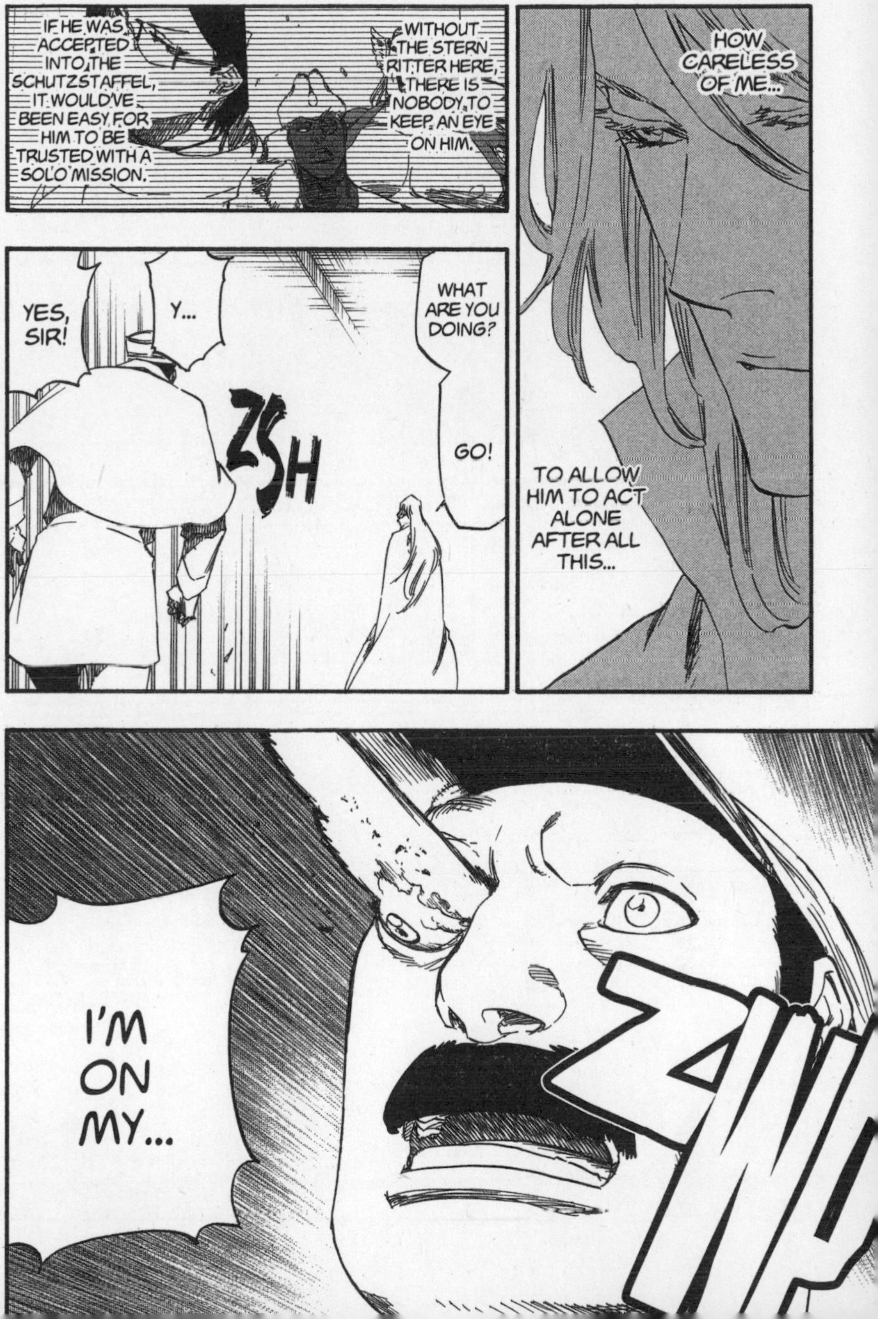

HOW CARELESS OF ME...
TO ALLOW HIM TO ACT ALONE AFTER ALL THIS...
WITHOUT THE STERN RITTER HERE, THERE IS NOBODY TO KEEP AN EYE ON HIM.
IF HE WAS ACCEPTED INTO THE SCHUTZSTAFFEL, IT WOULD'VE BEEN EASY FOR HIM TO BE TRUSTED WITH A SOLO MISSION.
WHAT ARE YOU DOING?
GO!
ZSH
Y...
YES, SIR!
I'M ON MY...

READ THIS WAY

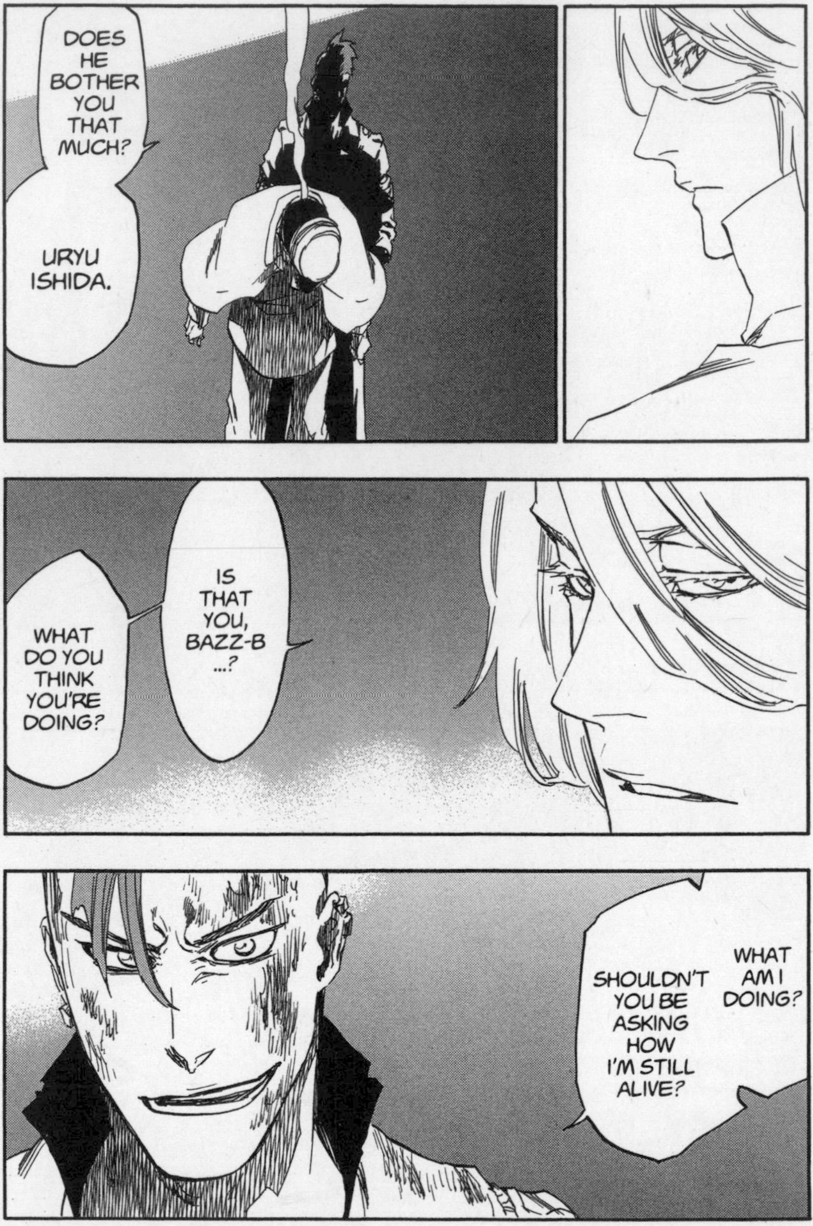
DOES HE BOTHER YOU THAT MUCH?
URYU ISHIDA.
IS THAT YOU, BAZZ-B ...?
WHAT DO YOU THINK YOU'RE DOING?
WHAT AM I DOING?
SHOULDN'T YOU BE ASKING HOW I'M STILL ALIVE?

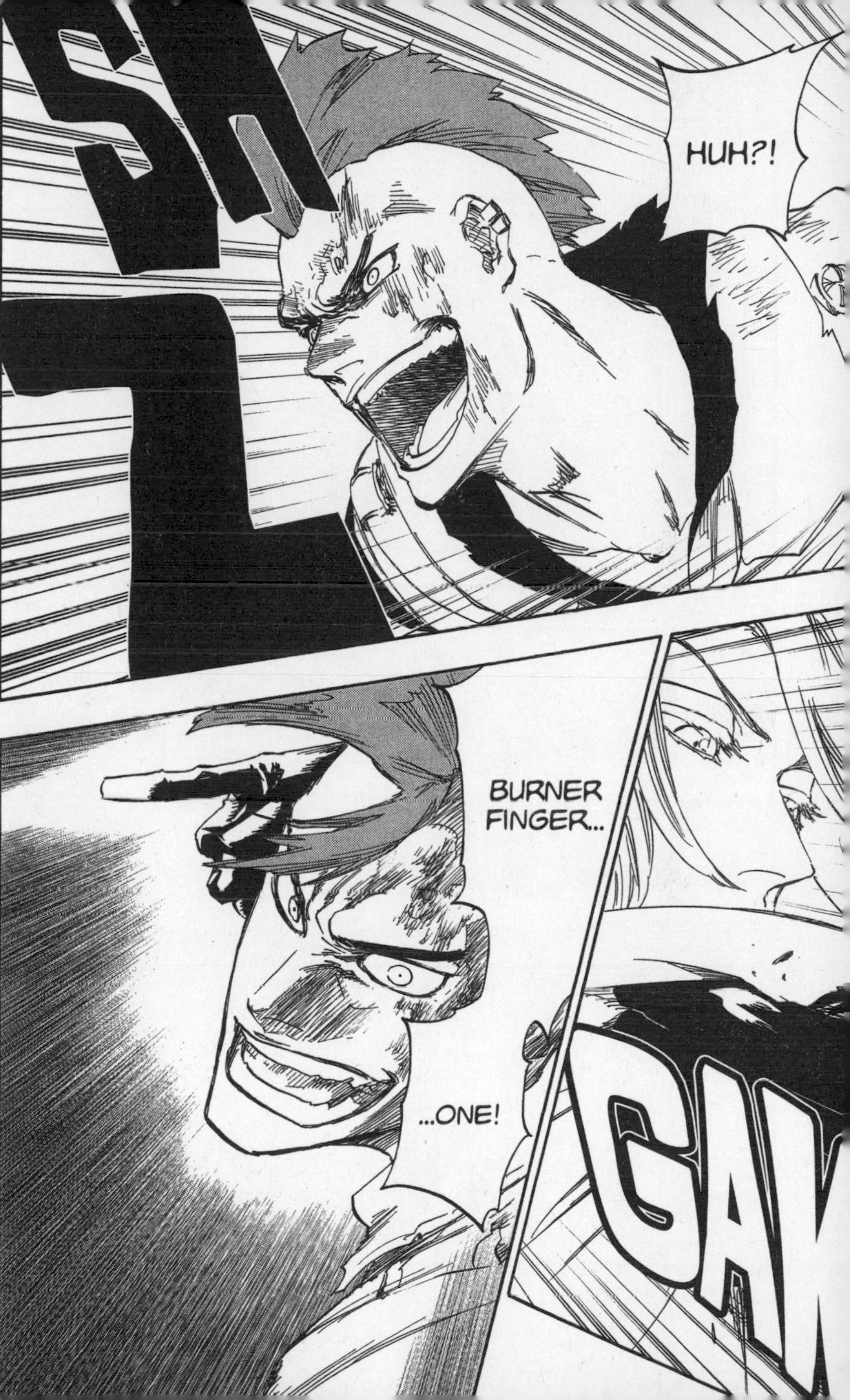
SH
HUH?!
BURNER FINGER...
...ONE!
GAK

READ THIS WAY

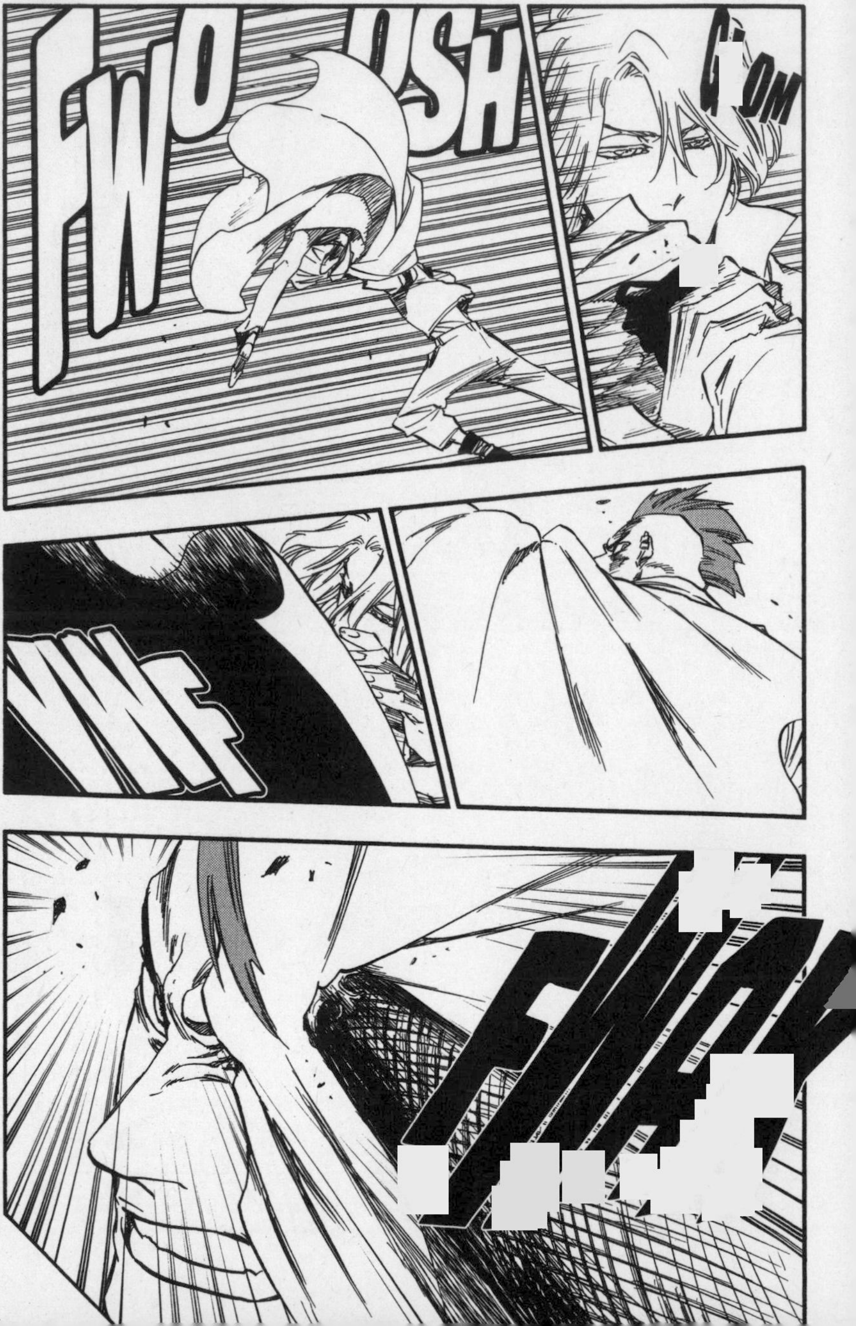

VWF

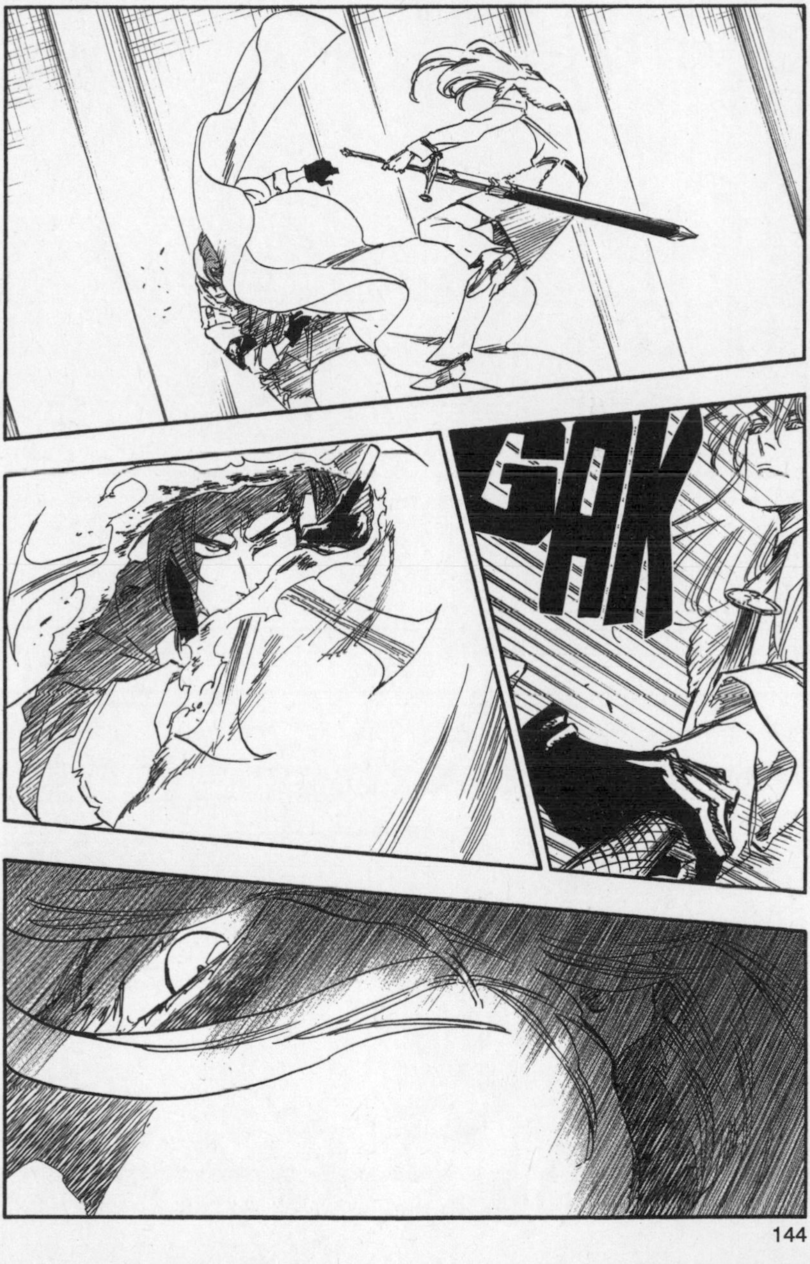
GAK

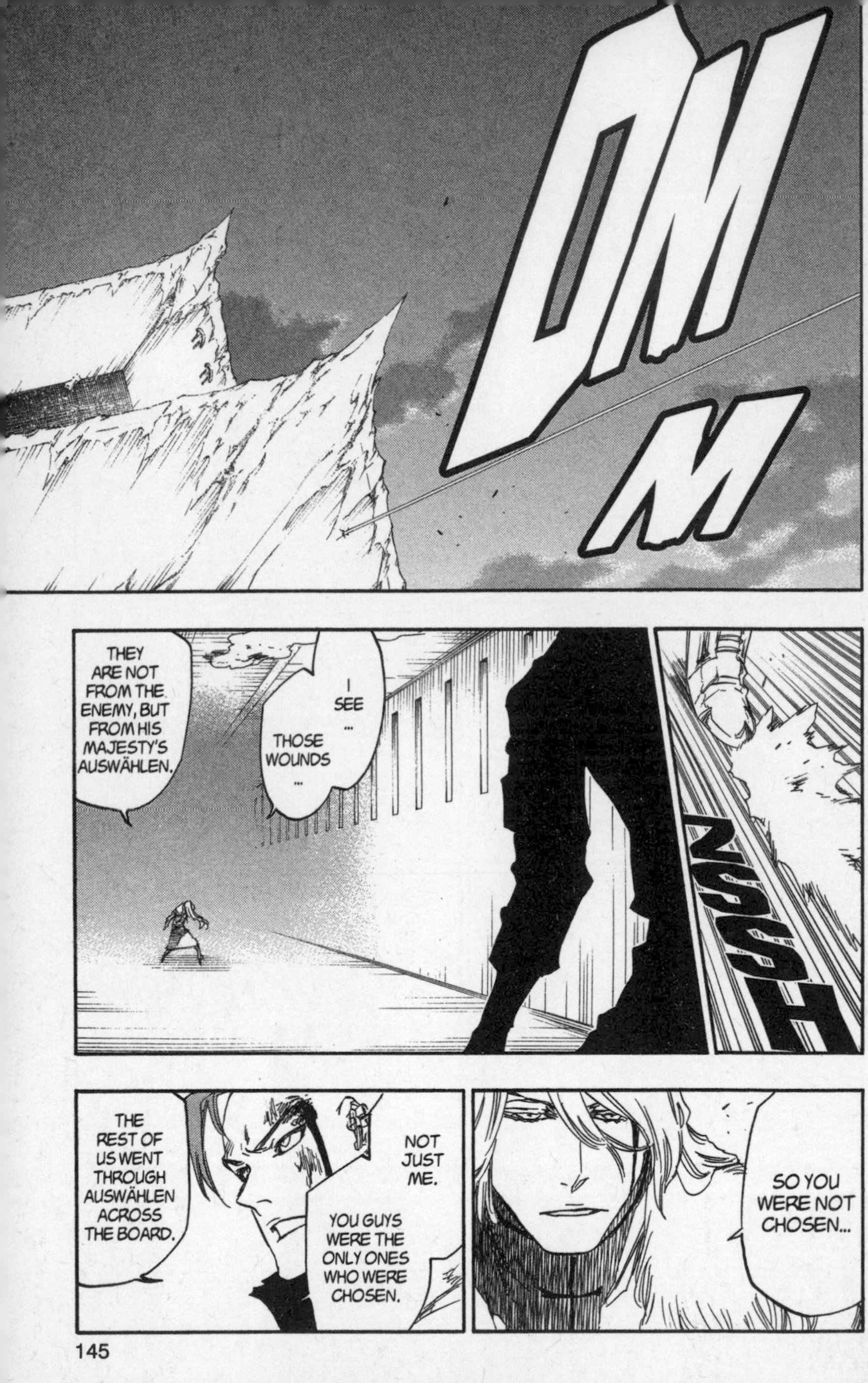
DMM
NSSSH
I SEE ... THOSE WOUNDS ...
THEY ARE NOT FROM THE ENEMY, BUT FROM HIS MAJESTY'S AUSWÄHLEN.
SO YOU WERE NOT CHOSEN...
NOT JUST ME.
YOU GUYS WERE THE ONLY ONES WHO WERE CHOSEN.
THE REST OF US WENT THROUGH AUSWÄHLEN ACROSS THE BOARD.

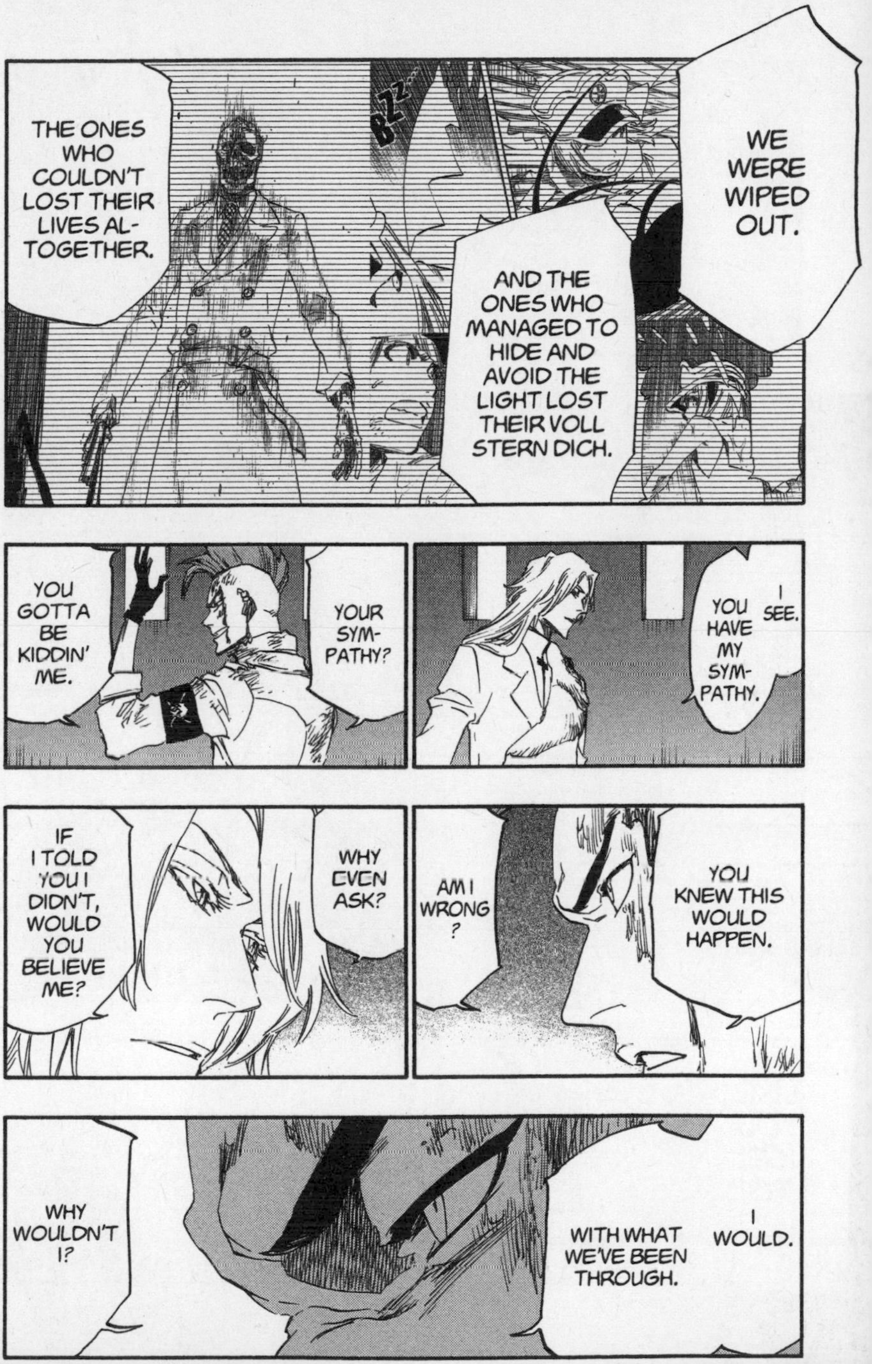
WE WERE WIPED OUT.
BZZ...
THE ONES WHO COULDN'T LOST THEIR LIVES AL-TOGETHER.
AND THE ONES WHO MANAGED TO HIDE AND AVOID THE LIGHT LOST THEIR VOLL STERN DICH.
I SEE.
YOU HAVE MY SYM-PATHY.
YOUR SYM-PATHY?
YOU GOTTA BE KIDDIN' ME.
YOU KNEW THIS WOULD HAPPEN.
AM I WRONG?
WHY EVEN ASK?
IF I TOLD YOU I DIDN'T, WOULD YOU BELIEVE ME?
I WOULD.
WITH WHAT WE'VE BEEN THROUGH.
WHY WOULDN'T I?

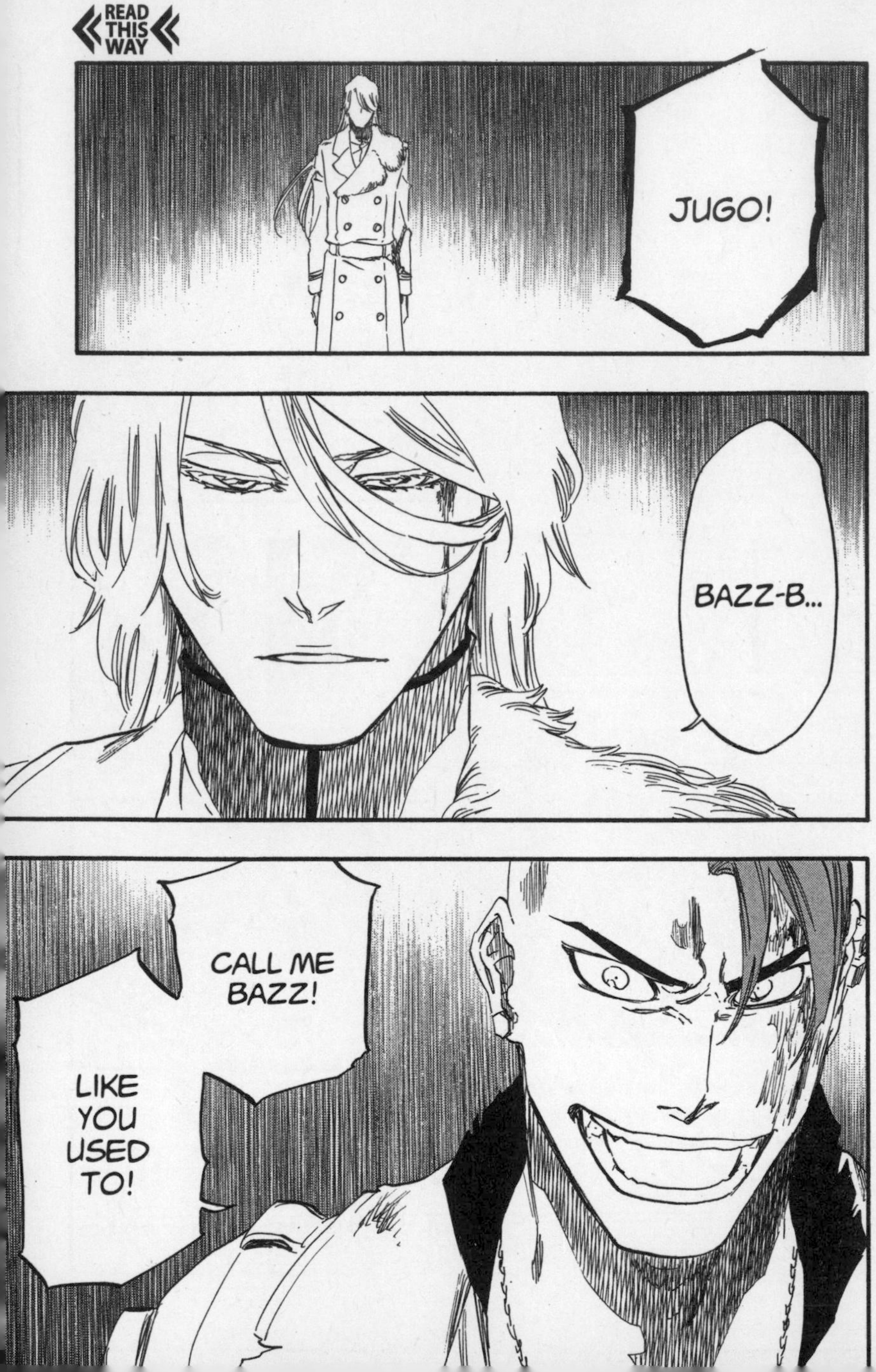
READ THIS WAY
JUGO!
BAZZ-B...
CALL ME BAZZ!
LIKE YOU USED TO!

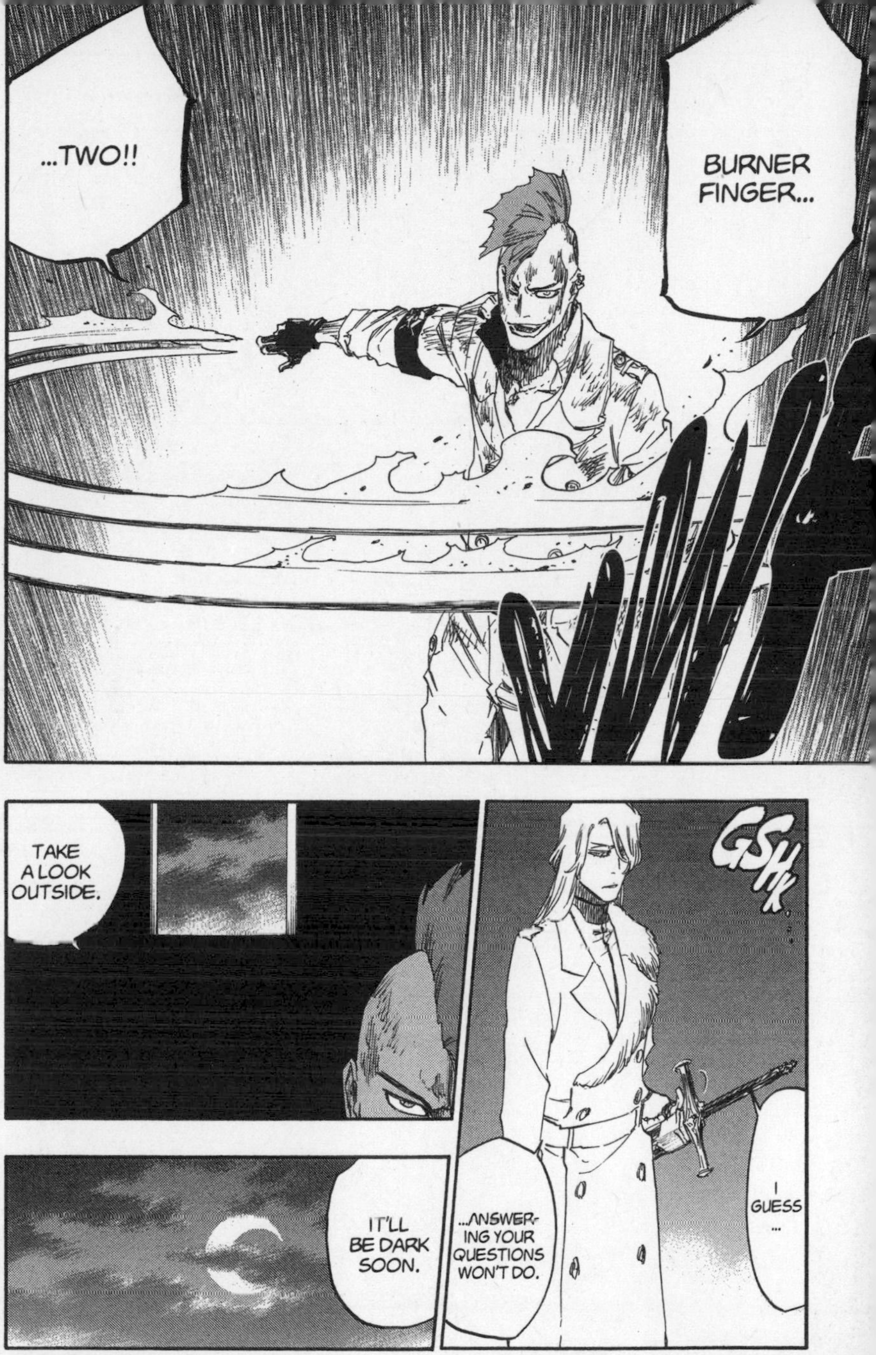
BURNER FINGER...
...TWO!!
GSHK
TAKE A LOOK OUTSIDE.
IT'LL BE DARK SOON.
...ANSWER-ING YOUR QUESTIONS WON'T DO.
I GUESS...

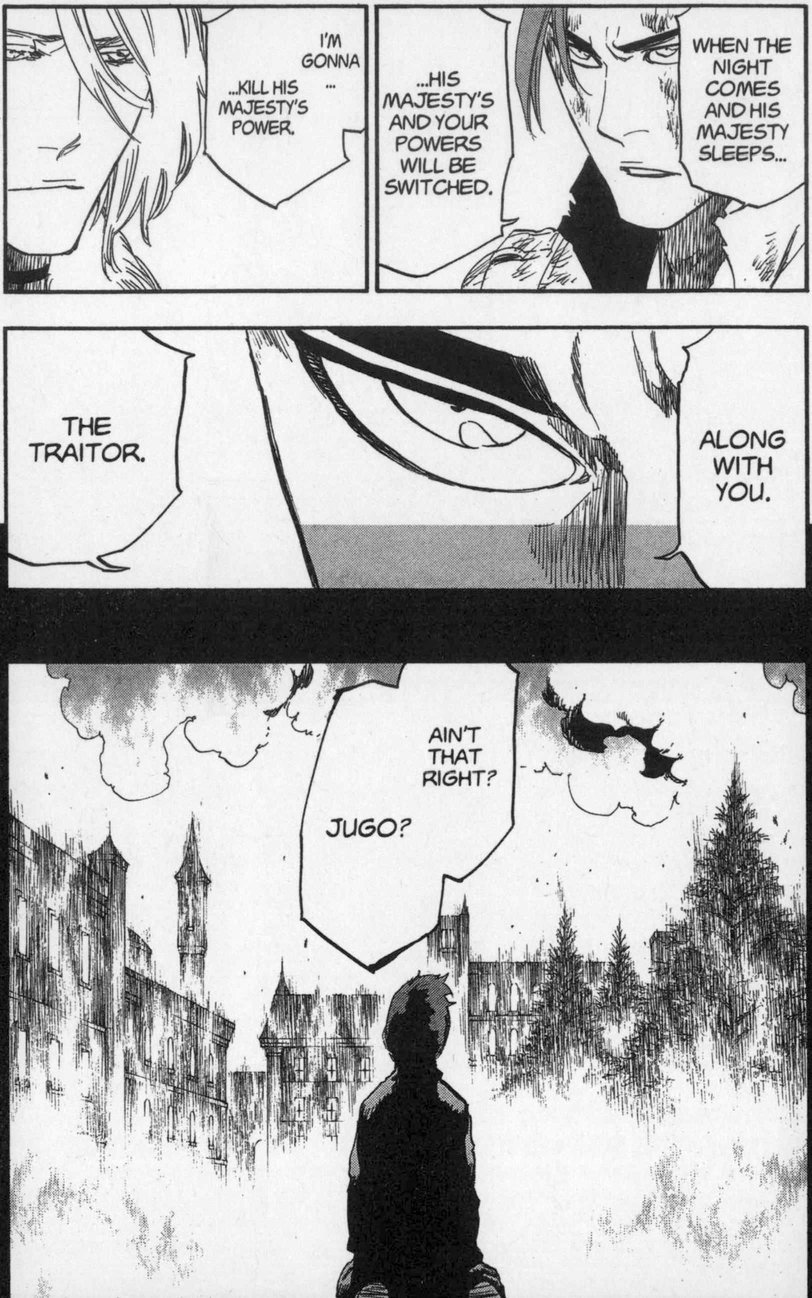
WHEN THE NIGHT COMES AND HIS MAJESTY SLEEPS...
...HIS MAJESTY'S AND YOUR POWERS WILL BE SWITCHED.
I'M GONNA ...
...KILL HIS MAJESTY'S POWER.
ALONG WITH YOU.
THE TRAITOR.
AIN'T THAT RIGHT?
JUGO?

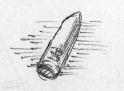

631.FRIEND

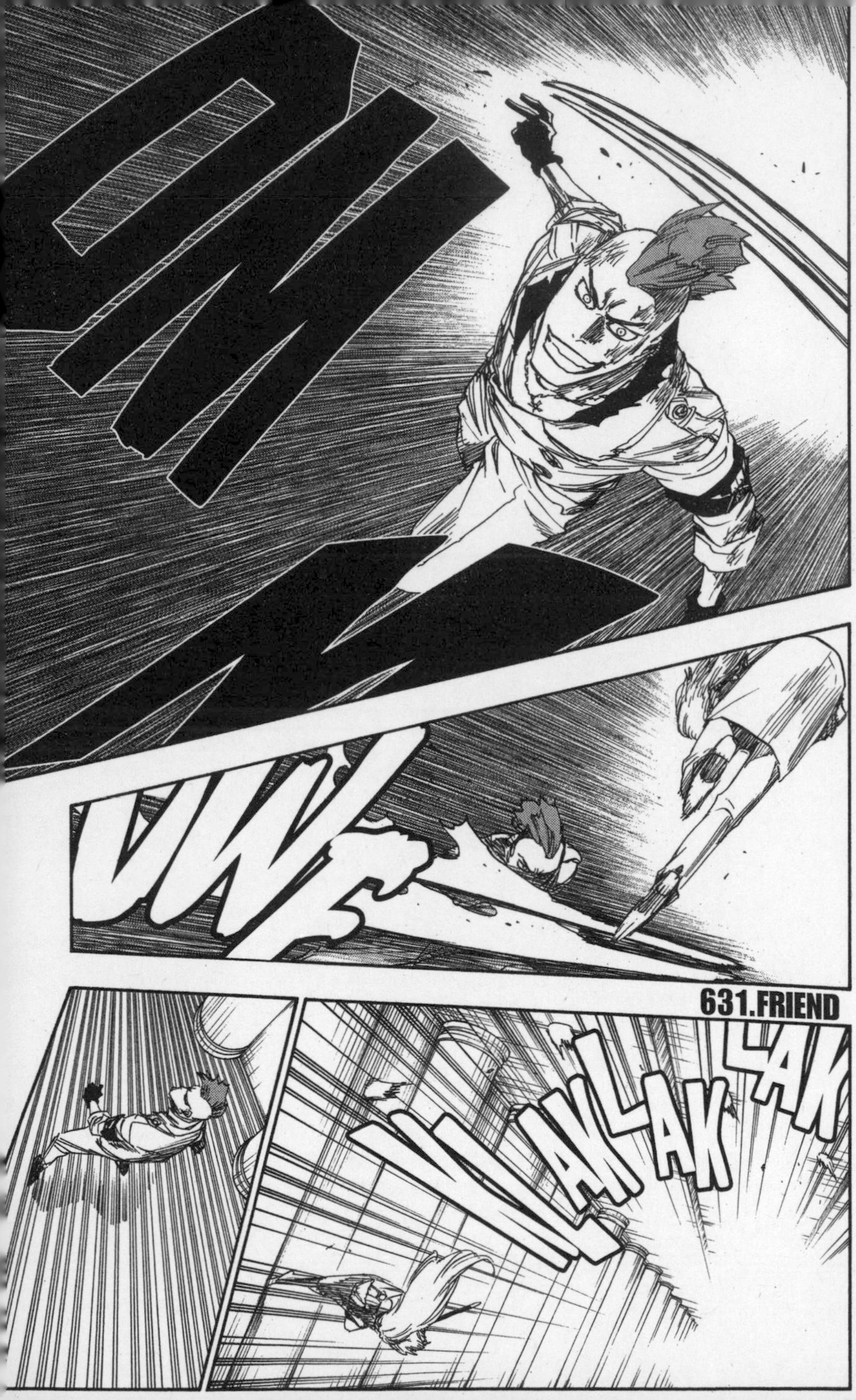

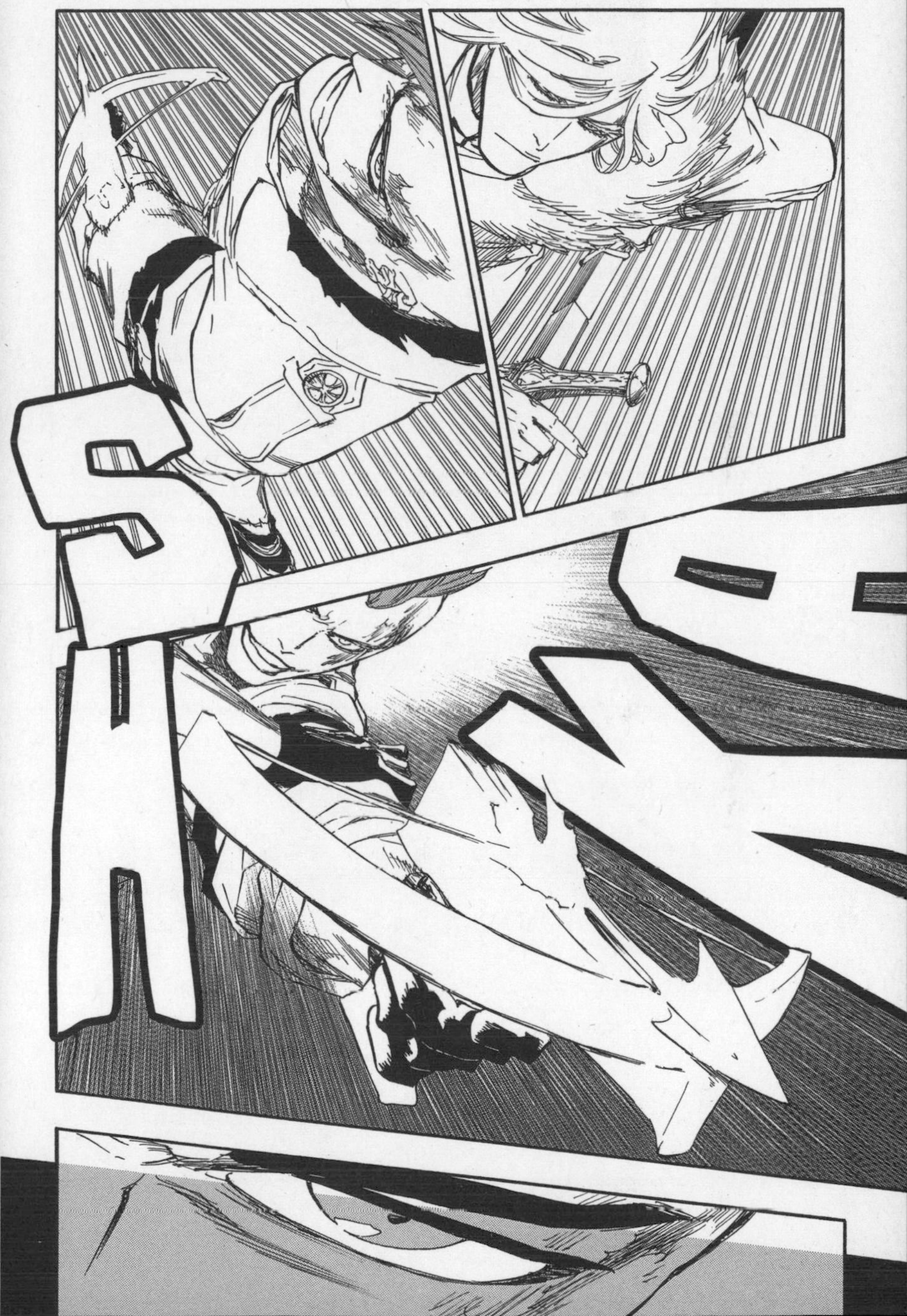

READ THIS WAY

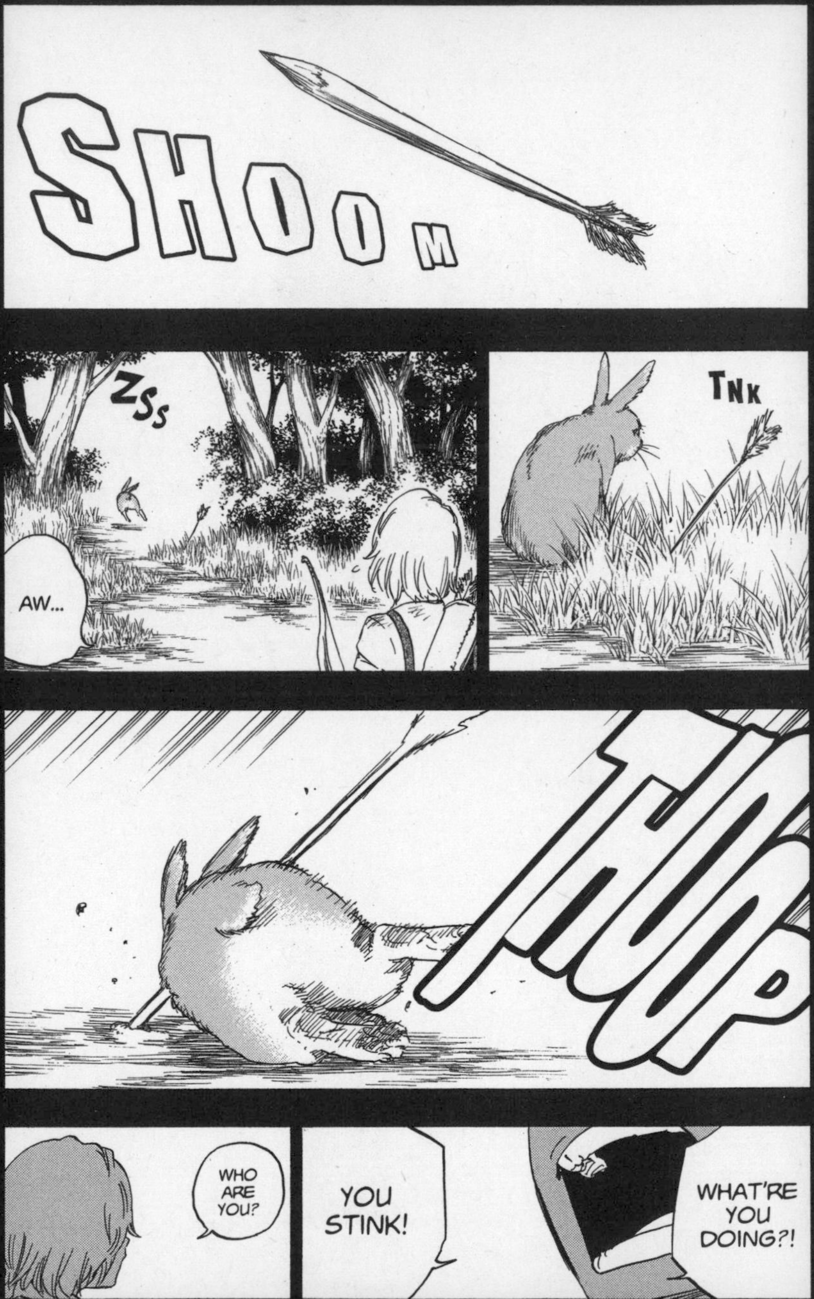
SHOOOM
TNK
ZSs
AW...
THUP
WHAT'RE YOU DOING?!
YOU STINK!
WHO ARE YOU?

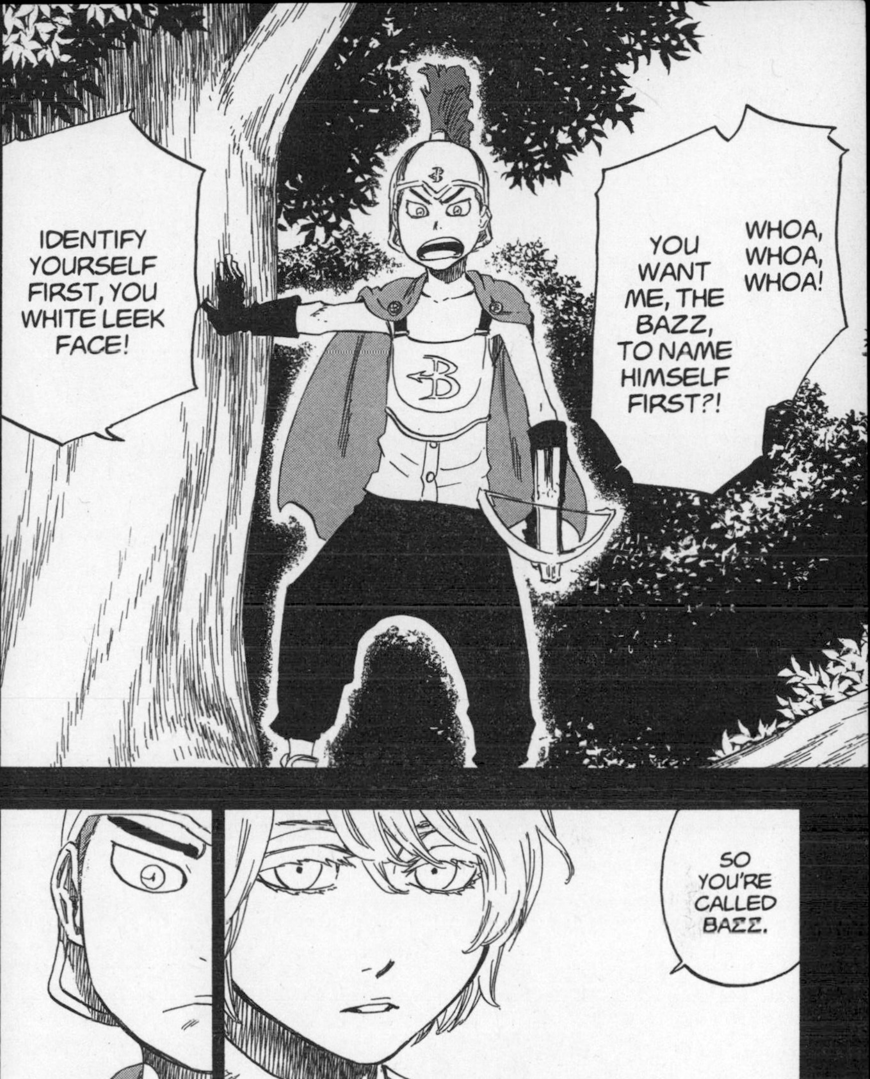
WHOA, WHOA, WHOA!
YOU WANT ME, THE BAZZ, TO NAME HIMSELF FIRST?!
IDENTIFY YOURSELF FIRST, YOU WHITE LEEK FACE!
SO YOU'RE CALLED BAZZ.

BLEACH 631.

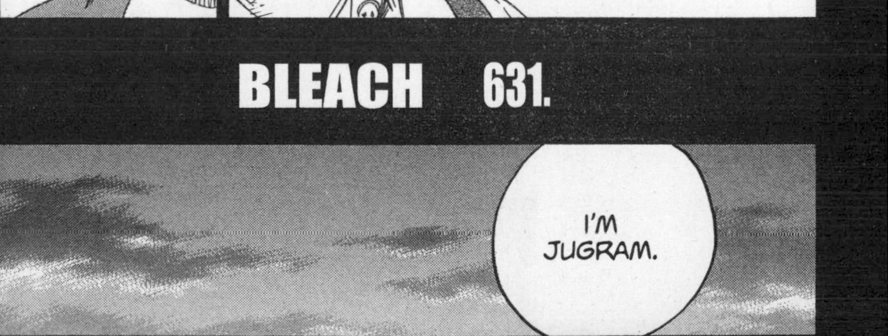
I'M JUGRAM.

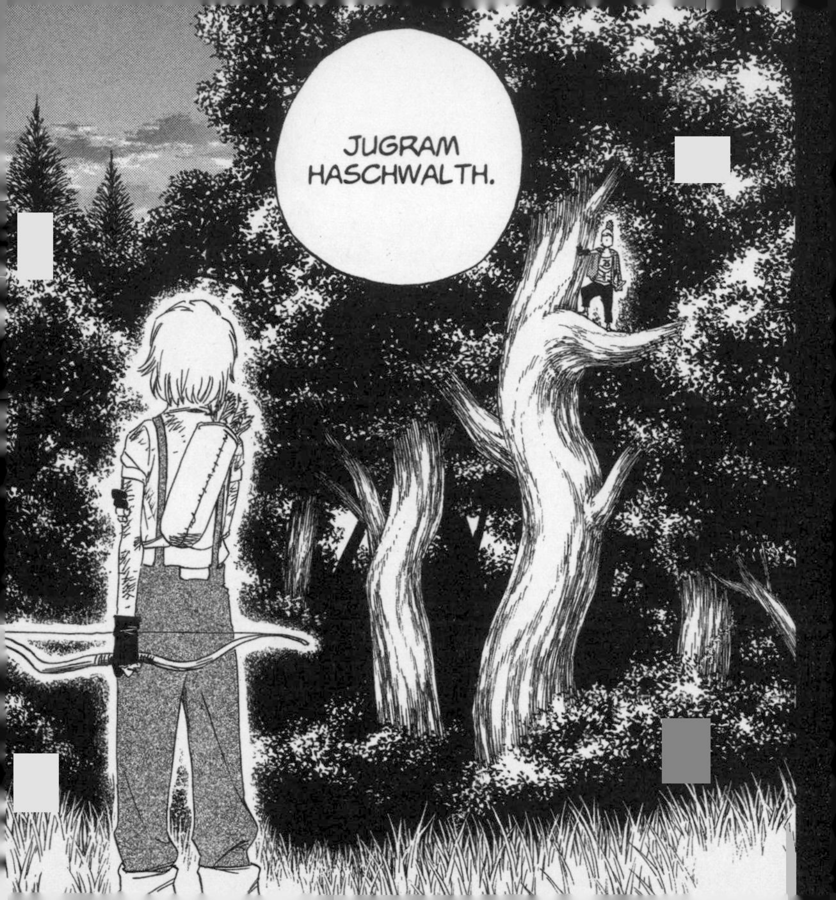
JUGRAM
HASCHWALTH.

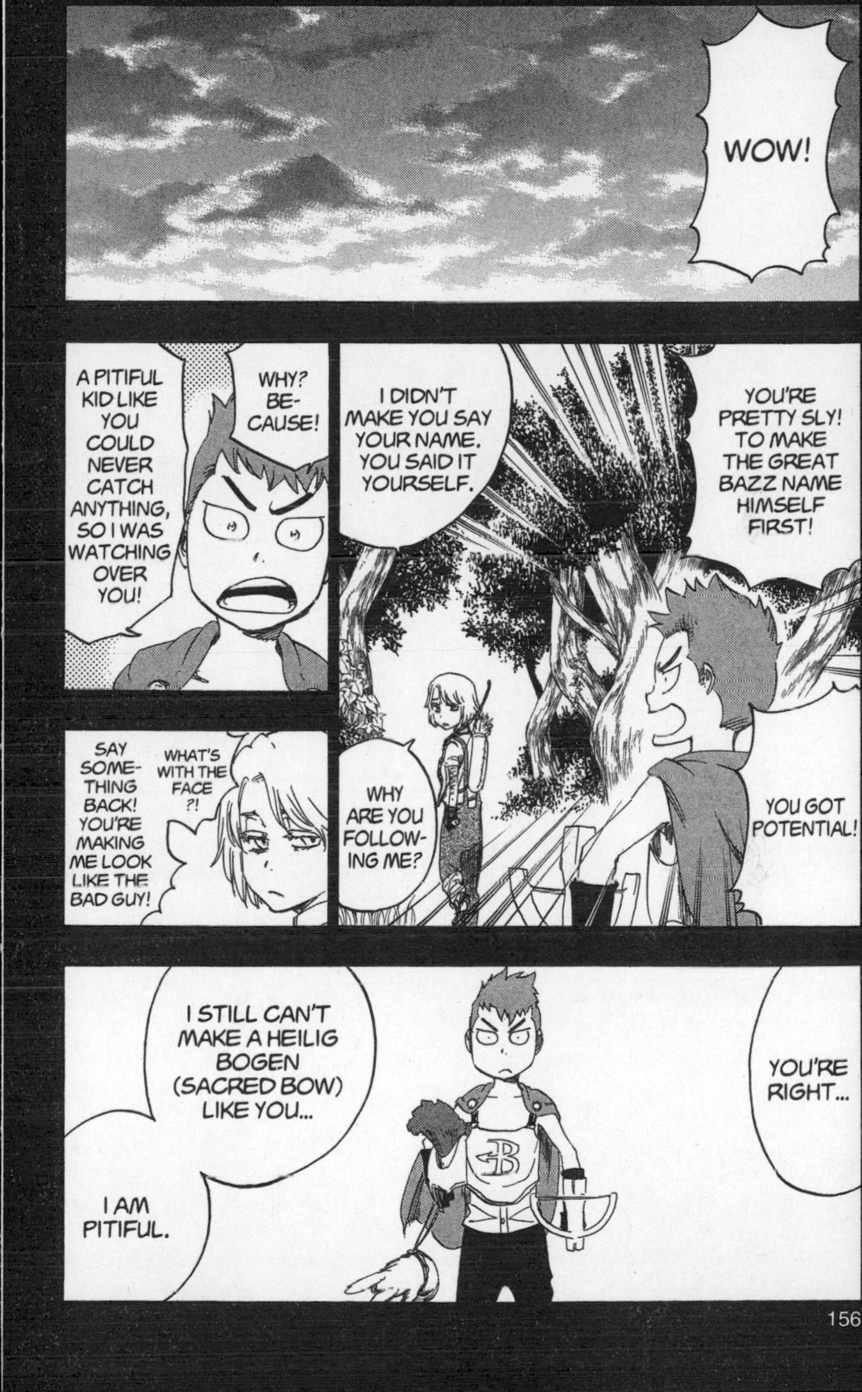
WOW!
YOU'RE PRETTY SLY! TO MAKE THE GREAT BAZZ NAME HIMSELF FIRST!
I DIDN'T MAKE YOU SAY YOUR NAME. YOU SAID IT YOURSELF.
YOU GOT POTENTIAL!
WHY ARE YOU FOLLOWING ME?
WHY? BE-CAUSE!
A PITIFUL KID LIKE YOU COULD NEVER CATCH ANYTHING, SO I WAS WATCHING OVER YOU!
WHAT'S WITH THE FACE ?!
SAY SOME-THING BACK! YOU'RE MAKING ME LOOK LIKE THE BAD GUY!
YOU'RE RIGHT...
I STILL CAN'T MAKE A HEILIG BOGEN (SACRED BOW) LIKE YOU...
I AM PITIFUL.

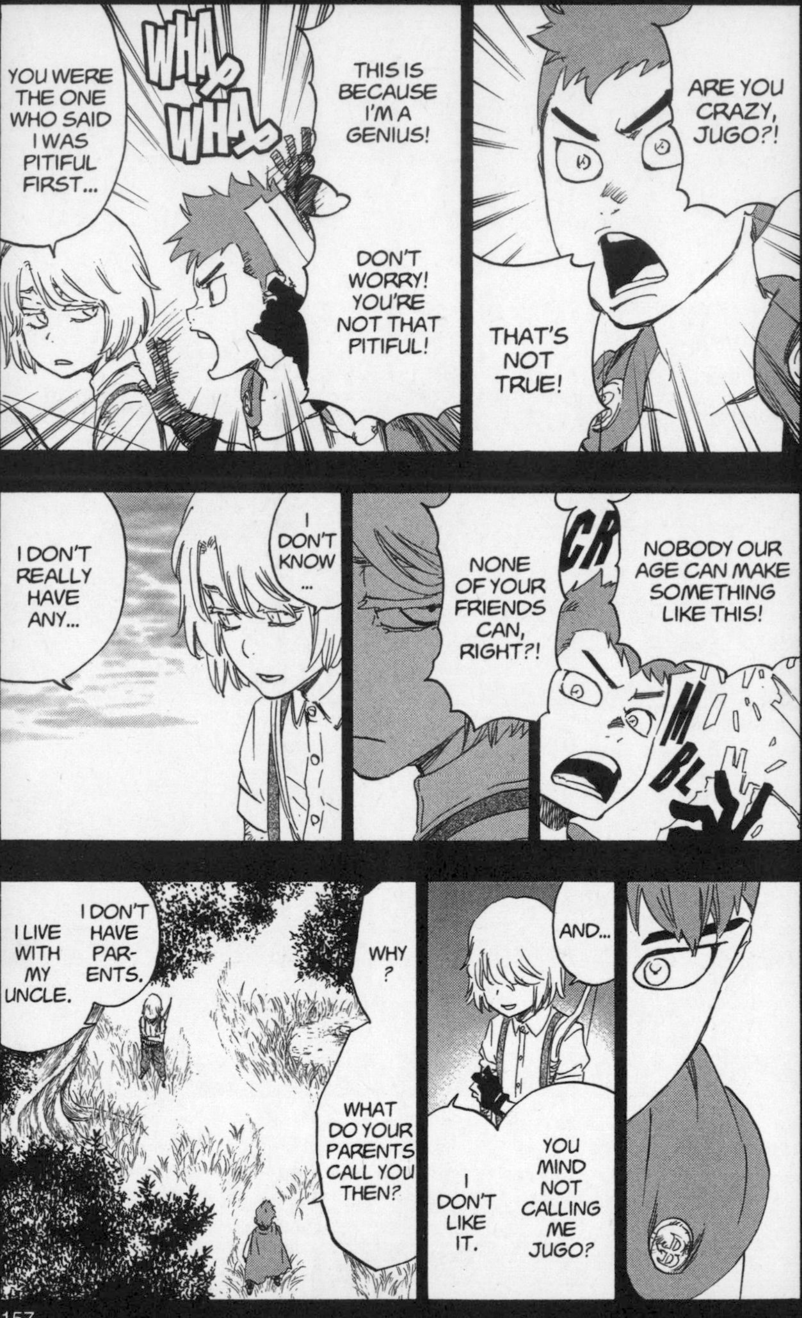
ARE YOU CRAZY, JUGO?!
THAT'S NOT TRUE!
THIS IS BECAUSE I'M A GENIUS!
WHAP WHAP
DON'T WORRY! YOU'RE NOT THAT PITIFUL!
YOU WERE THE ONE WHO SAID I WAS PITIFUL FIRST...
NOBODY OUR AGE CAN MAKE SOMETHING LIKE THIS!
CRMBL
NONE OF YOUR FRIENDS CAN, RIGHT?!
I DON'T KNOW...
I DON'T REALLY HAVE ANY...
AND...
YOU MIND NOT CALLING ME JUGO?
I DON'T LIKE IT.
WHY?
WHAT DO YOUR PARENTS CALL YOU THEN?
I DON'T HAVE PAR-ENTS.
I LIVE WITH MY UNCLE.

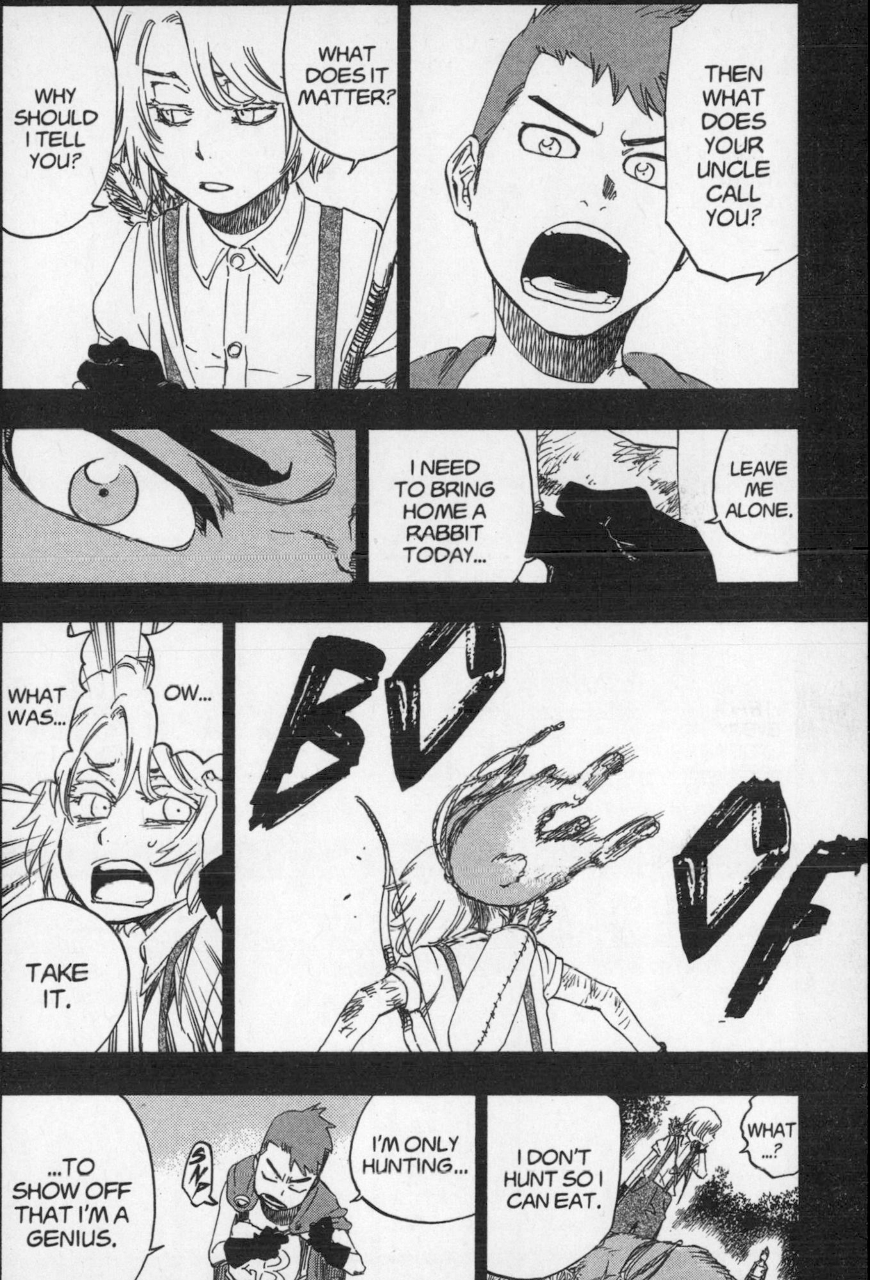
THEN WHAT DOES YOUR UNCLE CALL YOU?
WHAT DOES IT MATTER?
WHY SHOULD I TELL YOU?
LEAVE ME ALONE.
I NEED TO BRING HOME A RABBIT TODAY...
BOOF
OW...
WHAT WAS...
TAKE IT.
WHAT ...?
I DON'T HUNT SO I CAN EAT.
I'M ONLY HUNTING...
...TO SHOW OFF THAT I'M A GENIUS.

READ THIS WAY

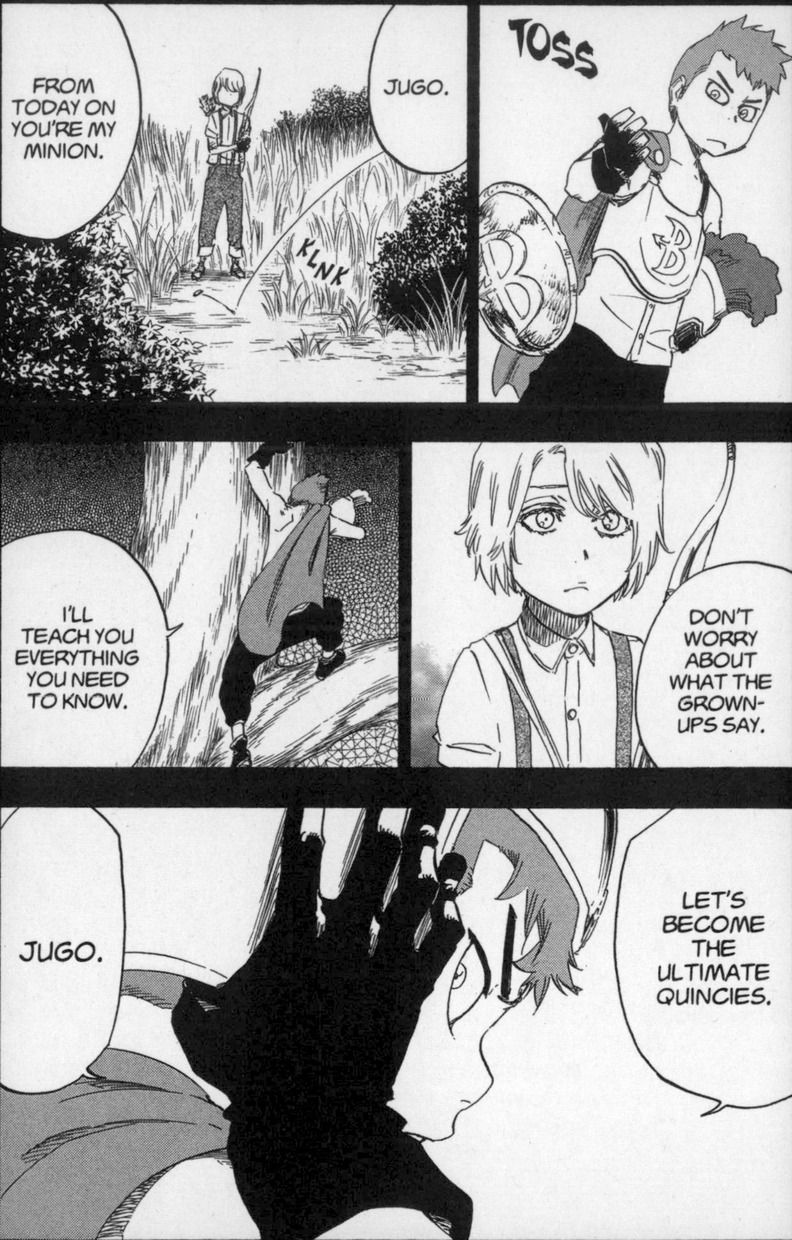
TOSS
JUGO.
FROM TODAY ON YOU'RE MY MINION.
KLNK
DON'T WORRY ABOUT WHAT THE GROWN-UPS SAY.
I'LL TEACH YOU EVERYTHING YOU NEED TO KNOW.
LET'S BECOME THE ULTIMATE QUINCIES.
JUGO.

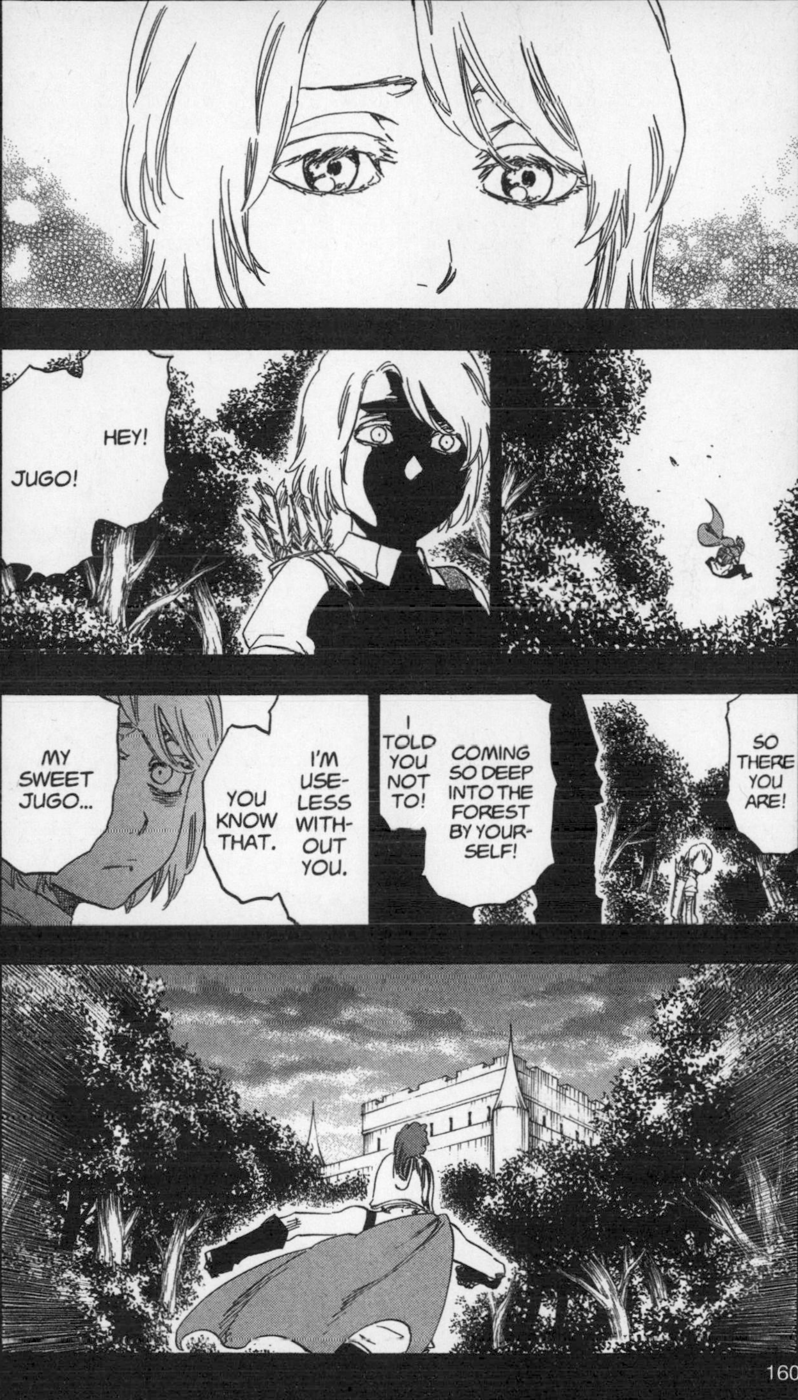
HEY!
JUGO!
SO THERE YOU ARE!
COMING SO DEEP INTO THE FOREST BY YOUR-SELF!
I TOLD YOU NOT TO!
I'M USE-LESS WITH-OUT YOU.
YOU KNOW THAT.
MY SWEET JUGO...

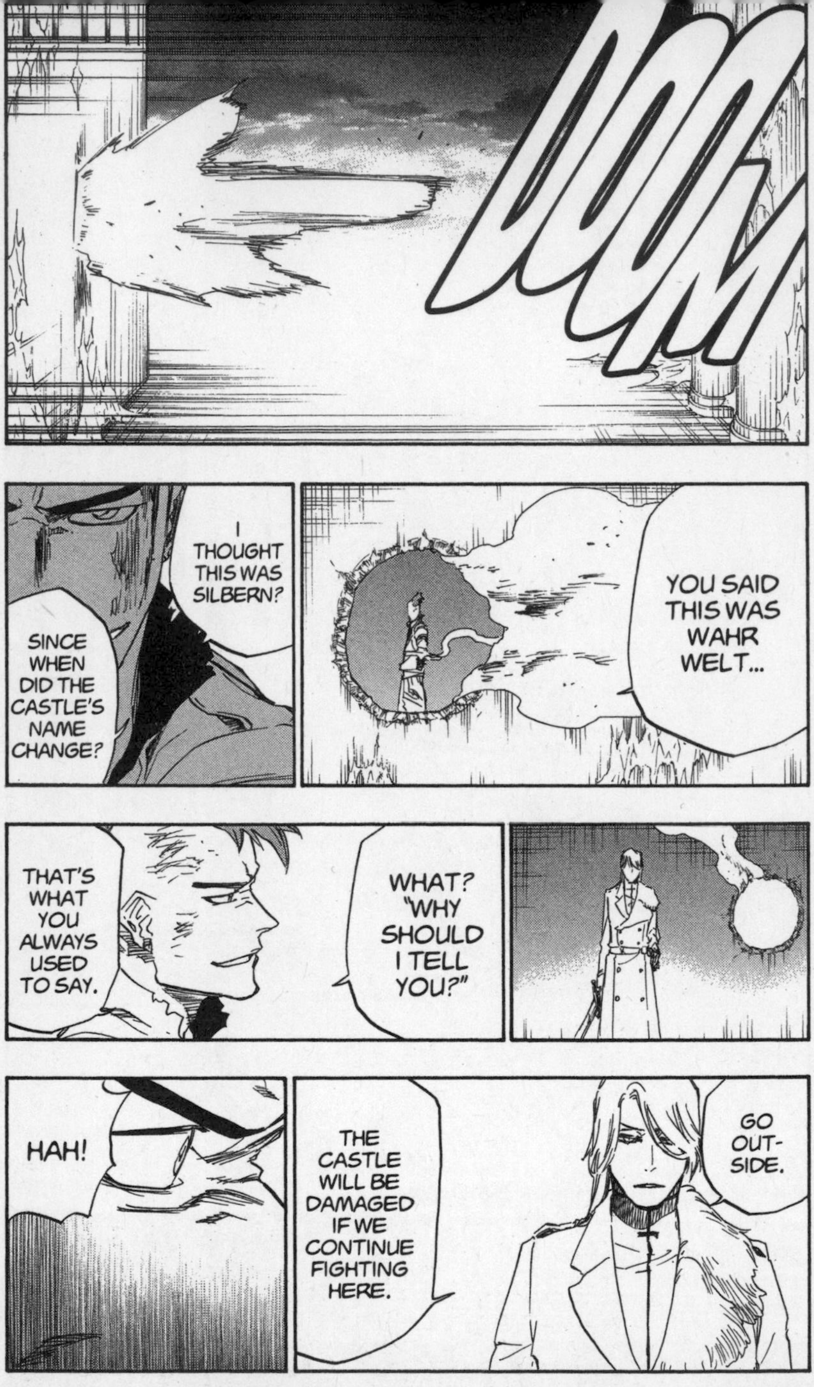
YOU SAID THIS WAS WAHR WELT...
I THOUGHT THIS WAS SILBERN?
SINCE WHEN DID THE CASTLE'S NAME CHANGE?
WHAT? "WHY SHOULD I TELL YOU?"
THAT'S WHAT YOU ALWAYS USED TO SAY.
GO OUT-SIDE.
THE CASTLE WILL BE DAMAGED IF WE CONTINUE FIGHTING HERE.
HAH!

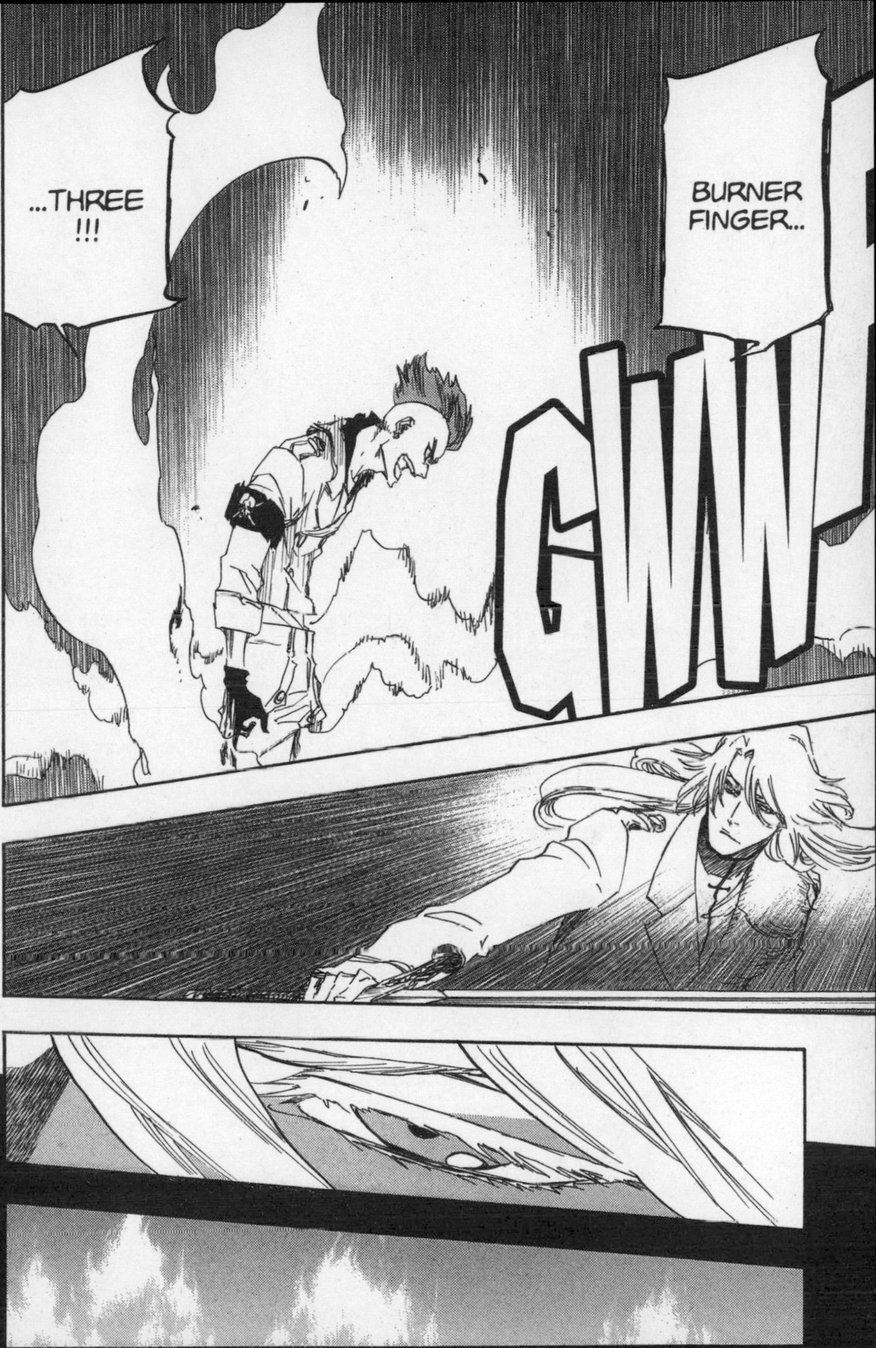
BURNER FINGER...
...THREE !!!
GWW

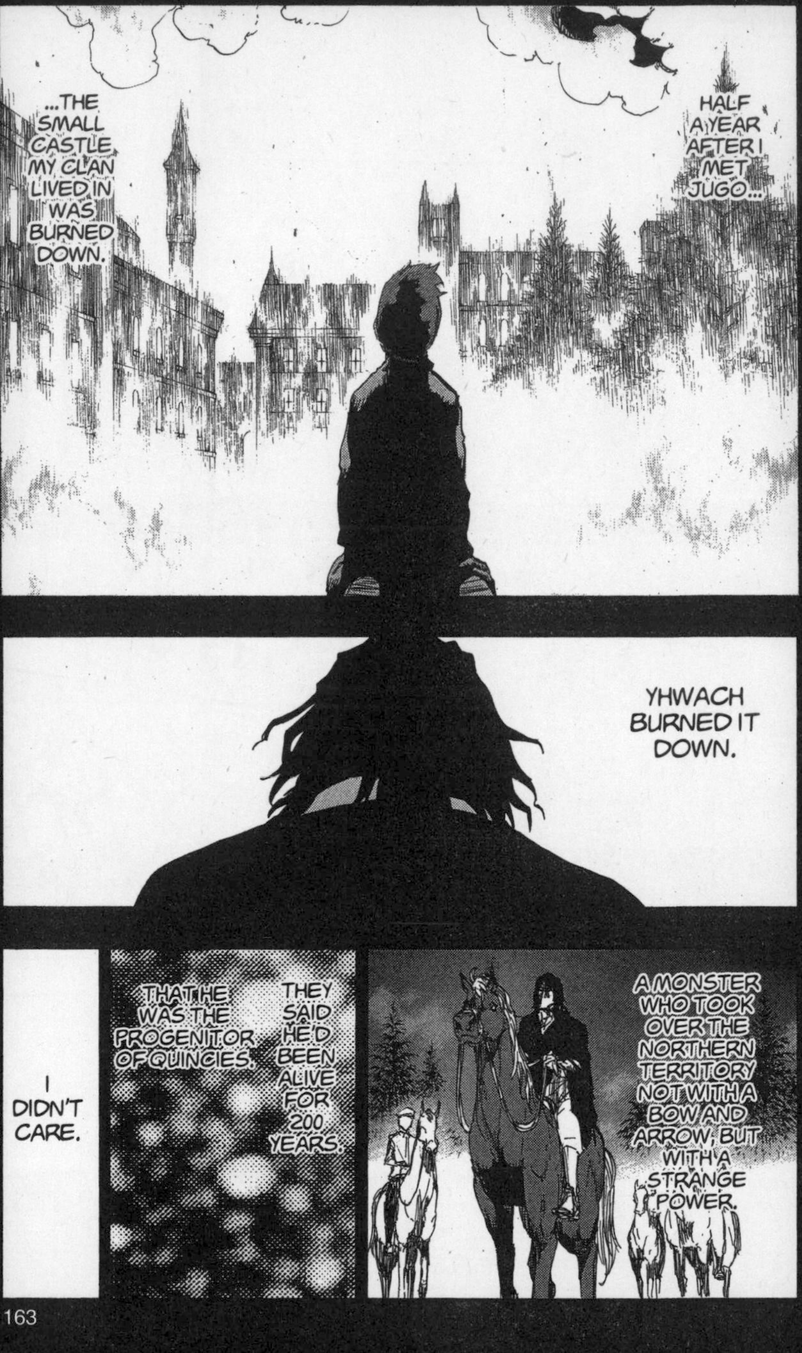
HALF A YEAR AFTER I MET JUGO...
...THE SMALL CASTLE MY CLAN LIVED IN WAS BURNED DOWN.
YHWACH BURNED IT DOWN.
A MONSTER WHO TOOK OVER THE NORTHERN TERRITORY NOT WITH A BOW AND ARROW, BUT WITH A STRANGE POWER.
THEY SAID HE'D BEEN ALIVE FOR 200 YEARS.
THAT HE WAS THE PROGENITOR OF QUINCIES.
I DIDN'T CARE.

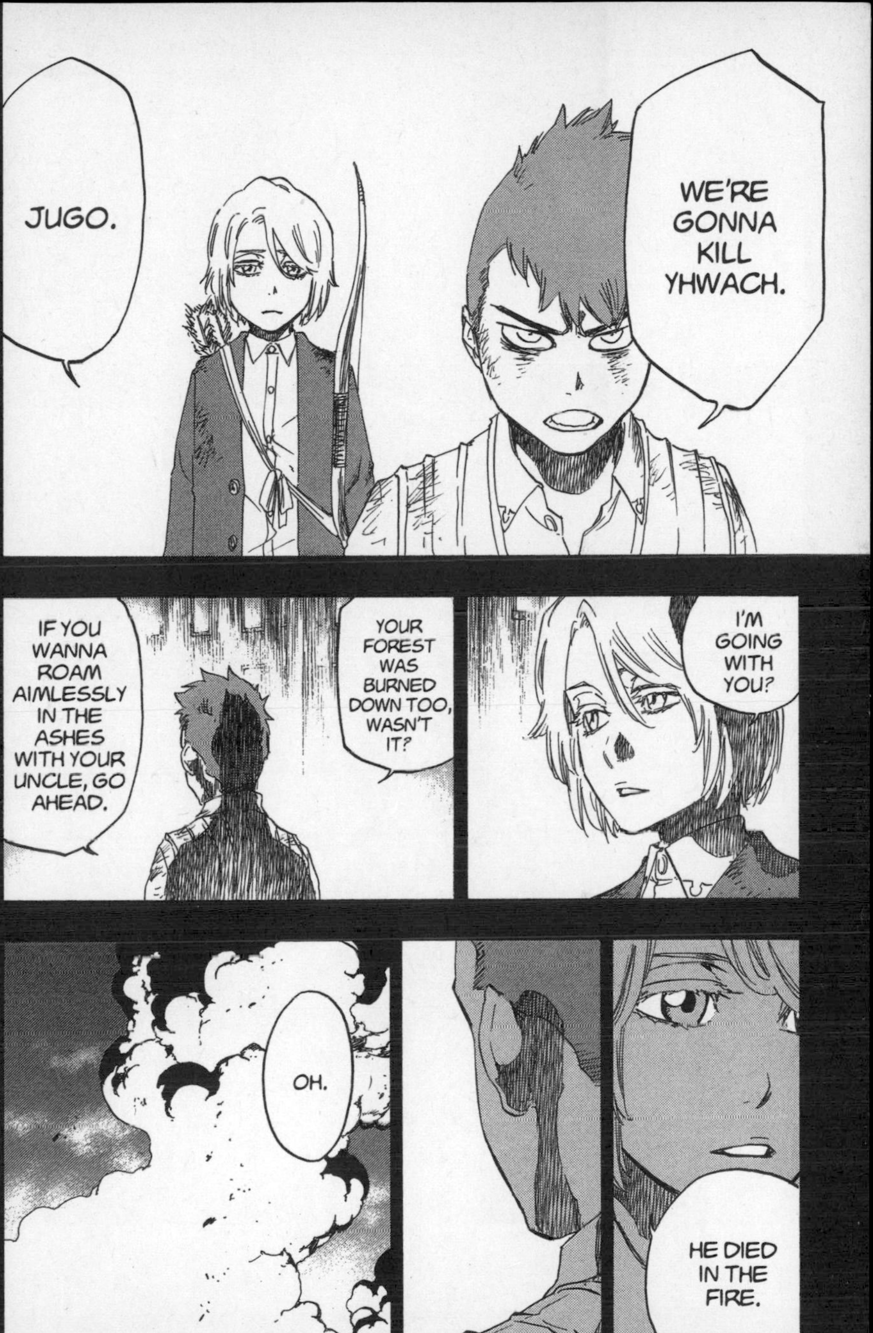
WE'RE GONNA KILL YHWACH.
JUGO.
I'M GOING WITH YOU?
YOUR FOREST WAS BURNED DOWN TOO, WASN'T IT?
IF YOU WANNA ROAM AIMLESSLY IN THE ASHES WITH YOUR UNCLE, GO AHEAD.
HE DIED IN THE FIRE.
OH.

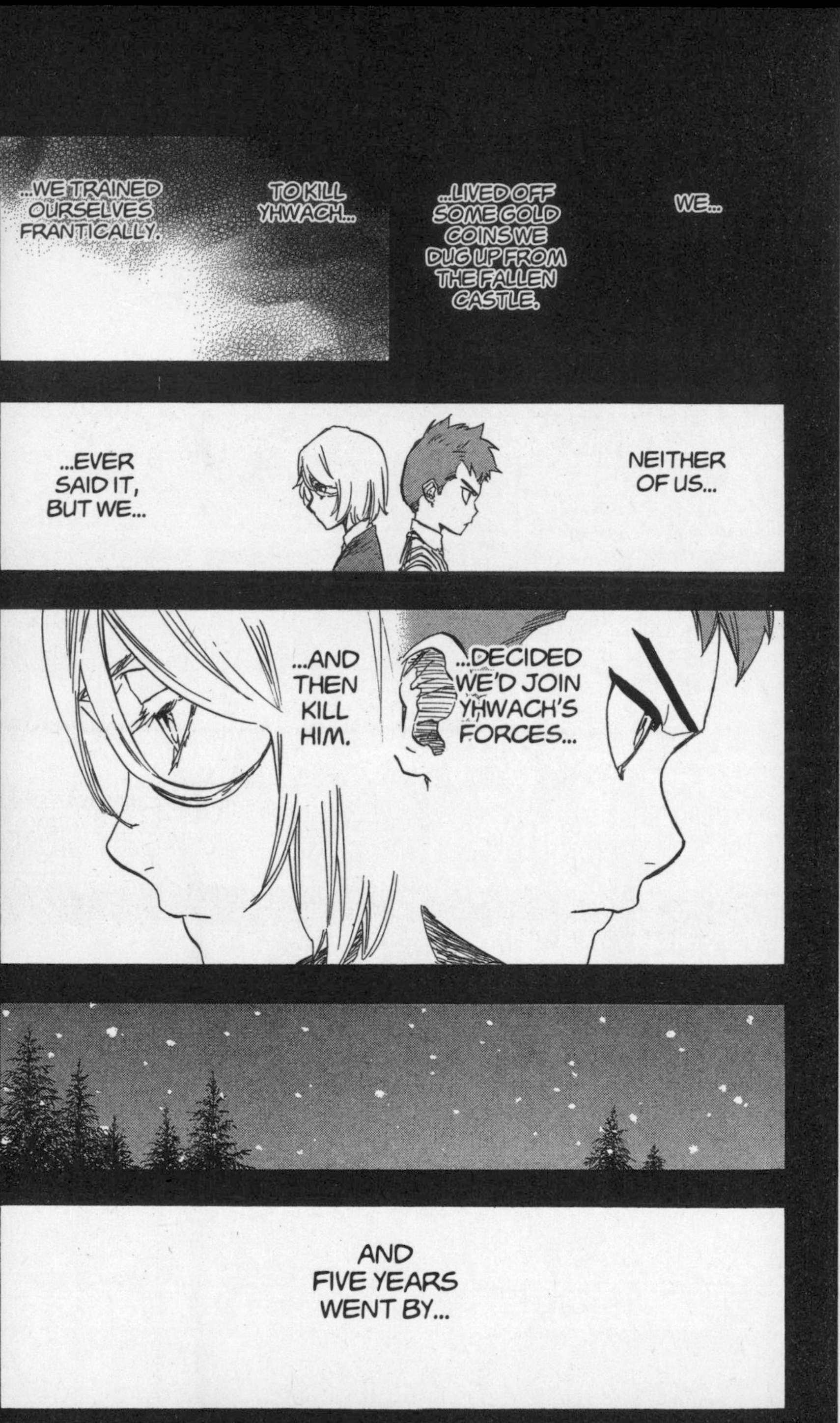
WE...
...LIVED OFF SOME GOLD COINS WE DUG UP FROM THE FALLEN CASTLE.
TO KILL YHWACH...
...WE TRAINED OURSELVES FRANTICALLY.
NEITHER OF US...
...EVER SAID IT, BUT WE...
...DECIDED WE'D JOIN YHWACH'S FORCES...
...AND THEN KILL HIM.
AND FIVE YEARS WENT BY...

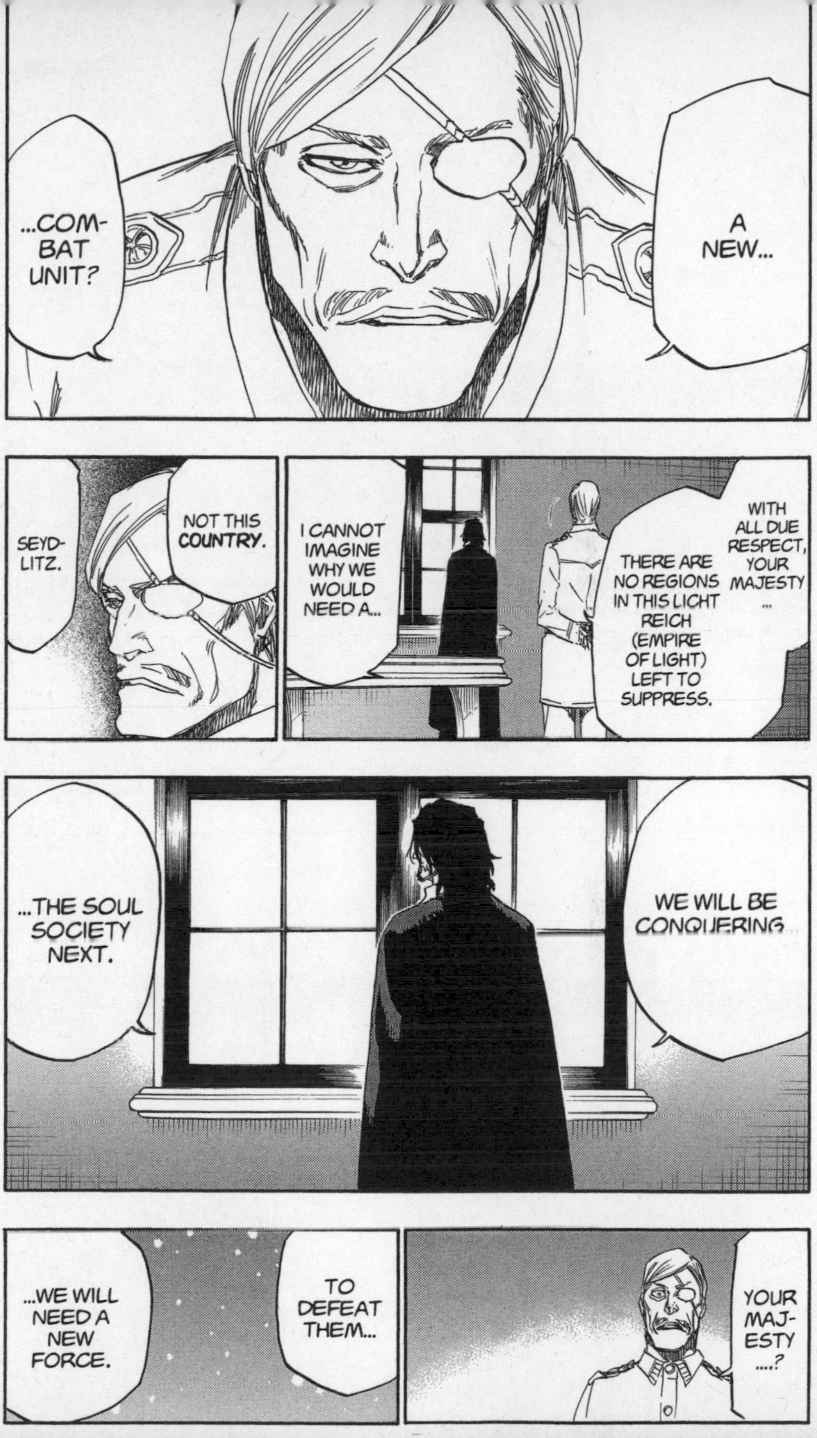
A NEW...
...COMBAT UNIT?
WITH ALL DUE RESPECT, YOUR MAJESTY...
THERE ARE NO REGIONS IN THIS LICHT REICH (EMPIRE OF LIGHT) LEFT TO SUPPRESS.
I CANNOT IMAGINE WHY WE WOULD NEED A...
NOT THIS COUNTRY.
SEYDLITZ.
WE WILL BE CONQUERING...
...THE SOUL SOCIETY NEXT.
YOUR MAJESTY....?
TO DEFEAT THEM...
...WE WILL NEED A NEW FORCE.

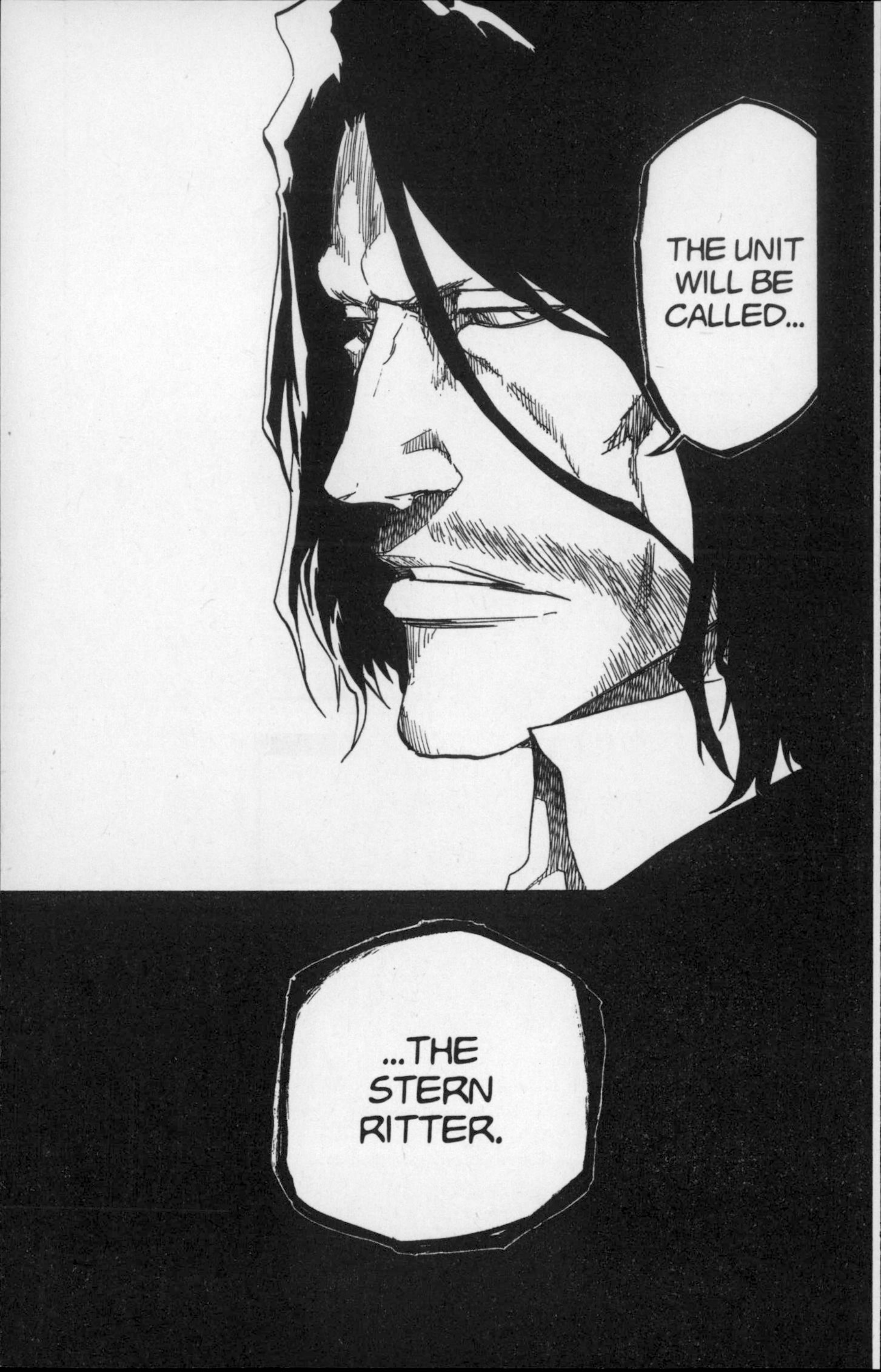
THE UNIT WILL BE CALLED...
...THE STERN RITTER.

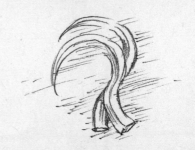

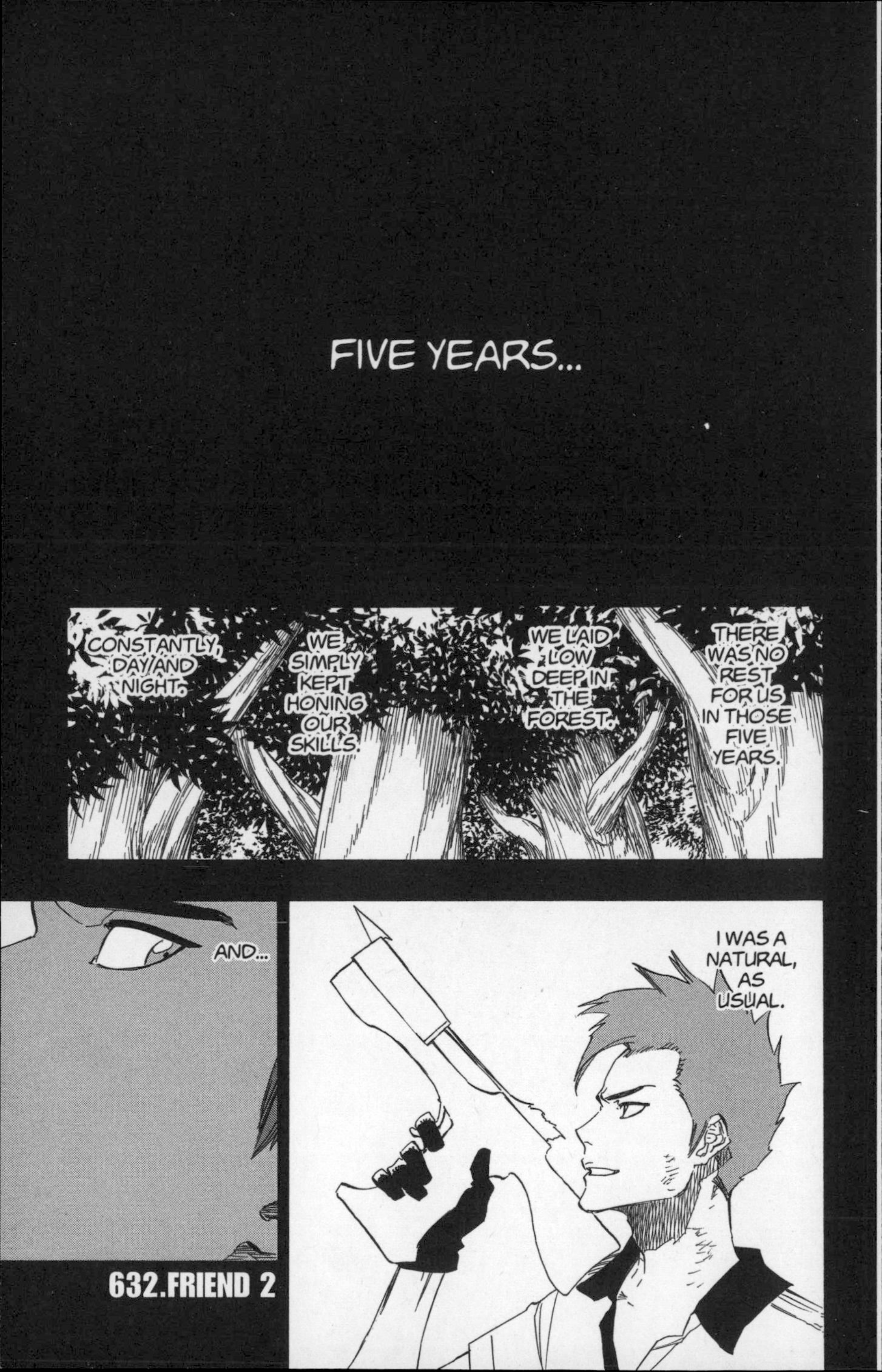
FIVE YEARS...
THERE WAS NO REST FOR US IN THOSE FIVE YEARS.
WE LAID LOW DEEP IN THE FOREST.
WE SIMPLY KEPT HONING OUR SKILLS.
CONSTANTLY, DAY AND NIGHT.
I WAS A NATURAL, AS USUAL.
AND...
632.FRIEND 2

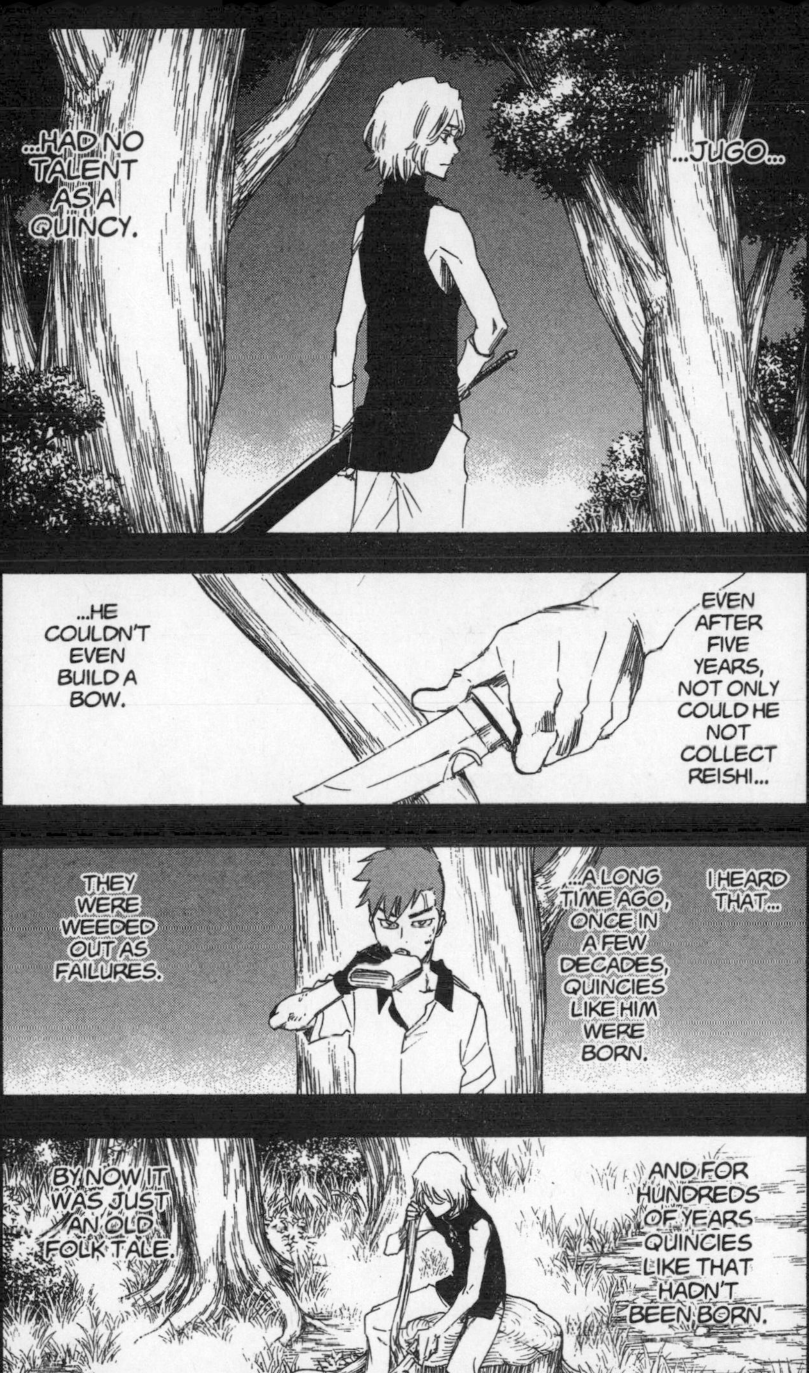
...JUGO...
...HAD NO TALENT AS A QUINCY.
EVEN AFTER FIVE YEARS, NOT ONLY COULD HE NOT COLLECT REISHI...
...HE COULDN'T EVEN BUILD A BOW.
I HEARD THAT...
...A LONG TIME AGO, ONCE IN A FEW DECADES, QUINCIES LIKE HIM WERE BORN.
THEY WERE WEEDED OUT AS FAILURES.
AND FOR HUNDREDS OF YEARS QUINCIES LIKE THAT HADN'T BEEN BORN.
BY NOW IT WAS JUST AN OLD FOLK TALE.

READ THIS WAY

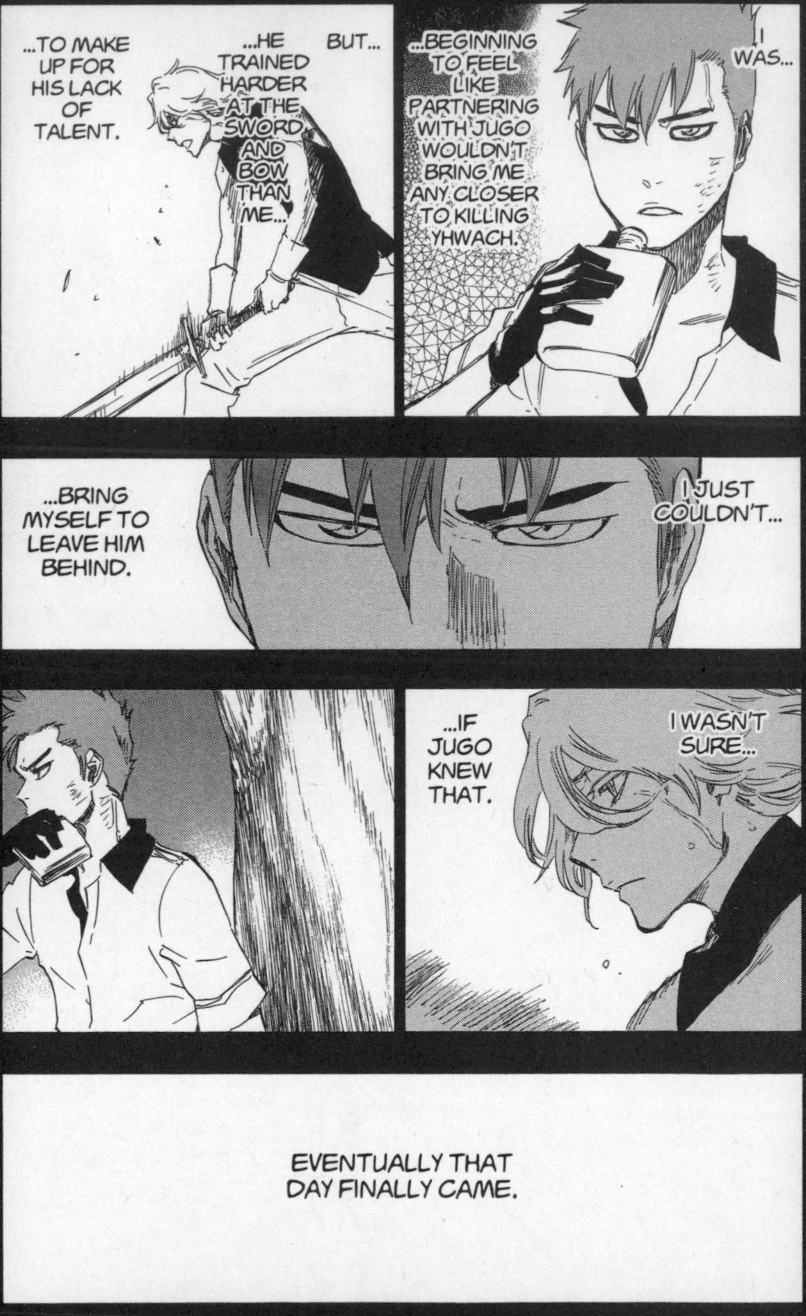
I WAS...
...BEGINNING TO FEEL LIKE PARTNERING WITH JUGO WOULDN'T BRING ME ANY CLOSER TO KILLING YHWACH.
BUT...
...HE TRAINED HARDER AT THE SWORD AND BOW THAN ME...
...TO MAKE UP FOR HIS LACK OF TALENT.
I JUST COULDN'T...
...BRING MYSELF TO LEAVE HIM BEHIND.
I WASN'T SURE...
...IF JUGO KNEW THAT.
EVENTUALLY THAT DAY FINALLY CAME.

bleach   **632.**

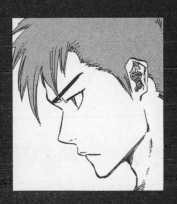 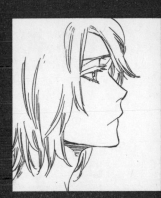

friend   2

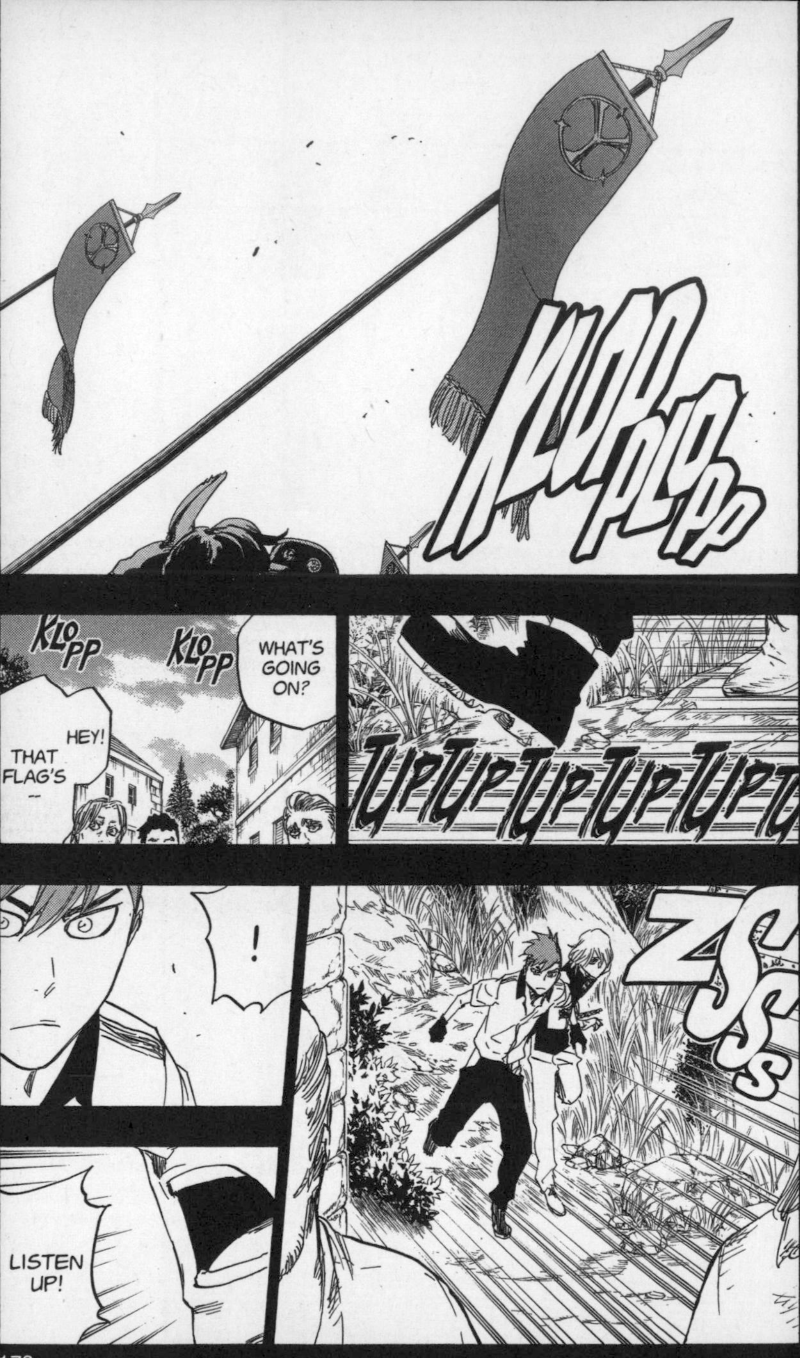
KLOPP KLOPP
TUP TUP TUP TUP TUP TUP
WHAT'S GOING ON?
KLOPP
KLOPP
HEY! THAT FLAG'S --
ZSSS
!
LISTEN UP!

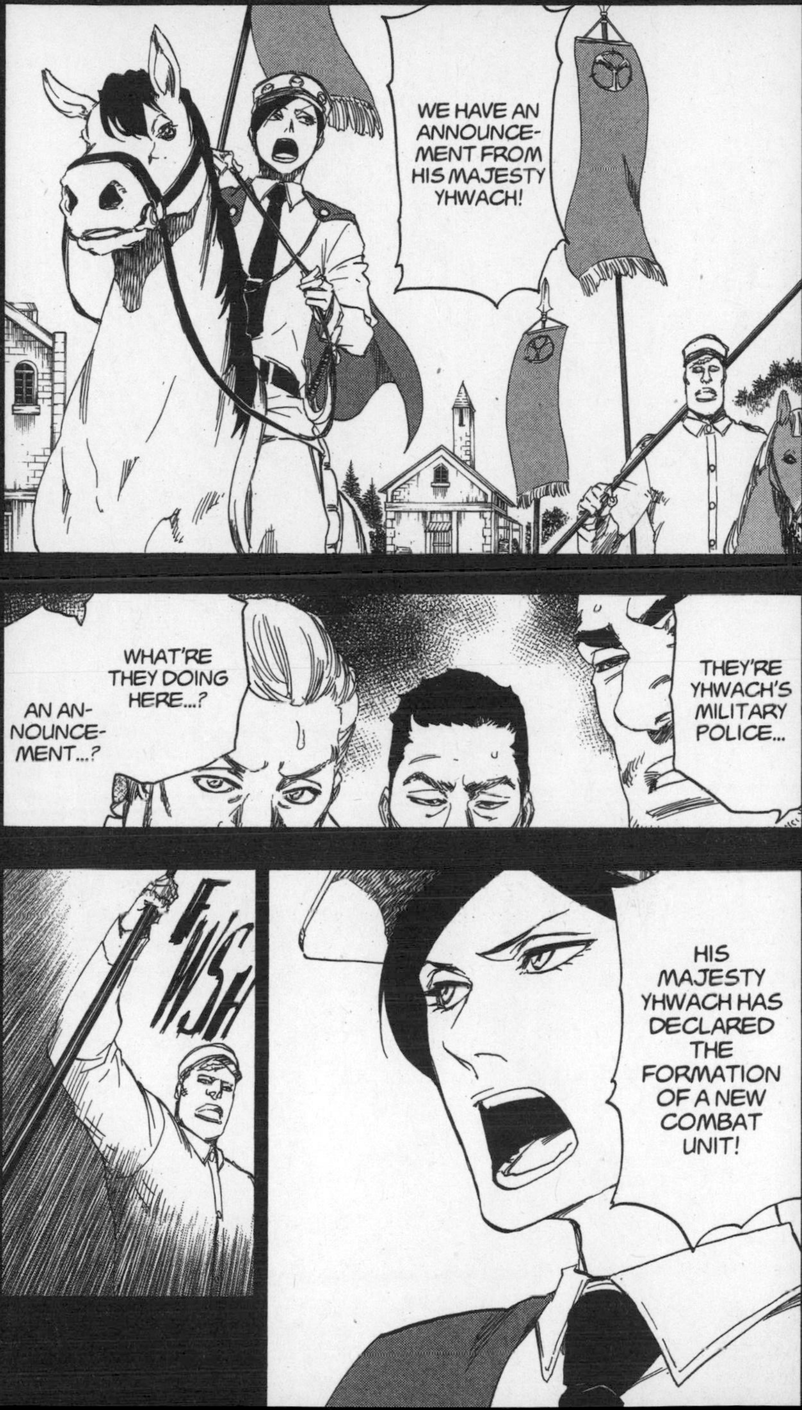
WE HAVE AN ANNOUNCEMENT FROM HIS MAJESTY YHWACH!
THEY'RE YHWACH'S MILITARY POLICE...
WHAT'RE THEY DOING HERE...?
AN ANNOUNCEMENT...?
HIS MAJESTY YHWACH HAS DECLARED THE FORMATION OF A NEW COMBAT UNIT!
FWSH

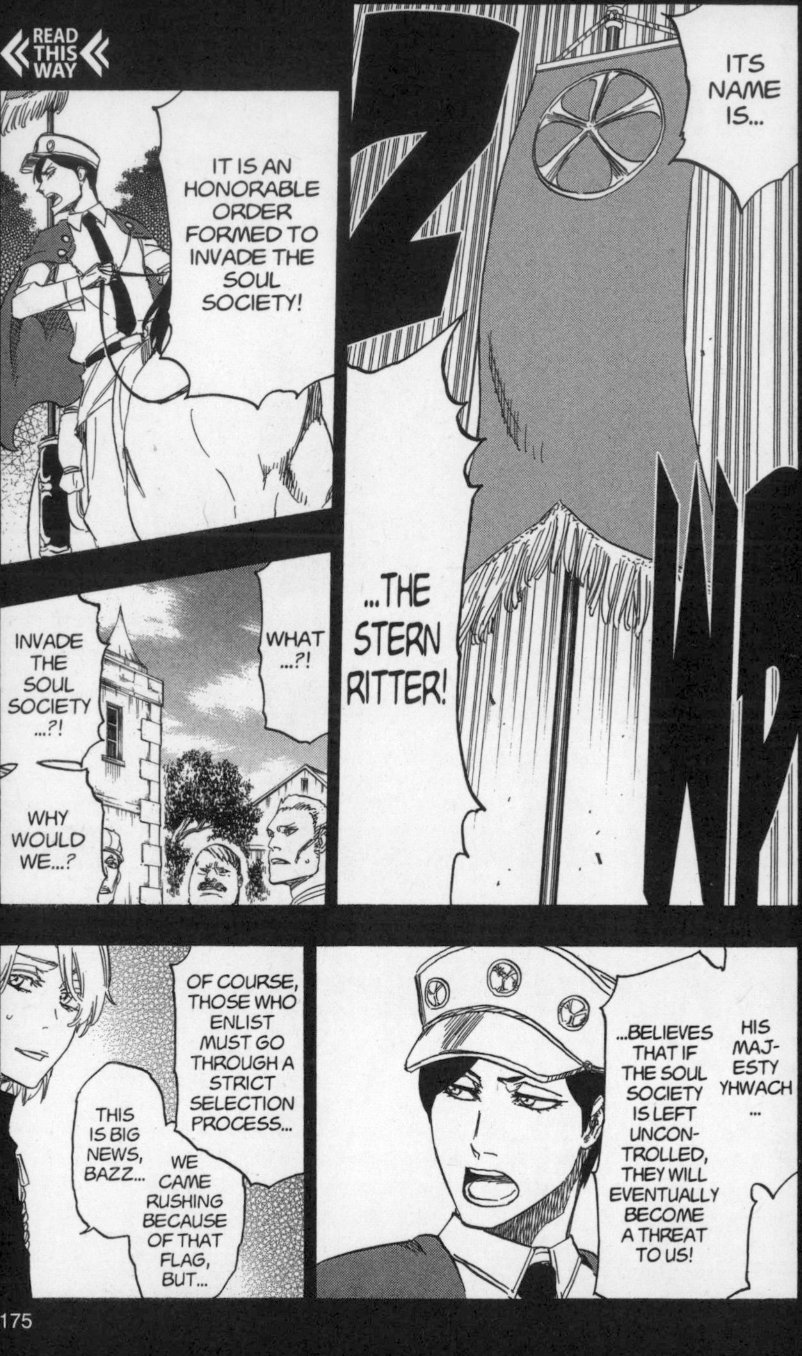
READ THIS WAY
ITS NAME IS...
...THE STERN RITTER!
IT IS AN HONORABLE ORDER FORMED TO INVADE THE SOUL SOCIETY!
WHAT...?!
INVADE THE SOUL SOCIETY...?!
WHY WOULD WE...?
HIS MAJESTY YHWACH...
...BELIEVES THAT IF THE SOUL SOCIETY IS LEFT UNCONTROLLED, THEY WILL EVENTUALLY BECOME A THREAT TO US!
OF COURSE, THOSE WHO ENLIST MUST GO THROUGH A STRICT SELECTION PROCESS...
THIS IS BIG NEWS, BAZZ...
WE CAME RUSHING BECAUSE OF THAT FLAG, BUT...

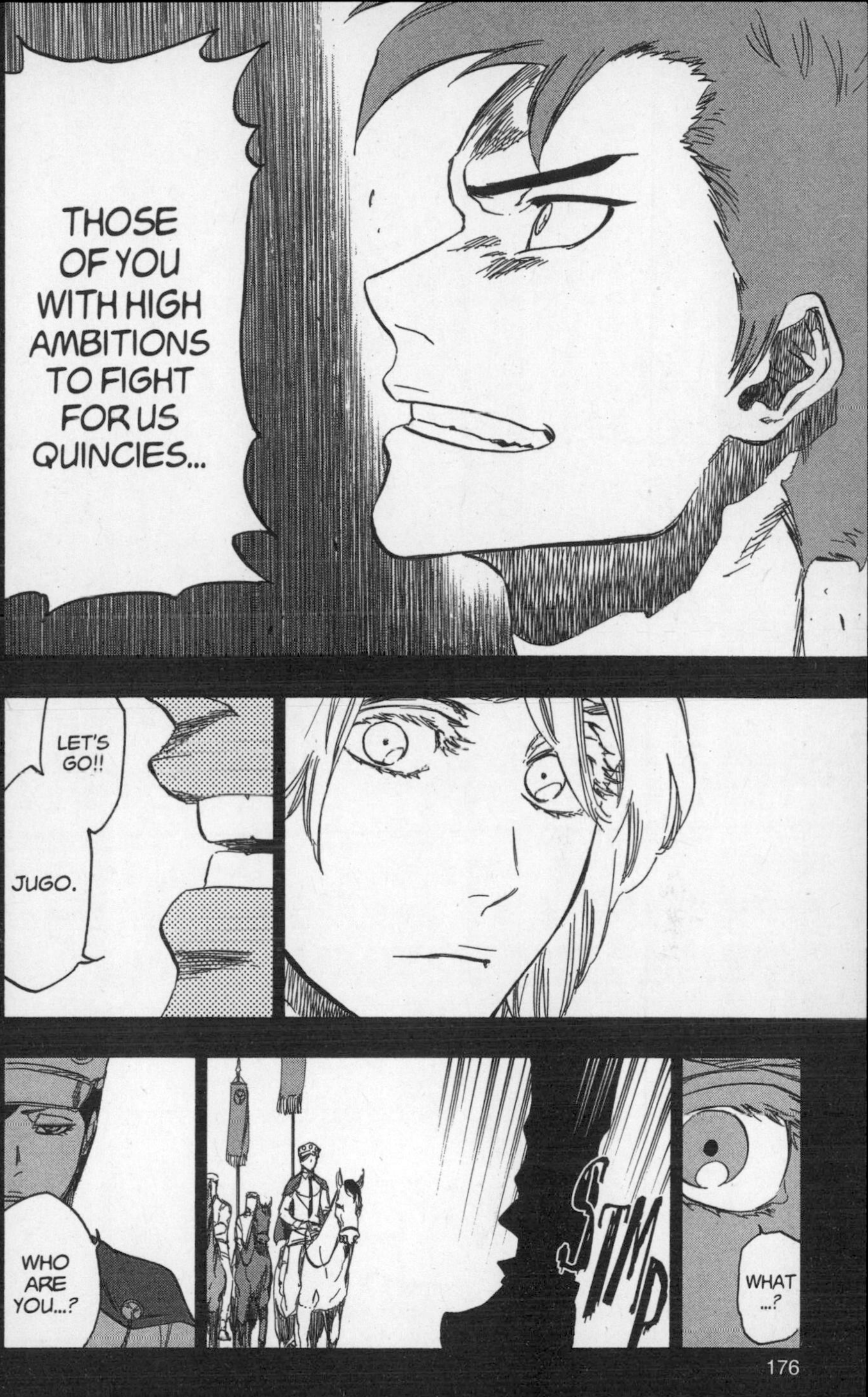
THOSE OF YOU WITH HIGH AMBITIONS TO FIGHT FOR US QUINCIES...
LET'S GO!!
JUGO.
WHAT...?
STMP
WHO ARE YOU...?

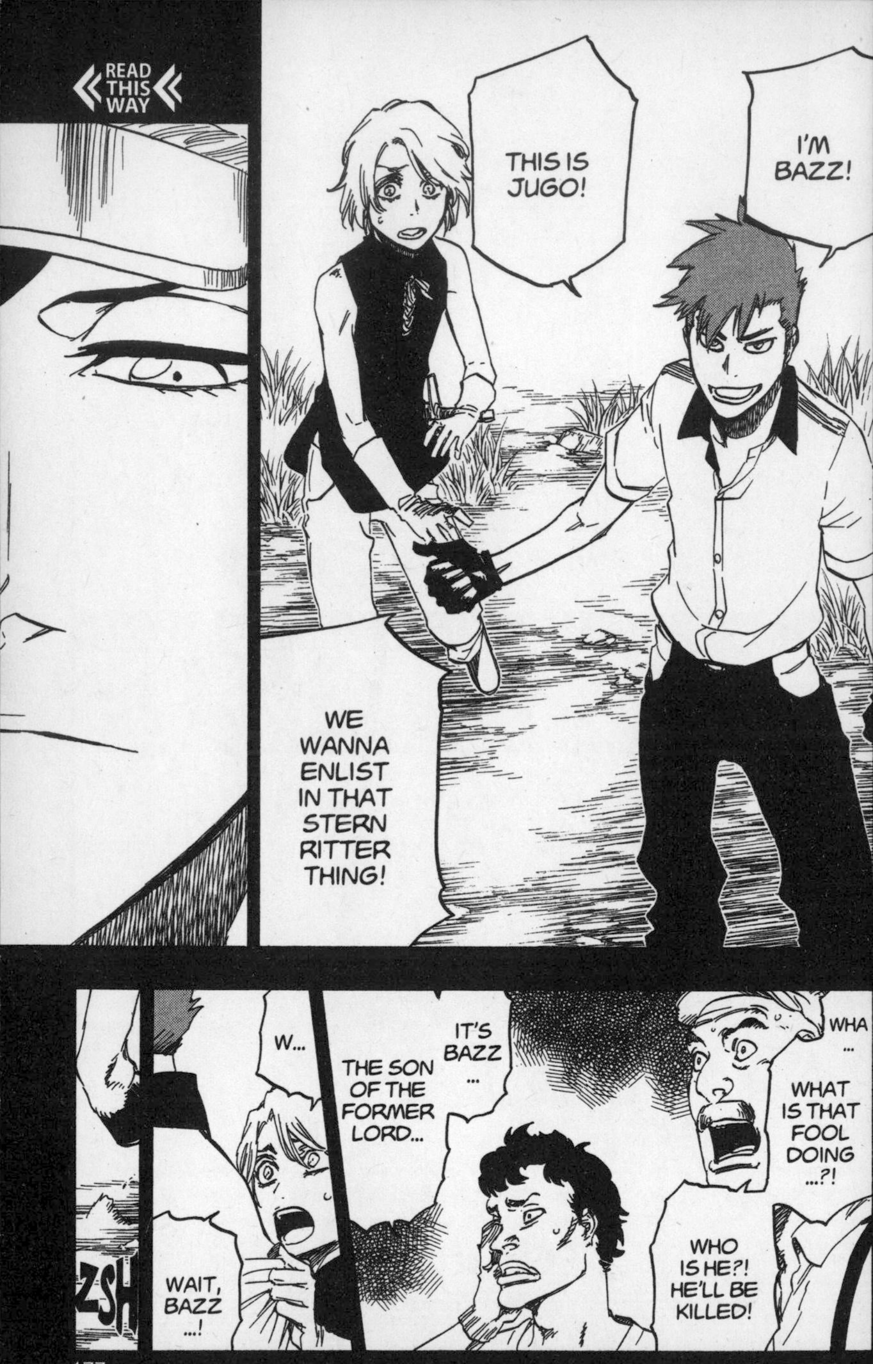
READ THIS WAY
I'M BAZZ!
THIS IS JUGO!
WE WANNA ENLIST IN THAT STERN RITTER THING!
WHA...
WHAT IS THAT FOOL DOING ...?!
WHO IS HE?! HE'LL BE KILLED!
IT'S BAZZ...
THE SON OF THE FORMER LORD...
W...
WAIT, BAZZ...!
ZSH

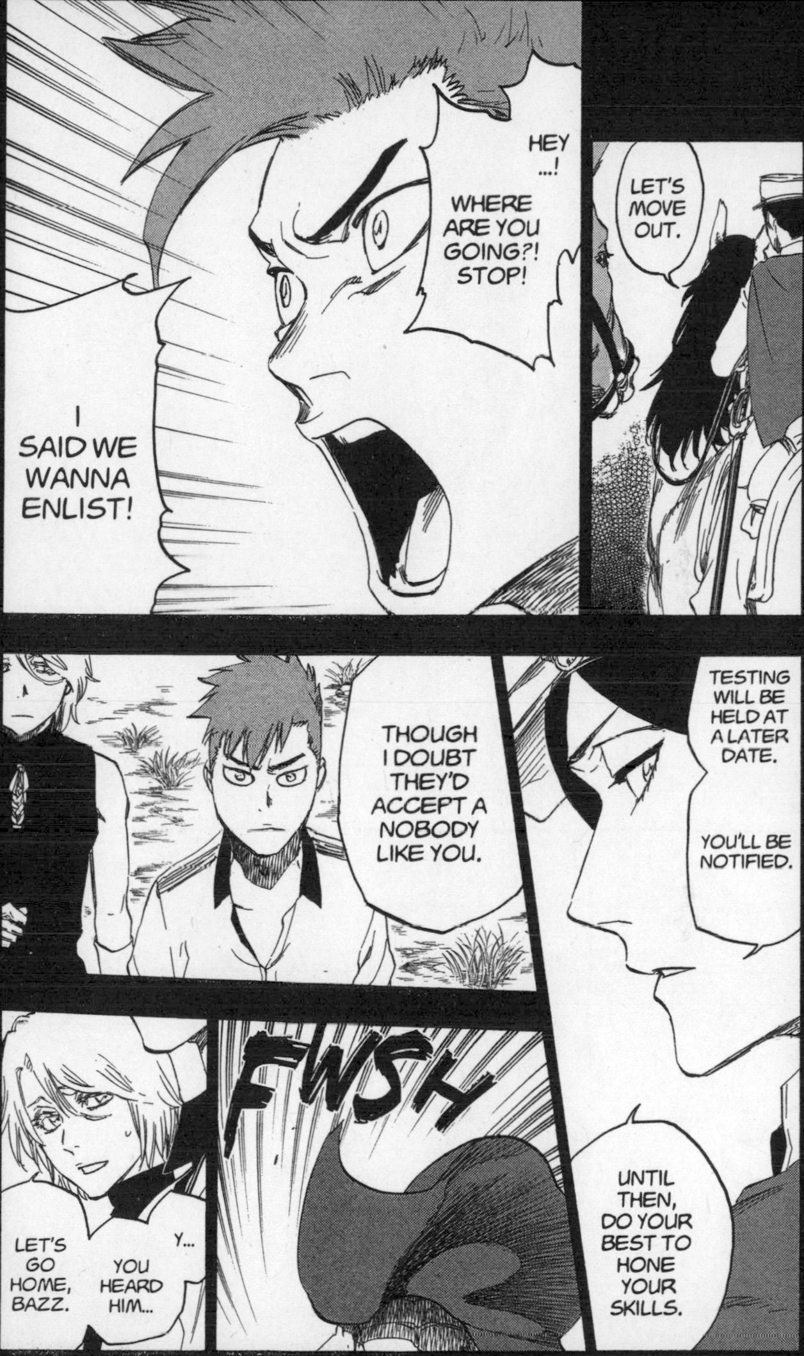
LET'S MOVE OUT.
HEY ...!
WHERE ARE YOU GOING?! STOP!
I SAID WE WANNA ENLIST!
TESTING WILL BE HELD AT A LATER DATE.
YOU'LL BE NOTIFIED.
UNTIL THEN, DO YOUR BEST TO HONE YOUR SKILLS.
THOUGH I DOUBT THEY'D ACCEPT A NOBODY LIKE YOU.
FWSH
Y...
YOU HEARD HIM...
LET'S GO HOME, BAZZ.

READ THIS WAY

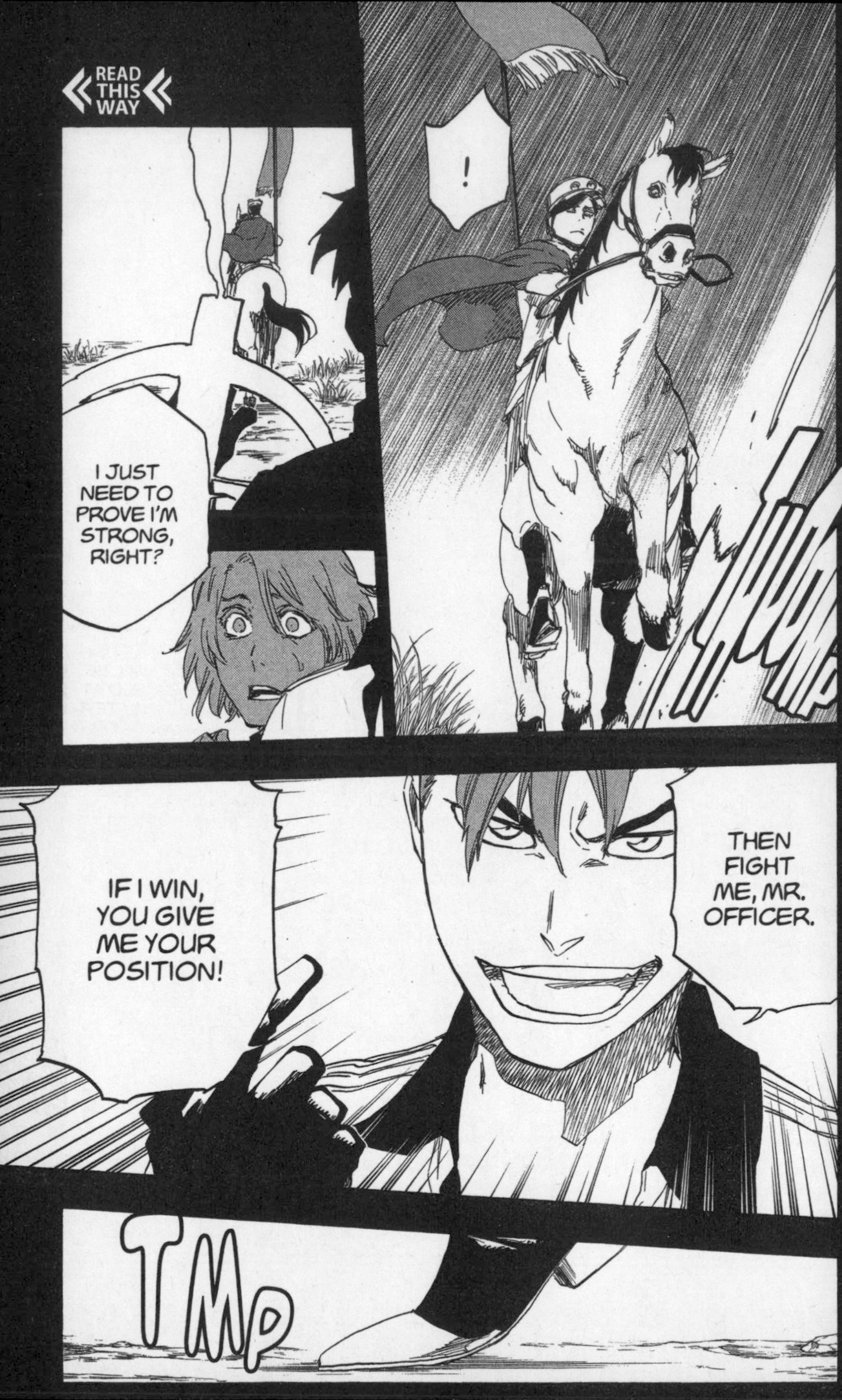
!
I JUST NEED TO PROVE I'M STRONG, RIGHT?
THEN FIGHT ME, MR. OFFICER.
IF I WIN, YOU GIVE ME YOUR POSITION!
TMP

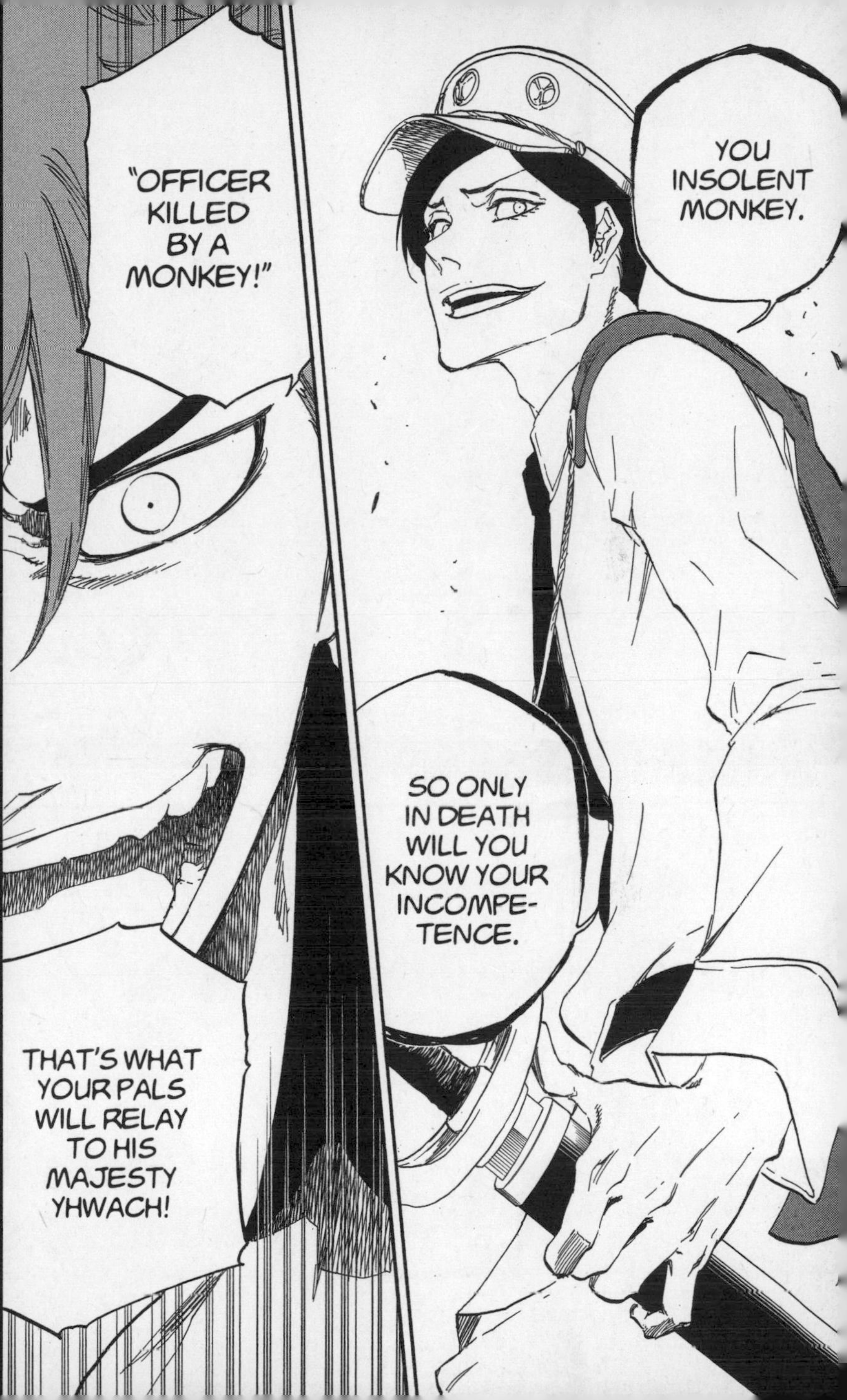
YOU INSOLENT MONKEY.
SO ONLY IN DEATH WILL YOU KNOW YOUR INCOMPE- TENCE.
"OFFICER KILLED BY A MONKEY!"
THAT'S WHAT YOUR PALS WILL RELAY TO HIS MAJESTY YHWACH!

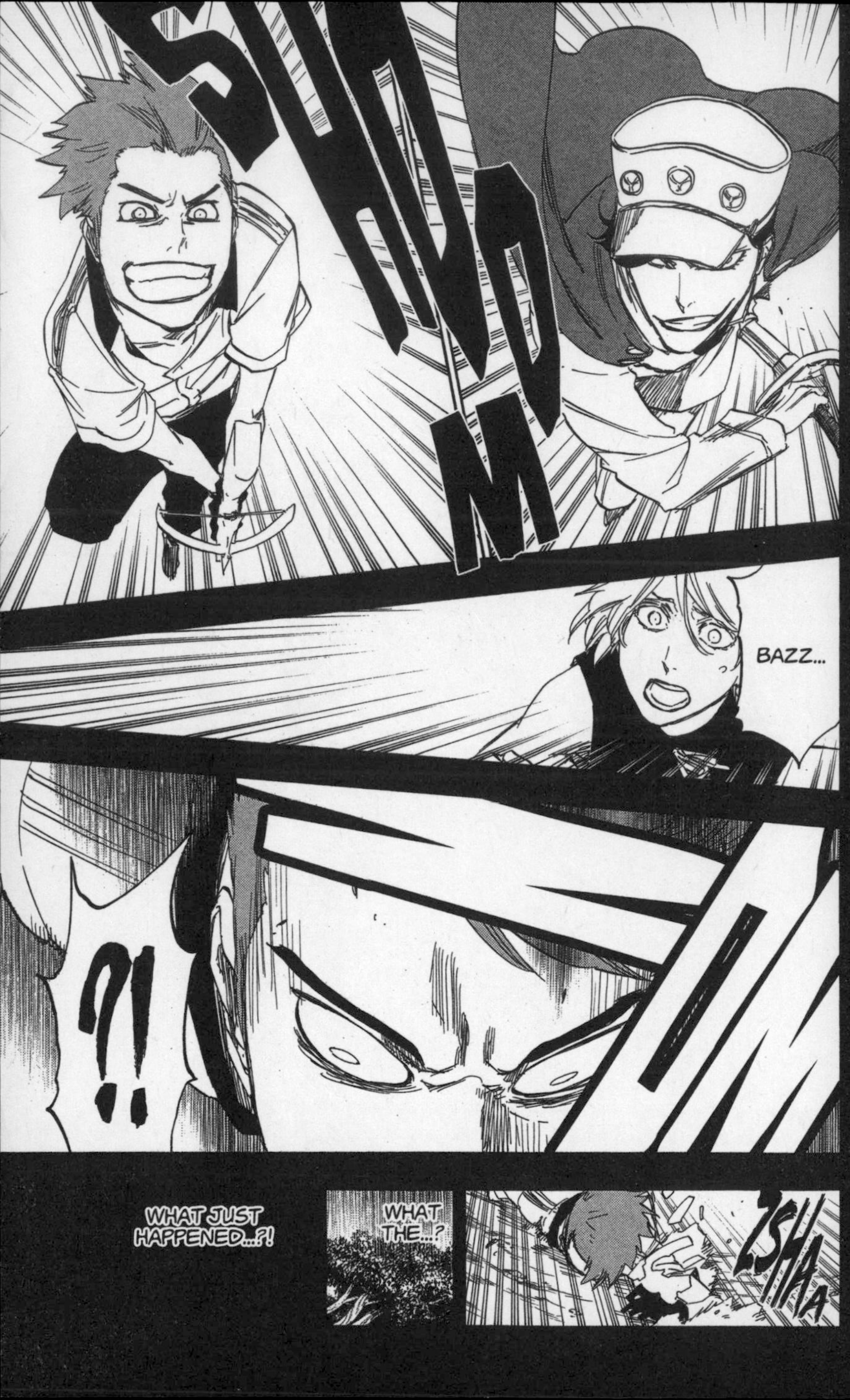
SHOOM
BAZZ...
?!!
WHAT THE...?
WHAT JUST HAPPENED...?!

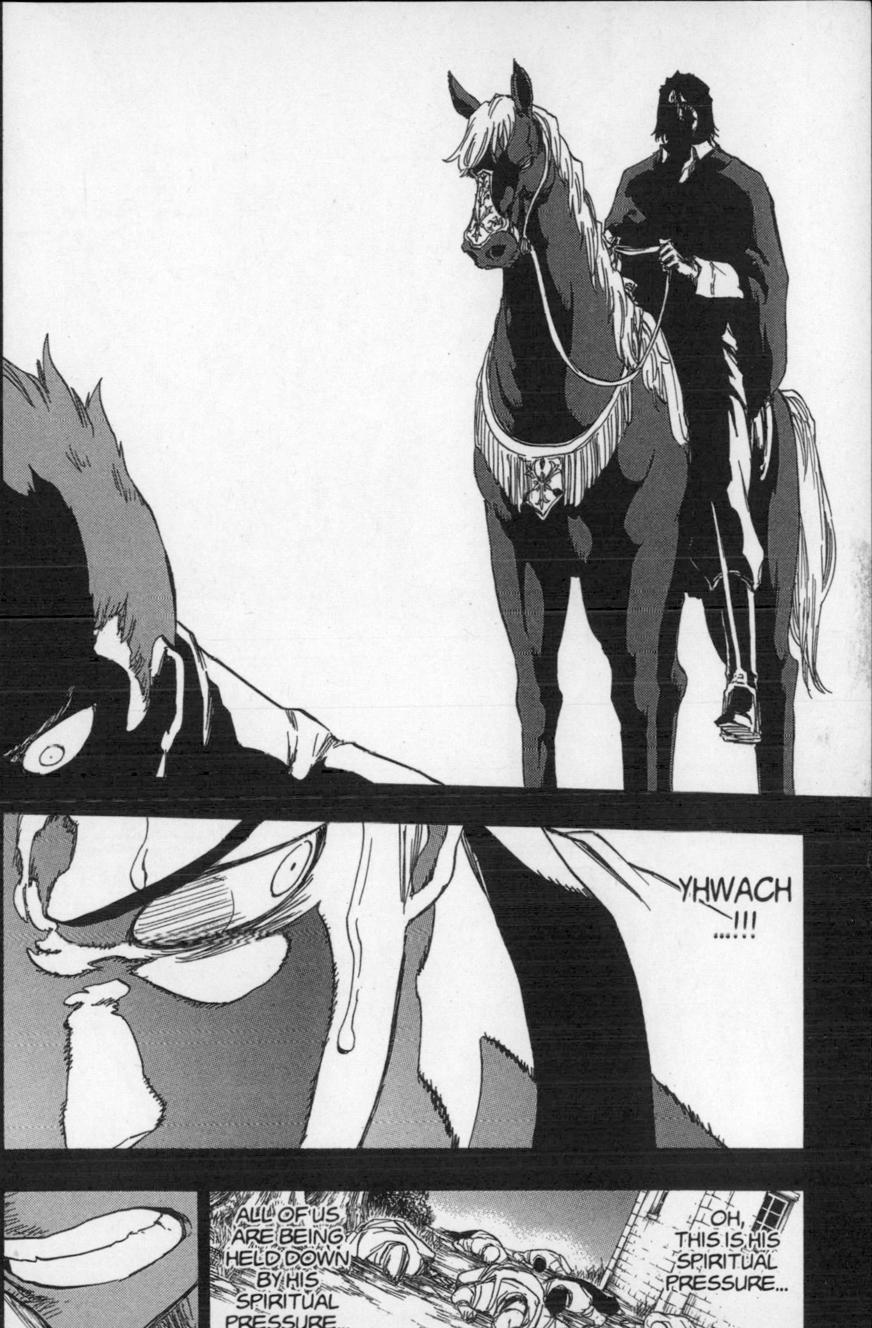
YHWACH ...!!!
OH, THIS IS HIS SPIRITUAL PRESSURE...
ALL OF US ARE BEING HELD DOWN BY HIS SPIRITUAL PRESSURE...

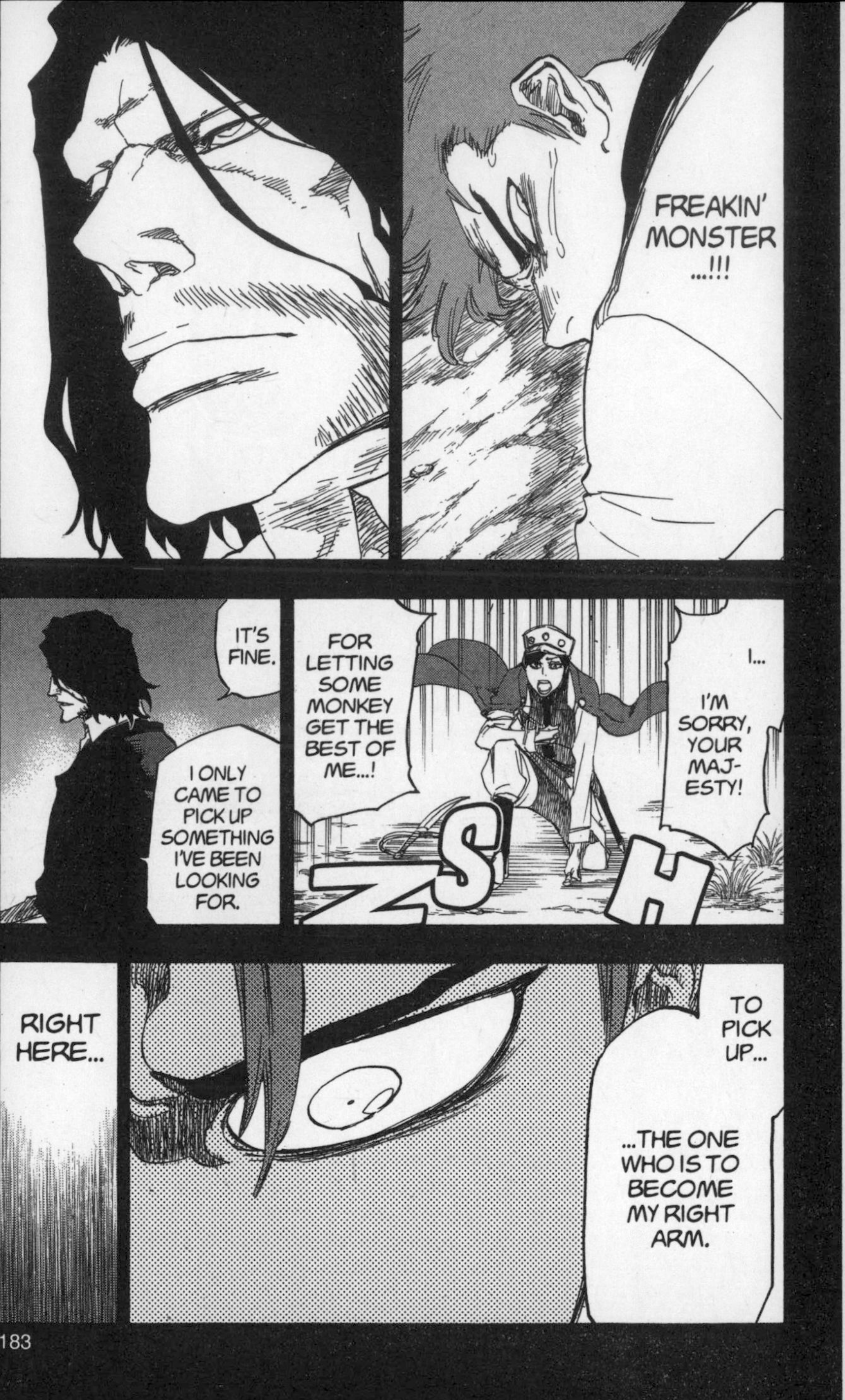
FREAKIN' MONSTER ...!!!
I... I'M SORRY, YOUR MAJ-ESTY!
FOR LETTING SOME MONKEY GET THE BEST OF ME...!
ZSH
IT'S FINE.
I ONLY CAME TO PICK UP SOMETHING I'VE BEEN LOOKING FOR.
TO PICK UP...
...THE ONE WHO IS TO BECOME MY RIGHT ARM.
RIGHT HERE...

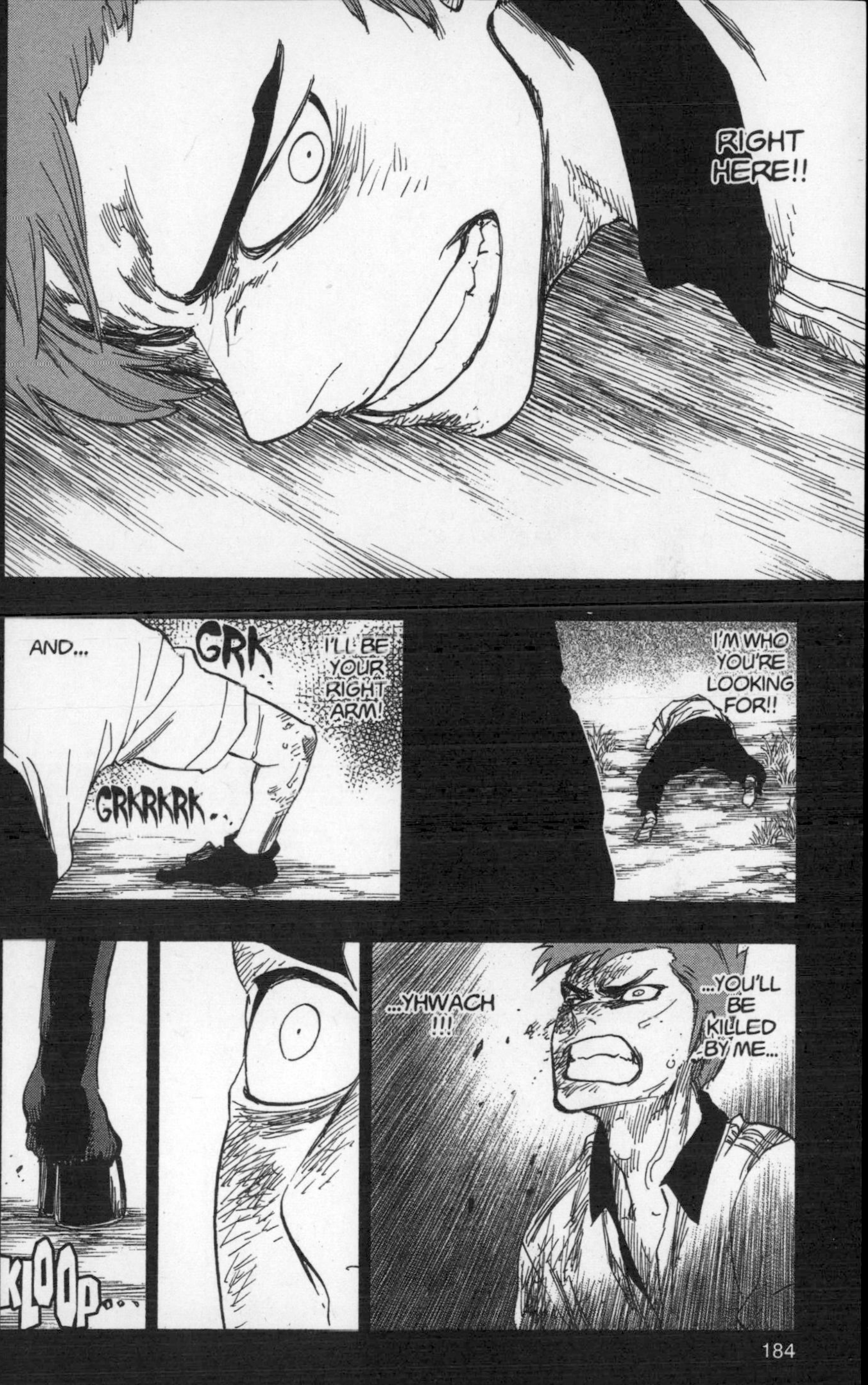
RIGHT HERE!!
I'M WHO YOU'RE LOOKING FOR!!
I'LL BE YOUR RIGHT ARM!
GRK
AND...
GRKRKRK...
...YOU'LL BE KILLED BY ME...
...YHWACH!!!
KLOOP...

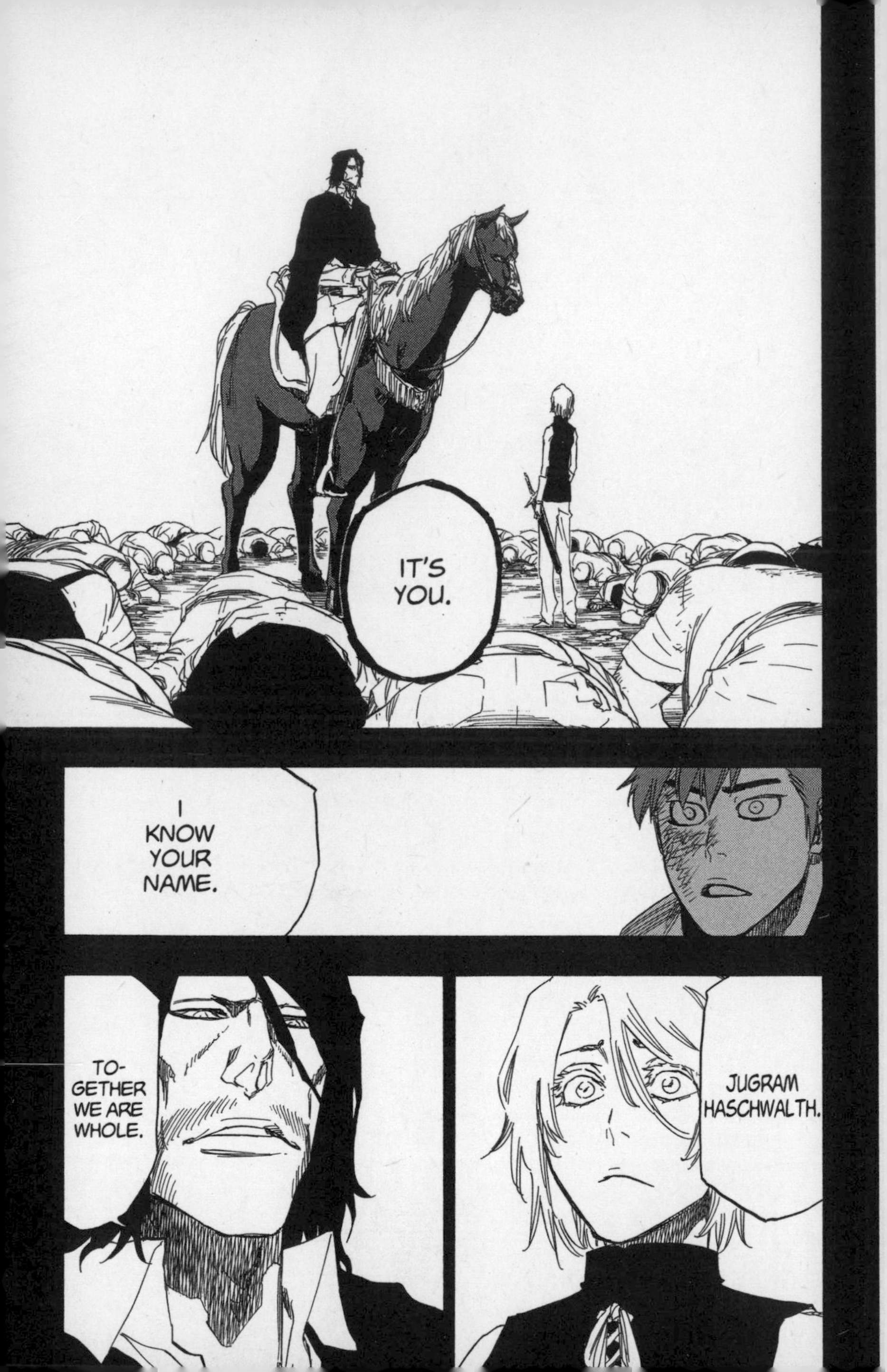
IT'S YOU.
I KNOW YOUR NAME.
JUGRAM HASCHWALTH.
TO-GETHER WE ARE WHOLE.

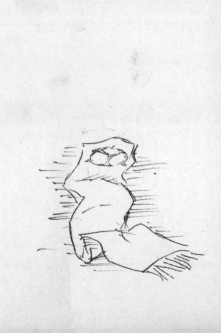

CONTI
NUED
IN
BLEACH
70

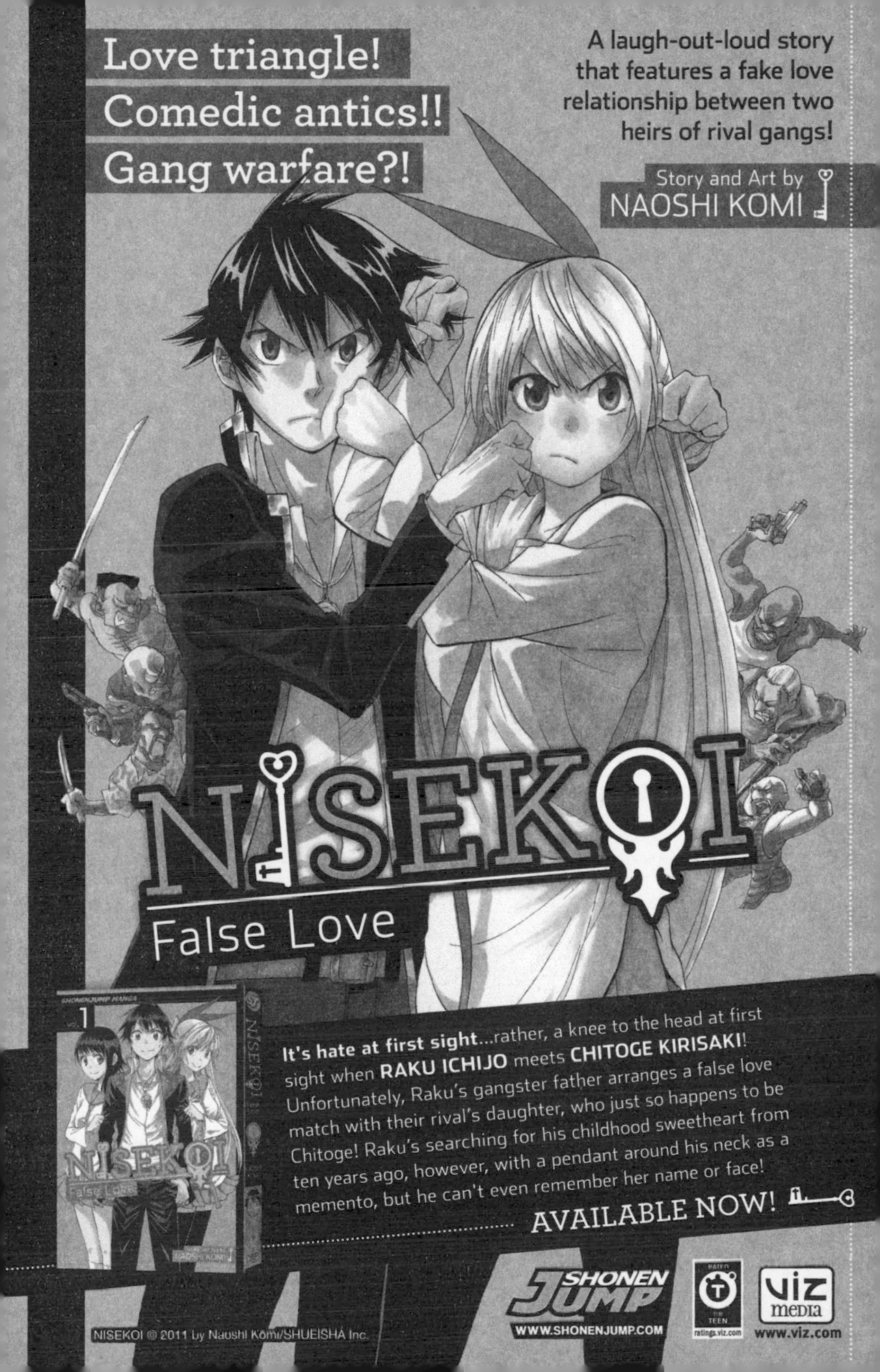

Love triangle!
Comedic antics!!
Gang warfare?!
A laugh-out-loud story that features a fake love relationship between two heirs of rival gangs!
Story and Art by
NAOSHI KOMI
NISEKOI
False Love
SHONEN JUMP MANGA
Vol. 1
NISEKOI
False Love
It's hate at first sight...rather, a knee to the head at first sight when RAKU ICHIJO meets CHITOGE KIRISAKI! Unfortunately, Raku's gangster father arranges a false love match with their rival's daughter, who just so happens to be Chitoge! Raku's searching for his childhood sweetheart from ten years ago, however, with a pendant around his neck as a memento, but he can't even remember her name or face!
AVAILABLE NOW!
SHONEN JUMP
WWW.SHONENJUMP.COM
RATED T TEEN
ratings.viz.com
VIZ media
www.viz.com
NISEKOI © 2011 by Naoshi Komi/SHUEISHA Inc.

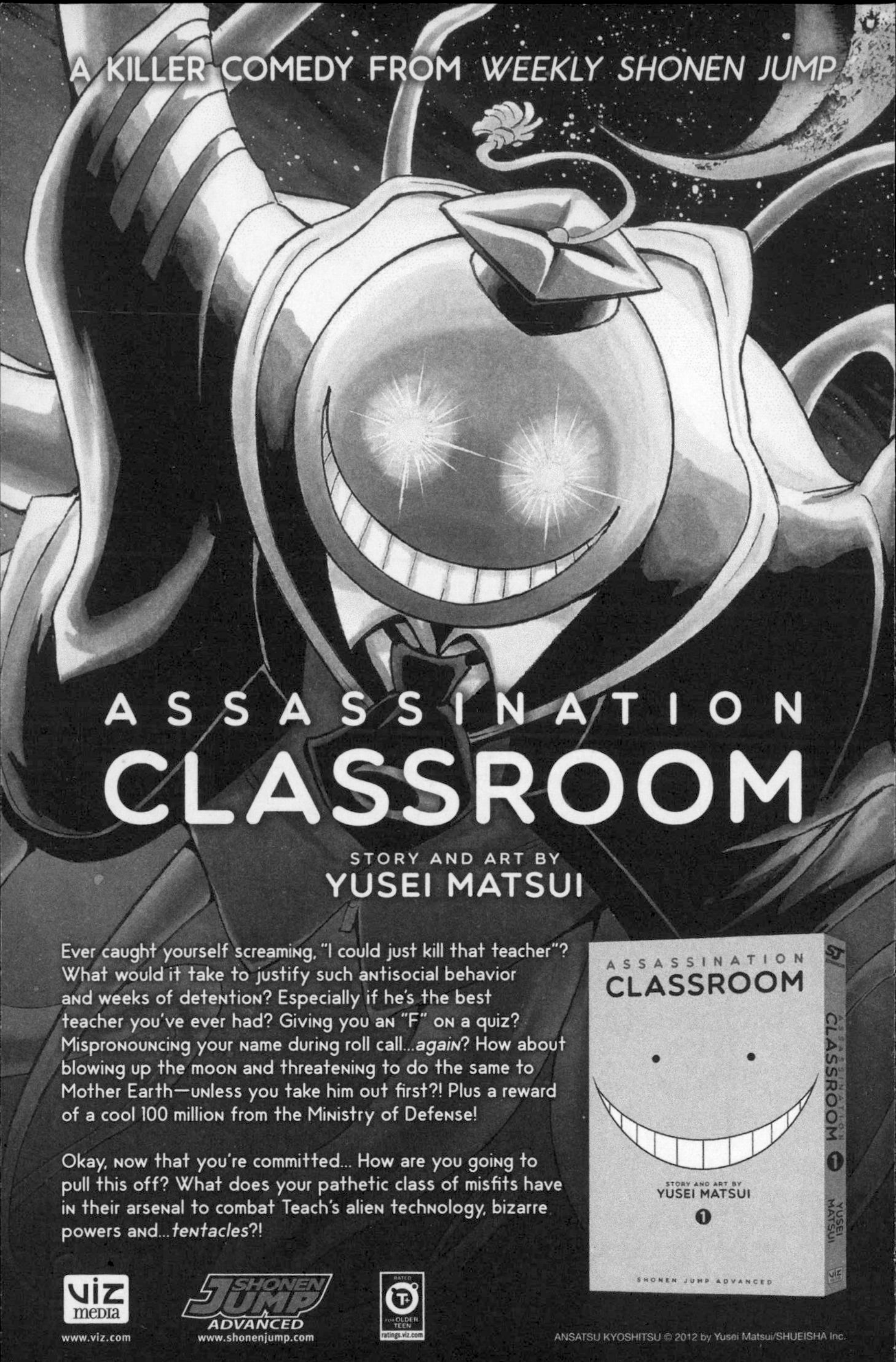
A KILLER COMEDY FROM *WEEKLY SHONEN JUMP*
ASSASSINATION
CLASSROOM
STORY AND ART BY
YUSEI MATSUI
Ever caught yourself screaming, "I could just kill that teacher"? What would it take to justify such antisocial behavior and weeks of detention? Especially if he's the best teacher you've ever had? Giving you an "F" on a quiz? Mispronouncing your name during roll call...*again*? How about blowing up the moon and threatening to do the same to Mother Earth—unless you take him out first?! Plus a reward of a cool 100 million from the Ministry of Defense!
Okay, now that you're committed... How are you going to pull this off? What does your pathetic class of misfits have in their arsenal to combat Teach's alien technology, bizarre powers and...*tentacles*?!
ASSASSINATION
CLASSROOM
STORY AND ART BY
YUSEI MATSUI
1
SHONEN JUMP ADVANCED
viz media
www.viz.com
SHONEN JUMP ADVANCED
www.shonenjump.com
RATED T+ FOR OLDER TEEN
ratings.viz.com
ANSATSU KYOSHITSU © 2012 by Yusei Matsui/SHUEISHA Inc.

NARUTO

Story and Art by
Masashi Kishimoto

Naruto is determined to become the greatest ninja ever!

Twelve years ago the Village Hidden in the Leaves was attacked by a fearsome threat. A nine-tailed fox spirit claimed the life of the village leader, the Hokage, and many others. Today, the village is at peace and a troublemaking kid named Naruto is struggling to graduate from Ninja Academy. His goal may be to become the next Hokage, but his true destiny will be much more complicated. The adventure begins now!

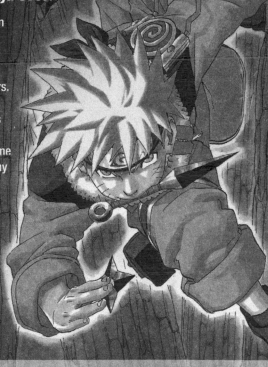

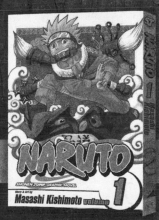

WORLD'S BEST SELLING MANGA!

www.shonenjump.com

www.viz.com

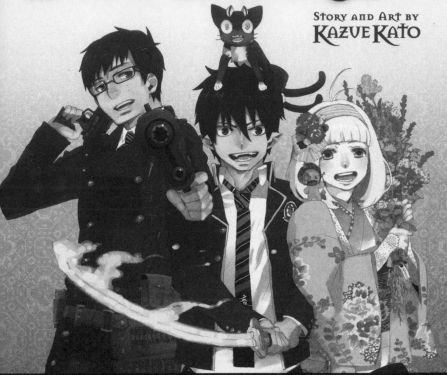
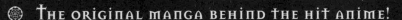
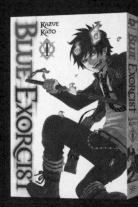

You're Reading in the Wrong Direction!!

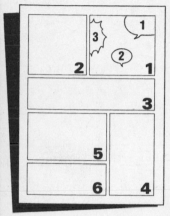

Whoops! Guess what? You're starting at the wrong end of the comic!

…It's true! In keeping with the original Japanese format, **Bleach** is meant to be read from right to left, starting in the upper-right corner.

Unlike English, which is read from left to right, Japanese is read from right to left, meaning that action, sound effects and word-balloon order are completely reversed… something which can make readers unfamiliar with Japanese feel pretty backwards themselves. For this reason, manga or Japanese comics published in the U.S. in English have sometimes been published "flopped"—that is, printed in exact reverse order, as though seen from the other side of a mirror.

By flopping pages, U.S. publishers can avoid confusing readers, but the compromise is not without its downside. For one thing, a character in a flopped manga series who once wore in the original Japanese version a T-shirt emblazoned with "M A Y" (as in "the merry month of") now wears one which reads "Y A M"! Additionally, many manga creators in Japan are themselves unhappy with the process, as some feel the mirror-imaging of their art skews their original intentions.

We are proud to bring you Tite Kubo's **Bleach** in the original unflopped format. For now, though, turn to the other side of the book and let the adventure begin…!

—Editor

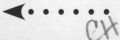

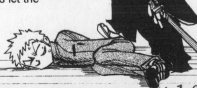

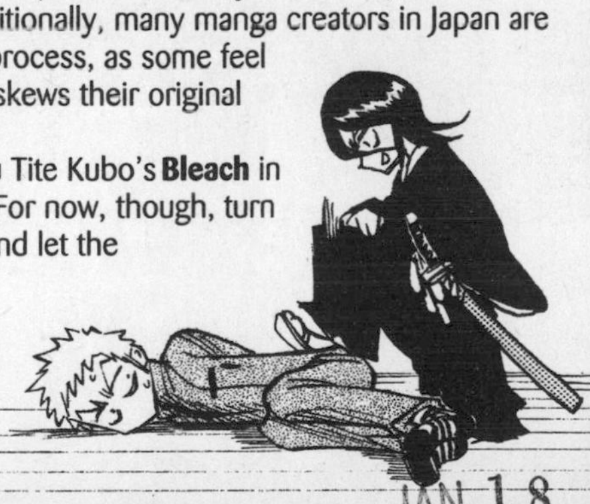